WORLD CITIES
LOS ANGELES

WORLD CITIES
LOS ANGELES

Series Editor: Maggie Toy

A.D. ACADEMY EDITIONS • Ernst & Sohn

ACKNOWLEDGEMENTS

Our thanks are extended to the many architects who supplied material for publication and in addition a special thanks to those who participated in 'Learning from Los Angeles'.

A selection of the text included in the social and planning history section of this book was derived from the Academy Forum and Symposium 'Learning from Los Angeles', 23rd October 1993, which was held at, and organised in collaboration with, the Royal Academy of Arts. We are grateful to the President, Sir Roger de Grey for his encouragement and support and to MaryAnne Stevens for her insight and participation.

Photographic Credits: Joe C Aker: pp220-221; Architectural Design: pp67, 69, 70 (above), 71, 73; Tom Bonner: pp76, 78-79, 81, 128, 129 (above), 148-155, 176, 178-179, 196-198, 200-203, 212, 216-219, 226-233, 244-249 (above), 250-251 (above), 252-253 (below), 255 (above), 256-257, 260-263, 266-269, 286-290 (below), 294-301, 304-307, 310-311, 314 (below), 318-321, 332-337, 342 (below), 344-345 (above), 351, 366 (above), 382-386; Donatella Brun: pp192-193, 195 (below), 208; Benny Chan: pp302-303, 316-317, 374-375; Todd Conversano: pp64, 92-107, 199, 209, 211, 250-251 (below), 253 (above), 343 (below), 356, 378-380; Peter Cook: pp214, 330-331; David Glomb: pp255 (below), 290 (above), 291-293; Jeff Goldberg/Esto: pp20, 172-175; Paul Groh: pp357, 381; Douglas Hill: pp272-273; Craig Hodgetts: pp80, 120-121, 129 (below), 142-143, 224, 372-373; Shen-Yuan Hwang: p207; Timothy Hursley: pp144-147, 180-185, 235 (below), 236-237, 274-283; Charles Jencks: pp125 (below), 126-127, 131, 195 (above); *La Cité*, May 1934: p40 (below); M McVay: p219 (above); Michael Moran: pp124, 132-135, 242-243; Grant Mudford: pp130, 156-157, 258-259, 270-271; Photo courtesy Dion Neutra, Architect and Neutra papers, UCLA, special collections: pp42-43; Yusuke Obuchi: pp376-377; Ron Pollard: p206; Marvin Rand: pp308-309, 322-329; Georgia Scott: p40 (above); J Scott Smith: pp204, 210; Stephen Simpson: pp188, 190-191; Douglas Slone: p189 (below); Tim Street-Porter: pp2-3, 8, 58, 136-141, 194, 213, 215, 234-235, (Esto) 238-241, 284, 312, 314 (above), 315; Photo courtesy Maguire Thomas Partners: pp28, 162-171; Adrian Velicescu: pp222-223, 340, 360-363; Alex Veritkoff: p205; Ulf Wallin: Front Cover, pp44, 125 (above); The Walt Disney Company 1993: pp158-161; Photo courtesy Warner Bros Studios: pp52, 347; Joshua White: pp338, 343 (above), 354-355; Annette del Zoppo: p189 (above and centre).

Published in Great Britain in 1994 by
ACADEMY EDITIONS
an imprint of the Academy Group Ltd
42 Leinster Gardens, London W2 3AN

Published in Germany by
ERNST & SOHN Hohenzollerndamm 170, D-10713, Berlin
members of the VCH PUBLISHING GROUP

Distributed to the trade in the USA by
ST MARTIN'S PRESS 175 Fifth Avenue, New York, NY 10010
ISBN: 1 85490 293 8

Copyright © 1994 Academy Editions *All rights reserved*
No part of this publication may be reproduced or transmitted in any form or by any means, whether by photocopying, recording or facsimile machine or otherwise howsoever without permission from Academy Editions

Printed and bound in Singapore

Series Editor: Maggie Toy; Art Editor: Andrea Bettella; Chief Designer: Mario Bettella; Editorial Co-ordinator: Pip Vice; Production Controller: Annamarie Uhr Delia; Editorial and Design Team: Ramona Khambatta, Katherine MacInnes, Jason Rigby, Laurence Scelles, Iona Spens, Owen Thomas

Front Cover: Los Angeles skyline, southern end; *pp2-3*: View of Downtown Los Angeles; *p4*: Eric Owen Moss, Lawson-Westen House, Brentwood; *p64*: Eric Owen Moss, 2 Rhino, Culver City; *p338*: Frank Gehry, Disney Concert Hall, Downtown.

CONTENTS

SOCIAL AND PLANNING HISTORY

Elizabeth Moule and Stefanos Polyzoides *The Five Los Angeleses* — 8

Diane Ghirardo *Architect as Demolition Man: Eco Cleansing in Southern California* — 20

Elizabeth Moule and Stefanos Polyzoides *Downtown In the Twentieth Century: The Struggle for Defining the Centre of Los Angeles* — 28

Kim Coleman *Los Angeles Made Visible* — 34

Kathryn Smith *Richard Neutra's Rush City Reformed, Los Angeles 1950* — 40

Academy International Forum *Learning from Los Angeles* — 44

LOS ANGELES AS IT MIGHT HAVE BEEN — 64

Maggie Toy *Random Conurbation or Planned Satellite?* — 66

LOS ANGELES AS IT IS — 122

Maggie Toy *Invention and Reinvention in LA* — 124

LOS ANGELES AS IT WILL BE — 338

Maggie Toy *Life in a Social Experiment* — 340

Maps — 392

Architects' Index — 398

ELIZABETH MOULE AND STEFANOS POLYZOIDES
THE FIVE LOS ANGELESES

Since its founding in 1781, our great city, El Pueblo de Nuestra Señora La Reina de los Angeles de Porciuncula, has been visioned, designed and built four times. However, with each successive layer of its development rased and little of the cumulative evidence remaining, the myth has flourished that Los Angeles has no history.

Nothing could be further from the truth, of course. Through more than two hundred years of existence, Los Angeles has indeed possessed a rich history and a complex culture reflecting the roots and the contributions of its diverse population. There are many reasons to explain the gap between the myth and the facts underlying the making of Southern California: the extraordinary speed of constructing infrastructure and buildings has promoted the practice of urban clearance and its psychic equivalent, collective memory lapses; the cultural heterogeneity and the sheer numbers of emigrant and immigrant people settling here (often for very brief periods of time) has resulted in underestimating the traditions of a common, native past; and the persistent emphasis on material and technological progress over a stable local culture has depreciated the value of the existing city and its natural setting.

The leading current architectural ideology of this city was established by a few historians and apologists of modernism, including Reyner Banham, Esther McCoy and John Entenza. Their paltry accounting and analysing of its origins and history simply ignored the facts. They would prefer one to believe Los Angeles a place without a past. The romance of a *tabula rasa* to be redeemed through modern form was irresistible to the cultural protagonists of the last era and still persists today. But Banham had it wrong when he proclaimed that 'apart from a small downtown and a few other pockets of ancientry, Los Angeles is instant architecture in an instant townscape'.[1] McCoy so exaggerated the contributions of the local pioneers of modernism that she created the distorted impression that they were the first significant architects of the region.[2]

Banham's arguments highlighted his interest in geography, pop culture and highly selected elements of infrastructure – the freeways, as the crucial determinants of urban form in the Los Angeles basin. His particular fixation on these freeways has perpetrated the bizarre view that this is a unique American metropolis driven (as it were) by the language of automobility. His argument was flawed then as it is now: Los Angeles was *not* the only place in the United States to be afflicted by automobile-induced sprawl. After 1954, every single urban area in the country was being as brutalised by the construction of the Interstate Freeway System. More importantly, the singularity of Banham's focus failed to account adequately for the preponderance of the city's fabric: the places in-between freeways, such as towns, neighbourhoods and districts formed out of the architectural riches of a local, centennial urban culture. Los Angeles is, and has always been, a typical American metropolis, not the no-past place of modernist historiography. In his interest to promote the architectural agenda of the post-CIAM generation, Banham caricatured Southern California as the epitome of a futurist paradise in our midst. Doubly ironic is that it has recently come to symbolise the most acute version of the international landscape of nowhere.

However, this current negative image is as undeserved as its more long-standing reputation as 'the city of the future'. It is not so much mobility that is this city's emblem but – as Norman Schwartzkopf aptly put it – the fact that quantity has a quality all of its own. What always has been unique about Los Angeles is its regional expanse and the accompanying dominance of its natural ecology by technology. It is also its political complexity, its demographic variety and the fluidity and multiplicity of its culture that has set it apart from most other places on this continent. Nonetheless, it is sheer size and its accompanying provincialism that makes Los Angeles difficult to describe and compare. Many visitors, let alone residents, do not regularly traverse this metropolis or take part in its diverse life. When they see vast distances, unfamiliar signs, local discontinuity and even chaos, what most observers overlook is a much larger territorial perspective; a vast infrastructural and natural context, and a tangible and coherent town structure and building fabric which would explain the wholeness of the metropolis' form over time. The propensity to ignore these signs of formal order in the urbanism and the experience of living in Southern

OPPOSITE: Bertram Goodhue and Carleton Winslow, Sr, Central Library, Downtown Los Angeles

SOCIAL AND PLANNING HISTORY

California is a failure of both knowledge and imagination. The city's ahistorical myth has led each new piece of architecture of the most recent period to take upon itself the extremely difficult burden of defining the image of Los Angeles as a whole and explaining it to the world. At the same time, architects faced with this impossible task have reacted by calling all issues of city-building as quixotic and untenable. This is an absurdly self-destructive purpose for architecture. It is in the domain of urbanism that issues of wholeness and commonality must be explored, if for no other reason than that it is this discipline that examines and forms the parts of the city that are *public*, not private, and hence, accessible to all.

What we believe makes Los Angeles truly unique is the peculiar process by which it has been constructed and reconstructed over time, each phase of growth displacing the one before it and generating the myth of its perpetual modernity. As we are currently entering yet another new era in the city's rebuilding, it is imperative that a compelling version of Los Angeles' history should be presented to both its citizens, its political leaders and its architects. Our city is too incomplete and in places too dysfunctional to leave it alone and too vast to imagine that it can be changed rapidly. Our only hope is to begin to transform it deliberately and selectively in awareness of its historical profile. The production of culture and of wealth can only be sustained by people who understand the burden of maintaining a city's continuity over time and in space.

The First Los Angeles 1781-1880: The Pueblo

After Cortez had conquered Mexico in 1519, Southern California was visited only twice by Spanish expeditionary forces, during the voyages of Cabrillo in 1542 and Vizcaino in 1602. It was not until 1769 that a combined religious/military group headed by Gaspar de Portola and Father Junipero Serra landed in the San Diego Bay. They headed northwards along the El Camino Real to found religious missions in the hope of both converting the native Californians and promoting the colonisation of their territory. Departing from this course, Captain Gaspar de Portola accompanied by Father Juan Crespi set out on a long march from San Diego to Monterey to find future suitable sites for settling. Later that year, Father Crespi arrived at a spot along the Porciuncula River where the coastal plain comes upon the hills of the Lower Arroyo Seco at the foot of the San Gabriel Mountains. Crespi considered it the most suitable site for a mission and large settlement. However, the Mission was not settled here but in San Gabriel in 1771, leaving Los Angeles a premier site for a pueblo.[3] Ten years later, the pueblo of Los Angeles was founded in a spot along the Porciuncula River where the coastal plain comes upon the hills of the Lower Arroyo Seco at the foot of the San Gabriel Mountains. This butterfly-shaped area shaded by alders, cottonwoods and sycamores had clear running water, fertile land for farming and grazing and had been described in the most poetic terms by Father Crespi in his diaries ten years earlier.[4]

Los Angeles was afforded the rare civic destiny of being settled by decree of the Spanish Crown. On September 4, 1781 Governor Felipe de Neve, having laid out the pueblo based on the guidelines for site selection and urbanisation coded in the *Laws of the Indies*, led a procession of other soldiers, eleven families of forty-four individual settlers, mission priests and some natives marching slowly around the pueblo site.[5] They invoked the blessing of the new community. Los Angeles became one of the few cities in the North American continent deliberately planned in advance and ceremoniously inaugurated for and by its new settlers.

The *Laws of the Indies* was a very sophisticated set of urbanising rules propagated by decree of King Philip II in 1573 and used extensively in the process of Spanish colonisation in America. The pueblo's location near a river and not near the ocean was deliberate, protecting the settlement from the unhealthy effects of swamps and from pirating.[6] Two separate precincts were delineated for each settler: a lot for the construction of an urban house and a plot of land in the adjacent countryside for farming. The residences encircled the plaza along with royal public buildings, the granary and a guard-house lining the southern edge. The plaza was rectangular with corner streets heading straight into the square. It was oriented at the compass quarter-points in order to protect the streets from the wind. A typical house-lot size was twenty by forty *varas*, about fifty-five feet by one-hundred-and-ten feet. The field lots were about five hundred-and-fifty-foot-squares, some of which were well-irrigated by the river and the *zanja madre* (or mother water ditch).[7] The *zanja madre* separated the fields from the plaza allowing domestic water to be distributed close to the new settlement. This enabled the houses around the plaza to be located on higher ground, further away from the Los Angeles river. This did not prove effective enough however, and in 1815 the pueblo was washed away by floods and its site was subsequently moved to its present location.[8]

This move to higher ground explains why today the plaza doesn't resemble the original plan. While the open space was retained, its shape was no longer rectangular; it became smaller and irregular. It was at this time that the

ABOVE: Kuchel & Dresel's California, 1857, showing the pueblo and its buildings; BELOW: Los Angeles city map, Edward OC Ord's survey, 1849

existing, larger church of Nuestra Senora de Los Angeles was laid out in its present location. The plaza became the site of a water reservoir, and because of the disarray over property lines, many houses were built encroaching on streets. A wealthy landowner built his house so far out at the north-west corner of the plaza that it required the Calle Principal (Main Street today) to angle further west as it headed north.[9]

Throughout the Spanish and Mexican years of its existence, Los Angeles remained a tiny and unimportant village. It was surrounded by an immense territory, dominated by its Catholic Mission and was subdivided into ranchos rich in agricultural production. The pueblo's public life was centred on the plaza and its church; the private life of its citizens focused on the spare adobe houses lining its streets and dotting the countryside. All of that changed rapidly, beginning with the Mexican-American War of 1846-47 and the subsequent annexation of California into the United States.

In one of its first acts, the new American administration under Governor Bennett Riley sent Lieutenant Edward OC Ord to survey Los Angeles in 1846 and later in 1849 to draw up a plan of the pueblo's expansion. His work was meant not only as a record of the existing settlement, but also as a document to establish the limits of municipally owned land in an as yet undeveloped and unplatted territory. Under American law, lots could be sold and taxes on those holdings could be levied to fill the coffers of the new municipal government. Ironically, one of the first municipal transactions under the US system represented a vision of the city's fate. In order to pay Ord, Los Angeles had to first gather monies from the merchants of the pueblo. Upon selling several lots in auction, the City paid Ord his full fee.[10] The principle of district assessment, and the primacy of real estate speculation were the legacy of Los Angeles from the start.

Ord's plan called for expansion to the north and to the south. Unlike most cities in the world, Los Angeles did not develop concentrically. This was due to the pueblo's proximity to the river at its east (and the continued desire for adjacency to the rich agricultural lands on either side of it) and the hills to the west. The platting called for blocks that were roughly three-hundred-and-twenty by six-hundred-and-ten-square feet and streets that varied in width from sixty to seventy-five feet. One of the blocks to the south declared unsaleable because of being located in the flood plain was reserved for a central park and is today the site of Pershing Square. The pueblo's buildings continued to be built of local materials, adobe and wood. The predominant building types were those of the Spanish American territories, one-storey structures arranged around courtyards with the street fronts lined with wooden arcades.

If the land divisions of the pueblo were rational and gridded, the delineation of the territories under the Spanish rancho system was more or less topographically derived. The *diseg̃nos*, picturesque land contracts of the period, were laid out by reference to all kinds of unique natural conditions, such as hills, stream beds, and coastal bays. Both the regularity and irregularity of territorial subdivision within the Los Angeles basin have their source in Spanish colonial practices.

The institution of an American banking and tax system coupled with the catastrophic drought of 1863-64 which destroyed the cattle and tallow business, forced the original California ranch owners into irreversible debt. The ranchos were taken over by American businessmen from the north-east and mid-west. The economy and the social structure of the region were changed forever.[11] The countryside began to be dominated by large-scale agricultural business. The pueblo slowly became a territorial outpost, a frontier town. An unstable population produced a violent present and an uncertain future. The culture of the pueblo under the American administration produced a settlement that began to resemble a spontaneous camp. Yet Los Angeles continued to develop despite its location, rather than as a result of it. The expectations that the water supply for the pueblo would be adequate did not turn out to be quite so reliable in a region dominated by a ten-year rain and drought cycle. In the future, all the vegetation, water, energy and institutions that would support the life of a resident population here would have to be imported or invented. Los Angeles would become the ultimate artificially sustained city of this century.

The Second Los Angeles 1880-1900: The Town

The eventual domination of Los Angeles by its recently arrived emigrant American population produced a settlement in the image of its former towns and homes. This Los Angeles was made possible primarily through the establishment of railroad connections to the rest of the continent as well as the radical expansion of local infrastructure that included new road networks, water distributing *zanjas* and horse-drawn trams.

The transcontinental railroad reached Los Angeles in 1876. The famous real estate boom that ensued in the 1880s transformed Los Angeles into a mainstream American town. Its centre was dominated by multi-storey brick Victorian civic, office, retail and warehouse buildings – expressions of the commercial interests that controlled its fate. Its periphery was formed by neighbourhoods of tree-lined

ABOVE: Bunker Hill from the east, 1890s; BELOW: Bird's-eye view of Los Angeles and environs, 1861

SOCIAL AND PLANNING HISTORY

streets of single-family wooden houses, like those of Bunker Hill, the West Adams District and Angeleno Heights, many designed in the extravagant styles of the turn of the century. Central Park (Pershing Square) overtook the prominence of the old plaza as the heart of Los Angeles shifted southwards.

The Stevenson map clearly illustrates this southward drift of the town and the slow displacement through development of the agricultural lands surrounding it. The railroad tracks were located alongside the Los Angeles river as a convenient path to the north and east out of the basin and to the south to the port of San Pedro. The decision to locate the railroad here has to this day kept the city from relating to the river as a recreational amenity. The eventual location of industrial uses next to the railroad tracks also precluded the contiguous, orderly growth of the city eastwards. The north and west boundaries of Los Angeles were provided by beautiful hills. The town during this period was contained and dominated by its natural surroundings, the urbanistic consequences of its Spanish foundation still visible.

It should be noted that four principal parks ringing the city were established at this time, but only because the lands from which they were formed had not been sold. Nonetheless, the building of Hollenbeck, Elysian, Westlake (now MacArthur) and Echo parks provided regional amenities for the neighbourhoods surrounding them and for the town as a whole. They also surrounded Los Angeles, establishing its size and a sense of itself by marking its urban edge.

In 1877, Brooklyn Heights, the first 'suburb' overlooking Los Angeles from across the river to the east was created. It was platted as a picturesque series of curvilinear streets focused around a neighbourhood park on the top of a knoll, Prospect Park, which is still in use. The entire subdivision is the first example of Los Angeles laying-out an area and landscaping all of the streets as a way of attracting residents.[12]

The surrounding open countryside, further away from the plaza was settled into small foundation towns, like Santa Monica, San Pedro, Wilmington, Pasadena and Claremont. They were strung out along the transcontinental railroad all the way to the edges of the basin. Although Los Angeles was the dominant settlement in the region, these other towns had strong separate identities, economies and populations. The city of San Pedro was especially well-developed, housing the area's harbour and a predominantly Anglo shipping and fishing industry. In fact, San Pedro and Santa Monica were linked by local rail well before the railroad connection to San Francisco and then to the rest of the continent.[13] From the early 1870s, Southern California was heavily promoted nationwide but particularly in the midwest for tourism and for health reasons. The cult of the climate of this land of perpetual sunshine had begun, and the claims of a closer, more perfect Europe made people flock here in great numbers. Pasadena was such a tourist destination and resort, developed in the midst of fertile fields of orange groves, the last rail stop before Los Angeles.

The land boomers were veterans of life in Wichita, Kansas City, Minneapolis and Chicago. A typical subdivision was made by trying to attract these buyers through building a hotel, laying out a few streets, sidewalks and curbs and planting rows of street trees, the fastest way to establish the presence of civilisation in the arid environment of the basin. By 1893 various fruits, vegetables, trees and flowers imported from Mexico, South America, Japan, Australia and Africa were dominant. A new, exotic image for Southern California was evolving through the use of this eclectic palette. The natural forms of the agricultural countryside were utilised in urban applications, such as in rows of street trees. The forerunners of the monumentally beautiful palm-lined streets like those found throughout the region (and made internationally famous through the promotion of Beverly Hills) were agricultural windbreaks and date groves. Strident contrasts of plant materials such as tropical flowering trees with native oaks began to appear.

From January 1887 to July 1889, over sixty new towns were laid out in the region on over 79,350 acres. But by 1889 the boom had run its course. Out of a hundred towns platted from 1884-88, sixty-two no longer exist except as minor suburbs and outposts.[14] The boom came in two distinct movements: the first in a normal course of railroad warfare; the second in an hysterical frenzy based on the first.[15] What is so remarkable about the rapid transformation of Los Angeles in this period was the desire to eliminate the vestiges of the pueblo and its buildings. In part, this can be interpreted as the need to erase the memories of the pueblo as an inhospitable and dangerous frontier settlement. Equally plausible was the desire to establish the dominance of an urbane Anglo-American civilisation in Los Angeles, by removing all evidence of its cultural origins in a minor rural, Hispanic Sonora Desert outpost. Only Olvera Street, the diminished and remodelled plaza and a few surrounding buildings survive today as remnants of the original pueblo.

Urban clearance prevailed as a principle of growth during the Second Los Angeles. However, an even more critically important aspect of Los Angeles' character began to emerge during this time: its regional expanse. The sheer amount

ABOVE: Main and Temple Streets looking east, 1880s; BELOW: Pershing Square looking west towards Bunker Hill, 1880s

of land made possible and accessible through the railroad encouraged land sales and subdivisions within the boundaries of properties related to the Spanish grant ranchos. These properties encompassed the entire land mass of Southern California. The majority of newcomers either became directly involved with agriculture or had inexpensive opportunities for living spread out across the land. Los Angeles evolved from this point on as a region anchored by a historic centre and surrounded by emerging smaller towns. Their building fabric was mostly compactly contained within pedestrian precincts, leaving the groves and farms among them open for cultivation.

The Third Los Angeles 1900-40: The City

Under increased pressures of migration, immigration and economic development, Los Angeles was transformed into a major new agricultural, commercial and industrial city on the west coast of the United States. Between 1890 and 1897, its streets and sidewalks were paved, and sewer systems were constructed. Intense infrastructural expansion fuelled urban development. In 1913 the City of Los Angeles completed construction of an aqueduct in order to bring Owens River Valley water to the city of sufficient capacity to service a population of 2,000,000 people.[16] In 1912 a deep-water port was opened in San Pedro. Lacking in wood or coal, Los Angeles became the first electrically illuminated city in America. Oil was discovered with the first well in production by 1892. In 1906, the Wilshire/Vermont area had one-hundred-and-sixty active wells, dramatically transforming the landscape.[17] Oil shipments made from the Port of San Pedro brought prosperity to the harbour and an increase in ocean-based trade. A major airport was established in 1930 and the region developed into the most important area for the design and production of aircraft in the world.

By 1909 the third layer of Los Angeles' centre which would become known as Downtown was already being built over its Victorian commercial heart, following a definite southerly and westerly bearing – again erasing most traces of the previous settlement. Development followed transit lines through available tracts of undeveloped land in the flat central plains of the basin.

In the same year, Charles Mulford Robinson, one of the foremost theoreticians and practitioners of the City Beautiful movement was commissioned by the City to offer guidelines for its further growth and orderly development. His contributions to the future form of Los Angeles were substantial: he conceived Downtown as a beautiful, commercial city centre of broad streets and parks, elaborate bridges and public works, grand civic buildings and continuous-fabric commercial blocks limited in their height to one-hundred-and-fifty feet.[18] Pershing Square was confirmed as the symbolic centre of the region and Broadway as its commercial and entertainment heart.

The essential character of Downtown as we know it today is based on the Robinson vision. Several important regional civic monuments were built during this time including the Central Library by Bertram Goodhue and Exposition Park. The City Hall and Union Station were proposed by him but were ultimately built in locations and in form different to his suggestions. *The Los Angeles Times* Building by Gordon Kaufmann, the Atlantic Richfield Building and others by Morgan, Walls and Clements and the many office buildings by John Parkinson on Spring Street are only a few of the monuments to commerce built at this time to the prescriptions of the 1909 plan.

Robinson also established standards for the development of vehicular boulevards and for the landscape and open space character of residential neighbourhoods, both of which eventually became central to the unique garden city image of the Los Angeles region. The early twentieth century was not just another period of routine growth. The city experienced sustained development based on the creation of a major industrial manufacturing sector. From 1920-30, one-and-a-half-million people moved to Southern California. This time they came on the new national transcontinental highway system. Consequently, seven new cities were created in LA County alone: South Gate, Bell, Torrance, Hawthorn, Maywood, Lynwood and Tujunga, mostly as 'company' towns for the new major industries.[19]

By the 1920s, an extraordinary 2,500 mile inter-urban train transit system called the Pacific Electric Rail or 'Red Car' was virtually complete, allowing people from all over the region to commute to its centre.[20] The intense growth of train suburbs and charter towns surrounding Los Angeles and the idea of a dense downtown employment district developed simultaneously. Glendale, Burbank, Beverly Hills, San Marino and many others were founded, planned and built as isolated, self-sufficient towns with a balance of civic, commercial, recreational and residential uses. Along with their equivalent neighbourhoods within the Los Angeles city limits, they offered a small-town lifestyle to their residents away from the congestion of the regional employment centre Downtown.

Simultaneously and for the first time in the city's history, an architecture native and specific to Los Angeles was being created. Architects with many diverse interpretations of a design idiom based on Mediterranean precedents like

ABOVE: Pershing Square, 1920s; BELOW: Broadway and Seventh looking north, 1940s

SOCIAL AND PLANNING HISTORY

Gill, GW Smith, Goodhue, Hunt, Neff, Kaufmann, Spaulding and Johnson produced some of the best residential architecture built in America. RM Schindler, in a rooted but modernist idiom, created truly unique and original residential and commercial forms. Their great houses and gardens, multi-family courtyards, public parks, magnificent streets, shopping villages, schools and other public institutional buildings intensified the sense that the Los Angeles region was one of the most amenable places to live in the United States.

Throughout this period, the automobile played a special role in the city's development. Used primarily as a means of local transportation, it allowed people to move easily around their suburban towns. Residents of the region typically used the train for the long commute to and from the centre while being picked up by the car to be brought home at the end of the day.[21] Boulevards, most notably Wilshire, served as the city's great motoring promenades. As they were linear they tended to connect some of the new subdivisions such as Westwood, Hancock Park, Larchmont and others to Downtown. Although commercial/retail activities began to spring up along them from the 1930s, they were limited compared to the major concentration of similar activities Downtown. As a consequence, Downtown remained remarkably dense. The constellation of towns surrounding it were connected primarily by rail transit, leaving much of the in-between and surrounding countryside virtually open until the 1940s.

The Fourth Los Angeles 1940-90: The Metropolis

In 1942, three years after the inauguration of the Pasadena Freeway, the word 'smog' was uttered in Los Angeles for the first time. Fuelled by massive post-World War II westward migration, the city began to spill over beyond its urban boundaries determined by rail corridors and pedestrian neighbourhoods and districts. Infrastructural changes, principally in freeway, airport and flood control projects, induced massive land development in Southern California.[22] Post-war national policy was designed to encourage such automobile induced sprawl. With a new federal mortgage programme in place, single-family housing was built at a very rapid pace. The basin was eventually covered by this homogeneous growth, giving the region an unlikely unity and shared values amongst its young, suburban residents.

A region-wide freeway system was promoted in denial of the certain air-pollution catastrophe that it would precipitate. Its role as a piece of transportation engineering was to parallel the functional role of the boulevards as well as of rail transit and to resolve their perceived shortcomings. The inter urban and intercity train lines in place were principally radial in order to service Downtown. Additional ring routes were required to connect suburb to suburb. The boulevards in place were seen to be too congested to continue to carry the ever-greater loads of passengers travelling to newly acquired lands further and further away and beyond the pedestrian reach of transit stations. As a result, the freeway system was adopted and developed in a unique pattern – both girded throughout the basin and concentric around Downtown. In the early 1950s, the transit rail system was eliminated as the transportation principle of 'uninterrupted flow' became gospel.[23] This was one of the most short-sighted and costly decisions made in the history of Los Angeles. A much abridged transit rail system is now being re-inserted into the region at the cost of hundreds of billions of dollars.

The first freeway, the Pasadena Parkway was built within and sunken into the fabric of the city and the natural landscape of the Arroyo Seco. However, the next generation of freeways built above the city on pylons and into enormously wide rights-of-way. Because many freeways were not built in straight lines (national policy set to keep drivers from falling asleep at the wheel), they severely damaged the social and built fabric of the areas they traversed. Not only did they create great serpentine gashes through the city, but they became walls through neighbourhoods and districts, often dividing one of their parts from another.[24] In the early years of freeway-building, the system functioned quite well. The limited commuting distances and the low number of vehicles allowed traffic to flow relatively smoothly. But eventually, and as the urbanised edges of Los Angeles moved further out and the number of vehicles in circulation skyrocketed, a severe case of low density congestion set in.

The city had annexed quite a substantial amount of land preceding this period. In an effort to respond to an enormous demand for housing as well as additional water rights, the San Fernando valley had been acquired. To gain access to a new industrialised port, the city had reached down a thin strip of land to San Pedro/Wilmington for incorporation. To acquire land for an airport, the city had claimed the beach area south of Santa Monica.[25] The universal directionality of motion encouraged by the freeway system allowed all open land within Los Angeles to become accessible, therefore, valuable and available for contiguous development. The Fourth Los Angeles grew by filling out the sections of the Jeffersonian mile-by-mile continental survey. Large boulevards lined with commercial activities surrounded exclusively

ABOVE: Completion of the Central Library and its gardens by Bertram Goodhue, 1930s; BELOW: The Red Car Station, Beverly Hills, 1930s

residential developments within this gigantic grid. This urbanising pattern was endlessly repeated until it collided with a distinct town like Santa Monica or a topographical feature like the foothills or an old rancho boundary. Los Angeles began to be developed as the enormous, formless in-between all the somewhere places of Southern California: a vast, privatised nowhere, lacking adequate open space or access to the regional landscape, spatially isolated from the necessary common, civic places. Every family in Southern California was sentenced to perpetual dependence on two or more cars.

In the spirit of modern planning, Downtown was judged to be overly congested. Since the early 1930s a grave confusion had prevailed regarding the phenomenon of congestion. The conflict of accommodating excessive numbers of people and vehicles within roads and sidewalks was judged to be a serious problem.[26] Unfortunately, it never occurred to anyone that large numbers of people were necessary to sustain an economically prosperous pedestrian city centre. The freeways were advertised as a means of easing access to, and circulation through Downtown. Instead, they allowed many people to bypass Downtown for their employment and retail needs, while flooding Downtown with cars and requiring vast amounts of parking. The same number of people, about 300,000 were employed at the beginning and at the end of the Fourth Los Angeles in the greater Downtown area. Where roughly two thirds of them accessed their jobs by transit in 1940, the same percentage accessed them by automobile in 1990.[27] Naturally, a decongested Downtown became physically, functionally and symbolically eroded. More than fifty per cent of its building stock was demolished in favour of parking. Many Downtown districts atrophied and decay set in.

Downtown continued to play a prominent role in the life of the region. But as accessibility by automobile became omnidirectional within the basin, a variety of other competing subcentres emerged. Economic growth was increasingly attracted to them, especially after the Watts Riots when whole populations moved westwards fleeing the inner city and its racial and economic problems. Their growth generated a sense of fragmentation within the metropolis. It was then that the word 'urban' began to mean 'poor' and 'suburban' began to mean 'affluent'.

By 1960 there was political consensus that the now decongested and declining Downtown needed to be replanned and redefined as a modern city centre befitting a car-dominated, up-to-date metropolis.[28] Bunker Hill, the oldest mixed-use district of Downtown was declared severely blighted and measures began to be taken to have it replaced through clearance and redevelopment with large separated blocks of commercial, motel (not hotel!), residential and parking uses. The hill was to be lowered in order to eliminate the necessity for an Angel's Flight and a super block-sized grid of highway-standard streets and ramps was to be laid over it for easy auto access. Pedestrians, automobiles and service vehicles were to be separated vertically in space by overpasses for 'safety'. New high-rise buildings were to be isolated in the centres of blocks, surrounded by plazas designed primarily for viewing, not human occupation.

Bunker Hill was indeed cleared, and a commercial citadel was built to replace it. It was all part of that most tragic and misdirected process of urban renewal that swept the country in the 1960s and destroyed so many centre cities throughout the United States.[29] The life of what was left of Downtown Los Angeles was sapped as commercial activity failed to multiply as expected, but just relocated to the newest quarters. Dozens of empty buildings were left behind, many of them significant architectural monuments, most of them still empty. The architectural form of the new Bunker Hill was finally established by the 'Silver Book' plan of 1972[30], so named because of the sleek colour of its cover representing the region's attachment to high-tech metaphors during this time. Its stereotypical modern buildings, isolated plazas and parking and car-dominated streets turned the centre of Los Angeles into a caricature of an international anyplace. Its housing prescriptions were never carried out. Downtown became increasingly dominated by non-residential uses. In combination with similarly conceived and constructed segregated islands of commercial development, such as Century City, South-coast Plaza and Warner Center, it erased the possibility for a genuine public, pedestrian life in Southern California for a generation.

At least the economic life of Downtown was stabilised. It re-emerged as the predominant West Coast financial and business centre of our country and one of the most important on the Pacific Rim. Yet, the homogenising influence of the automobile-oriented development standards, the erosion of a vital and popular public realm and the disinterest in retaining significant housing neighbourhoods undermined Downtown's special physical endowment. This became exacerbated by the predominance of suburban development models, such as sealed underground malls and office parks, which undermined Downtown at the expense of surrounding centres and bedroom suburbs.

The expansion of the territory finally transformed the city into the contiguous metropolis that we now call simply Southern California; at 5,000 square miles, one of the most extensive

ABOVE: Downtown in the late 1950s; BELOW: Los Angeles' Downtown as Central City 1990, from the Silver Book, 1970

SOCIAL AND PLANNING HISTORY

ELIZABETH MOULE AND STEFANOS POLYZOIDES

areas of suburban sprawl in the world. Within this vast spread of monotonous and undistinguished suburban house tracts, the region's public monuments, employment and shopping centres became engulfed by parking. Further out beyond the Jeffersonian grid into Orange, Ventura and Riverside Counties, these same public places gravitated away from populated areas, isolated from them by the phenomenal quantity of parking surrounding them. The commanding physical contrast between the densely-built city and the open countryside which dominated the Third Los Angeles was virtually erased and replaced with a landscape of nowhere.

On the verge of a Fifth Los Angeles, the metropolis quickly became dominated by those aspects of the built world constructed in the last fifty years to accommodate and favour the car: roads and car parks. The citizens of the region increasingly became subject to the cumulative negative effects induced by fifty years of sprawl: extreme distances and time delays, intense privatisation, social ghetto-isation and alienation and environmental pollution, now the typical experiences of current daily life. Random growth and uncritical dependence on technology brought Southern California to the brink.

The Fifth Los Angeles 1990 – : Region/State

The problems of Los Angeles are the very definition of the burgeoning urban and ecological crisis everywhere. The urbanism crafted out of a single-minded dependence on the car has been carried out as low density, land-intensive suburban sprawl on the one hand and as abandonment of the Centre City and the public realm on the other. The qualities that characterise the form of Los Angeles have been planned for exactly as they are: segregated land use by 'zones'; streets made primarily for automobiles; landscape as residual buffers, not for human occupation; neighbourhoods of racial and economic homogeneity and buildings without a human-scale. The resulting urban fabric is neither urban nor rural. Any sense of a vital urbanity associated with small towns or large cities and of unspoiled nature expected of the countryside is increasingly threatened by the omnipresence of 'nowhere'. The economics of building and maintaining such widely-spread infrastructure of freeways, roads and utilities is indeed unsustainable in the face of competition with other more compact cities and threatens our economic wellbeing. Los Angeles has pioneered in the short-term techno-centric economic development of immediate consumption over long-term, cultural development of social equity, quality of life and environmental responsibility.

The riots of the spring of 1992 indicated among other things that the systematic assault on the city and its public spaces destroyed more than just buildings. It destroyed our collective shared experience, a bond that bridges ethnic and class distinctions. The extremes of the intense hermeticism of the walled enclaves from Simi Valley to Mission Viejo and the disenfranchisement of the barren and alienating streetscapes of Florence Avenue must be seriously re-evaluated if the city is to become the integrated multi-cultural city which it aspires to.

Despite this, or in part because of it, evidence of an emerging transformation of this metropolis is to be found everywhere. A new regional, multi-modal rail transit system comprising four hundred miles of light and heavy lines, amplified by electric trolley buses, bikeways and an expanded bus service is under construction, partly in the old right-of-ways of the Red Car lines, promising a region-wide alternative to the car as well as greater development around the stations.

Rebuilding public space throughout Southern California coupled with the 'localisation' of retail activity is generating active pedestrian districts all over the basin. Cities like Pasadena and Santa Monica stand out as the best examples of municipalities actively directing the reuse of their downtown commercial districts. Through mixed-use projects and selective densification, commercial activities are accommodated adjacent to multi-family dwellings. The net result is that the making of liveable pedestrian centres preserves the character of the surrounding single-family residential neighbourhoods. Large new development projects such as Playa Vista are now emerging that use urbanistically and ecologically sound practices in land use, transportation, water conservation, garbage disposal, sewage treatment, pollution controls etc. At Playa Vista, the use of more dense housing types, duplexes, townhouses and courtyard housing in neighbourhood configurations, will generate a pedestrian-based community life familiar to the residents of Southern California's pre-sprawl towns. This same model has also allowed for an ample provision of neighbourhood and regional parks as well as the preservation and biological reconstruction of a significant portion of the Ballona Wetlands.

The city that we envision the Fifth Los Angeles becoming would be predicated on a few operative principles aimed at encouraging a dedication to place: supporting a sense of local economy and community, building upon our city's heritage and reinvesting in the public realm. These are the motivations of the Downtown Strategic Plan and Playa Vista, both led by our office and published herein.

Because our society has so fetishised the private spaces in this city, it is important to emphasise the need to also encourage its opposite. The public realm is made up of both

OPPOSITE ABOVE: Fashion Island, Newport Beach; OPPOSITE BELOW: Angel's Stadium, Anaheim, 1980s

SOCIAL AND PLANNING HISTORY

open space and institutions: it is those shared places which bring people together, that relate them to one another or, conversely, that separate them and secure their privacy. A city is a cultural artefact and a repository of places and things. It is what we are born into and what we leave behind. What a society holds in common is not only what it shares with the living, but what it shares with those before us and those after us.

Our system of governance upholds both our individual civil rights and our common interests as cities, states and nations. However, while our Constitution guarantees these rights, they are being constantly undermined by the sorry state of the built world around us. In order to maintain the vigour of our democratic ways, we need to elevate the construction of a Los Angeles suitable to the needs of its residents to the level of urgent priority. For too long, all levels of government have been preoccupied with abstract social and economic programmes divorced from the power of place. By building this common permanent place, the public realm of our built world, the urgent problems of our society can be addressed, our rights and responsibilities applied and a balance between public and private interests established.

If the Fourth Los Angeles was chaos by design, then the reversal of policies that destroyed this metropolis and degraded the quality of the natural world in and around it is in order. The following is an outline of operative principles towards the physical transformation of the Los Angeles region during the phase of its development we are now entering:

Layering: The Fifth Los Angeles depends for its growth on a new, regionally-centred entrepreneurial economy that is committed to the enhancement of local places. Similarly, it is also dependent on a government with a new purpose that measures its accomplishments by the positive physical change that its initiatives generate. The metropolis all around us represents over one hundred years of continuous investment in our well-being. To the degree possible, the architecture and urbanism of its future should be based on an ethic of conservation and gradual infilling. The unique physical fragments of Los Angeles as they exist today should become the point of departure for its further redevelopment and the source of its character and difference from other places in America. In research such as is represented by this essay, the historical images and facts about the ecological and urban history of the city must be documented and taken into account in design. And the lost, mythical-poetic dimensions of past Southern Californian cities and landscapes should also be imagined and brought to bear. No more attempts to turn Southern California into a memory-free zone should be tolerated.

Urbanism Formed by Architecture: Urbanism is the design of the public void of the city. A complex array of voids composed in particular figures is the essential character and experience of all cities, including Los Angeles. Architecture and landscape architecture are the means by which this *forma urbis* is incrementally formed. The collective figure of this void is more complete, permanent and important than the shape of any single one of the buildings that define it. Within this open space framework, roads, transit networks and infrastructure of all kinds should be designed to contain sprawl and to support pedestrian precincts of all kinds. Special climatic, ecological and cultural influences on the design of open space in this region should be taken into account in order to safeguard its local character. Internationalist diagrams of urban and territorial organisation favouring the automobile and all other forms of machinery should be discarded once and for all.

Architecture that Marks Time and Place: The architectural project today is most typically an isolated act which depends on objectives that benefit a limited cast of characters. And yet it is the means by which the city and the countryside are constantly and incrementally constructed day in and day out. Its effects, therefore, are essential to the well-being of all. Marking time and place is a means of fulfilling architecture's most noble purpose; that is, the establishment of the identity of a society through their constructed and natural surroundings. A mere personal expressive gesture is not enough to elevate architecture towards such a goal. Single buildings must be supported by a local typological code that takes into account both historical precedent and accepts the possibility of introducing new formal patterns. The linking of both typological memory and individual expression can relieve architecture of its consumerist burdens and revalidate it as an instrument for rebuilding the city.

Catalytic Projects as Transformers: The city grows relatively slowly. At the same time, this process of change is a potent, relentless and permanent one. For half a century, the dominant paradigm for city-making has been the violent imposition of either inert masterplans or formally complete, self-referential and spatially isolated objects onto the body of the historic city and the open countryside. It is now time for the acceptance of a new paradigm that is the reverse of our current practices. We should be designing the collective body of the city and nature, not exclusively its individual architectural parts. Buildings, landscapes and open space projects should be designed as small and incomplete interventions. Their programmes should accommodate with equal passion client interests, the

ABOVE: *Downtown's redevelopment district boundary, after the rasing of Bunker Hill, showing the first tower, Security Pacific;* BELOW: *The continued disintegration of Downtown's building fabric*

interests of the public and the invisible interests of the unrepresented. Their completeness should be defined by reference to their physical relationships to existing objects and places. All new projects should be considered as catalytic in promoting positive physical change, furthering economic investment, and improving the daily life of all beyond their property boundaries.

The Promise of Public-Private Cooperation: The State and the Market as we have experienced them in the twentieth century are the principal promoters and sponsors of 'nowhere'. The first priority for architecture is to reject both as isolated agents of urban growth. States by themselves are capable of little more than establishing normative standards. Similarly, the unchecked market produces mindless uniformity and repetition through the statistical validation of marketing recipes applicable everywhere and usually framed under limited ambitions and singular purposes. Long-term economic prosperity and the construction and maintenance of beautiful cities are linked. Private and public interests must actively cooperate in the regeneration of this region. Neighbourhoods and buildings should become the ultimate means of empowerment in our society, the illustration of our best social intentions.

However diverse the population of Los Angeles becomes, only dialogue can generate the agreements upon which a common, public future can be delivered. The public sector can sponsor a neighbourhood and district framework for political participation. The private sector can make it its responsibility to deliver architectural and urban form based on the common ground that such citizen involvement would generate. The Fifth Los Angeles can only fulfil our dreams if the needs of individuals and the diverse groups that comprise the city are met, at the same time as a sense of community is re-established by the deliberate rebuilding of the physical world within which we all exist.

Notes

1. Reyner Banham, *Los Angeles: The Architecture of the Four Ecologies*, The Penguin Press, Baltimore, 1971, p21
2. Esther McCoy, *Five California Architects*, Praeger Publishers, New York, 1975
3. Writer's Program of the Work Projects Administration, *Los Angeles: A Guide to the City and its Environs* Hastings House, New York, 1941
4. *Ibid*, pp25-27
5. Harry Kelsey, 'A New Look at the Founding of Old Los Angeles', *California Historical Quarterly*, Vol LV, No 4 (Winter, 1976), p335
6. *City Planning Ordinances of the Laws of the Indies*, issued by Philip II on 13 July 1573, translated from the original manuscript by Axel I Mundigo and Dora P Crouch, in their book co-authored with Daniel J Garr, *Spanish City Planning in North America*, The MIT Press, Cambridge, MA, 1982. Ordinance 41 suggests that maritime sites are unhealthy, not well populated with natives and dangerously exposed to pirates, p9
7. Crouch et al, *op cit*, pp157-58
8. W W Robinson, *Los Angeles from the Days of the Pueblo, Together with a Guide to the Historical Old Plaza Area Including the Pueblo de Los Angeles State Historical Monument*, California Historical Society, San Francisco, 1959, p9
9. Crouch et al, *op cit*, pp168-69
10. W W Robinson, 'The Story of Ord's Survey as Disclosed by the Los Angeles Archives', *Historical Society of Southern California Quarterly*, Vol 19 (Sept, Dec,1937), pp123-25
11. Robert M Fogelson, *The Fragmented Metropolis: Los Angeles 1850-1930*, Harvard University Press, Cambridge, MA, 1967, pp14-17
12. John Reps, *The Making of Urban America*, Princeton University Press, Princeton, NJ, 1965
13. Fogelson, *op cit*, pp110-11
14. Carey McWilliams, *Southern California Country: An Island on the Land,* Duell, Sloan & Pearce, New York, 1946, pp121-22
15. *La Reina: Los Angeles in Three Centuries,* Security Trust and Savings Bank, Los Angeles, 1929, p74
16. *Ibid*, p130
17. *Ibid*, pp129-30
18. Charles Mulford Robinson, 'The City Beautiful', *Report to the Mayor the City Council, and Board of Public Works,* Los Angeles Municipal Art Commision, 1909
19. McWilliams, *op cit*, p135
20. Spencer Crump, *Ride the Big Red Cars: The Pacific Electric Story,* Trans Anglo Books, Glendale, CA, p198
21. *Ibid*, p125
22. Mel Scott, *Metropolitan Los Angeles: One Community,* The Haynes Foundation, Los Angeles, 1949, pp69-79
23. *Ibid*, p94
24. David Brodsky, *LA Freeway*, University of California Press, Berkeley, 1981, pp101-31
25. Fogelson, *op cit*, pp223-28
26. Scott, *op cit*, pp105-10
27. *Factbook Downtown Los Angeles,* Community Redevelopment Agency, 1991, pp6,14
28. The Bunker Hill Urban Renewal Project, authored by the Los Angeles City Community Redevelopment Agency, was given its final approval by the Los Angeles City Council on March 31, 1959
29. A remarkable photo-essay of Bunker Hill just before its destruction is by Arnold Hylen, *Los Angeles Before the Freeways: 1850-1950, Images of an Era,* Dawson's Bookstore, Los Angeles, 1981
30. Wallace, McHarg, Roberts and Todd, et al, *Central City Los Angeles: 1972/1990; Preliminary General Development Plan,* The Committee for Central City Planning, Inc, Los Angeles, 1972

ABOVE: Continuous residential neighbourhoods of single-family houses in Pacific Palisades; BELOW: The end of the Fourth Los Angeles

DIANE GHIRARDO
ARCHITECT AS DEMOLITION MAN
Eco Cleansing in Southern California

Driving through the urban hinterland of Los Angeles, particularly heading east through the Inland Empire at high noon in the middle of summer, is an encounter with eye-straining dimness. Yellow-brown smog is illuminated by sunlight feebly piercing the thick layer of atmospheric pollutants. Smog envelops everything north, south, west and east of Downtown Los Angeles, but the farther east you travel, the thicker, stickier and more foul smelling it becomes.[1]

To Southern Californians, smog is a natural artefact, the price paid for a year-round temperate climate. But filthy air, far from natural, is instead a direct consequence of deliberate development policies relentlessly pursued in Southern California throughout the twentieth century. The urban form of the built environment in Los Angeles offers Angelenos the privilege of breathing foul air, thereby poisoning their lungs and those of their children on a level probably matched only by coal miners.[2] The building of Los Angeles and Southern California issues in yet other dubious achievements: it has required over-pumping and poisoning the rich artesian springs throughout the basin, and poisoning the ocean through toxic run-off and the emissions of a ring of refineries circling the south bay; it has such concentrated salts in water that eventually the Inland Empire will have to be abandoned as an agricultural and development gold mine; it has vanquished millennial ecosystems, consigning species of flora and fauna to extinction without a second thought; it has so recklessly reshaped and remodelled the landscape that Southern California is, much like the areas adjacent to the Mississippi River before July 1993, a series of disasters waiting to happen.[3]

If the intimate connection between these facts and architecture is not readily apparent, it is because for too long architects have abjured any responsibility for the manifold consequences of the buildings, airports, subdivisions, shopping malls, office parks, skyscrapers, new towns, factories and other artefacts that they design. Architects learn to bracket out of their consciousness anything other than the form and internalised function of the aesthetic objects they sweat to produce. The measure of their accomplishment is the affirmative judgement of their formal virtuosity pronounced by professors and by other design professionals. In other words, from architecture school onward, architects learn that only by massively simplifying, abstracting and ignoring most of the problems connected to their designs will they be able to achieve success as architects. The building of Los Angeles and its vast periphery, whether planned or unplanned, provides a towering counterpoint to the simple-minded verities of contemporary architecture.[4]

Banham's Four LA Ecologies

Although he drew entirely different conclusions from the same evidence, Reyner Banham was one of the first architectural critics to notice many of these characteristics of building and architecture in Los Angeles.[5] In *Los Angeles, The Architecture of Four Ecologies*, he chastised the conventional commentaries on architecture that ignored 'Pop ephemeridae . . . freeway structures and other civil engineering. . .' on the grounds that 'both are as crucial to the human ecologies and built environments of Los Angeles as are dated works in classified styles by named architects'.[6]

However bold his attention to the built environment, Banham was almost oblivious to the imperatives of the natural ecosystem, the unbuilt environment: 'Whatever man has done subsequently to the climate and environment of Southern California, it remains one of the ecological wonders of the habitable world.'[7] Wonder, indeed, but only for supreme pollution and environmental destruction. For Banham, the first ecology, Surfurbia, and its spectacular beachfront homes and generous beaches only required 'vigilance' to avoid becoming a dumping ground for cost-cutting industries and public services. Instead, the bay has been ruthlessly and systematically polluted by industries and cities, and the beaches themselves have had to be supplemented by infusions of sand, since the systematic control of the LA basin's rivers has interrupted the natural cycles whereby beaches are created.

Banham also celebrated the housing built along the flanks of the Santa Monica mountains and the Hollywood Hills as 'classic Los Angeles foothill settlements.'[8] Subsequent foothill developments – at Los Feliz, Beverly Hills, Bel Air, Pacific Palisades, Brentwood around the basin,

OPPOSITE: Downtown, Pei Cobb Freed & Partners, Los Angeles Convention Center

and then east to Highland park, Pasadena, San Marino, Sierra Madre and Monrovia – were simply variations on the same theme. Such hillside sites adjacent to wilderness areas 'seem to cry out for affluent suburban residences . . . Watered, it will carry almost any kind of vegetation. . .'[9] Architects responded to the design challenges of hillside construction with flair and originality, with some of the most inventive houses by Craig Ellwood, John Lautner and Pierre Koenig lifted off the ground to afford spectacular wide angle views of the city and the ocean.

Elsewhere, developers were less individualistic and more ruthless. Banham described the tiers and terraces carved into the mountains that surround Los Angeles in order to build houses on level surfaces, but even though he acknowledged ecological implications to this manner of building, he refused to adopt the position of the 'Jeremiahs at Berkeley and in the Sierra Club'.[10] With a classic faith in the power of people to move mountains, Banham insisted that regulations and codes could control the forces that led to major slides, and in any case, the worst construction had occurred in Northern rather than Southern California.

Events gave the lie to Banham's twin articles of faith in human ingenuity and well-enforced codes to contain the forces of nature on a rampage: mountains rather than people have done the moving. The San Gabriel Mountains, relatively young tectonically, are rising steadily, and as they do, masses of boulders, mud, gravel and sand, known as debris flows, stream down their flanks, ploughing right through the homes, streets, barricades and anything else Angelenos confidently perch nearby. All of the machinery and engineering might muscled against this relentless movement, including enormous debris basins and debris dams, amount to little more than pesky pebbles, temporary interruptions in the path of the mountains. And still the houses go up, streets are paved and homeowners profess ignorance and amazement when their garages and homes fill up with mud, gravel and boulders.[11]

On the other side of Los Angeles on the coast, in the stylish subdivision of Pacific Palisades, million dollar homes perch on sandstone bluffs two hundred feet above the ocean. Many of them perch about ten feet closer to the edge of the bluffs, winter rains twice the normal amount in 1993, saturated the thirty to fifty feet of topsoil upon which the homes sit and sent it sliding downhill toward the edge of the bluffs. Although the sandstone cliffs have eroded steadily and ruinous landslides have occurred throughout the century (1969 was a banner year for landslides in Pacific Palisades as well as the San Gabriels), homeowners refuse to move. Instead, they sue the city for damages, claiming that poorly maintained sewer and water lines, plus poor drainage, are the culprits, and the rest of the city, not the builders or the residents, should pay for the damage to their houses. Over six months, the city spent over $2.5 million to install a series of steel pikes to protect the city streets. In reality, the I-beams anchor the hill, and thus the homes, of politically powerful residents. Only political clout sends money and resources to people who shouldn't be living on what is widely known to be geologically unstable terrain, instead of sending it to devastated areas of post-rebellion South Central LA.[12]

Ubiquitous Unplanned Sprawl

The swath of territory to the north, east and south of Los Angeles was built up at different paces during the twentieth century, and roughly falls into one of two types of development: planned and unplanned. In this essay, I will examine the unplanned variant in the Inland Empire (Riverside and San Bernardino Counties), Orange, Ventura and Los Angeles Counties, and the so-called planned growth in Orange County in the city of Irvine.

Residential development exploded precisely in these seemingly remote areas from the late 1970s on – areas that could still be called the far fringes of Los Angeles in 1981 – smothering orange groves and agricultural land beneath concrete, asphalt and tract homes. In the post-World War II years, the tide of settlement flowed east from the San Gabriel mountains in a pattern familiar from early twentieth-century development in the LA basin but that spread, domino like, from there to the San Fernando Valley, beyond to the western edge of the Antelope Valley in Leona Valley, the San Gabriel Valley and then out on all sides, to the northeast of Los Angeles toward the Mojave desert, and to the south east in former agricultural areas such as Temecula. A vast ring of bedroom communities sprang up in order that the maximum number of people could live out the single family home version of the American dream. With the relentless typology of projecting driveway and garage prominently fronting the street, these pristine desert lands promised freedom from the urban ills associated with Los Angeles: traffic, gangs, crime. This soon proved illusory, as they eventually all followed the commuters right out to their new suburbs.

Concentric rings of commuter zones spilled out from Downtown Los Angeles, first twenty or twenty-five miles to the San Fernando Valley, some of the San Gabriel Valley and the northern section of Orange County; then in 1970 thirty or thirty-five miles, and by 1980 to fifty miles from Downtown, beginning to penetrate into Ventura, Riverside and San Bernardino counties.[13] Most recently, the commuter zone drove from sixty to ninety miles deep into Riverside County as far as Temecula, Hemet and Moreno Valley; into San Bernardino County to Apple Valley, Adelanto and Big Bear; and finally to the northernmost reaches of Los Angeles County to Palmdale, Lancaster and Antelope Valley. Although the Inland Empire of Riverside and San Bernardino counties, hemmed in by mountain ranges and blasted by searing summer heat, enjoys the most devastating smog, air quality only marginally improves in communities closer to Los Angeles such as Pasadena and San Marino.[14]

Almost overnight, tiny villages or plots of desert lands transmuted into endless acres of interchangeable tract homes in cities such as Palmdale, Moreno Valley, Rancho Cucamonga, Adelanto and Valencia, serviced by expansive shopping malls, discount and outlet stores. Developers even floated the idea of turning Kern County, just south of Fresno, into further bedrooms for LA's hungry labourer force.[15] During the 1980s, population in the Inland Empire almost doubled from 1.6 million to 2.9 million people. Exponentially rising housing costs within the LA basin intersected with increasing demand for low and moderately priced housing from 1978 onwards, as a mixed bag of junk bond laden nouveau riche yuppies, rust belt refugees, wealthy post-Khomeini Iranians, Korean and Southeast Asian entrepreneurs, Central American victims of Reagan policies and Mexican emigrants all converged on Southern California in the space of a few short years. The demand spilled over the San Gabriels into the Inland Empire, as communities closer to LA resisted attempts to increase the stock of affordable housing. The affluent communities of San Marino, Bradbury and Rolling Hills Estates even proposed to count maids' quarters and caretakers' cottages in a desperate bid to meet state-mandated quotas for affordable housing – without actually having to build any.[16]

These suburbs serviced the city by sending workers on commutes of up to four hours per day, insuring not only monumental traffic jams and slowdowns, but also the persistence of intense smog for the better part of the year. An eighty mile drive might only require one and a quarter hour's driving elsewhere, but here, it could easily consume up to three hours even in the absence of a major accident. In the building fever of the late 1970s and 80s, builders, politicians and residents were sublimely indifferent to the possible consequences of such development. In Southern California, where financier Michael Milkin and Savings and Loan King Charles Keating set the standard for fast money, developers, politicians and new homeowners have traditionally brushed aside such questions as barriers to progress and economic growth.

Opposition to the relentless expansion coalesces around two chief arguments: quality of life and environmental concerns. Residents of rural communities oppose the suburbanisation of mountains and deserts on the grounds that the quality of their life in these rural or wilderness areas will be irreparably eroded by what they perceive as the unmitigated greed of developers. Such is the case for the residents of Antelope Acres, located twelve miles north of Lancaster in the High Desert. First settled in 1948, Antelope Acres consists of about 400 mostly frame cottages on one and one-half to five acre lots, ample spaces for horses, chickens and even bird sanctuaries.[17] The city of Lancaster annexed 885 acres to the south of the town, and plans to have the Larwin Land Company of Encino erect 2,000 homes on the site, effectively turning the original community into a tiny oasis in a sea of tract homes.

Not far away, a heated debate throughout 1992 pitted opponents of a two million dollar mega-development in the San Jacinto Valley, Moreno Highlands, against other residents and even the City Council. Although the town of Moreno Valley exploded during the 1980s, the steady increase in smog and the erosion of open and wilderness areas brought planners, environmentalists and residents into violent opposition with elected officials. The site where two Denver and Chicago families, the Cohens and Crowns, plan a mini-city of nearly eight thousand homes, schools, business park and village centre, serviced by twenty-four miles of new roads, also happens to be the habitat of peregrine falcons, golden eagles and other endangered species. Even though developers claim that areas will be set aside for these animals, environmentalists and even state officials claim that the plans are totally inadequate for the needs of the area's fauna. The thirty thousand new residents planned for the area amount to an addition equivalent to one-fourth of the current population of Moreno Valley.[18]

The biggest white elephant of all is the proposed Tejon Ranch Development, on a parcel of land the size of the city of Los Angeles along the Grapevine between Los Angeles and Kern Counties. Although development is now in the preliminary stages, the *Los Angeles Times*, which owns a third of Tejon Ranch stock, is smoothing the way with cautious articles about the environmentally sensitive plans being developed by the company.[19]

One of the great shibboleths of such developments is the claim by proponents that they will provide much needed jobs in a time of recession.[20] But once the houses and business park have been built, there will not be nearly enough employment generated to support this new community, particularly in a time when the jobless rate inches higher every month. Such is the case elsewhere in the Inland Empire, where factory outlets, shopping malls and automobile dealerships can only absorb a limited number of workers. The steady decline in property values and the strains on Riverside County's social services hardly argue for yet more tracts of housing. Other losers from over-development include Southern California's few remaining traditional downtowns, such as the old urban core of Oxnard, a prototypical American downtown decimated by the proliferation of strip malls on the city's outskirts.[21]

Some visionary politicians and planners want to dump urban waste into the pristine desert and finish off the job that the mosaic of tract homes started.[22] Politicians and planners in Los Angeles county have their sights set on five desert areas in the Inland Empire as waste-disposal areas for Los Angeles. Waste-by-rail is scheduled for sites such as Eagle Mountain, an abandoned mine on the border of the Joshua Tree National Monument and at Amboy in the Mojave Desert, where trash is to be deposited in enormous caverns being dug for the purpose. Two more hazardous waste sites and one low-grade nuclear waste dump are scheduled for Highway 40, between Barstow and Needles.

Whether for waste or tract developments, the common view of the desert lands that extend to the Arizona border is that they are empty, barren and hence available for any speculative use, from a thoroughfare to Las Vegas or Palm Springs to a perfect venue for dirt bikes or off-road vehicles. Although not fitting a bucolic rural image, deserts are habitats for innumerable species of flora and fauna. Environmental concerns extend from the needs of endangered species to the problems of erosion and flooding to the most serious of all, contamination of ground water. Although city and county officials insist that they can devise adequate protection, anyone who has followed the saga of Rocky Flats in Colorado and other nuclear facilities is more than a bit sceptical of official assurances. The high fees that Riverside County will be able to charge for each ton of refuse convinced county officials to support the project, even though planners in the urban areas envision sending six trains and 200 trucks belching diesel fumes into the deserts of the Inland Empire every day.

During the booming economy of the 1980s, and indeed, throughout the Cold War years, when the proliferation of defence industry contractors, army, air force, navy and marine bases – the military industrial complex – cast the unhealthy illusion that economic expansion was destined to last forever, Southern California seemed miraculously immune to the economic swings or steady erosion that afflicted other parts of the nation. Even though the Southern California economy has seen its share of booms and busts, the length of this boom – almost fifty years – seduced politicians, entrepreneurs and citizens alike into believing that the boom would go on forever. Alas, if nothing else capitalism endlessly repeats itself: with the steady closure of defence bases, and hence defence industry suppliers, the decline of international trade in the wake of a world wide recession, unemployment has risen dramatically over the last three-year period, and property values have plummeted up to thirty per cent. The hopeful pursuers of the American Dream who purchased their dream houses in Palmdale, Temecula and Adelanto suddenly found themselves with mortgage payments greater than the value of their homes. When unemployment forced them to put their houses on the market, they often found no buyers at all, and no job possibilities in their new communities of little more than block after block of tract homes, the occasional strip mall, fast food outlets, mini-mall complexes and car dealerships sprawling out on acres of asphalt. The part-time, minimum wage jobs they offer barely keep an adolescent in Reeboks and video games, let alone food and shelter for a family.

The Planned Alternative
The human and environmental tragedies now being configured in these areas could have been predicted, and the disasters to come are being predicted today. Indignant urban planners and architects regularly decried the mindless sprawl that consumes hundreds of thousands of acres of pristine landscape every year. But planned developments in Southern California hardly offer an alternative. The city of Irvine was developed on the extensive lands of the Irvine Ranch Company, originally purchased in 1876 from drought-stricken Mexican-American ranchers and slowly transformed from range land to a giant agri-business.[23] As part of the post-World War II suburban explosion in Southern California, Myford Irvine began to turn the Irvine Company into a real estate development firm, in particular taking advantage of the miles of prime ocean front land between Newport Bay and Laguna Beach owned by the Ranch. Instead of selling the houses and lots, the Irvine Company offered long-term leases, retaining a degree of control unusual in American real estate.

Irvine's luxury subdivisions, with tennis courts, pools and club houses, differed substantially from the FHA financed tracts of repetitive homes for middle class homeowners that could be found in most of Southern California. But it soon became obvious that the biggest development money lay with the middle income homes, so the Irvine Company came under intense pressure to sell blocks of land to developers. Instead, it chose the option presented by the regents of the University of California, who wanted to build a university campus on Irvine land, the University of California at Irvine (UCI), with a new city to service it. William Pereira, who had originally proposed the site to the regents, was chosen to design a comprehensive land-use master plan for the university, the city and the surroundings.[24] The explicit programme was to build the ideal city of the future, drawing ideas from the best designers, the most experienced planners and especially from the errors of the past. Unlike ordinary, developer-built suburbs, Irvine would be neat and orderly: infrastructure buried underground, carefully bordered and trimmed roads leading to diverse types of housing, shopping centres and business parks. On these broad, uninviting corridors, no homeless wants to linger, no teenagers want to congregate, no hookers stroll. Those marginal groups that powerful interests have repeatedly tried to exorcise from the city would themselves opt out of occupying the streets of Irvine. Instead of a sea of tract homes, Irvine was to be divided into villages, each with diverse housing types and dominant architectural style, not to mention schools, shopping districts, churches and community pools.

Despite decades of scorn heaped on Levittown and its successors, the first thing the architects did in Irvine was contract an instant marriage with the key features of the average suburb – foregrounding the automobile amid identical rows of stucco townhouses, apartments and houses, with modest variations only emphasising their uniformity. They then embraced a second typical developer trope: the worst features of the average business park, with glass sheathed boxes surrounded by seas of parking. With astute prescience, the hit Sylvester Stallone film, *Demolition Man*, sets the violence free, dystopian fascist Los Angeles of the future in precisely these kinds of business parks, quintessentially expressed in James Freed's new Los Angeles Convention Center, which is the actual setting for much of the film's action.

The absolute abandonment of what designers touted as a comprehensive architectural vision in Irvine is breathtaking, but it served the Irvine Company's plan for an equally homogeneous class of inhabitants: middle to upper middle class white professionals, with a sprinkling of Asians and a tiny number of Latinos and African Americans. The glue holding all together is the typically Californian obsession with maintaining property values, a dicey proposition in 1990s Southern California. Hence the power of the homeowner associations, which aggressively contain any loose architectural or landscape cannons that might unwittingly roll in.

But even as the homogeneity of residents and residence configures the nightmare of modern architecture, the ideal of the perfect city crumbles in the face of market forces and real estate strategies. Although the initial idea was that residents could work and live in the same area, two things conspired against this goal from the outset. The housing prices and availability effectively limit the number and class of inhabitants, and the business parks, chiefly aerospace companies, electronics firms and research-and-development industries, have been so successful that far more people work here than originally anticipated. Irvine is therefore a net importer of workers. Add this to a general design absolutely dependent on the automobile for even the most trivial activity, and you end up with traffic congestion and pollution comparable to that of older cities – precisely the models that Irvine's design was intended to surpass. The Irvine Ranch and the city council steadfastly resisted mass transit facilities, let alone low-income housing. A lawsuit charging the Irvine Company with violation of state low-income housing laws was not settled until the Irvine Company came into new ownership in the late 1970s, and plans were outlined for a dramatic increase in development.

Although forced to admit a marginally more diverse population, Irvine maintains control over the environment and potential troubles, from gangs to homelessness, in part through the most suburban and most brilliant design strategy: there is no downtown, no central place to which residents and visitors can repair for an urban fix, no milling crowds or lingering strollers. Downtowns are far less susceptible to formal and informal measures of control than are suburbs under the watchful eye of Homeowners' Associations, and most of all, downtowns risk encouraging visits from precisely those groups that the planning process so mightly sought to banish. It is not difficult to imagine that for youngsters brought up in Irvine, Disneyland's Main Street in nearby Anaheim provides the only remotely urban experience they are likely to have.

The University certainly cannot fulfil the role of a public arena, sprawling as it is over a vast plain, with mostly second-rate signature buildings dotting the landscape and serviced only by a singularly unsuccessful mini-mall. For architects, the most notable feature of Irvine is the university's 'designer' architecture, with buildings by Frank Gehry, Rebecca Binder, Robert Venturi, Robert AM Stern, Eric Owen Moss and Charles Moore. With the exception of Gehry's Engineering Center and Binder's Lounge, however, most of the designs are dog-eared, uninspired variations on well-known themes. Set far apart from one another and amidst thoroughly uninspired landscaping, only the occasional bright colour distinguishes them from the nearby business parks.

Over thirty years ago, the Irvine Company brokered a deal to donate land to the University of California in exchange for development rights, just as President Donald Bren has recently donated 17,000 acres of land, including Limestone Canyon, in exchange for permission to develop adjacent land without cumbersome and irritating planning oversight. Only the occasional townhouses and apartment buildings in Irvine, Tustin or other Irvine Ranch Company bedroom communities depart significantly from the relentless expansion into the desert by tract developers. The marginal gestures to ecology and preservation of open space are little more than shrewd manoeuvres to defuse opposition to planned developments on other Irvine Ranch Company lands.[25]

It is no small irony that the Maguire Thomas Partners' plan for Playa Vista, just a few dozen miles away on the Los Angeles coast, has been presented as similarly bold, innovative and future oriented, even though like Irvine, there are no controls to mandate sales and rentals to those who will work in the area.[26] Architecture's cosmic claims, however, turn out to gush as noxiously and as steadily as fumes from a bus: hope springs eternal that architects can somehow pull magic solutions for new cities out of their hats. Irvine is an alarming indication of what Playa Vista might turn out to be, with much of the Ballona Wetlands, one of the few remaining in Southern California and certainly the only significant remaining open space within the basin, sealed in concrete except for a dainty preserve constructed *ex novo* as a sort of eco-amusement park for LA's prosperous westside.

Other parts of Southern California's little remaining coastal land are fixed in developers' sights, especially the enormous tracts of land owned by the federal government – US citizens, to be more precise – as military bases and soon to be sold to the highest bidders in order to make a dent in a national debt largely created by Reaganomics and politician sponsored S & L disasters.

Despite the growing problems with water, subsidence, pollution and waste disposal, the tide of single family tract house development rolls relentlessly forward, from long range plans for Tejon Ranch to eager plans to tame the Santa Clara river and to line it with concrete, malls and tract homes.[27] Although the plans for Tejon Ranch, a parcel of land the size of Los Angeles, are alarming for their scale and their intrusion into previously pristine mountains, north of Los Angeles, the Santa Clara River is probably the most typical example of development Southern California Style, casting into high relief the battle between developers and conservationists. The one hundred miles of the Santa Clara River are the longest, wildest and lined with the largest, best preserved riparian woodlands in Southern California. It supports five endangered species – three birds, one fish and one plant – and nourishes a $125 million dollar citrus crop.

But the competing interests waging a death struggle over the river's future are irreconcilable. Developers covet thirty miles of the river between Santa Clarita and Fillmore, which they envision lined with five commercial centres, a shopping district, an industrial area and thousands of homes. The owners of orchards, on the other hand, want the river controlled to protect their orchards – planted here precisely because of the rich river bottom soil – from the dangerous flooding that transforms the normally placid river into a raging torrent during the winter. Although growers have bermed and bulldozed the river for decades, like the Mississippi and other rivers, the Santa Clara meanders precisely where it wants to, often over adjacent citrus orchards.

Gravel miners plough up vegetation and disperse silt to raid the river bottom's hundreds of feet of aggregate, and they want to increase their take rather than limit it. Like developers and growers, they cite progress, development and cultivation as automatic social benefits that justify taming the river, and they have no patience with environmentalists' concerns for habitats, endangered species and complex ecosystems. The pro-development forces are convinced that the river can and should be controlled, but the US Army Corps of Engineers flatly rejects their arguments.

Fresh from the losing battle with the supposedly long-tamed Mississippi River and the ongoing struggle over the Atchafalaya River's attempt to become the new path of the Mississippi, the Corps has finally recognised that the grand engineering feats accomplished on rivers such as the Santa Clara always end up diminishing the resource and costing far more to preserve than is ever anticipated at the outset. Once tracts of homes go up along the river banks, extraordinary measures will need to be taken to protect the occupants from floods, and altogether too often, even the most elaborate measures fail. Rivers go their own way, or exact a terrible price of those who attempt to confine them.

Where will it end in Southern California? The natural barriers to endless development have been systematically battered without regard to short or long term costs, and the planning of Irvine only marginally improves on that of Moreno Valley or Palmdale. Developers still sweep up their profits, and leave the social, political and environmental costs for the taxpayers to shoulder. And nature, as the Mississippi demonstrated so tellingly, does not yield passively to the dictates of humans.

Notes

1. An early version of this article appears in *Cite*, the Rice Design Alliance publication from Houston, Texas, Winter 1993
2. The best study of the politics of air pollution in Los Angeles is Eric Mann and the Watchdog Organising Committee, *LA's Lethal Air: New Strategies for Policy, Organizing and Action*, Los Angeles: Labor/Community Strategy Center, 1991. A study is now in progress by this same organisation demonstrating that although air pollution spares no one in Southern California, other kinds of toxic poisoning disproportionately strike the poor
3. Norris Hundley Jr, *The Great Thirst: Californians and Water, 1770s-1990s*, University of California Press, Berkeley and Los Angeles, 1992, pp373-80; Donald Pisani, *From the Family Farm to Agribusiness: The Irrigation Crusade in California and the West 1850-1931*, Berkeley and Los Angeles 1984; Marc Reisner, *Cadillac Desert: The American West and Its Disappearing Water*, Viking, New York, 1986; Barry Commoner, *Making Peace with the Planet*, Pantheon, New York, 1990; John McPhee, *The Control of Nature*, Ferrar Straus and Giroux, New York, 1989, pp183-272. See also Tim Palmer, *California's Threatened Environment*, Washington DC, 1993; Richard Lillard, *Eden in Jeopardy – Man's Prodigal Meddling with his Environment: The Southern California Experience*, Knopf, New York, 1966. The best history of Southern California's development in general remains Carey McWilliams, *Southern California: An Island on the Land*, Peregrine Smith Books, Salt Lake City, 1973, original edition 1946. More recent critical analyses of Southern California and spatial change are Edward Soja et al, 'Urban Restructuring: An Analysis of Social and Spatial Change in Los Angeles', *Economic Geography* 59, April 1979, pp80-106; and Edward Soja, *Post-Modern Geographies*, Verso, London, 1990
4. I have written about the social and political role of design in Los Angeles elsewhere; see 'The Post-Modern Geography of Los Angeles,' *Design Book Review*, Summer 1991, pp86-91; 'Los Angeles Architecture 1970-90': *A & V* 32, December 1991; 'What Price Paradise?' *Architectural Review*, December 1987, pp85-89. The most compelling account of Los Angeles to appear since McWilliams is Mike Davis, *City of Quartz*, Verso, London, 1990.
5. Reyner Banham, *Los Angeles: The Architecture of the Four Ecologies*, Penguin, London 1971
6. *Ibid*, p22
7. *Ibid*, p31 Banham's four ecologies – surfurbia, the foothills, the Plains of Id and Autopia – playfully intersected with specific architectural styles
8. *Ibid*, p96
9. *Ibid*, p100
10. *Ibid*, p107
11. The best analysis of the debris flows is John McPhee's classic essay, 'Los Angeles Against the Mountains', in John McPhee, *The Control of Nature*, Farrar, Straus and Giroux, New York, 1989, pp181-272
12. Ken Ellingwood, 'It's an Uphill Battle', *Los Angeles Times*, 3 October 1993
13. A quick summary appeared in Rodney Steiner, *Los Angeles: The Centrifugal City*, Kendall/Hunt Publishing Co, Dubuque, 1981
14. When this article had already been written, an article essentially corroborating my account appeared in the *New York Times*: Seth Mydans, 'With a Boom in the Desert Over, Transplants are Feeling Stranded', August 26, 1993
15. *Los Angeles Times*, December 13, 1992
16. *Ibid*, April 23, 1993, section B, 1:2
17. Matthew Heller, 'A Quiet Getaway', *Los Angeles Times*, 28 May 1993
18. Patrick J McDonnell, 'Backlash Hits Growth-Loving Moreno Valley', *Los Angeles Times*, 13 January 1992
19. Jonathan Gaw, 'As It Turns 150, Tejon Ranch Weights Development', *Los Angeles Times*, 19 September 1993
20. McDonnell, 'Backlash'; Patrick J McDonnell, 'Referendum on Quality of Life', *Los Angeles Times*, 22 March 1993
21. Fred Alvarez, 'Looking for a Boost in Oxnard', *Los Angeles Times*, 2 February 1993
22. Paul Feldman, 'Trash Dumps May Intrude on Desert Serenity', *Los Angeles Times*, 28 October 1991; 'Ward Valley Nuclear Waste Facility Approved', *Los Angeles Times*, 17 September 1993
23. Among the classic histories of the Irvine Ranch Company and of Orange County are Robert Glass Cleland, *The Irvine Ranch*, San Marino, CA: Huntington Library 1962; Nathaniel M Griffin, Irvine: *The Genesis of a New Commmunity*, Urban Land Institute Washington DC, 1974; Martin J Schiesl, 'Designing the Model Community: The Irvine Company and suburban Development, 1950-1988', in R Kling et al, eds. *Post-Suburban California: The Transformation of Orange County Since World War II*, University of California Press Berkeley and Los Angeles, 1991, pp55-91
24. Pereira conducted two major studies for the new community and the university: William L Pereira and Associates, *A Preliminary Report for a University-Community Development in Orange County*, 1959, Government Publication Files, University of California, Irvine (UCI); and *Second Phase Report for a University-Community Development in Orange County*, 1960, Government Publications Files, UCI
25. Marla Cone, 'Public Gets Invitation to Secluded Canyon', *Los Angeles Times*, 8 May 1993
26. Andres Duany and Elizabeth Plater-Zyberk with Stephanos Polyzoides are the designers and planners associated with Playa Vista
27. Jonathan Gaw, 'Tejon Ranch Weighs Development'; J Gaw, 'Farmers Fear Development Will Go Unchecked', *Los Angeles Times*, 25 April 1993

ELIZABETH MOULE AND STEFANOS POLYZOIDES
DOWNTOWN IN THE TWENTIETH CENTURY:
The Struggle for Defining the Centre of Los Angeles

Downtown Los Angeles has been the historic centre of the Southern California region since its inception and Bunker Hill one of its pivotal constituent parts. The development and redevelopment of Bunker Hill in the last one hundred or so years, provides a special opportunity to observe the process through which the architecture and urbanism of Los Angeles was developed during various phases of the city's growth.

Bunker Hill was platted in the 1880s as part of the first wave of neighbourhood formation in Los Angeles. Its varied topography with elegant streets, single family houses, gardens, and its proximity to commercial establishments and governmental and cultural activities made it one of the most amenable residential locations for the elite of an emerging American town.

After 1900 and as the pattern of development in Los Angeles began to change, its urban and architectural character was seriously affected. By the turn of the twentieth century, Downtown was the centre of regional employment and retail uses in a Los Angeles slowly being transformed into a city. It included a multitude of twelve-storey building blocks which defined impressive streets and boulevards. Its overall building fabric was dense and continuous and generated an active pedestrian life.

Downtown was connected to a series of suburbs and independent towns strung along the stations of the 'Red Car' train system. These suburbs and towns were composed of discrete neighbourhoods and were surrounded by large tracts of beautiful, open and productive agricultural land. The myth of Southern California as a place that combined all the advantages of urban and rural life was born during this period. Meanwhile, the automobile was also being firmly established as a serious mode of transport. It was used both for short trips within individual towns and for longer trips between them.

In the early 1920s the imperative for establishing Downtown Los Angeles as the civic and cultural centre of Southern California became a political reality. A number of competing proposals were commissioned, but the most extraordinary one was prepared by the Allied Architects, a group of classicist architects who associated during this period for the purpose of executing civic architectural and urbanist projects.[1]

The Allied Architects' plan for a civic, administrative and cultural centre of the Southern California region is the most extraordinary architectural vision ever presented for Downtown Los Angeles. It was conceived at a metropolitan scale. Its sheer physical size, approximately one mile in each principal direction was amazing, with an equally ambitious building programme: all the major public buildings of Los Angeles were to be assembled in a complex composition dominated by public gardens and places.

The mythical, integrative power of the plan was also monumental. It incorporated El Pueblo, the Spanish foundation site of Los Angeles; Fort Moore, the hill overlooking El Pueblo where the American army camped during its occupation and annexation of the Mexican pueblo; a new train station, symbol of an industrial America that absorbed and transformed California; and new cultural, entertainment and administrative buildings, the symbols of a progressive, democratic US-centered civilisation. All of the above restated the principle that a beautiful city, a city of deep culture and a prosperous city are interdependent.

The overall formal idea of the Allied Architects' plan was landscape-driven. A powerful *Beaux Arts* composition of spaces arrayed on major and minor axes, it was very skilfully overlaid onto the grid of Downtown. In the north-south direction its principal axis was centred along the ridge of Bunker Hill along Grand Avenue. In the east-west direction, the public spaces and new streets erased the irregular pattern of small streets and blocks that were part of the original pueblo. Its overall configuration was mountain-like, an extruded pyramid with a flattened ridge and a series of linear gardens tiered along its slopes. There is no doubt about the fact that this was a massive clearance project. But its ambition was clearly directed at the public good: the monumental, almost millennial marking of the civic centre of the Los Angeles region.

The centrepiece of the plan was a seven block long public piazza called Las Alturas. On one end of its gently sloping ground stood a monument to Fort Moore and on the other, a major public building. Temple, First, Second and Third

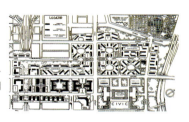

OPPOSITE: Pei, Cobb & Freed, First Interstate World Center, Downtown Los Angeles; FROM ABOVE: Plan for an administration centre for the city and county of Los Angeles, Allied Architects, 1924; Bunker Hill, existing, LA city planning commission, 1942; Bunker Hill, proposed, LA city planning commission, 1942

SOCIAL AND PLANNING HISTORY

Streets were tunnelled under Las Alturas and access to this largely pedestrian place was through local streets on its edges.

La Rambla was located on the first tier, approximately fifteen to twenty feet lower than Las Alturas. It was in effect a highly landscaped Olive Street, connected to Hope Street around a semicircular apsidal road wrapping around Fort Moore. Hope Street terminated at El Prado, a hilltop block-sized park in front of a proposed public library. If the precedent for Las Alturas was French, the inspiration for La Rambla, clearly suggested in its plan configuration, if not its name, was Catalan, perhaps a tribute to Father Serra.

La Ronda was located on the lowest tier, a rather simple connection between Hill and Flower Streets, also around Fort Moore. What is particularly wonderful about La Ronda is that as it circumnavigated Bunker Hill it became tangent to all the smaller piazzas and parks of the ensemble, El Prado, El Paseo and La Plaza, the extension and enlargement of the original square of the city's foundation. Driving or walking along La Ronda, one would have passed through all the great public spaces on its edge, sensing that they were cleverly placed perpendicular to Bunker Hill, sloping down and away from it, visually connecting the city beyond.

La Ronda also intersected a massive city hall building on the west side of the project. The city hall, of an identical *parti* as the one constructed on its current site later in the decade, dominated Las Alturas with its elaborate plan and imposing biaxial massing. This could have been a powerful and complex building, combining a traditional formal role in terminating the east-west axis and a thoroughly modern one in its overlap and multi-level intersection with Flower Street on the north-south axis.

The Allied Architects' plan incorporated fifty new buildings. They were used mostly as *poche* between the body of the existing city and the extraordinary figures of public spaces that the plan defined. The most developed combination of buildings and gardens unfolded on the cross axis. Three spaces reminiscent of the sequence of squares at Nancy, France, were formed by the county buildings: El Paseo, a linear Carrière-like square without a name and La Alameda, both of which depended upon the formal inflections of the buildings which surrounded them. The fronts of the buildings were massive, continuous and uniform in scale, their backs combining to form beautiful civic gardens. All kinds of public uses were intended for the fifty buildings. It is hard to ascertain the use for each one, as the plan is without an index. Most buildings are described as normative, with the exception of the buildings intersecting the axes and the train station to the east which dominates La Alameda.

The easternmost portion of the plan was an attempt to turn La Plaza into a formal park containing the important remaining historic building fragments of early Los Angeles. The integration of monuments with new buildings and gardens was a strategy well worth pondering in the future reconstruction of the foundation settlement of the city.

The idealistic character of the Allied Architects' work can be sensed not only by its astounding programmatic scope and overall form, but also by its attitude towards the existing city. The plan proposed clearing Bunker Hill in its entirety. It avoided any engagement with the areas of Downtown where commercial uses predominated. Pershing Square, its commercial centre, was drawn uncontested on the edge of the plan. Eventually the plan's civic dignity fell victim to crass politics, bureaucratic confusion and real estate interests that favoured the development of the open land between the many towns of Southern California.

The city and the county judged the project too large, too expensive, too complicated and opted out for a scaled-down alternative, a version of which remains incomplete seventy years later. By the mid-twenties, real estate interests had began to sense the potential of the automobile to give universal access and value to the endless tracts of land in the Los Angeles basin. Beginning with the extension of Wilshire Boulevard westwards from Downtown and the construction of an extensive network of all-weather surface roads in the 1920s, the fate of the Allied Architects' plan was sealed. The city was going to sprawl and it didn't need, perhaps it didn't even deserve, a Civic Centre appropriate to a world-class city.

By the end of World War II and the beginning of massive freeway construction, Bunker Hill was a neighbourhood of a vital mix of uses, people and buildings of a kind quite typical of other American urban centres. The dream of a great civic centre to challenge and dwarf San Francisco's was long gone. But the temptation to re-energise the economic potential of Downtown by rasing it and reconstructing it in a thoroughly 'modern' form began to pick up support.

By 1942 the Los Angeles City Planning Commission set in motion the intellectual and political agenda for revitalising Downtown. The architectural and urbanist instrument for accomplishing this task was the theories promoted by CIAM, the International Congress of Modern Architecture, of which the progressive Los Angeles architect Richard Neutra was an active member. The 1942 illustrative site plan of Bunker Hill by the Planning Commission combines two tragic

FROM ABOVE: Military parade on Broadway during World War I, c1915; Angels Flight crossing through Bunker Hill, c1950; Bunker Hill, urban renewal proposal, community redevelopment age, 1959

ELIZABETH MOULE AND STEFANOS POLYZOIDES

trends: clearance and the international formal language of Le Corbusier's Ville Radieuse. Not only did the plan propose the obliteration of one of Los Angeles' most interesting and vital inner neighbourhoods, it also replaced it with the normative and arbitrary modern slabs that eventually robbed every American city of its public realm. It would be many years before architects and planners realised that the public realm in such schemes was not to be replaced by parkland but by huge streets and parking.

The spark that ignited the 'Urban Renewal' catastrophe at Bunker Hill and everywhere else in California was the enactment by the state legislature in 1945 of a Community Redevelopment Act. It authorised the creation of local redevelopment agencies to acquire properties (using eminent domain proceedings, if necessary), clear them, and resell or lease them to private developers in order to build anew, using the maximum densities of the most productive uses available, most typically office and commercial retail. Redevelopment was a wealth-generating instrument, through which Community Redevelopment Agencies would come to control the disposition of monies accruing to them by the tax increment difference between the value of the new development and the existing improvements on the land.

The theory of redevelopment was based on questionable assumptions regarding physical and social decay. 'Blight' was variously described during this period as being caused by mixed uses, old fashioned street patterns (the grid), heavy automobile traffic, a run down (but affordable) housing stock and adverse environmental conditions. In retrospect, all these criteria were offered as rationalisations to hide the true motivations behind massive urban clearance. It was in fact the associating of dense city form with social heterogeneity and social dysfunction that precipitated the mass demolition of America's Downtowns after 1945. The existence of 'urban problems' should have been addressed in place everywhere. Instead, Bunker Hill was cleansed only to have its social pathologies appear south, east and west of Downtown in ever more virulent forms, particularly as the poorer citizens of the city had lost faith in the ability of their city's leaders and planners to listen to their needs and respond to them.[2]

The urban theories of Modernism emerged as the antidote to blight. The Bunker Hill Urban Renewal project was approved by the Los Angeles City Council on March 31, 1959. The two formative concepts of this new urban plan were described as follows: 'First, automobile and truck movements will not be permitted to destroy the usefulness of the new development. A division between pedestrian activities and vehicular travel will be controlled through grade separation, escalators, super blocks, pedestrian malls, peripheral and sunken parking garages, public transit and off street truck loading. Secondly, human scale and beauty will be the keynote of the 'new city within the city'. Removal of all height limit restraints will permit skyscrapers with breathtaking views. (The hill will be regraded but will remain a hill.) Building coverage controls will provide much more usable open space, light and air among the structures, than has ever before been realised in the centre of a major city. Parks and other recreational areas and aesthetic features will state that this Downtown is not only for trade but for livability and comfort as well. In short, it will be built for people.'[3]

This absolutely chilling description of the Bunker Hill project is the clearest description of the method by which most classic American urban centres were destroyed. They were replaced by a fragmented version of the Ville Radieuse, an imported, internationalist urbanism. The operation was in full swing in the 1960s, 70s and 80s. The resulting urban environment was catastrophic throughout the country but particularly in Downtown Los Angeles: more traffic and smog than before; streets dominated by freeway standards and faceless, huge garages; buildings designed like bunkers, inaccessible to the sidewalk, massive and scaleless; rooftop parks, inaccessible to pedestrians; districts of Downtown fragmented and separated from each other, their pedestrian life extinguished; hundreds of significant landmarks and buildings rased; the natural profile of Bunker Hill graded by twenty feet and destroyed; blight spread throughout the centre of the city. The cleared redevelopment sites remained virtually empty for almost fifteen years, an image of desolation offered to millions of commuters that fuelled the decline of Downtown as the region's symbolic centre.

In the mid-1960s, Floor Area Ratio (FAR) legislation was enacted by the City of Los Angeles into its zoning code. In the interest of delivering urban form dominated by the monumental towers and random chaotic residual open space of modernism, entitlements were coupled to abstract, mathematical ratios of density – the multiples of the ground area of a given property that can be built. By this decision, density was de-coupled from form guidelines such as height, built to lines, land coverage and block profiles. It was such codes that historically had kept buildings within typological limits and had allowed the incremental construction of the public realm as individual buildings were put in place. The ugliness, scalelessness, unfriendliness, lack of street

FROM ABOVE: LA pacific ticket office, 1910; aerial view of Bunker Hill, 1955; view of Bunker Hill demolished, from City Hall, c 1965

SOCIAL AND PLANNING HISTORY

landscape and public parks, the insecurity, in short most of the perceived ills of Downtown as it has recently existed can be traced to this disastrous piece of FAR legislation. It allowed the introduction of isolated buildings and residual open spaces unsympathetic to its existing building fabric and public open space network. The resulting Downtown Los Angeles of Urban Renewal was chaos by design.

In 1972 the Community Redevelopment Agency published 'Central City Los Angeles 1972-90, Preliminary General Development Plan', popularly known as the 'Silver Book'. This document became the blueprint by which the detailed architectural development of Bunker Hill took place. It was a planning effort sponsored by the major corporate powers located in Downtown Los Angeles with the support of the heads of all the technical Departments of the City. This was a document with predictable recommendations, considering recent political and planning history. It took advantage of all the legislation of the 1950s and 60s and eventually delivered a stereotypical modern downtown whose skyline matched Houston's, Atlanta's, Kansas City's, and those of most other American cities. Happily, the plan's provisions for the development of housing in South Park were not realised. They were to be based on the design of a nine block sunken park surrounded by high-rise apartments. Another violent imposition of a new formal order on the body of Downtown involving the clearance of at least twenty-five blocks.[4]

In 1984 Maguire Thomas Partners and the Community Redevelopment Agency negotiated a complex agreement for a project on the southern edge of Bunker Hill. It involved the construction of two office towers, the renovation and extension of Bertram Goodhue's Central Library, the construction of three major parks including the renovation of Pershing Square, and the revitalisation of the streetscape along three blocks of Grand Avenue and three blocks of 5th Street. Now complete, the project is a remarkable accomplishment in beginning to reverse the ravages of Urban Renewal. It is focused on the public realm of Downtown which it repairs and enhances. The various projects are dispersed enough to have already attracted further private development. They are architecturally ambitious and beautifully layered onto the body of the existing city. They encourage pedestrian life, a source of enjoyment, safety and civic pride in any city. It is a model of catalytic development of the kind that includes a mixture of building, open space and landscape projects, and which has the power to reverse recent trends and enhance Downtown Los Angeles' position as the centre of a region with which it is inextricably linked.

Since 1989, an Advisory Committee appointed by Mayor Bradley has been working on a new Strategic Plan for Downtown Los Angeles that will guide its growth to the year 2020. The plan represents a consensus among all major community, business and public interests regarding the future of the city centre. The process of planning brought to one table the Committee along with consultants in the various aspects of Urbanism: architecture, landscape architecture, transportation, economic planning, environmental planning, homelessness and social services and policy implementation. It was the first time in more than fifty years that single purpose planning was displaced by the simultaneous consideration of all the technical aspects and all the particular economic and social interests relevant to the reconstruction of Downtown.

The Strategic Plan intends once again to link the economic prosperity of Downtown to the beauty and unique character of its public realm for the benefit of all the citizens of Los Angeles. It directs all future public and private investments and actions to the task of coordinating this reconstruction. The scope of the plan covers all ten neighbourhoods and districts of the centre of the city and is not limited to Bunker Hill. Considering that at five square miles the project area is quite enormous, many of its provisions are surprisingly physical. The new train transit system, a proposed Downtown trolley bus circulator and the pedestrian-friendly streets that parallel them are presented as the primary means of linking the disparate pieces of Downtown to each other. A whole open space network of metropolitan, civic and neighbourhood parks can be leveraged out of individual building and infrastructural projects. Building design prescriptions are based on both the adaptive reuse of significant existing buildings as well as the design of new ones that define public space on their street sides and private space in the interior of blocks. The grain of development is purposefully kept small so that the maximum number of citizens can participate in the development process.

The Downtown that can be generated out of the physical provisions of the Strategic Plan depends on an urbanism of new-found realism whose nature is only now becoming clear. It replaces the compositional formality and rigidity of classicism and modernism with the idea of collective form accomplished out of multiple incremental projects. It rejects the modern fixation with designing all buildings as isolated monuments in favour of few monuments rendered within a continuous urban fabric, stressing the importance of shared public space serviced by a variety of transportation modes. Finally, the plan depends on the intense mixing of uses in space and on the conservation and reuse of the existing city as an irreplaceable cultural and economic resource.

ELIZABETH MOULE AND STEFANOS POLYZOIDES

The current need to rebuild Downtown Los Angeles is not based on a romantic notion that the concentric city of the past should be reconstructed. Instead, the struggle to redefine the centre of this metropolis is emblematic of the need to direct our society's energies toward a commitment to permanence of place. That is, the agreement to deal with the problems and opportunities that are presented by the world we inhabit in its current state. Despite the rhetoric that has dominated our recent history, it is not possible to escape the issues of the day nor is it possible to continue to build ever further into nature; and most certainly, it is ultimately not possible to make or remake a city out of uncoordinated, single-interest, single-purpose projects whatever their size or however celebrated their author.

Notes
1 Robert M Fogelson, *The Fragmented Metropolis*, Cambridge, Mass, Harvard University Press, 1967, pp263-72
2 Mel Scott, *Metropolitan Los Angeles, One Community*, The Haynes Foundation, Los Angeles, 1949, pp108-10
3 John Baur and Russell Belous, *Los Angeles, 1900-61*, The History Division, Los Angeles County Museum, 1961, pp53-54
4 Wallace, McHarg, Roberts and Todd, *Central City Los Angeles 1972-90, Preliminary General Development Plan*, The Committee for Central City Planning, Inc, Los Angeles, 1972

View from Downtown Los Angeles

KIM COLEMAN
LOS ANGELES MADE VISIBLE

I spent my first year in Los Angeles with an AAA map open on my lap, just trying to find the city. Gertrude Stein's 'there is no there there' was a constant mantra reverberating in my head. The absence of visible 'place-making' was particularly hard-felt because the two cities I had just left, New York and Charlottesville, Virginia, both have very tangible and architecturally exciting qualities of place. But the order I initially perceived on the map – that of grids and shifted grids, of straight streets becoming curvilinear as the Basin meets the hills, of diagonal patterns as the streetcar right of ways of Exposition and Electric superimpose on the more prominent system – eventually pervaded my sense of the city as points of reference and orientation in the way that building landmarks do in older American and European cities.

The lack of typical urban forms in Los Angeles, those which are traditionally believed essential to a great city, positions it as an ideal laboratory for speculation. The search for processes which continue and enrich its unique urban structure is at issue in a two-part design proposal submitted for the Olympic West Design Competition. Each stage of the competition is a vehicle for the exploration of ideas and is approached differently. The resulting proposals, which are seen not as a visionary scheme but as a possibility, test methods for reconstituting the city.

Olympic West

The Olympic West Garden District International Design Competition was sponsored by a City of Los Angeles Councilman and two private developers in an effort to demonstrate that quality development can occur in an atmosphere of cooperation, and that neighbourhood concerns can be incorporated into design values. The competition, the ultimate goal of which is the design of an office building, focuses initially on the urban design of the boulevard and prescriptions for the use and arrangement of future buildings along the boulevard. It provides the opportunity to design both the public setting for the architecture and the architecture itself.

The competition brief identifies areas appropriate for redevelopment and those off-limits to the proposal (having relatively new buildings close to or exceeding the proposed maximum building envelopes). The urban design scheme is to be phased in over time, and the proposal as a whole should not depend on any property not under the control of the competition organisers. The site of the first stage is the redevelopment of a district, ten blocks of Olympic Boulevard immediately west of the San Diego Freeway near the Santa Monica border with West Los Angeles. The second stage concentrates on a block-sized parcel within the District – and the design of an office building with some mixed use on the ground floors. In both stages the primary programme elements, office space and parking, are malleable typologies with conventional variations repeated endlessly across Los Angeles.

Site

The Olympic West District is characterised by the closeness of industrial, commercial, single- and multi-family residential uses. Good weather, cool ocean breezes, convenient access and proximity to prosperous residential neighbourhoods make the area desirable for development. The area has been known primarily for its large Japanese-American population and the preponderance of family-run small landscaping nurseries. More recently it has become an area of large discount stores housed in warehouses, high-rise bank and insurance company buildings and upscale health clubs and shops.

The best way to see LA is from the freeway, particularly on a Sunday morning when the air is clear and the traffic sparse. The freeway from the beach to Downtown at times carves into the land, at times moves along the surface, and at times rises above it, providing a sequence of very different impressions of the city. Beginning at the Pacific Coast Highway, an asymmetrical path with the flat horizontal span of the ocean to one side and the high cliffs of the Santa Monica Palisades on the other, the thoroughfare dives into a tunnel and emerges surrounded by high embankments of dark green. The Christopher Columbus Transcontinental Highway (a mouthful of a name if you're only going to Centinela, but better known as the 10, or Santa Monica, freeway) moves below the surface of its surroundings through Santa Monica, and rises to natural grade near the border with West Los Angeles.

At Bundy and Barrington, the area closest to the Olympic West District, the freeway has climbed above the rooftops of the surrounding apartment buildings and the driver's seat provides a dramatic, if moveable, perch from which to survey the city. The new buildings along Olympic Boulevard are silhouetted against a backdrop of the Santa Monica foothills and are pronounced presences of the skyline. There is a feeling of exhilaration at this point – no sound-deflecting walls as there are in Santa Monica, but a burst of space as the freeway rises above the houses and trees. On days when the air is clear and there is snow on the mountains beyond, the freeway heading toward Downtown looks like the road to Oz.

Method

The technique of transformation is used in both proposals to explore a domain for architectural design which applies to both artefact and concept. Applied to making architecture in the city, the process of transformation parallels the evolving nature of urban growth and change. A city is always in the process of becoming: encouraging, allowing, describing possibilities for human action, reaction and intervention, rather than a fixed condition which determines a closed system. Transformation may describe the place of formation which exists in the city between historical fact and future vision.

The goal of the process is to explore methodologies which establish a multiplicity of readings within an overall hierarchy. The multiplicity mirrors the manifold diversity of scale, overlay and culture of Los Angeles, where urban life occurs in pockets of activity, rather than as a continuous pedestrian experience. The intent is to re-engage the structure of the city to experience.

Land-ship

The word landscape (derived from the Dutch word, *landschap*: land which is created) is a term which initially applied to seventeenth-century paintings representing natural scenes. The painter, as the maker of an artificial nature, creates the artefact through an image which structures his or her ideas. Thus, landscape is not nature *per se*, but defined as land + -ship: land which is constructed by man.[1] The term Land-ship may also suggest the idea of a ship (as opposed to -ship), a complete living environment which establishes boundaries and areas of programmed human activity. A ship suggests density and intensification of use, and multiple activities, from formal to casual, occurring simultaneously. Landscape suggests interface: a thread between interior to exterior. Land-ship, then, implies a living environment where many activities occur, which is integral to the land it inhabits.

Stage I: The Machine in the Garden

Land-ship I, the design for the Olympic West District, establishes a dialogue between two forces inherent in the American Dream: the pastoral ideal, represented by the landscape garden, and technological reality, exemplified by the automobile, steel and glass buildings and the lights of the city. The idea, articulated by Leo Marx, of the machine overriding the garden, is a pervasive theme in American literature.[2] As a city primarily of the twentieth century, Los Angeles has been built on technology, that of the railway, the automobile, the engineered viaduct, the oil well and the aerospace industry. Technology has been the ideal in the city's growth, not the image of an idealised country life.

Our first year in LA, my husband and I traded our loft in New York City for an enormous loft in an industrial area of Inglewood and a car. An auto-body shop flanked the loft on one side, an auto-upholstery shop on the other. The median strip in front on Florence Avenue was concrete, painted green. Railroad tracks ran ten feet behind the building, and every night at 12.35 a train went by, the engineer waving if he saw our lights on. My primary route to the city was up La Brea Avenue through the Baldwin Hills. A surreal area, the hills are populated with oil pumping machines, bobbing like birds pecking at the ground in slow motion. There are parts of the hills where you cannot see the city at all, only the yellowish haze and the machines. The hills themselves went through radical transformations in the course of that year: from brown, dry and dusty, to mud with houses sliding, to an incredible green fuzzy carpet in spring. The constant throughout was the rhythmic movement of these machines, up and down, around in circles, day in, day out, gracefully dancing on the landscape. The train, the oil-pumping machinery, the traffic patterns, the

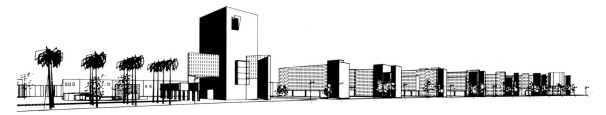

Land-ship I, View of the Botanical Park, office building and studio-loft buildings looking southwest from Olympic Boulevard

SOCIAL AND PLANNING HISTORY

noise of the generator in the auto-body shop next door: the movement of machines became established rhythms which moulded a routine, a way of life, in a new place.

Land-ship I proposes the process of industrialisation in reverse: instead of the nineteenth and early twentieth century intrusion of technology, it proposes the re-infusion of the landscape experience – its sequences, open and closed spaces, and explicit relationships to the environment – on the technological city. New building typologies are developed which link inside to outside, garden to office, roof to ground.

Design intentions for Land-ship I are encrypted into emblematic diagrams, the form and structure of which imply the formation of artefacts yet to be made. Marco Polo, in Italo Calvino's book, *Invisible Cities*, designates a gesture as an emblem to denote a generative idea, the coding of essence or underlying order opens it to the receipt of other information.[3] The forms which encode a design project become repositories of meaning which go beyond functional requirements or formal diagrams. The emblems imply function, order and a set of ideas which may become the framework for buildings yet to be developed. In an urban design scale proposal such as this, where a large area is studied, the designer formulates an attitude about every area and denotes a response through the representation of a building mass. Land-ship I includes such masses, but behind each one is a construct, an encoded emblem. The reading of formal intention through these emblematic diagrams establishes a threshold for the design idea.

In the first stage the context made visible is the context of architecture – of spatial constructs being woven into the fabric of the area, germs of building forms developed from diverse backgrounds: elements from Hejduk and Jefferson, Philip Johnson's Glass House juxtaposed with Comlongen, a medieval Scottish castle. The parking garage with recreation facilities and gardens on the roofs is an icon for the merging of landscape and technology inspired by Leonitov's visionary city at Magnitogorsk. Building and design are seen as a repository for memory, for spatial archetypes which go beyond their prior uses and *loci*. Precedents in architecture are the DNA for the future development of schemes; transformations of formal order are adapted and grounded in a context and use which forces the fundamental transformation of design intention.

Computer-integrated design is influential to the methodology for the first stage, because it facilitates relationships and transformations which would have remained dormant without it. The evolutionary process of life growing and developing many permutations is a model for computer use in the project. Design transformation studies executed by members of the project team prior to the competition are further transformed, forming the germ of ideas for each of the parcels along Olympic Boulevard from organisations akin to the genetic material of organic matter.[4] The use of the machine of the computer, and the repetition and permutation of forms which it allows and encourages, both parallels and contrasts the metaphor of the garden. A computer-integrated process of design exploration expands the opportunity to test options, and also facilitates the transformation of artefacts from one context to another.

Stage II: The Landscape made Visible

Changes in weather alter one's perception of Los Angeles because they dramatically effect the sense of the space of the city. On some days, particularly in summer and early fall, the city appears as an endless sprawl with no boundaries, only continuous streets stretching out straight and flat to infinity. No edges are apparent. But on days which are clear, especially after it rains, the edges of the city come into focus, as if the collective population simultaneously removed scratched discoloured glasses with incorrect prescriptions. Significant markers and boundaries, like the Hollywood sign, the mountains or the ocean become visible and add scale, contrast and background to a city which on other days seems reduced only to a middle ground.

The implied structure of the existing city and the memory of that structure is the reference for the making of Land-ship II, a proposal for a single block at the north-west corner of Olympic

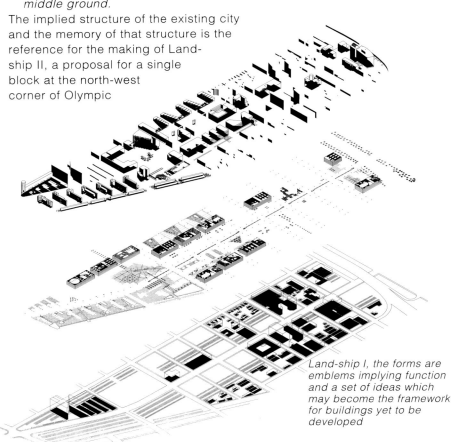

Land-ship I, the forms are emblems implying function and a set of ideas which may become the framework for buildings yet to be developed

Boulevard and Barrington Avenue.[5] The focus of ideas is the order inherent in the physical history of a city which, as Jan Morris observes, does not lie thinly on the ground, but neither (like a true Southern Californian) does it reveal its age, which is only implied by the names of its streets and boulevards.[6] Los Angeles exists as a layering of fragmented pre-existing ordering systems, which are typically obscured or erased as subsequent development seeks to satisfy current objectives often at the expense of the reinforcement of those elements critical to sustain the city's fabric. Land-ship II proposes a prototypical methodology for development which resurrects layers of history which have been typically obliterated in Los Angeles in the name of progress. The proposal asserts and makes more legible the critical underlying syntax of the existing context in a reconstructive process, which builds on traces of former texts.

Land-ship II attempts to simultaneously look back and look forward, acting as a window through time like Khan's atlas and mediating between the city that was and the city that could be. The goal of the project is not to synthesise forms into a homogeneous structure, but, in fact, to maintain the disjunction in scale, method of construction and response to the site which characterises Los Angeles. The autonomy of its systems gives LA its unique urban structure. In the sequence of orders imposed by development – chaparral, agriculture, parcelisation, railway, freeway – each system is not marked in the overlay of the next. The context is transformed over time, weaving new densities and required infrastructure into existing community patterns and activities. This evolution suggests an appropriate methodology for making explicit the urban structure of the city, one which allows the user to experience the spaces between orders – the plurality of development and time.

When you live in the hills, your awareness of the underlying order of lunar cycles and changes in weather is more profound than when you live in the flats. Nights are dark and still; there are no street lights, and the sounds of the city are far away. But on nights when the moon is full, the volume of the sky is awash with light, and the howling of the coyotes is sometimes deafening. A single one starts, and soon the canyons are filled with eerie baying.

On days when the Santa Anas have been blowing for a while, or in early fall, with the one heat wave of the year, when our colleagues or the drivers behind us or the people in the check-out line at the supermarket are noticeably irritable, changes in animal activities in the hills are intense. Deer walk up onto the lawn at midday, searching for water. Rattlesnakes emerge from their hiding places in the canyons. Bobcats are emboldened to walk into back yards. Roadrunners wander into houses, looking for food and water, when doors are left open for the occasional breeze.

Michel Foucault's description of order parallels a process of making visible the city. 'It is only in the blank spaces of this grid that order manifests itself in depth as though already there, waiting in silence for the moment of its expression.'[7] The intent of the process is to uncover not only prior orders, but also previous experience and sense of place. The proposal for Land-ship II brings to the surface the reading of the site and replicates time in a laboratory setting to explore a design process which looks at past layers of growth.

Speculative office building design is driven by economic and market forces which favour undifferentiated space, producing a building type which is non-hierarchical and does not suggest articulated accommodation.[8] In cities across the world, homogeneous steel and glass office buildings literally mirror the forms around them without expressing their own forms. Instead of mirroring, the types of office space developed in Land-ship II spatially represent the scale and delineation of space around them. The sequence of development in Los Angeles has transformed large tracts of farmland to small ones, then sold individual parcels within blocks for small industrial and commercial buildings and is now, with the current demand for office/parking developments, recollecting the parcels for development at the scale of the block. Maintaining the massing of the individual parcels within the block allows Land-ship II to mediate between the scale of the boulevard and that of the residential neighbourhood to its north. The spatial integrity of the neighbourhood prevails at the pedestrian scale, while the identity of the mid-rise tower predominates at the scale of the boulevard and the freeway. Desert chaparral and irrigated orchard gardens on the

Land-ship II, X-ray drawing

SOCIAL AND PLANNING HISTORY

plaza suggest the landscape order at the scale of previous large land holdings.

Land-ship II develops differentiated interior and exterior public spaces which encompass a full range of scales within an urban continuum. The new context is made by restating multiple structures of development, combining the scale of the neighbourhood and existing parcelisation with the imposition of a new scale, the urban scale of the freeway, of multi-parcel development and of the new public gardens and amenities that only large-scale development can provide. The strategy allows for a combination of densities which can both reinforce existing patterns and overlay new amenities in an integrative process. A sequence of public spaces: park, plaza and garden imposed over a ground of a modern, vehicular, non-pedestrian scale provides an identity for the proposal which operates at many scales: weaving into the existing neighbourhood, providing a positive contribution to pedestrians in the form of significant public spaces, and marking the site with a landmark that identifies it from the automobile and the distance.

Conclusion: Visible City

The schemes for Land-ship I and II do not depend on a singular vision of what might be, rather they suggest increments of change which refer to and replicate growth in the city itself. They outline not a particular design model but a structure and methodology which would allow for other designers and other programmes to work within an overall strategy.

Land-ship I proposes an additive process, of infusing, adapting, transforming constructs and artefacts to enrich an urban condition. Land-ship II proposes a method which is subtractive, its authors interpreting, uncovering, speculating on the past growth of the city. The landscape is conceived to be uncovered from the existing condition rather than superimposed upon it. Forms are derived from the juxtaposition of conditions found in the context.

Leo Marx observes that twentieth-century American writers extend the myth of a wild or rural landscape as a repository for values, while acknowledging 'the power of a counterforce, a machine or some other symbol of the forces which have stripped the old ideal of most, if not all, of its meaning'.[9] Land-ship inverts this process, becoming a counterforce which, as an ordering system, reinfuses meaning and value to the city. The overlay of contextual forms with spatial archetypes – housed in the collective memory of architecture – makes an architecture of meaning, but one which is also specific to place. The work references both the particular place and forms which resonate across time and culture. As the living sounds and scents of the bustling city mingle with its past at the Largo Argentina in Rome, so might the magic and mystery of Los Angeles merge with forms of enclosure appropriate to provide security in a crowded environment and make visible the erased layers of history.

As you climb into the hills, the built landscape falls away, exposing the natural condition of the land. For a few years we lived in a house in the hills above Brentwood. Five minutes north from Sunset Boulevard and you feel you have left the city, but open the door to the house, look out, and the Los Angeles Basin opens out at your feet. On a good day, you can see from Downtown to Malibu, from Long Beach to Catalina and, once or twice a year, to the Channel Islands off Ventura. During the day, the view is an enormous horizon line, with sea level a thousand feet below. The sky and its edge with the Pacific Ocean is the central view. But at night, the sparkle of the city at your feet is hypnotising, and distinct patterns of habitation and movement, blurred in hazy sunlight, are made visible. Streets high up in the hills do not have street lights, so the picture of the view is perceived as if in a darkened movie theatre: framed by a black foreground. In the moving picture, different streets use different temperatures of street lights and all appear to be twinkling, car headlights and tail lights move fast on some

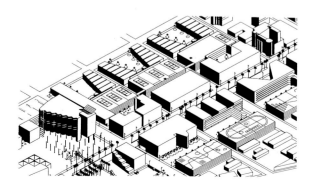

LEFT: Land-ship I, isometric detail; RIGHT: Land-ship II, sketch

streets, slowly on others. There are dark masses where trees are thick contrast to brighter areas of no trees, palm trees or deciduous trees in winter. Sweeping spotlights signify the opening of a new movie, fast food restaurant or gas station. The blinking red and white lights of aeroplanes make visible the systematic order of arrival and departure from LAX. The patterns of the city, a network of orders both moving and stationary, all come alive from dusk to dawn.

Networks of Land-ships would make visible Los Angeles, beginning and ending in the natural edge of ocean or mountain, chaparral or desert which bound the city, implicitly tied to transportation, establishing an identity for each street and each neighbourhood. Land-ships I and II propose prototypical networks of spaces which are continuous from the scale of the freeway to the scale of private, contemplative spaces of courtyards and back yards. Land-ships may extend as fingers into the residential, commercial and industrial areas around the city. Linked as a network, landscape is treated as a continuous mechanical system – woven through the city like sewers, electricity or train tracks. The inverse of the nineteenth-century arrival of the machine in the garden is the insertion of Land-ships on the city: expanding at hubs, narrowing to threads or lines, linking public to private spaces, sprouting through every crack in the sidewalk in the asphalt expanse which is Los Angeles.

Notes
1. *American Heritage Dictionary*, Houghton Mifflin Company, Boston, 1991
2. Leo Marx, *The Machine in the Garden*, Oxford University Press, New York, 1964
3. As the seasons passed and his missions continued, Marco mastered the Tartar language and the national idioms and tribal dialects. Now his accounts were the most precise and detailed that the Great Kahn could wish for and there was no curiosity which they did not satisfy. And yet each piece of information about a place recalled to the emperor's mind that first gesture or object with which Marco had designated the place. The new fact received a meaning from that emblem and also added to the emblem a new meaning. Perhaps, Kublai thought, the empire is nothing but a zodiac of the mind's phantasms. 'On the day when I know all the emblems,' he asked Marco, 'shall I be able to possess my empire, at last?' And the Venetian answered: 'Sire, do not believe it. On that day you will be an emblem among emblems.' Italo Calvino, *Invisible Cities*, Harcourt Brace Jovanovich, Orlando, 1974, pp22-23
4. For further discussion of work with the computer and design process, see Mark Cigolle & Kim Coleman 'Computer Design Studio: Work in Progress', in *Journal of Architectural Education*, vol 43/3, pp26-33. Stage I project team: Mark Cigolle and Kim Coleman with Manuel Mochon-Zaga, Marcela Oliva-Aguilar, Maria Baldenegro, Nazeen Cooper, Victor Diaz, Tina Go, Stacey Gong-Wong, Alicja Hrabia, Olivia Tay
5. Selected as one of five finalists for the competition, Cigolle & Coleman proceeded to the second stage with a modified team, set of intentions and tools for developing the scheme. The computer was used as a tool for presentation, but was not a force which impacted strongly on the design of the project, which was developed through conventional methods of drawings and study models. Stage II project team: Cigolle & Coleman with Architectural Collective, Gruen Associates, Associate Architect, Emmet Wemple and Associates, Landscape Architect
6. Jan Morris, 'Los Angeles: The Know-How City', *Destinations*, p84
7. Michel Foucault, *The Order of Things*, Random House, New York, 1970
8. In West Lost Angeles, parking need is assumed at one parking place per worker, which makes the floor area required for parking approximately equal to the floor area for the building.
9. Marx, *op cit*, pp362-63

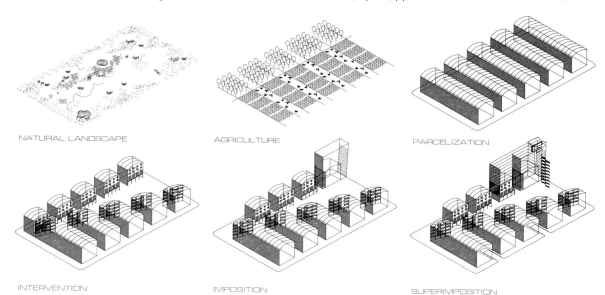

FROM L to R: Land-ship II: Natural landscape; Agriculture; Parcelisation; Intervention; Imposition; Superimposition

SOCIAL AND PLANNING HISTORY

KATHRYN SMITH
RICHARD NEUTRA'S RUSH CITY REFORMED
Los Angeles 1950

'The studies for Rush City Reformed *were made over a dozen years and are based on a statistical investigation of the flaws of American urbanism which differs fundamentally from what was realised in Europe during the industrial-capitalist era.'*   Richard Neutra, 1934

The major work of Richard Neutra's early career was his plan for *Rush City*, which he later referred to as *Rush City Reformed*. This was a scheme for the high-speed city of the twentieth century and contained his views on transportation; the zoning of residential, commercial and industrial areas; and the issue of centralisation versus decentralisation. Most of Neutra's later architectural innovations and achievements reflect the ideology of this project. As a work of city planning it was well within the approach which was set forth by Le Corbusier's theories of the post-World War I period. Although it is known primarily through a series of utopian perspective drawings which date from the late 1920s, by 1930 had Neutra applied his notions to the development of Los Angeles in the year 1950.

Neutra left little written record of the details of *Rush City* with the exception of a brief article which was published in 1934. The principles of his plan can be traced to the social and economic ideas of progressive European thought influenced by his American, and predominantly Southern Californian, experience. His buildings, especially the multiple-family dwellings and public schools have been taken seriously, unlike his views on social organisation. A complete study of *Rush City* has not been published.

Neutra started work on proposals for urbanism as early as 1923, in the aftermath of World War I and the scarcity of building commissions in Europe. His ideas were further developed after he arrived in the United States in 1924, with a short stay in New York followed by a longer stay in Chicago. He continued to refine his notions after he settled in Los Angeles in 1925. Elements of *Rush City*, as it was originally titled, appeared in Neutra's first book, *Wie Baut Amerika? (How America Builds?)*, published in Germany in 1927, and others in his second book, *Amerika*, in 1930. Some were a result of projects or opportunities which arose over the years. One such was the incorporation of his entry for a competition held in 1929-30 by the Lehigh Portland Cement Company for the design of an ideal airport. Rush City was further worked out in detail for presentation at the third annual meeting of CIAM (International Congress of Modern Architecture) in Brussels in 1930. The theme of the meeting was land-planning and the issue of low-rise versus high-rise housing and urban density. Neutra participated as the Los Angeles delegate side-by-side with Walter Gropius representing Berlin and Le Corbusier from Paris. The scheme, with Neutra's accompanying text, entitled 'Rush City Reformed', was published as an article in the Belgian journal *La Cite, Revue d'Architecture et d'Urbanisme*, in 1934.

In the interim, Neutra had come to the attention of the curators of the International Style exhibition at the Museum of Modern Art, Philip Johnson and Henry-Russell Hitchcock. In the spirit of the CIAM conference, Neutra proposed to exhibit a series of apartments at MOMA, showing how the bachelor, the married couple and the family should live. Rejecting this idea, Johnson suggested the Ring Plan School, already a component of *Rush City*. A detailed model of the project was constructed and then shown at the museum exhibit, *Modern Architecture – International Exhibition*, which opened on February 10, 1932.

Los Angeles 1950
The 1930 CIAM conference called for entries devoted to the replanning of cities according to advanced thinking. 'We replanned Los Angeles as we imagined it might be in 1950 . . . in 1930, the year 1950 was so remote and shrouded in mists, one could imagine anything possible', recalled Harwell Hamilton Harris, who worked on the drawings. For this presentation, Neutra added the plan of a typical section and an aerial perspective, placing the city in a specific topographical setting. In 1934, Neutra admitted that he did not intend to create an ideal American city, but rather he hoped to explore the problem of regional urban planning.

As early as 1928, Neutra began to attract a dedicated following as a teacher at the Academy of Modern Art in Hollywood. When students from these classes continued to work with him as apprentices, he encouraged them to pursue different architectural and theoretical problems

OPPOSITE ABOVE: Richard Neutra, aerial perspective of Rush City, *c 1930; OPPOSITE BELOW: Model of* Rush City Reformed, *constructed by SCI-Arc*

SOCIAL AND PLANNING HISTORY

associated with his ideal metropolis. Three of his students, Harris, Gregory Ain and Raphael Soriano went on to become prominent architects in the 1930s and 40s. In his 1934 article, Neutra gave them and four others credit for their contributions to the studies for *Rush City*.

The drawings and plans which were produced by Neutra's studio depicted a city of one million people organised along a transportation spine, anchored by an airport or air-transfer station at one end and a commuter railway station at the other. The aerial perspective reflects the horizontal development of Los Angeles along Wilshire Boulevard in the plains below the Santa Monica Mountains. It differs from the present day environment in its brutally repetitive commercial blocks, in the separation of pedestrian and vehicular traffic within the residential zones and in the idea of an uninterrupted linkage between the modes of air, rail and automobile transportation. As Neutra pointed out in 1934, regardless of the election of Franklin Roosevelt, social and political conditions in the United States did not exist that would allow urban-planning ideas of this type to be carried out.

The business centre, consisting of uniformly oriented twelve-storey buildings which ensured maximum exposure to the sun and reduced shadows from neighbouring buildings to no more than forty per cent of street width, was concentrated along the transportation spine. The horizontal slabs were elevated on pilotis to allow traffic to flow freely below. Shops were located at the second and third floors, bordered by pedestrian bridges and were accessible from elevators located at the intersections.

The typical section represented a repetitive one-and-a-third mile area responding to California climatic conditions accommodating a population of 22,040. Each section consisted of a commercial zone of rectangular slab office buildings bordering the central linear corridor; three residential zones for families, couples without children and singles; and a greenbelt containing schools, recreation and a sports stadium. Particular attention was devoted to the residential zones which were grouped into the following categories: (A) hotels for nonresidents, (PTS – Prefabricated Transportable Singles) low-cost, prefabricated mobile housing units for single people, (FD1) courtyard housing for families of the first decade – in other words, with children to the age of ten; (FD2) row houses for families of the second decade – that is, children aged eleven to eighteen. Neutra's plan and drawings seemed to indicate a very rigid system of units but he emphasised that there were numerous possibilities for grouping the zones. He provided two alternatives which he called Type 1 and Type 2, as a response to varying populations and conditions. In effect, we can extrapolate that his plan was not to be taken literally, but as a planning kit for the most technically developed area of the world.

Transportation

Los Angeles was the perfect arena for Neutra's ideas because the latter depended so heavily upon a hierarchy of movement and the separation of the pedestrian, vehicular, rail and air transportation. Neutra believed that organising the city around means of continuous mobility was the key to the future. *Rush City* was planned with the super highway leading directly from the airport to the city and the railway station beyond, with trains and cars travelling on different levels. Early in his career he became aware of the role aviation and railroads would play in a world-wide system of transportation. He felt the need not just for airports and railway stations, but for facilities where one means of transportation would connect with another. As a result, the air-transfer station and the commuter railway station (stub-end station) were the anchors of the plan. 'Rail delivery of a passenger was to a plane's own waiting room directly above its loading bay', Harris explained many years later, 'not to a grand concourse or an immense waiting room as in the railroads' union station. Our grand concourse was for shops and restaurants and occupied a different level in the deep concrete trusses that spanned the loading bays'. Cars, buses and taxis entered below the concourse for arriving trains, and the planes occupied the upper level. Although the airport was designed as part of a competition, Neutra conceived of it from the beginning as an integral part of *Rush City*.

Neutra was familiar with trains from his childhood in Vienna and made an investigation of them during his stays in New York and Chicago. He was particularly concerned with the accommodation of both commuter and long-distance travel in one terminal which he did not believe was adequately addressed in America. He associated trains with the idea of subways and commuter traffic – transportation which was used on a daily basis. His design for a commuter train station (stub-end station) was based on his analysis of traffic patterns and the uninterrupted movement of pedestrians, taxi cabs, buses, automobiles and long distance and commuter trains. He believed strongly in the separation of arriving and departing carriers which is reflected in his design. A twelve-storey hotel with six-hundred-and-twenty guest rooms was incorporated within the train station, providing rooms for business meetings and trade shows as well as facilities such as a restaurant, post office and other personal services.

Perpendicular to the linear corridor were the

ABOVE: Richard Neutra, aerial perspective of Radial Avenue, c 1928; BELOW: Richard Neutra, aerial perspective of a typical section, c 1930

major expressways, which Neutra called Radial Avenues, with bridges connecting arterial streets. These separated each residential, commercial and recreational zone. Tremendous detail is evident in the circulation within and around the residential zones, allowing children to play as well as commute to school and the park without crossing streets. Between the urban and residential zones lay service zones.

The most important circulation artery was Radial Avenue. These expressways were placed every 3,400 feet dividing the suburban zones and joining the super highway with ramps. They formed the local neighbourhood service corridor and were meant for shopping, services and social interaction. The central area of the roadway was below grade twenty feet and intended for high speed traffic. Left and right-turn ramps were spaced along the route to allow access to businesses where parking was available. The office buildings or stores on each side were connected by two-level bridges which separated automobiles and pedestrians. As a result, shopping and business could be conducted on foot with distances between home, office and the store no more than a mile in most cases. With these services adjacent to each residential zone, it is possible that a family would only have needed one car for commuting to work while most travel could have been conducted on foot.

Industrial Zone

Local industries and branches of industrial chains such as laundries, hardware stores, automobile and truck repair shops were located in a zone paralleling the electric-junction railroad and the typical commercial truck boulevard.

Housing

Neutra's greatest attention was devoted to the details of housing. While high-speed movement was the guiding principle of *Rush City*, tranquillity was sought in the residential quarters. The hotels or bachelor apartments (A) were conceived of as twenty-storey blocks only two rooms wide, but with private balconies, which maximised both views and daylight within the interiors. An area adjacent to the hotels was set aside for single people. This was the Prefabricated Transportable Singles group who were housed in low-cost dwellings of light-weight concrete, twenty by forty-five feet, each with its own garden and garage.

Married couples with children under ten (FD1), considered to be thirty-two per cent of the population, were housed in two-storey apartment blocks facing a courtyard ninety-six feet wide and one hundred-and-eighty feet long. On the sides were six detached two-car garages bordering the alley fifty-feet wide for cars. There were two rows of six houses, receiving daylight from two sides through wide expanses of glass, each open to the courtyard with terraces and a balcony on the second floor. The focus of each courtyard was a clubhouse, meant to serve by day as a kindergarten with an adjacent wading pool for the twelve families, and by evening as a social hall. Attention was focused on the separation of walkways and driveways so that children could have complete freedom of movement.

Married couples with children over ten (FD2), calculated at twenty-four per cent of the city, were housed in patio dwellings with attached garages. This neighbourhood was adjacent to FD1 and bordered the greenbelt. Each FD2 section consisted of four rows of six units oriented with two rows of houses facing a central community centre. Each unit was thirty-five feet wide by one hundred feet long with a double garage in the rear and an entry facing the common green. The plan included a living room which opened onto a garden, two bedrooms, a bathroom and a kitchen. The houses were grouped in rows of twelve on each side of the community centre, which was connected to the common green by covered walkways.

Neutra placed great importance on the residential courtyards where neighbours could greet one another in the manner of the man-made squares of many European cities. These traffic-free plazas covered a greater area than the public parks in *Rush City*.

The recreational and educational needs of the neighbourhood were met in the greenbelt. With the exception of kindergarteners who met in their neighbourhood clubhouse, each typical section was provided with four elementary schools for five hundred students each and one high school for 1,500 students. Other park facilities included swimming pools, open-air and enclosed auditoriums, a sports stadium and ample parking.

The most developed of these buildings was the Ring Plan School conceived by Neutra in the late 1920s, but refined in detail for the 1932 Museum of Modern Art exhibition. The school was planned as a circle, hence its name, and comprised a series of classrooms with sliding glass doors, enabling each classroom to open onto a garden, providing an indoor-outdoor relationship for a variety of activities. The furniture which was neither fixed nor heavy, could be easily moved in and out, providing great flexibility. In addition to the openness of the plan, the one-storey concept eliminated stairways and fire escapes and substituted a covered outdoor corridor for an enclosed hallway. Neutra promoted the building as earthquake-proof, well-lit and well-ventilated. Many of Neutra's innovations in the Ring Plan School were incorporated into later schools in Los Angeles.

ABOVE: Richard Neutra, railway station for commuter and long distance travel, before 1926; BELOW: Richard Neutra, aerial perspective of courtyard housing for FD2, before 1930

ACADEMY INTERNATIONAL FORUM
LEARNING FROM LOS ANGELES

The International Forum on Learning from Los Angeles, chaired by Edward Soja and Paul Finch, was held at the Royal Academy of Arts, Gallery III, London on Saturday 23 October 1993.

Paul Finch: Welcome once again to the Academy Forum, sponsored by the Academy Group and Academy Editions. Our subject for today is Learning from Los Angeles and this is the third 'Learning From. . .' symposium that we have held this year. The title of Academy's book on Los Angeles and the *World Cities* series should probably be a simple quote like 'Los Angeles is the pits!' – I am sure there are others here who can argue to the contrary, and of course from a certain perspective of people brought up on the movies, the image of Los Angeles veers between a rather violent place where policemen are likely to hit you over the head as soon as they look at you, in the kind of films made from Raymond Chandler novels and a city of neon-lit angels in which the freeways can be as heavenly as they may be hellish, as in Steve Martin films. I was thinking about the former in relation to the kind of Rodney King situation because the idea of police beating up anybody, be they black or white, would seem entirely natural for anybody brought up on Raymond Chandler.

We are going to start the afternoon off with a presentation by James Steele who will lay out some sort of groundwork about the way the city operates.

James Steele: The personification of Los Angeles is that the Mexican and Spanish settlement in 1781, which began as a scattered *pueblo*, was basically following the lines of blood flows in the south-west without the Cartesian grid system. After the Mexican defeat of 1848, Los Angeles slowly started to grow with the oil boom, developing a dispersed kind of outline because of the railroad which brought settlers to the city from the east. Then with the movies at the turn of the century, with figures such as Charlie Chaplin, the development of the studios began the coalescence of Los Angeles and the image of the perfect dream. The perfect American dream was in a sense capitalising on the idea of the Western movement and the repository of everyone's hopes and wishes. The studios are still visible and they front mostly onto boulevards. Paramount, for example, fronts onto Melrose reflecting this relationship with the large surface streets. The movies increasingly became everybody's image of what America was and then became the depository of dreams in the country, with the studios developing into large cities on their own. Universal Studios is one of these cities within a city and has projects going on to make it further into a city.

After the Second World War the Downtown area started to develop. If you were to beam down from outer space and parachute into Downtown Los Angeles you would find it to be virtually indistinguishable from any other city in the United States, lacking the prerequisite landmarks which are characteristic of cities such as New York, Detroit and Philadelphia. The development of areas such as Olvera Street has now become a cleaned up Hispanic area where tourists like to go to – it shows the process that has taken place of cleaning up and of sanitising ethnicity in the city. The grid system which exists in certain parts of Los Angeles is contorted by the geology, geography and typography of the city, so now there is an overlay over the *pueblo* and the fifty-three ranchos which existed in the area in the Spanish period. The boulevards still follow this outline. Douglas Suisman has written a wonderful little pamphlet entitled *Los Angeles Boulevard: Eight X-rays of the Body Public*, in which he discusses how in the two or three layers of Los Angeles the order is not apparent and you have the overlay of the grid, the contours and enclaves of green (near Century City for example). It is very characteristically Los Angeles where an urban pattern exists and then behind it something totally different, something totally out of the ordinary crops up like, for example, a golf course. Wilshire Boulevard to the west again has these boulevards, these surface streets that were involved in the 20s which shows the kind of pretension of the city, the boulevard using the French idea. Developments like Venice and Marina Del Rey are places where someone like Abbott Kinney would come and try to do 'Venice in California' to try and entice tourists, to attempt to bring people into Los Angeles from the east. So revamping the city, or Los Angeles revamping itself, has happened

Los Angeles skyline at dawn with Hollywood Freeway, viewed from Hollywood Hills

SOCIAL AND PLANNING HISTORY

again and again, five times at the last count where the city has gained a new personality to go with its developing aims and yet there are the elemental aspects of the city that just cannot be ignored: the ocean, the mountains, the torrential rains and the earthquakes – everything seems to happen to excess here even in nature and there is the thin blue line of the final frontier of America, the final stopping place.

The other aspect of Los Angeles, Long Beach in Los Angeles proper, is the reduction experience. In Hollywood itself Charles Moore opened a new museum that will hopefully turn around this emptiness, making it a tourist attraction. The freeway system which began with the Arroyo Seco in the 1920s is a thin little valley that travels up to Pasadena and encompasses most of the city; for some people the experience of the city *is* the freeway and the car takes up an enormous amount of surface area – it is the one public place that Los Angeles has. The San Fernando Valley is the place that Mike Davis has called the last green paradise on earth – he talks nostalgically about the orange groves in this area but this was a part of California that was an extremely important part of its psyche. The same area is now where the developers have come in and basically destroyed the paradise, putting a car park over it and this is exactly what is going on all around the rim of the city. It is interesting to note that Los Angeles was one of the first cities in the United States to have a transport system. The little red cars that were such an important part of the city in the 20s, were scrapped after the war and then the entire emphasis was put on the freeways, and now that logic is being overturned with people trying to get back to the metro system and get rid of the freeway as a major means of transportation.

What Frank Lloyd Wright did when he came to Los Angeles was very instructive of the kind of attitude many architects have when they worked in Los Angeles, coming in from the outside. His first instinct was to deal with nature, to react to the elements: to the sun, to the earthquakes, the rain, the sea and so on, and make a different kind of architecture, as with the Hollyhock House. He attacked the kind of typology that he thought would be appropriate for Los Angeles and came up with a courtyard house around an interior court that is basically a replication of the Spanish hacienda courtyard, very appropriate for this area. On the other hand, his own residence nearby, which is quite similar to his Prairie style houses, displays a sort of schizophrenia that is endemic of many of the people who react to the city by being overwhelmed by both nature and the environment. The Imperial Hotel directly across the Pacific acts as a reminder of this period. In a sense Los Angeles and its counterpart across the Pacific are two sides of the same coin. His concrete block Ennis house, the Store Houses and the Malade House are examples that show Wright struggling with the idea of the machine and nature. This dichotomy I think, is one of the elements of Los Angeles that is still being struggled with by many architects. In a sense Wright was trying to marry the two together. These concrete blocks in actual fact are not machine made but are made by one person pressing down on a really crude plywood form to try to make each block by hand. In a sense they are hand-crafted houses just as much as if they were made of wood.

RM Schindler for example, who escaped the Holocaust, escaped the Second World War and came to Los Angeles early before all of that had changed and created many important works, including his own house, the Translucent House, and a portfolio of apartments. Neutra, on the other hand, with his Lovell Health House in 1929 was very much affected by what happened in the Second World War and came to Los Angeles later, bringing a whole different psychology to the city. Schindler introduced the first International Style monument to America in the creation of lightweight steel houses that follow the tradition of the Gamble House, using very light steel members. The Eames House is a continuation of that tradition and follows Neutra in moving to metal. The interesting thing about the inside with its retaining wall is Eames' second impression of the site. His first impression was to build a bridge across the site which he then turned away from because he saw an exhibition of Mies van der Rohe's work in which Mies had already done that, and so not wanting to be derivative, he pulled the house into the hillside, created a wall and attached it to the land. This factor of taking a building out of context and putting it back into its context is indicative of the attitude of the modern movement of taking the context seriously.

Of course the one missing character in the play today has to be mentioned: Frank Gehry, the medium of the consciousness of the city during the late 70s or early 80s. His own house, the Gehry Residence, and the Spiller House in Venice are a commentary on the social problems of frame structures. America cannot get its act together to do a prefabricated house, still relying upon the wire-nail construction of a hand-built one-board-at-a-time and it cannot use the high technology necessary because of unions, costs and so on. Also the toughness of the Venice area, where this is built, is reflected in the building.

The Aerospace Museum is in a way a city within a city, in the sense that it relates to the museum itself rather than out to the city – it turns its back on the city, it turns its face towards the music to make a community there.

The Law School is also a recreation of a classical city inside Los Angeles. It is inside a gateway so it can be isolated and this is the difference between the architects in the past – Neutra, Eames and Wright, who related to nature, to the environment and to the elements – and those architects, beginning with Gehry perhaps, who turned their backs on it to create another world almost like the movie lots do, turning inside and making an entirely different environment. This is best exemplified by the Schnabel House, a New England village in Bel Air which relates to itself only. It is an idealised town that Gehry would ideally like Los Angeles to be. Rather than finding what is actually there and portraying that, he recreates something that he wants to be there.

The Disney Hall is a perfect example of the role of the institution in the city in the way that it should relate to everyone and not just the people who can afford to buy the tickets; anyone can come into the foyer and participate in the process of entertainment even if they cannot afford to see the performance. The building is isolated on its site in spite of all the attempts to try to relate it to the outside by lifting up the hem of the building to allow people under it. It is an object, a sculptural object, albeit a beautiful one and yet it is still isolated, it is still separated, it is still disconnected.

The Museum of Contemporary Art (MOCA) building by Arata Isozaki on the other hand, very humbly and carefully fits into its site and does not try to be aggressive, relating to its surroundings very well. There is a kind of paranoia that Los Angeles has with New York, the cultural capital of the East Coast, and this dialogue between New York and Los Angeles is an important issue because basically Los Angeles is trying to replace New York in the psyche of America culturally and in every other way. Los Angeles is now the gateway to the States in the 21st century where Ellis Island was the gateway in the 1800s, and instead of people moving from the east to the west they are now moving from west to east and so everything has now changed and the country has turned around and in on itself. The aspect of Gehry again with this relationship to Japan is also extremely important because, like Schindler, Wright and many other architects before him, he also looks across the Pacific Ocean.

Bart Prince's Japanese Pavilion (Los Angeles County Museum of Art – LACMA) is a good example of this kind of looking to the east and yet trying to make an Americanisation of it. The other aspect of turning inwards is shown by Morphosis' Arts Park Performing Arts Pavilion with an introspection and turning away and burying the building in nature, rather than opening it up to the outside world. Why is there this dichotomy of turning away from the paradise that is there, that other architects had found in the past?

I think I should mention the interior of restaurants as one other public space in the city where people get together. The restaurant has its own particular social milieu and if you do not have it on the outside, the one way to obtain it is to sit in a restaurant and share the publicness of that. Kate Mantilini by Morphosis is a commentary on the cosmic or the international nature, of relating to the other parts of the world, a conspicuous part of Los Angeles as a capital of the world today, not just the United States. The houses that Morphosis have done also relate to this idea and also relate to Charles Eames in a sense of burying the building partially in the ground and relating it in part to the outside; and so for those who think there is neither tradition nor history in Los Angeles, look again at the architects who have worked there in the past and the way that new architects relate to it. On the one hand there are the hermetically sealed boxes like Cesar Pelli's Design Center, while on the other hand you have people like Charles Moore doing the opposite with craftsman churches. So another aspect today is tradition versus the object building, tradition versus the building out of its context and separated from it – and that is very much a visible part of it. Once you begin to get through the layers of wackiness in the city, you begin to see that these two dichotomies, these two camps can be clearly defined.

The recent building by Richard Meier, the Getty Center, promises to be a civic Acropolis, at least that was the idea of it working with the Getty Center people – Meier had very little leeway to design the building himself and it is a perfect example of architecture by committee. Eric Owen Moss' 8522 National Boulevard Office Building of the-building-within-the-city-within-a-building shows how the building becomes the shield for the city; cities with plazas that are now internal and isolated from the outside for security reasons as well as many other social reasons.

The idea of the public plaza is also given over to the car rather than the people and the attitude towards nature and the environment is seen, for example in the snatches of light illuminating the interior courtyards which are carefully monitored so that the light, as well as nature, is regulated. This idea of the object building is spreading to areas in the desert where building would not have happened before – for example Joshua Schweitzer's Monument and buildings that relate to the idea of the image in the city, which is still very strong where art-imitates-life-which-imitates-art, and it goes on. So the architecture there is very much related to the film, related to image, related to the third dimension. Today there is the psychological tendency to make one united Los Angeles, not a city scattered with several separate centres. The new metro line is thought to be the way to establish this unity, yet within the unity there are the self-contained medieval conclaves where people live and work together with different incomes from the lowest to the highest, from the homeless to the millionaire. According to this scheme they will all be living within one block of each other. So, the city has come around full circle wanting to be whole and yet developing cities within cities.

Paul Finch: Thank you very much. I wonder if the same sort of thing is happening in urban terms – this reluctance to engage in a public architecture because for the people who live and work there it may not be necessary. Edward Soja would you like to respond to that?

Edward Soja: I would like to make a few statements about the dimensions of interesting things to learn from Los Angeles as I see it. I think the first step is to realise that since 1965 Los Angeles has probably transformed itself more dramatically than any other major metropolitan area in the world. The patterns which have changed have been dramatic and it has been the attempt to make sense of those changes which I think we have been trying to understand. What I want to do is explore what I think are the main arenas from which to learn from Los Angeles – all of them are associated with the dramatic changes that I and others have called an urban structure in Los Angeles. This new urbanisation process of the city is a particularly vivid exemplar of what London could become tomorrow.

The first of these new arenas is essentially a new urban form taking shape – not just in the US, it is here in the UK already, despite it being less vivid or clear or exaggerated as it is in Los Angeles. This is reflected in part by a whole series of new titles and names that have been written or discussed on the subject. The most recent popular one is in a book by Joel Garreau called *Edge City*. In it he highlights some of these situations and preoccupations where the city is growing outside the old city and discusses how the city-without-a-city no longer has the characteristics that we have attributed to cities for the past few thousand years. These changes are perhaps sufficiently dramatic that all our conceptual categories and vocabulary have to be rethought and challenged. What we have is a city turned inside out and outside in at the same time, where the periphery of the city is now the centre of the city, and the centre of the city is now the periphery. The centres of cities, even in New York City, are emptying out and the old urban is becoming the suburban – are these words useful any more? My Orange County colleagues have invented the term 'Post-Suburbia'. Los Angeles is one of the places where these transformations are more dramatic than in most other places, more vivid, more visible and more educational.

Secondly, not only is the form of the city changing but there have been some very dramatic changes in the function of cities in the core of the very nature of the economy, at the base of life in the way production is organised and the way the economy is organised. We have had a dramatic change in the very nature of the urban economy and this is a vital part of the nature for this new organisation process and it feeds into everything else that is going on.

Basically the argument is associated with another influx of new vocabulary, words like 'flexible production' and 'flexible manufacturing systems', 'a new industrial era' and the concept of Post-Fordism. This second era I am talking about in relation to learning from Los Angeles is perhaps defined by this notion of a Post-Fordist city organised by small and middle sized firms and established nets of connected firms and subcontracting firms in little industrial complexes. Techno-poles is the term that is used frequently in Southern California and these are the energetic production centres of the new city. The very nature of the base of the city is another very significant element if one compares Los Angeles to places like London or New York, as since about 1930 Los Angeles has led every other metropolitan area in North America on both sides of the Atlantic, decade by decade.

Third is a kind of transformation, not in form or in function but more in terms of what I would call a scale or urban life – the scale of the city is dramatically exploded in places like Los Angeles and it has not only become a kind of massive regional metropolis with 14 million people, but it is one of the mega-cities. This is another new word that is being thrown around these days but it is now called a global or world city and globalisation is a word that is also being born by this process in which the local is global. The city itself is now more global than it has ever been and this is reflected, for example, in the composition and cultural context of Los Angeles. Los Angeles is the most heterogeneous city anywhere in the world.

The fourth arena has to do with the changes and the social structure, the class structure. There has been a restructuring of social relations within the city, creating whole new groups bursting with new vocabulary. An old word that has been around for many years to indicate one growth second to the population is the word 'yuppie'. Other words for this urban professional managerial class that has exploded in New York with brokerages and in Los Angeles with high-tech industry are words like 'dinks' – double income, no kids. An even more rapidly growing segment is that named by a South American sociologist, the 'permanent urban underclass'. A major process of polarisation is going on in the region of Los Angeles.

I have ripped off the fifth arena from the very interesting computer game SimCity – the computer game for planners and urban designers. Los Angeles is evocative of the 'reality' of the true SimCity or perhaps borrowing from Baudrillard we should call it 'hyper-real life', because essentially everyday life in Los Angeles and elsewhere is increasingly being captured by a simulation of reality.

You are all familiar with Hollywood, with Universal City and with Disneyland – these are very old fashioned, these are examples of hyper-realities where one enters enclosed spaces, pays for the tickets and experiences one's fantasies; now hyper-reality visits you at your home in your own space. An example of this over the last few decades is the advertisements in the newspapers in the real estate section inviting you to buy a home under the banner 'Welcome to . . . come and buy a house and you will live on a green island . . . ' The grand place for this is Mission Viejo which has been one of the fastest growing cities in the US over the last decade; you would buy into it and sign a massive document when you purchased your house – if you promised never to change the colour and you promised never to change the motif they would supply all the ingredients and they even hired people to walk around and look the part. This is a kind of suspension of our over-reality – reality is no longer what it used to be. Simulation is promising to have something that you do not have and that is why SimCity is a useful term here. It is creating a very confusing situation because this is being legitimated – it is now the basis for American elections, the American political system runs on this; the media are all involved in this and it is also producing new words like 'spin doctors' and 'sounds bites' – this is all part of this process of alternative reality. Los Angeles has probably pushed every conceivable urban problem to its greatest depths and yet at the same time there is the feeling that if any place is going to solve these urban problems then it is going to be Los Angeles.

Allen Scott: Let me just pick up on what Ed Soja said at the end. There is a very real sense of Los Angeles being at a critical turning point in its history and it's been at a number of these turning points. It is going through a very profound economic crisis and most people think of that crisis as being related to the fact that there are defence cutbacks in the world of international détente – the Pentagon is reducing its defence contracting and that is having a very negative effect on the Los Angeles economy. However, the crisis is very much deeper than that and is related to the fact that over the last 30 or 40 years in Los Angeles, there has been a trajectory of development in the economy and in the social life of the city in which wave after wave of immigrants have arrived, bringing a tremendous amount of vitality and cultural diversity, but combined with Los Angeles' peculiar economic order what has been created is an economic system that has moved progressively towards low wage, low skill manufacturing and service activities. In other words, despite the very impressive economic growth of Los Angeles over the last forty years there has been a sort of race to the bottom in a very significant part of the economy of Los Angeles and today the most dynamic part of the economy – by dynamic, I mean simply expanding quantitatively – is precisely in this area of the low wage sweat shop jobs.

Now in the 20th century, I would argue there have been two great phases of urbanisation in the United States. Two great phases if you like, of capitalist development. Two great phases of social and economic order. The first was a phase that many social scientists today would call a phase of 'Fordist Mass Production', which was a phase of American capitalism in which the paradigmatic cities of America were cities like Detroit, Chicago, Pittsburgh, Buffalo, Cleveland and so on. Overgrown industrial metropolises focused on large growth-pole industries. These enormous industries were themselves based on mass production, and mass production institutionalised *à la* Henry Ford. The Chicago School of Urban Sociology saw one small part of the city, but did not really look at the economy of the city, appraising instead something which was an outcome of the process of massive industrial change that was taking place in Chicago and other cities at that time. They looked at the city as an ecology of communities locked in a Darwinian struggle for survival, that was something of both the way we thought about those cities and something of the reality of those cities. Today, I think the pattern of urbanisation in the United States has changed and these significant changes, I would argue, can be related to the demise of that peculiar set of social relationships called 'Fordist Mass Production' and the rise of a new version of American capitalism and European capitalism for that matter. By Post-Fordist flexible production I mean a form for economic activity and manufacturing industrial activity based on small units of production but re-integrated with one another into clustered networks of economic activity. This very much constitutes the basis of economic order in Los Angeles and it also constitutes the basis of this whole new pattern of urbanisation of which Los

Angeles is perhaps the most advanced example, but which recurs across the American sun-belt.

Now in Los Angeles, or more generally Southern California, there are really two species, if you like, of this model of Post-Fordist flexible production. First a group of industries which we will call labour-intensive craft industries (they are industries like textiles, clothing, jewellery, furniture and movie-making, television, music and so on) are all based on very labour-intensive, craft-orientated forms of production and they constitute an enormous part, and perhaps the most successful part today, of the economic base of Los Angeles.

The second of these Post-Fordist flexible forms of industrialisation driving forward the whole dynamic and character of contemporary Los Angeles is based on the high technology industry, and above all in the aerospace and defence industries which since about 1987 and 1988 have been losing employment at a very rapid rate and are falling into rapid crisis. The industrial geography of Los Angeles shows a group of these labour-intensive craft industries at the centre, and then moving out into suburban Los Angeles are the high-technology industrial districts or techno-poles. In addition, there is an older industrial fabric in Los Angeles of the metallurgical industries which stretches from north to south, from the San Fernando Valley in the centre of Los Angeles down to Northern Orange County.

How did this peculiar pattern of industrialisation come into existence? There are really two main factors that we need to take into account when we look at the emerging economy of Los Angeles, we need to look at the film and the aircraft industry. Those are the two industries that developed rapidly and successfully in the 1920s and in the 1930s, providing the basis of the modern development in Los Angeles. They have been, if you like conduits, through which we can begin to understand the modern development of Los Angeles.

In the 1920s and 30s the film industry was organised in very large studios, what economists would say were vertically integrated studios, that is to say all of the functions of making a film were integrated into those studios, even the stars. The stars of course were under contract and from an economist's point of view the star system in the studios can be regarded as a form of product standardisation and a stabilisation of markets. In other words you could go every week and see the new Gary Cooper movie and because it was the new Gary Cooper movie you had a guarantee of standardisation and stability. The studios were very conscious of this and created a star system as a way of trying to create a captive market in an economic system that was otherwise liable to extreme instability and variation.

The other major industry was the aircraft industry which emerged in the 1920s and 30s when a whole series of technological breakthroughs occurred in the aircraft industry. By the 1940s, these industries were in positions of world leadership. After the Second World War the movie industry became a focus of growth for the TV and the music industries, and has grown to become a dominant global industry in Los Angeles at the present time. The growth of these three industries encouraged the rapid expansion of other labour-intensive craft industries like clothing, jewellery and furniture. There came into being a cultural products industry and all the different media picked up on what the other was doing and hence, image, memories, visions, symbols and all of the rest of it became created commercially.

The cultural products industry and the high-technology industries are the basis of the Los Angeles economy today and are at the focus of its Post-Fordist economic structure. They have both created fantastic economic growth since the 1940s. From the 1940s to the end of the 1980s Los Angeles was far and away the most rapidly growing metropolitan area in the United States. This had a number of implications because as these industries developed, a sort of bi-partite system of labour markets grew which consisted on the one hand of very high-skilled, high-wage managers, engineers, technicians and so on and on the other, and more dramatically, a mass or marginalised dispossessed low-skill, low wage worker, most of whom were immigrants. So we have a very polarised economy with very highly-skilled workers at the one end and an expanding underbelly of sweat shops at the other. The polarisation of Los Angeles society today is not something which just happened willy nilly – it is a structured outcome of the peculiar dynamics of Post-Fordist industrialisation that has driven the development of Los Angeles since the Second World War. The ideal type of the Post-Fordist metropolis then, of which Los Angeles is the outstanding example in the United States today, is that it has a flexible production base which is structured in such a way that it creates a segmentation of occupational structures in the metropolis. These low-skilled and very high levels of multi-culturalism sometimes appear nothing more than an expression of desperation. After all, in the Fordist city, one always had the hope of upward mobility and assimilation. The idea of the melting pot in America was thought to be what would ultimately happen, with everybody being assimilated into Los Angeles. The thought of assimilation is really out of the question for many people, given the way they are locked into low-skill, low-wage jobs and necessity is turned into a virtue by calling this multi-culturalism. This situation is likely to carry on for a long time. Indeed, we have a twofold intertwined crisis in Los Angeles today which is the crisis of the economic order and the crisis of the social order which has been created by that peculiar trajectory of development in Los Angeles.

A French writer Michel Arbert, in *Capitalism against Capitalism* wrote that the world capitalist system today really has bifurcated into two versions of capitalism. There is something he calls German-Japanese Capitalism and something he calls Anglo-American Capitalism. The German-Japanese model is a model in which social solidarity is constructed by the incorporation of all relevant social groups into a society where everybody is given a deal and where there are certain sorts of guarantees that if the basis of your particular social fraction happens to go to hell, at least there will still be a place for you somewhere in society. The Anglo-American version, but particularly the American version of capitalism, is described by Michel Arbert that if you go to hell you go to hell and nobody is going to look after you. This is a dog-eat-dog world and Los Angeles is a peculiarly intense, and I would say vicious, expression of this particular version of world capitalism today, raising the question: is there an alternative for Los Angeles today? I believe there is.

I think Los Angeles is at a turning point in its development. There is a realisable future, a realisable and progressive future that is available for people in Los Angeles and that is a form of capitalism which builds on co-operation and collaboration, on looking after the collective order of the city and of the urban economy, and in particular investing in technology and skills and attempting to halt this vicious circle in increasing low wages, low skills and decreasing competitiveness. This in turn is met by trying to push further down on skills and wages and by much higher levels of social and economic co-ordination in the interests of avoiding self-destructive competitive strategies that have driven the Los Angeles economy since the 1950s and 1960s. I would move towards a social democratic Post-Fordist metropolis and I think that the vision of a Post-Fordist social democratic metropolis in Los Angeles is not an impossibility.

Eric Owen Moss: It's curious to me that if Los Angeles is as topical as some people think, it is never topical in Los Angeles. The discussions take place in Vienna or Tokyo or Buenos Aires, but never in Los Angeles. I want to return to the question of architecture and to find a way to get underneath, at least for me, what is a more elemental basis for discussion of a city or the meaning of city-planning or conceivably, a discussion of what architects are doing in the most elemental way. I think architecture is the first act of a desperate man – that does not mean in the lexicon of Manhattan of somebody who takes on that problem – but that act of desperation as being glorious or esoteric.

There are a lot of discussions about why cities come and why cities go, and what we are looking at in Los Angeles may be inevitable in a kind of disintegration. It is dangerous, it requires some courage, it is fascinating, it has an enormous amount of energy but everybody is not necessarily holding hands and kissing goodnight. Akiro Kurosawa's rendition of *King Lear* is of everything coming apart: the woman, if you recall the film, is blind at the end but she is blind like Tiresias in that she comes to see and to understand everything that was previously disconnected and disassociated. During the Los Angeles riots we saw the disconnection of the citizens from their own city, so the city, like gravity is the adversary. What the city means, what the city espouses and what the city stands for, is not what these citizens aspire to, understand or stand for: they see it as the enemy and they want to burn it down.

So there are these disparate parts and Los Angeles can hold and tolerate and absorb these contradictions, both heaven and hell can co-exist, but it cannot exist as in a sequence in a chronology. It cannot exist simultaneously in the heads of the people who inhabit the city. Of course there are always those, or at least a few, who would argue that a pattern which we probably do not understand but which exists or has a history, should be the way of moving forward – if there is a forward – a way of moving into the future which takes away the fear, the danger and the issues that I think Los Angeles very much embodies now. These issues should be put in with Duany and Zyberk and soon into a substantial portion of Los Angeles with 10,000 housing units and so on. Hence, there is tension not only between the forces in Los Angeles that move it, but between forces that exist very strongly inside and outside. In *Foucault's Pendulum*, Umberto Eco's novel, I thought it was, if not the apotheosis or the quintessence of Los Angeles, certainly suggesting that we know everything. The Rosicrucians, Brazilians, Voodoos, all of these pieces floating around and we do not know what to do with them or how to order them or how to make them intelligible. This is the problem in some ways that I think architecture could set for itself, in the environment of Los Angeles and other places too. In the area called Culver City which is a civic jurisdiction somewhere between Beverly Hills, West Hollywood, Santa Monica and West LA, I am quite interested in a series of sculptures that Henry Moore did called *Helmet* – there are a number of them and they get into this

discussion of inside and inside, inside and inside/outside and I think these make the point that Los Angeles is very much the city of the introvert, meaning that it is up to the architect first to make the definition because the definition cannot come from outside.

I think Los Angeles in a fundamental way has learned, or is learning to build instability into its architecture and in a sense, by putting that experience down, they make it available to the next architects, the next city who will pick it up and take it somewhere else.

Wolf Prix: I think Los Angeles is everywhere and before I went there someone told me it was 'Raymond Chandler' and 'Rita Hayworth' but then when I went, these two images were reduced to a double decaffeinated espresso! What does it mean? (Actually it is the most perverse thing for a Viennese to have a double decaff!) It reminds me of the box, the stealing of the box, outside it looks like a building, it smells like a building but it is not, a building is just a box and I think this is what Los Angeles is for me, it is just a box. Secondly, as a city I agree that we cannot win the future city in the centre anymore, the centre in European cities is museums, so we have to travel to the periphery and actually redesign all the city tools we have like symmetry and axes and change it by using other words – maybe to vectors and tensions – but once again if we look at this city as a field of anticipation, for me Los Angeles is the best example because the whole area of Los Angeles is just a field of anticipation.

Conrad Jameson: I really want to know what I am going to learn about Los Angeles from those people who say that unlike yourself, here it is, it can go on as it is. I went there and the more I studied it, the more frightened I became. I think the possibility of the disappearance of the citizens is the second most frightening thing, the idea of flights from the city centres. I mean we know about this from many cities, but here it has totally collapsed with the change of the ethnic and racial mix of the city. This is not an illiberal remark, I have to say this: Los Angeles drowns in bogus liberal rhetoric about melting pots. It does not mean melting pot in the slightest, it means mosaic, a heterogeneity of some kind but it is certainly nothing to do with melting pots. Melting pots mean we all become Americans. You went to a school to become an American, now there is no such place to go to, these schools have just collapsed. It was all very interesting, all *Blade Runner* stuff – very, very frightening because how do you get a citizen out of this, how do you get even the articulation of the set? It is rather frightening because you have an immigrant population who finds it very difficult to take care of itself. These are the things which are actually frightening. The architecture, to me, is just an extra phenomenon; to me it is just a very light thing, there is nothing to it. I do not think any of us take architecture that seriously. You want to know what the city is about and one of the things that comes out in the open is that architecture is a very passive detail whichever way it is going and it is going in a terrible direction at the moment. We will see what sort of architecture is there, there are different types and one of the things that I find disconcerting – and it came out in the opening remarks – is that architecture has not got together to agree anything at all. That is terrible. You have the mini-Utopians, you have the theoreticians of some kind, the urban context which fits into a hillside, it is just claptrap, talk, this is not the interesting stuff, interesting things and the architecture come into the city when you know what the city wants.

Edward Soja: Is that architectural consensus you are referring to obligatory? Do all politicians have to agree with one another?

Conrad Jameson: There are different types of disagreement. In a political discussion you have the means for creating a proper discourse and without the discourse you get babble; now what we have here is babble, it is like the end of a film, you see flickering images of philosophies coming at you wildly. That is not what the forum is about. The forum requires a certain discipline, it does not necessarily require consensus but it does require agreement on how to argue and this is not even here. It is lacking and it is rather frightening.

Edward Soja: My suggestion of new words was not that I think we should all try to understand. A series of changes is taking place in all of our cities, challenging our own vocabulary. The new vocabulary is not preferred, it is not babble. If there's any point to it it's that it's forcing us to rethink what we've been comfortable with as tried and true and dependable.

Conrad Jameson: What you are trying to do is to retain moral discourse instead of concentrating on scientific discourse, which is trying to look at some new phenomenon and give it another name. Let us stick to our vocabulary and then when we really get stuck, we can find another word.

Eric Owen Moss: It is conceivable perhaps that at a certain point in the discourse the language is inoperable. Stravinsky might tell you that, John Cage might tell you that, even James Joyce might tell you that. There are points in the discussion where the language does not work,

Still from the film Bladerunner, *with Harrison Ford*

and in order to say what needs to be said, it adjusts either delicately or in some cases radically. If it is difficult for you to understand, it it may be because you want to pick it up too fast, in other words it may be more durable than you think and the concepts that you want to hang on to may be more ephemeral than you think but they are easier because you know them already, so it's conceivable that adjusting the language adds to the discourse – it does not debilitate.

Charles Jencks: I do not think Conrad is insisting on forcing values. The discourse of the public realm has to be in a place like Los Angeles, it has to be established in dialogue with people speaking slightly different languages or people slightly misunderstanding each other and negotiating the images and accents in two languages.

One of the poignant things I heard after the riots was the Koreans saying, 'Well, we tried to become part of the American dream but the Americans really wouldn't have us, we don't fit in.' In the end, they are hybrid Americans, that feeling of otherness which is both and not American is a result of this very difficult situation of heteroglossia and what we want in dialogic is a multiple discourse engaging in discussion. I do not know the political process that well but I would like to know whether people are disenchanted with any attempt to talk across these discourses, do they misunderstand each other completely, is it privatised, is it commercialised? With politics in Los Angeles is the public realm possible?

Edward Soja: I think there is the possibility of creating a public realm and that is what I think Allen and I were saying towards the end. I am still concerned however about the other comments of being frightened by Los Angeles; if that is the attitude that dominates well hell, Mike Davis has not completely brainwashed you in Britain has he?

Eric Owen Moss: The role of architecture is now defined for us as a bedding for the local police and the gendarmes; thanks to Karl Marx and Mike Davis, this has been pushed for quite a long time and not with any great subtlety. Why are we taking this guy so seriously? What did he tell us?

Allen Scott: The great thing about Mike Davis' book, despite the extraordinary vision that he portrays of Los Angeles, is that for once somebody has written about Los Angeles like a normal human being writing about other normal human beings. I think that the great power of *City of Quartz* is the way he brings Los Angeles back down to earth; this is something we have to accomplish and to begin to understand it for what it is not, for the nightmarish images that we think it provokes.

Wolf Prix: I would like to go back to the language again because it is very interesting. I am wondering why all these new words we have been discussing concerning cities have come from Los Angeles or the United States. I have never heard any new words coming from Vienna or Berlin. Perhaps this is because of the differences between the German and English language, the German language being more complex. However, I think we have to find new words for new situations. For example, if we go to Los Angeles and we are looking for public space, there is no public space as such, yet paradoxically there is a lot of public space in that it is not space but something public happens there. If you listen to the radio there are people talking to one another, but this is not a public space and it seems a little bit curious if we define the public space in Los Angeles by looking at its restaurants. I think this is the wrong way to look at it, and as long as we continue using all these old conventional terms we will never get a grip on the future city. I do not know whether Los Angeles will be a future city, it is not my concern if this is the capital of the Third World – I believe Mexico city will be the capital of the Third World, it's much more dangerous, much bigger – but I do not know whether we should learn from Los Angeles because what can we learn in reality? Maybe we can learn something from the city we like the most.

Allen Scott: I just want to take issue with a few things you have said. The first remark I want to make is that the problem is not a problem of terminology, it is not a problem of finding a new vocabulary. That problem can be put safely to one side while we ponder the problem of what substantively it is that constitutes the reality of Los Angeles and what it is substantively that constitutes similar realities somewhere else, independently of whatever vocabulary we want to apply, or not, to these problems. I want to try and focus this issue of what I think is a sort of essence of the reality of Los Angeles, and yet is also very characteristic of other major metropolitan areas in the contemporary world. It is not just that Los Angeles somehow magically became more characteristic. Something changed in America and in the world, that in turn drove forward that particular change and what changed in America and the world was a whole series of social and economic revolutions from about the end of the 1960s. If we want to address the question 'Learning from Los Angeles', we have to situate that question in the context of a wider sense of what it is that composes the large metropolis in the modern global economy and what it is in particular that creates the predicaments in that metropolis and how we might go about solving and truly learning from one another. I reiterate that this position is a response to what I thought I was hearing before, that somehow the problem is a problem of vocabulary. It is not a problem of vocabulary.

Eric Owen Moss: In the most primitive, most fundamental way, you have to tell us what you value, what you love, what you aspire to when you make an evaluation of a city. If the archetypal city is now about the new world economy, where is the individual in this model? The person who is born, who lives and dies for thousands of years, where is that person in the discussion? I picked up the *Herald Tribune* today and there is an enormous contingent in the United States which has made a powerful statement condemning unequivocally Martin Luther's anti-semitism – it has taken five hundred years to finally get around to it. Where is that in the economy of the world city? What do you value besides economic models and who makes up these economic models? Mike Davis was valuable because he personalised Los Angeles. He has allegiances, we know what his allegiances are, he has political objectives, he hates America, he hates Los Angeles and very specific pieces for the very specific reasons that the more people who come in from Mexico, the more the city starts to come apart.

Edward Soja: This is frightening, I think we need somebody to intervene because I think what has happened is an extraordinary language problem that has polarised the discussion. I have seen it happen before and I will take the anti-architect's side again but in doing this I fear that in the process of understanding this question or the topic of 'Learning from Los Angeles', we return to the spiritual arrogance of the individual in the creative architect's interpretation. It is the antithesis of the learning process, it is a withdrawal into ego and it gets covered with the same didactic pedantic fluff that others are accused of doing.

Eric Owen Moss: Nobody said that every architect who drew a line was esoteric and profound and nobody said that you have to demonstrate the use and meaning of architecture when you look at it. Does it stretch out the definition, does it allow us to understand if life is personal, is individual? Why are you so terrified by the conception of originality? Originality does not impose learning. Originality is not only ego. Originality does not prevent people from understanding what maybe is something else. If you cannot get it from the world outside you, then the only way you can get it is to be an introvert, because if I cannot depend on you, then I am forced to depend on myself.

Edward Soja: You are saying the process of learning from Los Angeles is the process that takes an understanding of the city of Los Angeles and of urban life and then forcibly translating it into a language and a terminology and a creative and original spirit, it makes something available, you can pick it up or you can walk by it, but there are collective audiences.

Demetri Porphyrios: About two weeks ago if I could have contemplated where I would find myself this afternoon, I never thought I would be here, and yet from somebody who knows nothing about Los Angeles, from somebody who may well be able to find out something about it and may well want to learn about it, I find something sadly lacking. If one wants to learn something, one has to be a fine teacher and the second necessary thing to learn is that one has to be told what to learn. It would be very nice at least to look specifically at one to two of these issues and then get some more complete suggestions or ideas regarding merits or demerits out of formal discussion; economic statements make rather more sense.

Charles Jencks: What we have not touched upon is why it is so incredibly wonderful to live in Los Angeles, at least for me who does not have to live in Los Angeles. I have been going there for 20 years and I really love it, especially coming from London as I do. A lot of foreigners have come to Los Angeles and stayed for three months every year or more, and live in it partly so that they do not have to put up with the part that Mike Davis finds so insufferable. It is a luxury to be able to travel in and out but what we have not discussed is what is so wonderful about Los Angeles and why it has attracted a million immigrants in the last ten years. We have not really touched on it, it is behind everything that we have been saying but we have not really brought it out. I want to suggest that the reasons for it being so wonderful change approximately every ten years because the city is being restructured so fast. It used to be the land of opportunity, the land of sun, the four ecologies of Banham. A wonderful book I recommend to you all is called *Divorce Among the Gulls*. Anyway, William Jordan, who does live in Los Angeles says in his essay in the book 'New Eden, City of Beasts', that there is more sheer animal diversity in Los Angeles than in any other city in the world. There is a city in Costa Rica that comes close and Sydney is also close but none of them has the same variety of animals,

SOCIAL AND PLANNING HISTORY

real animals on the streets, in the back streets or alleys because it is a one-storey city with the gardens forming a system of highways which rival the freeways. So here we have animal life, Los Angeles, that is incredibly diverse and differentiated and 95 per cent of the population of Los Angeles has come from elsewhere and if you compare that ecology of animals to the ecology that existed before 1781 you find in some sense it is more diverse and I would urge you to consider a city in relation to nature.

About a month ago I saw that Basil Hume, the Cardinal, was saying when many Anglicans were potentially moving to the Catholic church: 'Well we welcome them, but of course they must know they can't have Catholicism *à la carte*'. You have to take the whole part or none of it. Now the answer to the 'so what?' question, has to be, 'Well you can have Los Angeles *à la carte* and please take the parts you like if it is paradigmatic and criticise the parts that most of us do not like'. Let us think in those terms. There is the notion that Los Angeles has become the unique city, as they used to say of London because it has, like London, a lot of villages and townships and so on and that heterogeneity is its most recent incarnation. I only discovered after I wrote the book on heterogeneity what it was I was writing about; it is one of the curious things that I did not understand until too late. I think it is important to see it as it were in a series of impossible heteropoli, like Berlin and London, a secret heteropolis; or Moscow with its ten or so cities. The globality is very important, they have to be global cities of over seven million which have mixed radically mixed economies. Los Angeles has been called the capital of the Third World, more Third World than Mexico City or Hong Kong, but radically mixed, it is the largest manufacturing city in America for the last twenty years.

My teacher Reyner Banham, whom I mentioned before, wrote the famous book, *Los Angeles, The Architecture of the Four Ecologies* and he wrote it without even mentioning an animal or a plant, which is an extraordinary idea that one can talk about ecology without nature because Los Angeles has the greatest amount of different flora and fauna of any city in the world. There are more plants here from Japan, South Africa, Asia, South America and China, and the people who had the ethnic statistics and so forth, did not have anything on flora until I finally called a research corporation whose job it is to study pollution. They had studied the flora because they wanted to know what plants would keep the pollution down and they gave me the statistics to show that ninety-four per cent of the species in Los Angeles is foreign, just about the same number as the indigenous population, whatever that is – so heteropolis has to include the variety of nature.

Heterophelia, the love of difference and the style of difference, is an understanding which sees that you can turn difference into something creative; in other words it does not look on it only as a site for a conflict struggle and an ethnic struggle but for something that can be positively represented and turned into a new inventive language in the case of the Los Angeles school of architects and also a little bit of work for that in terms of building types and economic and social types. When I wrote the book a year ago I was using statistics from the United Nations which stated that after the Second World War, there were sixteen million people on the move. It said then that there were twenty million people on the move. This mass migration creates heteropoly – this is why Berlin, amongst a number of European Community global cities is heading in this direction. However, this summer the United Nations revised its statistics, revealing there were actually one-hundred-and-two-million people on the move – mass migrations of such proportions are unique in history and they are caused not just by population but by all sorts of other structural things. Every year the human success story extinguishes twenty-seven thousand species – one hundred a day – and this is again a unique event in history and a background in which we should see the representation of Los Angeles; as an incredible garden of exotic species and flora which have all come about in the last sixty or seventy years. We are now in the sixth major extinction and again that is the situation against which we should look at Los Angeles because global forces to a certain extent are now cosmic forces. The language of heterogeneity is one which somehow gives a creative result out of difference itself, acknowledging the differences in frames of reference language.

The four ecologies as to why people went to Los Angeles in the 20s and 30s, because of Le Corbusier's three essential joys: sun, space and greenery, and of course the fourth most essential one, the land of opportunity was the American dream at large, but you can see it was not – the importance of the foothills, the Pacific Ocean and the sun should not, however, be underrated. If one studies ethnicity differences you can see the so-called white population is located somewhere along the coast west of Los Angeles, while the black population is in South Central Los Angeles. Of course these classification systems highlight the internal differences of ethnicity, for instance the fact that 10 per cent of the 'whites' are Iranian and eleven per cent are Russian and so forth and they do not like to be classified as white, especially today. It is important to see this question of minoritisation because Los Angeles has one-hundred-and-fifty ethnic minorities and thirteen of the minorities are major minorities. The most major minority is the Hispanic one which is over thirty per cent of the population and the Asian minority, which is of course made up of mostly Japanese, Korean and Chinese who don't like to be necessarily lumped together as Asians, see themselves first as a different sub-category.

So, the important thing about heteropolis is that it is a radically minoritised city where there is no clear fifty-one per cent majority. Hence, the dominant, the notion of the centre and the dominant culture has only recently disappeared. I think in the 60s it was much more clearly defined with much fewer ethnic groups, so the heteropolis can change very quickly. The diversity index is greater than other cities. And there are more areas of differentiation, freeways, identity areas which I will not go into but they cut it up yet again with more differentiation.

There are, I believe, three basic architectural ways to deal with this. One is what I call representational heterogeneity, and Post-Modernists like Venturi carry this out at the medical research centre for UCLA campus, using four or five of the different languages that are local to the area or particular to UCLA. Venturi in a sense takes into account that pervasive modernist vocabulary of very big, mass-produced machines for welding which characterise all of this part of Los Angeles.

There are other ways of representing difference which are more analogous and that is what I want to look at. Some of them are traditional methods of informality which the Japanese have developed, or some are more radically conflicting. Moss, perhaps more than any other architect, is a regional local Culver City architect on the one hand and someone who enjoys the global discourse on the other, so when he designs parts of his buildings you can see a very creative inventive use of conflict of codes in his work. Gehry, although he does not like to claim paternity or to be a leader of anything, always disclaims any responsibility for any of the other Los Angeles schools of architects. From the outside it is clear that there is a common language of informality in his or the others' work, there is a very inventive use of difference which is an analogous difference.

Lastly, if representational and analogous heterogeneity are two methods, then the third method is the representation of difference in terms of displacement. In other words, instead of confronting directly the other groups of difference in terms of displacement, you say, 'Right, I'll use the difference to create something that the groups haven't thought of, so I'll displace the question to a new level.' Gehry's Disney Hall was the building which when designed for the competition, was meant to heal the wounds of this incredibly conflicting situation. An impossible task was put on it: it was meant to unify Los Angeles culture. Clearly it cannot do that but what it can do is use a language of otherness which is not recognisably Anglo or Italianate, in any case contaminated by any obvious association, and do it in a way which is inventive and opening out to the city with an organic or partly organic metaphor, partly a metaphor of broken crockery because Schnabel is part of the code of architecture and there are other codes too.

The drawings of Leon Krier show a fourth method, of course a traditional method, where true polarity exists, not only in having mixtures, which he characterises as false polarity, but in keeping some areas decontaminated from other areas so that you can enjoy difference at a macro level too. It seems to me that without going into it too deeply, the relationship between modern liberalism and traditional liberalism on the one hand and multi-culturalism in the politics of difference on the other, is the difference between these two versions of legitimacy and it strikes me that if we face this question straight, we have to admit that there is no resolution.

These are two different discourses, they are ultimately opposed to one another in terms of the law, in terms of our identity, in terms of their traditions. If one can guarantee a certain civility and legal control of the first, of rights and of what modern liberalism insists upon, then one can move on, as Charles Taylor the philosopher said, to the politics of difference and a true Post-Modern liberalism or liberalism that transcends it which would include both of them together, the politics of universalism and the politics of difference.

Chris Moller: You mention that Los Angeles restructures itself constantly, is it Los Angeles that is restructuring itself or is it the restructuring of the maths of Los Angeles?

Charles Jencks: Both. We have to learn them both ways, we must look at the discourse and we must look at the reality in, for example, the flora. It is fundamentally necessary to expand the definition of a city in a more radical and natural way. As Thomas Berry, an important theologian in America keeps saying, democracy is a conspiracy of the human species against the thirty-nine point nine per cent, and if it is true of Los Angeles that it has this diversity then where is it in our myth, in our mental language? We have to get it back.

James Steele: I think we can intellectualise about the centres of the cities but they do exist. There is a lot of energy going into the Downtown strategic plan and the planners are going to be very upset to hear it but basically people do not look at the image of the city. I do not think it is

very hip to talk about suburbs or whatever name you want to use for it. But it is also very important now for Los Angeles because the centre of the city is the focus of everyone's energy.

Kevin Rhowbotham: How do we politically empower people who occupy the city? There is all this talk about how you centralise by projecting a political sense which is controlled in the centre. It is going to blow apart. Now, your problem is how to incur these people who will fragment it, surely that provides the opportunity of actually returning to that central political control – the legitimacy of the centre?

Edward Soja: I agree with you that the question has to come back to the political issues of collective social political organisations instead of retreating into the individual and personal impressions, but I am saying my comments before had to do with a kind of shuddering at the notion of blaming Los Angeles for the problems that are internal to London; you should blame the people who are destroying London for destroying London and that is a political question which is going to require mobilisation in London – regardless of Los Angeles – to attempt to address it and it is going to have to be a political kind of movement. The question of learning the positives and negatives from Los Angeles is fine but that is not going to be possible if you start with the problem of seeing Los Angeles in this simplistic way, as evil, as the place from which problems emanate. No? Well, that is what it sounds like – blaming Los Angeles: a block to learning from Los Angeles if it is believed.

Maxwell Hutchinson: Please don't flatter yourself too much and think that we do think that you're the root of all evil and all problems. If I have learnt anything this afternoon it is the lack of consensus, vision and planning and I certainly share Kevin Rhowbotham's view about the city. If you have come to the end of your long statistical analyses about the number of settlements and claim that they should be given their individual identity and somehow the city of Los Angeles should be disintegrated into its past so there could be some sort of plan for those individuals, then I feel some optimism. But all I go away with at the moment is feeling sympathy and thinking, 'goodness me, we are going to try and help you sort out the issues?' I worry so much about your problems because in this country most of us actually do not want to be Europeans, we want to be Americans, we want everything that America has to offer, we will go on holiday to Europe but basically we are mini-Americans and the way that you romanticise your problems worries me enormously because Los Angeles somehow becomes even more romantic the more problems it has. The more romantic it is, the more it becomes a paradigm for a changing Europe and that worries me a great deal.

Eric Owen Moss: Your last statement is a good point but it would not be a surprise if people who come from Los Angeles romanticised their issues themselves. It is true that Los Angeles now exists in pieces, like a number of people have said, whether it is the flora, the animals or the Afro-Americans. When I was a kid, the latter were known as negroes, then they were to be called blacks. In the evolution this is interesting in terms of what Mr Jameson was saying about the form of the language and I think Mr Soja is from UCLA, so if he doesn't say African-American in the street he's in real trouble. He is afraid of that, not literally, but in the environment in which people work in – so the problem is that there is a kind of tension between the pieces in something which tends to try and pull it together or to try to make a form where the pieces can connect with other pieces in ways other than as adversaries. This means there is a Los Angeles singular and not in the peculiar sense one, and there is a Los Angeles multiple, both; and you would have to admit to both and it actually inspires both. I think that the problem now, in terms of what I gather Professor Erskine was saying, is that of myth: largely a myth floating around in Europe for quite a while about what constitutes an American city or a coherence; or we left all that in Ireland or we left all that in Italy, so this is now, we did not leave it in Mexico, we brought it with us. There was a very famous politician in Los Angeles who said, 'Wait a minute, we were here first.' This is a politician whom the Mayor of Los Angeles was trying to appoint recently and he said, 'Smell the refried beans, the next step may be that California belongs to Mexico'. This is not inconceivable in the argument at the moment and so it is divisive and I think the best that one can do would be to try and diffuse that and find mechanisms for people who work together. You may not be able to do that why history moves in bad directions. This may now be moving in a dangerous direction.

Conrad Jameson: Why don't you practise what you preach? You talk, you make this wonderful gesture, you say, 'Look, what are your values, what do you believe, what is this city?' I cannot give you a definition of the city but even if you asked these questions – for example in a non-rhetoric manner, like should a suburb become a town? – then you could actually argue whether this is something you are proposing or not. We are not getting actual proposals.

Eric Owen Moss: Well, it is non-rhetorical

Hardy Holzman Pfeiffer, Los Angeles County Art Museum

SOCIAL AND PLANNING HISTORY

because I do not know the answer to the question, I think it's an aspiration . . .

Conrad Jameson: It is very difficult giving a series of descriptions here because again it is very difficult to know how your values are entwined inside. We all want to know about Los Angeles and we also know what the difficulties are, there is a sort of hate Los Angeles ethos as well as one for London and Europe and generally speaking, this is very healthy.

Edward Soja: I don't understand the concept of a European feeling that Los Angeles can be dangerous to us. I am curious about the logic of that observation.

Conrad Jameson: Look at the Docklands . . .

Charles Jencks: Milton Keynes of course is the classic case of a city designed to be Los Angeles so it is quite true that this discourse can create new cities in Britain.

Edward Soja: I am not defending Los Angeles, I am just curious. . .

Conrad Jameson: What I hear from Charlie is that he likes flora and fauna, but what about the people? We want to see some kind of city and Los Angeles is collapsing into the sort of thing we often see in Britain and this is frightening. We see a middle-class Britain collapse into rich and poor, particularly in London and don't want to see this so we are very frightened.

Edward Soja: I think the problem may be a political one, it sounds as if you are not willing to blame yourselves on these issues.

Paul Finch: It is not a matter of blame, it is a question of what lessons there may be, for good or ill, which are coming our way and this seems to me to be an incredibly positive thing to look at. The reason for looking at this city or indeed any other kind of city is not to say, 'Oh my God this is really frightening!', but to see how the people in that city respond to problems which we all face, whether of the car, unemployment, immigration, constitutional arrangements or whatever. That is why it is interesting and that is what we need to look at.

Ralph Erskine: As an ex-patriot British person, my observation is that the British are very busily destroying London and have been at it for quite a time, but this situation is endemic in nearly all the cities in the world, both in the industrialised and the non-industrialised world. One of the big questions I should have thought, which would be interesting to discuss but difficult to solve, is, are such cities actually well fitted to the needs of the human being? We know the real needs, not the constructive needs, we have very powerful propaganda apparatus which we do not call propaganda – we call it advertising. You talk about the impact but I have seen the figures recently and the number of American films shown in Europe compared with the number of European films shown in America, and obviously the American film industry is making it into one of the dominating cultures in the world. The dominating cultures in the world have always had terrific influence and presumably have always been met with certain fear from certain people. But finally I think it is the question, how much do we really discern the potential possible risks for the future, how much do we try with intelligence to influence the future?

I have not personally been to Los Angeles and I get the feeling from this discussion that there is a tendency to assume that one has to follow what is happening. I came from Holland recently and it is a very different situation over there; the small towns are very conscious of their destiny. Apparently fairly general in Holland is that first, they are revitalising their centres, people like the results and are moving back into the centres. They forbid, of course, any larger supermarkets to be constructed. In Sweden we are following the American vision of reality and so they definitely have a policy of influencing people and not allowing indiscriminate commercial development; for example, an office building cannot be built on the edge of a road. We are also working on a competition in Germany where we discovered that if a building was built right on the ground, vegetation is taken away: it is part of building law. What I am talking about of course is the intention of our society and trying to influence it within some sort of proper situation where there is a common interest. We are obviously at an advantage in a small town in Holland compared to Los Angeles.

I think it is interesting to discuss Los Angeles on the basis of attempting to find elements which are useful guides for our future behaviour, or alternatively and rather regrettably, if we can find things to avoid. It is one of the sensible things the Swedes did before but do not need to do so now; they look around the world and being a very small country and assuming that they did not know everything, they found out what to do and what not do by looking at other countries. Now of course, they are doing the wrong thing by copying Margaret Thatcher after MT's almost dead! This seems to me to be the two reasons for looking at Los Angeles, the first is to find anything which is valuable for the human being and of course the second is to acknowledge that the human being who, as well as establishing psychology and so on, has not altered very much and does not alter very fast either. So we have to question the pace of change and whether we accept that we should follow this basis of change. Can we really cope with this pace? Is Los Angeles (and Western culture generally) very valuable? Should we not try and avoid as much as possible following the line of development of Western culture and like the analyst from Samoa discern all the things that are happening this century and advise against foreign discourse? This would be a very interesting discussion for me.

Edward Soja: I think the central point is the point we all share and that is to try and make liveable cities from the human standpoint.

Wolf Prix: I have to say, returning to the linguistic approach, that the focus on the centre of the city as well as restricting the language or the terms, points to a very conservative attitude and I am really afraid that we are confusing language, political language and strategies. I know a research group who carried out a survey on the prices of land close to the cultural centres, Gehry's Opera and the Getty Center, rated the price of the land which raised, in spite of the economic crisis – that means somewhere they have to decide to spend the money there and not somewhere else. So actually there is a cultural, not fight, but battle, between South Central and the Wilshire: these are the real political facts. On the other hand I have to say, and insist, that architecture and the spreading of architecture is a political thing, you cannot deny it that there is a political aesthetic if you just like; for example, I do not know how far Gehry is going with that but when he started, it was a political statement.

Kevin Rhowbotham: It is not political in every context.

Wolf Prix: If you take it just as a formal expression you have to discuss. Right now I meant a French philosopher – he said stay away from this form of discussion, we have to discuss the content of the buildings which is much more interesting than the shape. If the shape of course is connected to the content it is a political expression. Whether it is a solid box or an open box, it is connected to money and money is a political expression; so every expression, cultural expression, in the language is a statement.

Kevin Rhowbotham: We are constantly debating a single issue here instead of asking questions about the micro territories, the micro territories of Los Angeles, the micro territories that exist within an established institution. You could say quite clearly that you can refer to a centralist condition, because those institutions are actually present and the school system has its own micro territories, they are very well known; they are published every day in Los Angeles hence there's a crime, there's a series of criminal tendencies and many other tendencies within those institutions which constitute micro territories but we choose to see them as negative.

Wolf Prix: But what is universal? It is calling for leadership again, and first, it does not exist – this is the advantage of Los Angeles that it is the city of no problem, if you hear the words 'no problem', you had better run because it takes a long time to get what you want.

Conrad Jameson: Los Angeles has a special problem that puts us in the liberal left on the hock. You were not supposed to use the words illegal alien; you said undocumented worker. In other words you had a liberal view of this wonderful settling in of immigrants from everywhere and now we realised that it depended upon this tremendous train, this tremendous engine of economic growth which would somehow create employment. We have now lost faith in this. Los Angeles has pulled in cheap labour, different coloured skins, different nationalities and so on, and now we have the problem of what we are supposed to do. I can just think of Eric Osborne and the Socialist Bank of India, who came back and said whatever it was . . . it is the bravest nation state as it were in attempting a new melting pot.

Edward Soja: Earlier Charles Jencks referred to something I had used before as I guess the model of how to look at Los Angeles, how to learn from it. And perhaps I will repeat it again to begin the discussion because I think it is relevant. He referred to, and I refer to, a short story by Jorge Luis Borges called the *The Aleph* which is essentially narrated by someone who is Borges himself. He talks with a friend and the friend says, 'You must come to my house, I've got the most fantastic thing on earth'. He says, 'Where is it?' The other replies, 'In my cellar'. His friend says, 'I stole it from someone when I was a child and I still have it, you must come over'. So he goes over and he goes down to his friend's cellar and he sees what his friend called the Aleph which his friend described as the space that contains all other spaces. It is the simultaneity of everything included within one space and one place and he goes down and he is amazed by it and says, 'I can't believe what my eyes have seen'. Then he makes an interesting comment, he says 'This is the beginning of my problem. After seeing the Aleph I have this

SOCIAL AND PLANNING HISTORY

deep, deep problem, how can I explain the Aleph to you? I can explain it in language whether written or oral, because language is sequential, it's not simultaneous. And what I saw in the Aleph is simultaneous above all else. Every space at the same point at the same time'. The argument then was: I will just tell you what I can remember guided by my own project and in a sense that is also the lesson and something I think that was behind some of the efforts both this afternoon and this evening to make sense of Los Angeles, to try to share that sense with others and to try to sort of think this up into questions of learning from Los Angeles. The first, I think, is a characteristic architecture focused particularly it seems, on creative architects who are working a lot and have many projects that people who maybe are not involved in major projects at the moment have a less self-centred personal introverted point of view. The danger is indeed that this translates into self-indulgence.

I was scolded for making-up words. This is a word which I do not think exists in the dictionary but really should, because it is an old kind of word that is rarely used: 'propriospective'; that is perceiving the world so entirely within oneself that one loses sight of the outside reality. I think this is a problem with this particular kind of approach and as I said, I will leave open any particular attachment or decision on whether that was reached at all.

The second mode of thought I guess, was a sort of rational analytical approach to making sense of Los Angeles. I was part of that process and I think Allen Scott was very clearly part of that process this evening and this indeed is another mode of trying to make sense of and learn from any city. In a sense this is attached to maybe a new urbanist tradition, which most of Anglo-American architecture has lost contact with. That urban tradition is certainly, even the old urban tradition, although they're trying to increase the context with a new urbanist tradition. I think that's an interesting side point. This rational or analytic – perhaps not the best words to use – I think also is something to learn from. But dangers exist as well and the dangers here have to do with narrowing and with putting too many eggs in one basket of causality and a kind of powerful dependence upon singular kinds of theoretical argument and analyses; so all of Los Angeles, all of urbanism, is a way of life, all urbanisation comes down to the structured outcome of a particular cause. One is cautious about this but it is a very powerful and important way of learning.

I would attempt to define the third mode with the word eclectic, perhaps sporadically eclectic, that is to celebrate the maximum of diversity, heterogeneity, difference, and all sources of possible understanding and interpretation of the city. Again, an interesting approach, perhaps best expressed in the very term that Charles Jencks uses in *Heteropolis*, the emphasis on almost constantly seeing difference and diversity and heterogeneity at the centre. I think this indeed captures a tremendous amount of what can be learnt from Los Angeles, and it also becomes a very important base for learning from Los Angeles and connecting it up into other kinds of issues, areas and problems. This also poses dangers and the dangers are perhaps obvious: that it leads to a kind of chaotic eclecticism and complete lack of discipline, but everything fits in no matter how diverse and unusual and strange – the stranger the better, let's connect them all together. This becomes a danger in this eclectic mode. The best way to describe it I think is to compare it to the bumper sticker, 'I love (heart) New York' or London. I can imagine a bumper sticker which has 'I' and then this sort of a devil 'hate Los Angeles' and the kind of blinding force that comes from fear and loathing Los Angeles. I choose fear and loathing because they are so connected to what was often the euphemism or the substitute or the alternative to 'I hate Los Angeles' which is 'I hate Venturi and Las Vegas and Post-Modernism and all images and everything else that is associated with that whole bag of tricks'.

Therefore Los Angeles is an ogre and the idea of learning from Los Angeles is almost inconceivable. I think the most interesting factor about this negative learning process is that I thought wrongly, foolishly, and mistakenly became political. The 'propriospective' personal introverted mode was not only non-political, it was most anti-political. It produced arguments that of course could not be political if political meant some kind of collective action, because it was always drawing in, always introverting the argument, perhaps exclusively into a free creative spirit – a very logical kind of process but one that is fundamentally anti-political; and I think that there was always a comment that Los Angeles was the least ideological place. Well I disagree. It is a place that is filled with politics and ideology and it is just not the same way as it may be in many other places but I think the same is true with the rational analytical approach that I mentioned, by overly narrowing the interpretive matrix. There is a tendency to lose sight of the connections, the real politics that should be associated with the process of learning from Los Angeles. How does one learn from Los Angeles things that are relevant politically, because I think that is a very valid question and one thing we do share is an interest in trying to make urban life better, to improve urban life and conditions. I presume that is what we all share and what should be learnt from Los Angeles very vividly; and so vividly perhaps as much as anything else that can be learnt from Los Angeles is that in order to make things better in the city, you have to be political. What can be learnt from Los Angeles is (a) that what is happening in Los Angeles, whether you like it or not, is happening here: it is not coming from Los Angeles, it is coming from changes that are taking place from all over the world, in every metropolitan area at different rates, different times, different intensities but it is happening, it is part of existing in the late 20th century. And I am not saying these particular manifestations are inevitable but what I am saying is that these processes of change are occurring.

How they occur in a particular place depends upon that particular place, politics, geography, a variety of other factors; it depends on how the local reacts to these global processes of change and an organised political will which effectively shapes the restructuring processes, instead of denying that they exist. Improvement, rather than destruction is creative and lends itself to an aware political process. It is a process that sometimes I do indeed associate with Post-Modernism, not the Thatcher/Reagan form of Post-Modernism – they indeed were brilliant Post-Modern politicians – but with a radical Post-Modernism of resistance, one that does not deny the processes of change and does not deny the restructuring, but attempts to understand it and fight it on its own grounds, rather than assuming that the blame is elsewhere.

The Watts riots were the first and the most violent urban uprising riots in the 20th century. What they said (and they were followed by many more) was that it was business as usual, the postwar boom was over, it could no longer work; we had to find different ways to restore boom conditions and to achieve social control. All over the world, the period 1965-73 (1968 in Paris, 1969 in Italy and Mexico and so on) witnessed a sequence of events which culminated in the 1973 recession. That whole sequence of events was the first stage in a crises-generated restructuring. Many places like Los Angeles restructured very, very rapidly, others very, very slowly. Los Angeles boomed through this period when many parts of the world were actually declining. I like to define 1992 in Los Angeles as a kind of book end on this period, marking the beginning of a restructuring generated crisis. It is a radically different landscape to the one twenty-five or so years ago.

1965 saw the worst urban violence in the 20th century to date and then it exploded again in the worst urban violence in the 20th century ever in 1992. That tells the world that in the absence of organised politics, this is the only way to begin to break open the political situation. As I say this, I am not inviting you all to riot but I am arguing that this is one of the lessons, ideas, ways of learning politically from Los Angeles. It *is* directly relevant to the situation we are in here in Britain. It is indicative of something that is likely to have a major effect wherever you are, and since we are here, I think the connection is obvious. I will end with a hard political note and not have any regrets. Thank you.

Paul Finch: On that note I think we're going to wrap up on a rather chicken and egg remark about immigration and economic growth. I first visited Los Angeles in the summer of '69. It was the summer of Woodstock, the summer of black panthers in Boston. And when I arrived in Los Angeles I had a very hazy idea of quite what it would be like other than the fact that I would probably get taken to Disneyland at some point, which I did. But I was staying with somebody in the San Fernando Valley so my notion that Los Angeles would just be like London was rapidly destroyed, because it was *I Love Lucy* and it was trying to match that up to the discussions on late night television about the Vietnam War. The sort of family treat I was given at the end of my stay was to be taken to the local ice-cream parlour. It was a particularly good ice-cream parlour because if it was somebody's birthday (and amazingly enough it seemed to be somebody's birthday every night) then all the Italian waiters sang some verses from opera. That summer was certainly a rather bizarre introduction to the America of Vietnam and Woodstock and the ice-cream parlour. I always think about that because those are the images of Los Angeles which are impossible to dispel, like the remark somebody made about *Blade Runner* – if Harrison Ford can fly off into the distance with the girl, then perhaps we could do that too? Mike Davis' book has had such an effect here in London because he focuses on these issues of involvement and commitment and power, of which architecture is inevitably a part. And even if the architecture is looking inwards, it can no more avoid its relationship to the context in which it finds itself than if it looks outwards.

Finally, perhaps I could just remark that the difference between involvement and commitment, which I think has been a kind of sub-text through some of the remarks this afternoon, is rather well demonstrated by thinking about a plate of bacon and eggs. If you think about the eggs, the hen was involved; if you think about the bacon, the pig was totally committed.

LOS ANGELES AS IT MIGHT HAVE BEEN

RANDOM CONURBATION OR PLANNED SATELLITE ?
Maggie Toy   66

CULTURAL CENTRES
Morphosis
Yuzen Vintage Car Museum   76
Hodgetts + Fung
Arts Park LA   80

MIXED USE DEVELOPMENT
Studio Asymptote
Steel Cloud   82
Dagmar Richter
Century City   84
West Coast Gateway   88
Eric Owen Moss
Hayden Tract   92
Hayden Tower   94
Hercules Theater and Offices   98
S.P.A.R.C I T Y   100
Samitaur I & II   104
The Jerde Partnership
Hollywood Promenade   108

PRIVATE RESIDENCES
Dagmar Richter
Devine Residence   112
Hoffs Residence   114
Frank Gehry
Familian Residence   116
Cigolle + Coleman
Mills Musingo House   118

RESTAURANTS, BARS AND SHOPS
Hodgetts + Fung
Cookie Express   120

RANDOM CONURBATION OR PLANNED SATELLITE?
MAGGIE TOY

The point of arrival for the majority of Los Angeles' international visitors is LAX. This building was designed by the Luckman Partnership in 1955-61 and is unique in its ability to maintain its futuristic image. Poised as if about to take flight, the Luckman Building stands as a monument to the design of the airport as it might have been – an airport uncluttered with buildings above ground – and thus a representation of many architectural and planning schemes for this city which have been created, partially implemented and yet have been superseded by the next fashion. This is not necessarily a negative trait. The airport does in fact work. Its simple organisational system is sufficiently flexible to accommodate the inevitable rapid growth both in quantity of traffic and in size of aircraft. Versatility was the key element in its inherent design. The restaurant building remains the crowning jewel, now a historical landmark.

It is important to recognise that whilst Los Angeles is the second metropolis of the US it is also a very young city and in some ways maintains the open formlessness of that youth. Arthur Golding has claimed that the social structure is 'remarkably open for a major city'. There are no old families, no really major concentrations of power and in this context, change has become the norm. The city is not without its traditions but the predominant tradition in Los Angeles is the tradition of the new.

K Paul Zygas argues that the popular image of Los Angeles as a city with more than its fair share of curious, bizarre and entertaining buildings is in fact an illusion – a mental image widespread among Angelenos and visitors alike. In actual fact, the majority of the city is composed of indistinctive architecture which fails to create an impression, with the consequence that even a mildly unconventional style creates a memorable image.

So, the planning of the city comes into discussion again. Edward Soja has argued that J Portman's Bonaventure Hotel is a microcosm of the overall planning of the city. Bonaventure is perceived by Soja to be oppressive, devoid of a sense of place, billboards which in theory should be positioned to assist the public only serve to confuse them. As Soja reflected, one is left with a sense of being controlled, 'there being a body in control which is exerting their power of you'.

Contrary to public perception there is, in fact, grounds for debate over the urban origins of Los Angeles. Some argue that it is oriented accidently, others maintain that it was preplanned. The majority, however, finds itself in the battle ground in-between. Richard Neutra, whilst arguing for his own plans to be utilised in 1943, insisted that there was no preplanned development within the city. David Gebhard and Harriette von Breton on the other hand, believe that Los Angeles is a planned non-city.

Looking at the city in the midst of worldwide conflict that was to prove so critical to its subsequent growth, Neutra describes Los Angeles as having a long history of 'rampant disorder' which was seized upon by entrepreneurs. This commercially-minded group exploited the city's lack of organisation through wholesale land speculation, assisted by boosterism and carried out through the press, enticing people to invest their life savings and move 'westwards'. The new settlers arrived to find soaring land prices and the parcels they had bought as squares on a map were without access to water but, it has been said, they were 'surrounded by oil derricks swarming over the hills and down the beaches'. Wastefulness developed with greedy politicians seizing land grants on the basis of low productivity and by record-sized plots of land being sold for residential use, fuelling the American dream of a home of one's own with uncluttered horizons.

Neutra points out that the people who were enticed by Los Angeles were different from the pioneers who had moved to the mid-west from the east coast, because the former had little or no expectation of enduring hardship or difficulty, expecting instead a domestic paradise. They were born to 'shape life less harshly, more comfortably, and above all informally'. Unlike immigrants to New York, the new Angelenos dreamt of being individual homeowners. This in itself begins to explain the desire to create not another city, but a series of semi-rural rustic regions. The architectural implications of this melting pot of homeowners was a lack of organisation in approach to style or design, since each immigrant brought his or her own experience, resulting in a cacophony of styles: 'and so this

OPPOSITE: The Schindler House; ABOVE: The Luckman Partnership, Theme building and restaurant, LA Airport

LOS ANGELES AS IT MIGHT HAVE BEEN

landscape is generally dotted by many strange phenomena: half-timber English 'peasant' cottages, French provincial, Georgian missions on 50 x 110 foot lots, with Mexican ranchos adjoining them on sites of the same size. A Cape Cod fisherman's hut appears side by side with the estate agents' offices, seemingly by Red Indians. It almost goes without saying that all of these buildings are neither constructed of adobe or of half-timber or masonry, as they appear to be. Almost uniformly, they have been composed of two-by-fours covered with black paper, chicken wire and a brittle plaster veneer or on some occasions a brick finish crowned with a multitude of often synthetically-coloured roofing materials'.

Interestingly this observation made by Richard Neutra in 1943 is equally pertinent to the city's residential area today, particularly north of the centre in the foothills, where every architectural style imaginable is stacked upon the mountain side. Neutra's own solution to this chaos was to introduce the first International Style dwellings to be built on the West Coast. He was prolific and successful, probably his most notable examples include the Lovell Health House, his first and most important commission. During this period Neutra had written extensively about the promise of a new architecture and the constructive possibilities of a new age and this house was presented as the first ever built in an industrial material (steel frame). Stefanos Polyzoides reflects that this innovative house incorporated 'many gadgets widely admired abroad as symbols of progress'. This success was followed by, among others, the VDL Research House, Strathmore Apartments and Landfair House, which, true to Modernist principles, lacked reference to an historical period or local content. Much the same principles are executed by Thom Mayne of Morphosis and Eric Owen Moss today, although with quite different results. These had an all important influence in the case study houses that would follow, but his distinctive style failed to inspire the design for new housing after the war as it did not fulfil the contemporary desire for individuality coupled with a romanticised past.

Neutra was an unabashed admirer of Irving Gill, as was his fellow countryman Rudolph Schindler (who was responsible for bringing Neutra to Los Angeles). Both young architects responded positively to the clean surfaces, flat roofs and freedom from ornament, evident in Gill's Dodge House of 1916 and the Horatio West Apartments of 1919. Had Neutra attempted to expand on Gill's attempt to marry Modernism with the mission style, he might have been able to appeal to a wider audience. However he obviously misunderstood the national need for reference to the past, whether real or imaginary.

Irving Gill had served his apprenticeship with Sullivan in Chicago before moving to San Diego in 1893 and although he had limited education and minimal architectural training he was able to develop a simplification and refinement of both space and detail in architecture. He proceeded to develop his work in a direction rarely taken in this area of America, imposing his style on low-cost housing and public institutions of major importance. In the Dodge House he blended a concern for purity and single reading of form with his practical experiments in concrete construction and his appreciation of the surrounding landscape as an extension of the building. The Dodge House was a place to return to in order to understand the turn of the century architectural mind. America was robbed of a monument when it was demolished. Reyner Banham poetically describes how the loss was felt right to the core of America, even two 'hippies' politely expounded their disappointment in the County of Los Angeles on discovering that the building standing before them was about to be demolished.

Although Neutra admired Gill's work, there was a fundamental difference: whilst Neutra strove to design an International style, Gill knew and worked with local materials, climate, fauna and customs. Gill had an heroic agenda to invent a new architecture that was indigenous and yet a great departure. Los Angeles accommodates change, with little being preserved, even if there is a desire to do so – a stark reminder that architecture is not controlled by architects but is in fact, a 'dedicated follower of fashion', in the immortal words of The Kinks in 1966.

Hollywood is cited by Neutra as an example of the ingrained ambivalence surrounding the future of Los Angeles' populace. He uses the dubious analogy of the blind alleys in Vine Street and Hollywood Boulevard, extending it into an argument focusing on the separate urban centres in the region which are linked by arterial freeways. Neutra failed to appreciate Hollywood's capacity to symbolise American aspirations and its consequent potential in shaping American consciousness. Just as the Cape Cod House could embody a half-glimpsed ideal rather than a remembered reality of heritage, Hollywood concentrated the hopes of the American subconscious into celluloid images of a perfect past, and provided a role-model for social harmony.

Unlike RM Schindler who arrived in America before the war, Neutra suffered considerably through the Second World War in Europe, an experience which significantly affected his view of the world. Schindler's work was influenced by the *fin-de-siècle* which was sweeping Vienna, combining the pragmatic views of Otto Wagner

OPPOSITE: Morphosis, Yuzen Vintage Car Museum, composite drawing detail; ABOVE: Irving Gill, Dodge House

with the *zeitgeist* tendencies of Joseph Maria Olbrich. Schindler exploited the general feeling in Los Angeles to expound his theories which were partly set out in *Modern Architecture, a Programme*, written in 1913. The book demonstrated his belief in modern constructional methods and his faith in concrete: 'by introducing concrete construction, the twentieth century took the first step to disregard construction formally. The constructional problem has been reduced to a mathematical equation . . . construction has lost its interest . . . Monumentality is the mark of power. The first ruler was the tyrant . . . Today a different form of man demands its monument. The mind's creative power has broken the tyrant's power'. Expressing the freedom which constructing with concrete gave him, Schindler explains that the aesthetic of his forms derives from the exploration of space. However, after the Lovell Beach House, Schindler was forced to abandon his experiments in concrete due to excessive cost. Instead of moving to steel construction or the appearance of steel construction favoured by Neutra, Schindler began to explore the most readily available building medium in Los Angeles at that time – the wood frame usually covered in stucco. His work for the next three decades concentrated upon these materials, and when large areas of glass and a steel beam were used, often combined with a post-and-beam construction.

Another key architect of this time whose influence cannot be ignored was Frank Lloyd Wright. His work was not quite so closely connected with the International Style but like Gill, he designed for the site and the region. Wright had experimented with conventional pattern blocks previously in the Midway Gardens in Chicago, and between 1921 and 1924 he constructed the 'block houses', signifying a brief but important stage in his career. The textile blocks used in the Los Angeles houses have no precedent in his work. He probably felt the need to regionalise his design and achieved this by creating a new building method for his work in the city. These forms have retained a certain place in our memory as they are so different to his other works. The Ennis House has been used as a backdrop for many films to create an atmosphere of dignity and power. The plans were strongly influenced by their Prairie predecessors but the innovative construction process left one or two points open to criticism. The blocks were pre-cast individually on site, a time-consuming and demanding exercise, in which consistent quality was difficult to achieve. The majority of uneven exterior surfaces were exposed to weathering and crumbling. The reinforcing was often too wide to cover and became easily exposed to the elements. Today some of the walls lack reinforcement because of prolonged steel oxidisation and are only held together due to the creeping vines which are allowed to envelop them. As Jim Tice stated, 'the concrete blocks as a constructional experiment seem somewhat akin to Wright's infamous furniture – the effort is always more successful as a *plastic idea* than as a solution to *pragmatic fact*'. But, hey if you're going to experiment you're in the right city!

The two women, to my knowledge, to have any kind of architectural impact on the city at the time were Julia Morgan and Ray Eames. The surfaces of Julia Morgan's buildings have an ornamental finish but they exhibit the underlying motivation of Modernist planning. She, like Gill, designed to achieve a regional effect. Her most prominent building was the Los Angeles Examinar in Downtown in 1915. As with the Herst Castle in San Simeon, 1919-42, designed for William Randolph Herst, Morgan's Hispanic regional decoration responds to the environment, but the plan follows the basic principles of Modernism. Derek Walker describes the partnership of Charles and Ray Eames as being the most internationally stimulating team to have emerged out of celluloid city: 'they are designers, inventors, craftsmen, scientists film-makers, educators. Yet in all their diversity, their creation is not a series of separate achievements but a unified aesthetic with the organic growth of a beautiful tree.' Their case-study house is still as breathtaking today as when it was first introduced to the architectural scene in 1949.

These were all architects influential with individual buildings constructed within the urban framework that was Los Angeles. The wider planning schemes were confronted by the likes of Neutra. Romanticism of the *fin-de-siècle* was affected by the horrors of war, Neutra showed more of the social agenda of the best-known Modernists, as his 1943 article suggests, 'In Los Angeles prior to the second World War there was hardly conspicuous evidence of "marching battalions of industrial workers" but rather a motorised, variable, non-organised army of commission salesmen trying their luck in the offering of local and eastern products, of all kinds of services, and last but by no means least, real estate'.

The panacea for the social problems was, according to Neutra, in planning the region. It cited a quarter-of-a-million unemployed during the depression as evidence of a lack of regional balance. In a characteristically analytical fashion, Neutra abstracted the intensity of human tragedy. This emotion was portrayed effectively by novelists such as John Steinbeck, in *The Grapes of Wrath*, who highlighted the desperate escape of families from the dustbowl of the midwest to the fertile lands of Southern California.

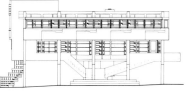

ABOVE: RM Schindler, view of Lovell Beach House; BELOW: Front elevation

The people who were dismissively described by Neutra as 'newly-baked Angelenos' were, in fact, often wizened by the droughts that plagued the central plains, and not only hoped for, but relied upon discovering a better way of life.

A less stereotypical view of the people who settled in and shaped Los Angeles is presented by the historians David Gebhard and Harriette von Breton. They have agreed that the well accepted paradigm of postwar Los Angeles as a 'decentralised city with a number of regional hubs' was intentional rather than arbitrary. The principles behind the prototype of Downtown Los Angeles as the central business district was to allow for the development of other larger commercial centres within the same area, assuming primacy of the automobile as the principal means of transportation between them. Gebhard and Von Breton point out that planners who have exerted an influence in Los Angeles since the turn of the century, ingeniously realised that the route to a position of power lay in controlling the configuration and growth of transportation, water and energy, rather than in built form. The first zoning code in the region was enacted in 1904, and in 1909 Los Angeles became the first city in the US to adopt an all encompassing zoning ordinance. The City Planning Commission itself was formally established in 1910, and its regional equivalent was recognised by legislation in 1923, all in a city commonly felt to have been created without an overall plan. Zoning differed in Los Angeles, in that it emphasised residential land use. As Gebhard and von Breton highlight, 'the agreed upon consensus was that land was a speculative commodity and that the highest use (the use most highly profitable for the speculator) should determine how it was to be used. The planning philosophy of the highest use also carried with it the built-in connotation that land use was non-static and thus ever changing'. It seems the only occasion on which the residents of Los Angeles ever put a stop to this laissez-faire attitude was with the sanctity of the house and residential use of the land. The result was the creation of suburban enclaves such as Rancho Park, Los Feliz and Laughton Park. The unseemly edge to this semi-rural Utopia was that the deeds to properties came with restrictive covenants that excluded ownership by African-Americans and Hispanics – these 'laws' have only recently been broken. The identity of these communities has stayed so coherent and distinct that recent attempts to unite the LA region with a mass transit rail system have been resisted by each one in turn.

Los Angeles differed from the majority of US cities in that it did not have a main street running in a linear fashion through its centre. Main streets in decentralised areas are joined together into a centrifugal chain by means of freeways. The concentrated patterns of land use which dictated the linear form were dispensed with in Los Angeles, allowing such extended growth to take place. The impetus for the freeway system began in the early 1930s, when the state division of highways, at the prompting of the Los Angeles Regional Planning Commission and its urban counterpart, began developing a network of superhighways. By the end of that decade, they had achieved a masterplan for a metropolitan parkway system. The idea behind these highways was that they should be beautifully landscaped, free from the staccato interruptions of the existing traffic systems that characterised the boulevards and surface streets, since over and underpasses allowed the free flow of traffic. Entrance and exit by gently curving lanes also ensured the absence of barriers in the freeway traffic. The first freeway, the Arroyo Seco Parkway (or the Pasadena Freeway as it is now known) was planned in 1934 and completed in 1942. It was paired with the Cahuenga Freeway and pieces of the Santa Ana and Ramona Parkways were also added. The success of the Arroyo Seco Parkway encouraged its replication following the Second World War, largely due to the accessibility it provided for prospective residential areas, fuelling the economic impetus that had proven to be the primary *raison d'etre* for Los Angeles. The connection between the freeways and the land values of the areas contiguous to them was symbiotic – new business centres sprung up virtually overnight as the concrete and asphalt were laid. The Arroyo Seco today looks quaint, with entries to underpasses detailed in intricate Art Deco Style. This level of attention was mirrored in each new freeway that followed, albeit in a more rationalised way, in the evolution of what may only truly be called the one architecture for the masses in the region.

The innovation of the freeways signalled the demise of the public transportation system that had given excellent service to the suburban areas of the city and had virtually established the boundaries of greater Los Angeles. The first transit line had opened in Los Angeles in 1874, but by 1885 some of these original lines were being replaced by cable cars and a funicular cable system called 'Angels Flight' was opened in 1901. The first electric lines were opened in 1888, most of them installed by private developers to promote the sale of land and property. By the turn of the century the Southern Pacific Railroad had purchased the majority of the railway and streetcar lines and streetcars and electric cars ran side by side through most Downtown streets. This, coupled with the increasing popularity of the private motor car, inevitably caused congestion and traffic con-

ABOVE: Richard Neutra, view of Lovell Health House; BELOW: Elevation

LOS ANGELES AS IT MIGHT HAVE BEEN

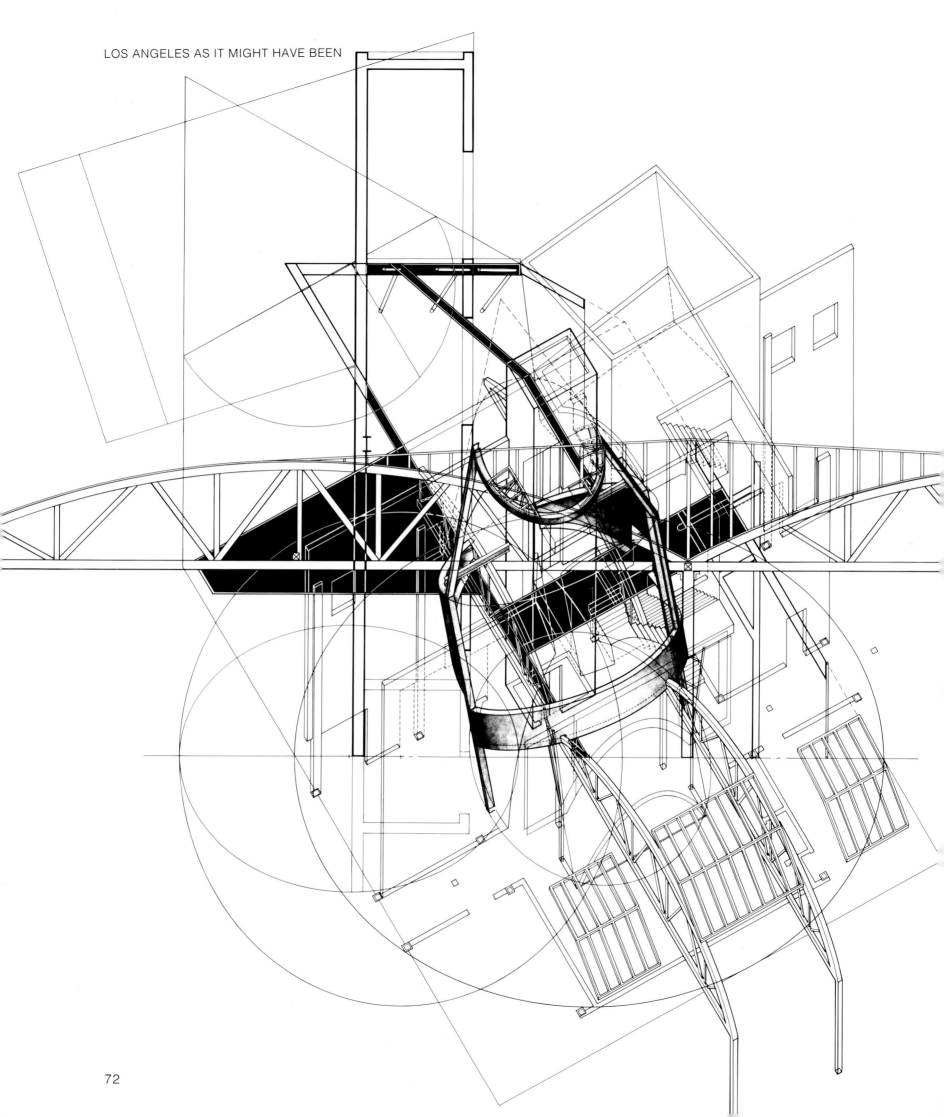

flicts. Speed restrictions were imposed on rail systems which left an opening for the next popular form of transport, the bus lines. Many of the latter's routes substituted the old streetcar lines and the service patterns remained very similar. Although the buses were comfortable they still could not compete with the luxury of the individual hermetically-sealed environments that motorcars afforded the user. Automobiles had begun to take over from the Pacific Electric Trains as early as 1915, although it was not until 1961 that the latter was finally destroyed, and the freeway attained true supremacy as the only viable means of communication between Los Angeles' districts. In recent decades the concentration of transport planning has been on the development of the freeway system and its objective of achieving a continuous circulation flow. However, it is important to recognise that despite the sophistication of the network, the proliferation of the private vehicle has had a knock-on effect, causing additional environmental problems within the city, which demonstrates the necessity to acknowledge freeways as only a partial answer to the solution of urban transportation. Although the total number of people entering and leaving the central city has not increased dramatically, decreases in vehicular occupancy have resulted in a net increase in the number of vehicles using the freeways. Numerous requests and attempts have been made to reinstate a comprehensive public transport system. As Graeme Morland observes, 'the romance between Los Angeles and the automobile is not only being questioned but is facing its most severe test'.

Gebhard and van Breton illustrate that the growth of Los Angeles was primarily dependent on its supply of water. Reyner Banham in the classic *Los Angeles: The Architecture of the Four Ecologies* points out that 'the politics of hydrology became . . . a deciding factor in fixing the political boundaries of Los Angeles. The city annexed the San Fernando Valley, murdered the Owens Valley in its first great raid on the hinterland waters under William Mullholland, and its hydraulic frontier is now the Colorado River'. The importance of water in the development of the region is particularly highlighted in the annexation of the San Fernando Valley, allowing water to flow into the orange groves, the symbol of Southern California as paradise on earth. Ironically, these groves have been supplanted by suburbs made possible by the initial access to water.

The engineering equivalent of the freeways that arose from the need for water was the Hoover Dam, completed in 1935. The motivation behind the decision to authorise the construction of an aqueduct to bring water from the Colorado River in the midst of the depression, was based on greed, ambition and the exercising of political muscle. Nevertheless it indicates the priority placed on this vital commodity which had helped to produce the 'eternal spring' of California. Since growth and development of the land – and therefore the city – had always been dependent upon the water, it was necessary to obtain the certainty of its provision. Angelenos are justly proud of the engineering statistics of the dam and despite the gloomy economic climate, the project created a characteristic optimism and desire to move onwards and upwards.

The overall landscape of the city gives little evidence of the original form and character of the land, except perhaps in parts of the Santa Monica and San Gabriel Mountains. It is only here that one can begin to see the land as it was two hundred years ago, and it is these places which become the centre for research of the native plant and animal communities. Just as the city has been decorated with every conceivable architectural style from all over the world, so has the landscape. After having been eroded by the technology of earth movers and covered with asphalt and concrete, plants have been introduced from all the far-flung corners of the world with each newcomer bringing a new specimen, perhaps as a reminder of home. Over the years, men such as Theodore Payne have attempted to preserve and propagate indigenous species, promoting an appreciation for plants such as the wild lilac, toyon, poppy and lupin amongst others. The most obvious crop associated with the area is, of course, the orange and there seems little danger of this being forgotten.

The best examples of landscape architecture are to be found in Los Angeles' private gardens. Angelenos have developed – perhaps partly through Irving Gill – the theory that their gardens and houses need to be extensions of one another. The temperate climate has always been coveted and the occupants make the most of the opportunities afforded to them.

There are many physical problems which have to be negotiated regularly within the Los Angeles Basin although the two most potentially destructive are fire and earthquake. The geology of the region contains expansive soils which contain swelling clays and thus absorb water. The expansion leads to a loss of interstitial strength, often damaging structures in the process and then deforming to produce landslides and flood damage. Eroded slopes slide on to residential areas. In addition fire alters the surface and provokes sliding. Surface erosion decreases fertility and therefore productivity of the soil and its water retention capacity. The resulting silt damages the habitat in streams and increases

OPPOSITE: Eric Owen Moss, I Rhino, Culver City, composite drawing; ABOVE: Harbour Freeway corridor looking west; BELOW: Santa Monica harbour interchange

flood potential as drains and waterways are clogged. Of the tectonic dangers, earthquakes are accepted as the greatest danger by Californians, the consequences of volcanic eruptions and tidal waves are not so widely recognised.

Tsunamis (tidal waves) are caused by earthquakes in the Pacific Basin, but only pose a minor threat to the populated coastal regions. There is a continuous threat of major fires which cannot be assuaged even with the best preventative measures. The climatic and topographical conditions of the adjacent areas are natural targets for conflagration. When the eastern winds occasionally sweep over the outlying desert and come into contact with the mountainous areas, the situation becomes hazardous and leads to treacherous fire-control problems. These factors all contribute to the make-up of the city. Although these incidents do not happen every day they are a perpetual threat to those who reside in the area and need to be appreciated within an understanding of the city. However, familiarity with potential situations has created a slightly blasé atmosphere in Los Angeles, with an acceptance that the geologically unsettled environment in which the Angelenos exist is in fact a small price to pay in comparison to the lifestyle and climate which they enjoy. Angelenos show their resilience in the situation by turning a disaster into an advantage – when an earthquake in 1992 shook a vineyard and disrupted the crop, the grapes were harvested, wine was made and labels were designed to illustrate the marketing strategy which was to sell the wine, highlighting its unusual life.

The optimistic attitude of many Angelenos was epitomised in the Hollywood dream, which not only weathered but benefited from the depression. The Hollywood environs lived up to the screen image and created their own aura of fantasy in the suburb of Beverly Hills, while contributing to the persona of a city where one is encouraged to believe that dreams can come true.

The ephemeral quality that Hollywood reflects continues to pose the same questions for observers of urban form as it did for Richard Neutra who wondered if Los Angeles was a metropolis paradise or a blight masquerading as beauty. He predicted that the city would always defy the most determined attempts to define it, and as its edges continue to grow faster than geographers can map them, others protest that Downtown, where the whole satellite began, is the area with the greatest potential. While the planners of the 1930s were 'apologists for economic laissez-faire-ism' and 'God-figures' who could determine what was good for the community planners in contemporary Los Angeles are preoccupied with changing social equations and the need to find an equilibrium while there is still time to do so.

It is against this historical background of influences that we present architectural lost opportunities, potential constructions not implemented by the city. We have limited this selection in many ways but also to a study within recent years. The occasion to contemplate what might have been occasionally affords one a sense of disappointment but other times a sense of relief. Perhaps whilst not necessarily inferring that the schemes presented here should be exhumed from their graves where in some cases they peacefully lie, but they might form food for thought in the assessing of present and future proposals and perhaps in one or two cases the reinstigation of discussions may occur.

The use of space as a transition between residential and commercial is one of the key community intentions of the Yuzen Vintage Car Museum by Morphosis, as with the majority of the work from this practice it uses the language of the street to draw its aesthetic. A homage to the development of the machine whose influence dominates this city will now not sit on this site in Sunset boulevard and the attempt as described by the architects to create a building which would give back to its environment a serving building which looks to knit an area together has been missed.

The competition for the LA Arts Park produced a selection of spectacular examples. We present here the entry by Hodgetts + Fung which demonstrates the ability to form an environment which is progressive and representative. The competition set out to create a cultural environment for the community which moved on from the popular culture of the Television experienced by the majority of the citizens of the city and to provide the opportunity for a wider and broader direct cultural experience. A series of museums and performances arenas is provided amidst a backdrop of plant and animal life. The Hodgetts + Fung example, executed in collaboration with artists provides a particularly elegant solution to the quest for a place for the encouragement of broader intellectual discoveries.

By way of comparison and demonstration of diversity The Cookie Express is another innovation of the Hodgetts + Fung partnership. This was to a be a series of drive-in fast snack bars which would be scattered across the Southern Californian region. Their identity had to be consistent but the iconography not as overt as the infamous hotdog or doughnut stands, thus a series of spaces was created which can be replicated and adjusted to any required site. Eric Owen Moss is demonstrating his ability and talent across Los Angeles today and inevitably there are a selection of schemes which will not have the opportunity to be realised.

S.P.A.R.C I T Y is one such scheme: the proposal for Southern Pacific Air Rights to develop a stretch of land which is losing its life and to renew the area with a new breath of life into a dying portion of the city and design an environment which will allow the inhabitants to develop financially and thus environmentally. In addition there is the goal to begin again and attract new life into the area. The plan was keenly viewed by the local City Council but at present stands on hold.

Dagmar Richter's studies for interventions on Century City are also bold positive plans which address the statements and consequences made by previous designers and the principles. She takes the clinical precision of 'Modern' design and its formal planning and ideology with its integral independence and applies to this a scheme drawn from the study of the site in great detail but in a perhaps nonconformist approach. Richter's design for Hoffs House demonstrates her method of intervention on a smaller scale, illustrating the methods used when confronting an existing structure and the careful modelling which achieves the necessary spatial and visual extension. Cigolle & Coleman demonstrates its more restrained approach to residential extensions with the proposals for the Mills Musingo House which alter the perception of this previously undistinguished home.

These proposals from micro to macro illustrate the schemes that have been previously conceived but now remain dashed aspirations for this American city of dreams.

Bibliography

Richard Neutra, 'Los Angeles Inventory' *California Arts and Architecture*, Vol 60, Nov 1943, pp16-20

David Gebhard and Harriette von Breton, *LA in the Thirties*, Peregrine Smith Inc, NY, 1975 pp26-35

Reyner Banham, *Los Angeles: The Architecture of the Four Ecologies*, Penguin, London 1971

Graeme Morland, 'Movement Systems', *Architectural Design*, 51, 8/9, 1981, Los Angeles p12

Dimitry Vergun and Derek Walker, 'Catastrophe LA', *Architectural Design*, 51, 8/9, 1981, Los Angeles, p20

Emmet L Wemple, 'The Landscape Salad', *Architectural Design*, 51, 8/9, 1981, Los Angeles, p35

K Paul Zygas, 'The Eclectic Tradition', *Architectural Design*, 51, 8/9, 1981, Los Angeles, p47

Stefanos Polyzoides, 'The Sources' *Architectural Design*, 51, 8/9, 1981, Los Angeles, p50.

James Tice, 'Frank Lloyd Wright', *Architectural Design*, 51, 8/9, 1981, Los Angeles, p62

Arthur Golding, 'The Big Offices', *Architectural Design*, 51, 8/9, 1981, Los Angeles, p88

Architectural Design, 52, 3/4, 1982, Los Angeles, p2

Jayne Merkel, 'Architecture of Dislocation: The LA School', *Art In America*, February 1994, pp33-39

David Gebhard and Robert Winter, *Architecture in Los Angeles: A Compleat Guide*, Gibbs Smith Layton, UT, 1984

RM Schindler, *Composition and Construction*, edited by Lionel March and Judith Sheine, Academy Editions, London, 1993

Michael Sorkin, *Exquisite Corpse: Writing on Buildings*, Verso, London, 1991

LEFT: Dagmar Richter, Hoffs Residence

LOS ANGELES AS IT MIGHT HAVE BEEN

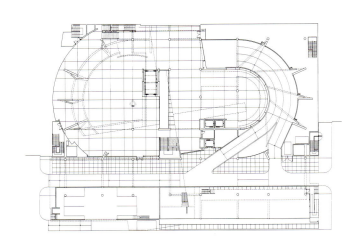
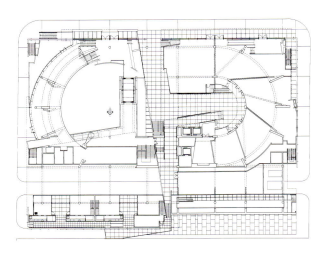
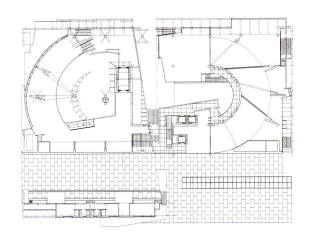
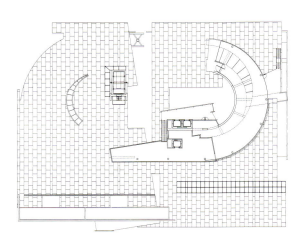
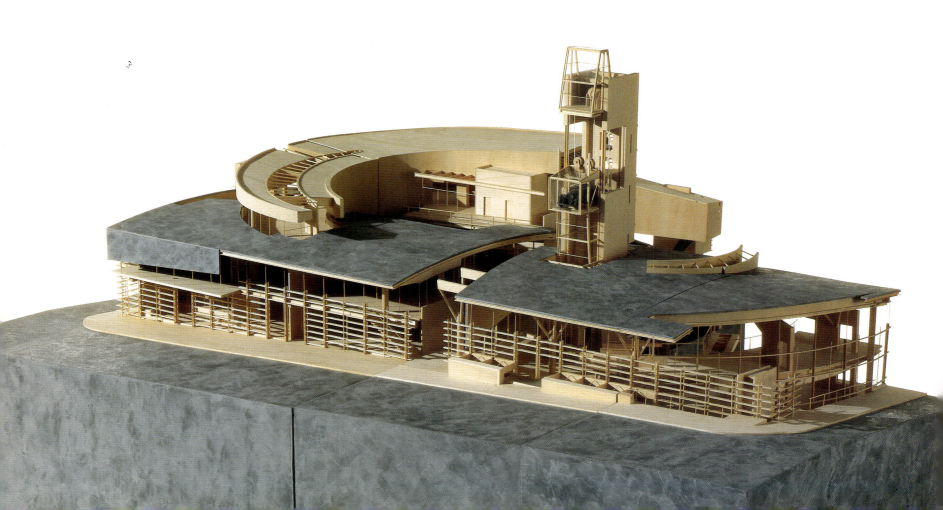

CULTURAL CENTRES

MORPHOSIS
YUZEN VINTAGE CAR MUSEUM
West Hollywood

The solution to the Yuzen Vintage Car Museum represents a formal mapping process, used as a means to accommodate the city's wish to suppress the considerable mass of the building. One of Los Angeles' prototypical conditions is that low residential neighbours exist directly behind heavily commercial streets. The building was used, in this instance, as both a transitional element and as an extension to the site as a landmass. It serves to mitigate against the busy main street to the north, and the houses to the south, using the thirty-degree drop in elevation from north-west to south-east to best advantage. The parking ramp, the structural grid and the exterior surface walls produce the architectural language, responding to the existing fabric of the street. The elevator tower acts as a scale device producing a transition with existing peripheral buildings. The exterior wall, which is intentionally scaffold-like, is a reference to the extensive excavation required to retain the rectilinear boundary of the site, and is about construction and making. The curving roof, viewed from the residential neighbourhood, becomes a warped piazza forming the perceived boundary of the site, allowing for the protrusion of a series of smaller-scale structures which reflects the scale of the residential fabric to the south, while creating a more formal street front along Sunset Boulevard.

The building is cut at its centre, producing an entry space orienting the pedestrian to the museum functions on the west and various ancillary commercial functions on the east. Entering the main space of the museum, one is made aware of the bifurcated elevator connected by a sixty-foot truss structure. The lower cab transports passengers and automobiles from subterranean storage to the museum floors. The upper cab is used for an interchangeable presentation of vintage automobiles. The cab assembly moves vertically within the tower, piercing the roof line and serving as a kinetic sign announcing the building's primary function.

OPPOSITE FROM L to R: Sub-grade floor plan; first floor plan; second floor plan; third floor plan; RIGHT: Exploded part axonometric

LOS ANGELES AS IT MIGHT HAVE BEEN

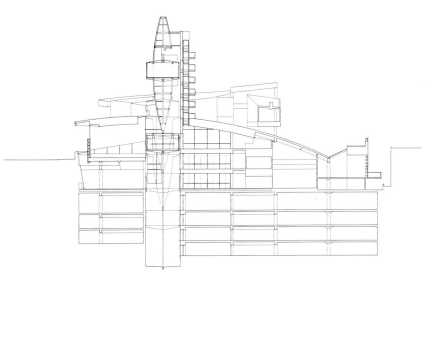
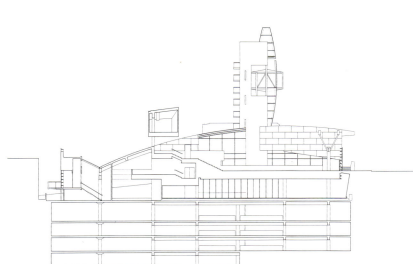
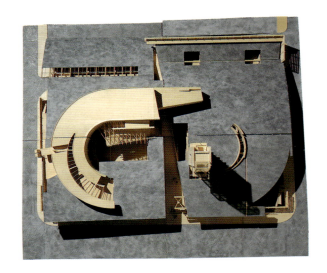

CULTURAL CENTRES

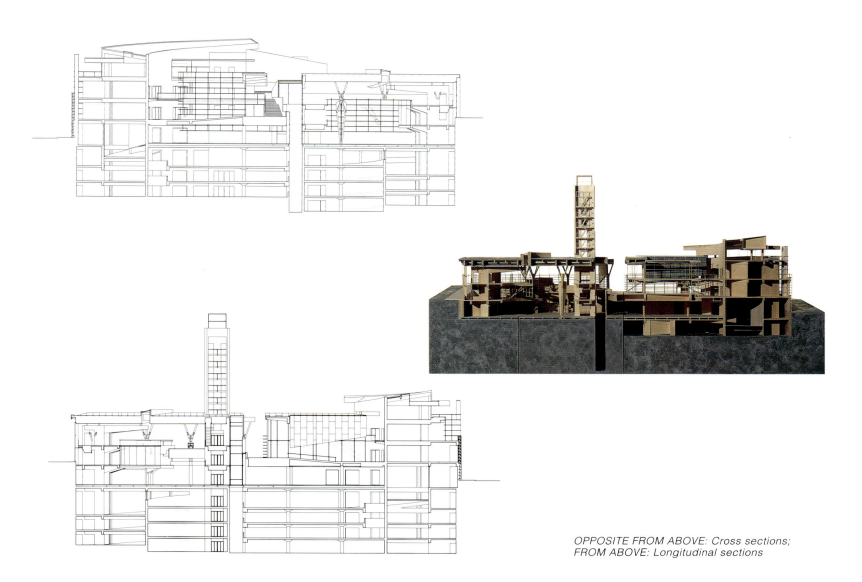

OPPOSITE FROM ABOVE: Cross sections;
FROM ABOVE: Longitudinal sections

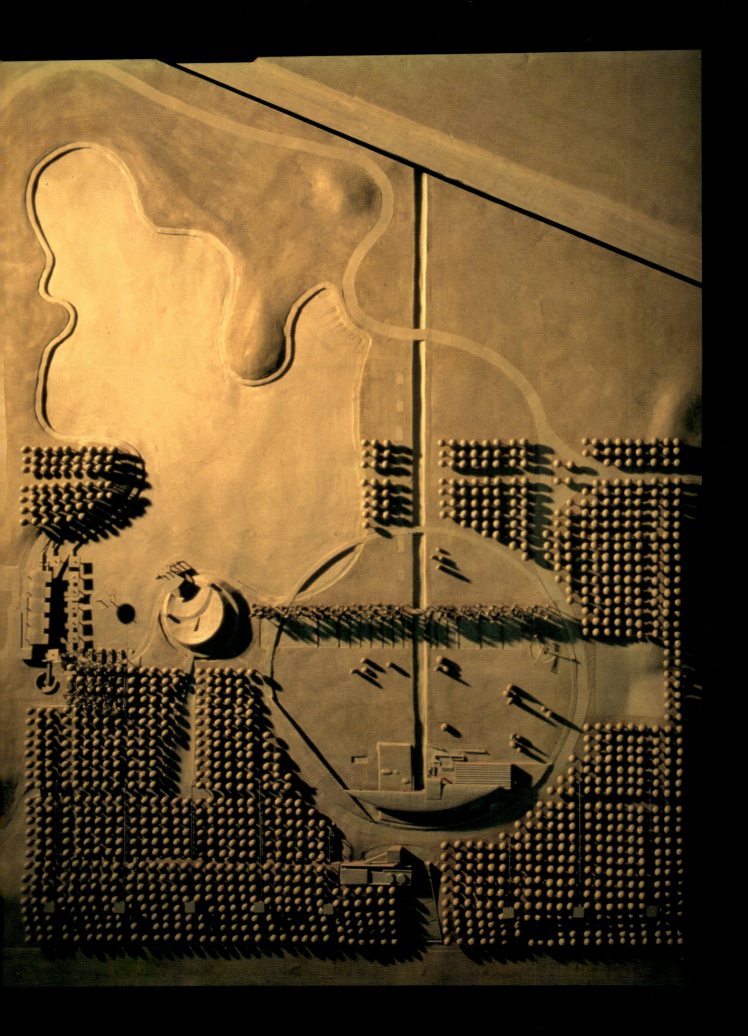

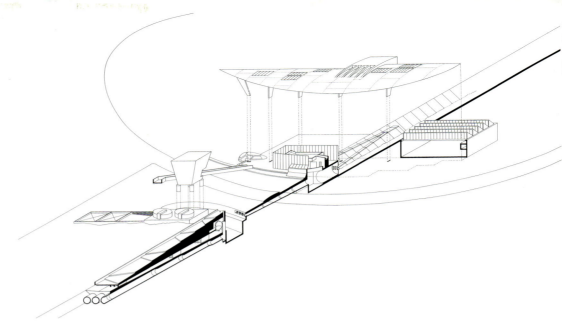

HODGETTS + FUNG
ARTS PARK LA
Sepulveda Basin

A team project with architect Adele Santos, sculptor Mary Miss and the landscape firm of Rios and Pearson, the programme called for a new fifty-acre art and cultural centre including a natural history museum, a children's museum, performance glen and open amphitheatre and media centre. An open-ended master plan was developed which included a large man-made lake, open park and the reinstatement of the orange groves once so prevalent in the area. The site plan exploits the unique relationship of architecture to water, exemplifying the interrelationship of man, building and nature.

The Natural History Museum presents an aid to dialogue between man and his environment rather than a demonstration of technical and design prowess. The museum strives to inspire both the curatorial staff and the public to engage in the sustained dialogue necessary for real learning.

Glen and Grove is a series of ecological rooms linked by structured paths which enhance the exploration of the adjoining facilities. The Glen and its amphitheatre form a natural destination for the meandering voyage through the park. It is the conceptual anchor for the matrix of activities surrounding it, and exploits the unique relationship of the building to the land and the water's edge, making the lake a background for theatrical events and a setting for commissioned art barges.

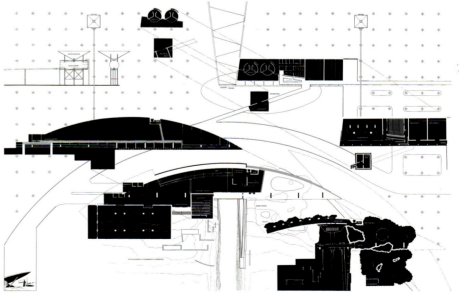

ABOVE: Exploded and cut-away isometric; BELOW: Composite drawings of various aspects of the building

LOS ANGELES AS IT MIGHT HAVE BEEN

STUDIO ASYMPTOTE

STEEL CLOUD
Hollywood

The American freeway is a by-product of an enduring desire for freedom and conquered terrain. Both the automobile and domicile are places of detachment and escape from an otherwise alienating urbanity. Los Angeles in particular is a city where privacy and evasion have formed a place of extremes, comparable with Disneyland where glamour and fantasy are offset by the danger of the unanticipated.

The Los Angeles West Coast Gateway/Steel Cloud is a 'prop' for this city so abundant in grand fictions and utopian possibilities. It is an episodic architecture inspired by optical machinery, simulators, surveillance technologies and telecommunication systems. Here the instantaneous has reconfigured the speculative, thereby providing a ground for this architecture to emerge from.

The 'Monument' occupies an invisible realm of anticipatory order above passing motorists on the Hollywood freeway. Here one experiences a simultaneity of events where each moment collapses onto another, as in Duchamp's axiom: 'the super-rapid position of rest'. This is a 'space' for the information age, an infinitely oscillating field without perspective or depth, a space of ambiguous signs formulated from a hyper-reality. The project is calibrated within this 'theatre of operations' where the corroded horizon-line must be vindicated. The Steel Cloud project seeks to unearth this dichotomy of the actual and the simulated, the violent and the picturesque.

FROM ABOVE: Site plan; section; Immigration Museum elevation

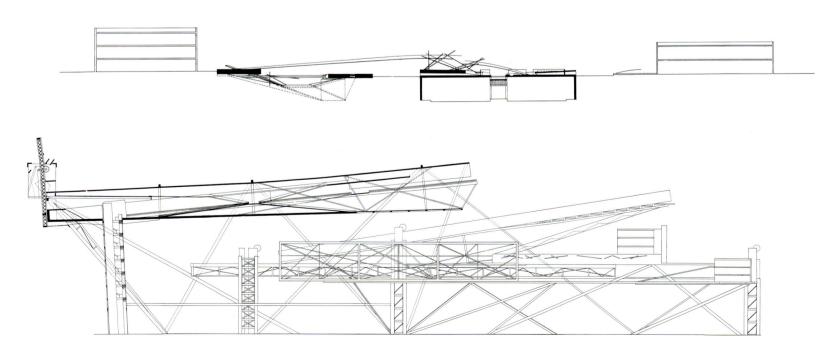

MIXED USE DEVELOPMENT

DAGMAR RICHTER
CENTURY CITY

Before 1958, Century City was the site where Century Fox Film Studios had a whole array of simulated environments, including entire cities and lakes made to order. Thirty years later after a 'successful' planning effort, we are today confronted with a 'prestige address for business, shopping, luxury living, theatre-going, dining and guest accommodation'. Century City is described by the local Chamber of Commerce as a landmark for modern urban development.

Thirty years ago when Twentieth Century Fox Studios faced near-bankruptcy after their box office disaster *Cleopatra*, Welton Becket was hired by the developers and SP Skouras, the chairman of the board of the Studios, to create a concept that would transform the back-lot of the dream factory into a futuristic city and thereby, through real estate transactions, rescue the film industry. The planners envisioned a total community, anchored by a strong business base. Today, Century City stands as the ideal outcome of modernist planning and formal ideology. The emphasis lies on cleanliness, open spaces, verticality, a car-orientated infrastructure and its independence from the rest of the city.

Century City proved to be an interesting text for the architect to read. Most striking was the contrast between the sleek, mirrored, antiseptic anonymity of the current development and the haphazard, rather tawdry and vulgar nature of the self-conscious artificiality of its previous existence as a film set. A working process was employed that used three forms of site readings, one historical and two contemporary. First, maps from various times in Century City's past were copied and overlapped. These contained the traces and markings of forgotten landscapes: dislocated film towns, movable lakes and film production sheds, oil fields, orange groves and one-family bungalow structures. From these residues, a new topography of traces was elaborated that incorporated the previously hidden elements which had been bulldozed by the developers. Century City's current state was next used. Two recording methods were employed: firstly, the shadows of the site, the uncanny, a transformed trace of the object of study was recorded. In a ritual of recopying the obtained information, different speeds and directions transformed the text, to reflect the experience of the place as it is perceived while driving through. The shadows can be seen as a manifestation of a hidden order, an axonometrical collapse of the vertical object onto a projection screen – the space in-between. Secondly, as a final study of Century City's current site condition, a photographic, or rather filmic, technique was used to allow analysis of the area's image. The dominant singular objects, the skyscraper's forbidding skins, celebrating their verticality and spatial control were filmed, enlarged and recopied. This process revealed spaces of folding and layering in the sleek surfaces of the buildings that would otherwise have gone unnoticed.

During the further process, emphasis was put on two distinct architectural properties: spatial boundaries and infrastructural and structural elements. A filmic method, not necessarily used in

Site Plan

LOS ANGELES AS IT MIGHT HAVE BEEN

its direct sense, as with cutting and splicing, but in its inherent structural logic, makes it possible to develop a space solely for the purpose of visual pleasure and as the carrier for human activity. The choice of working with veneer and surface can be traced back to the site's former history as a ground for film-making where conceptually, the surface used had the sole purpose of 'not letting the character fall off'.

Construction was used merely within the second set of copies, where the attempt was made to copy an order of structure and infrastructure onto the site. These structures developed an existence of their own. In film sets, as in newer architectural sections, the importance of the space in-between, the space of fasteners, insulation, air-buffer zones and second structures, becomes apparent. Different generic sections through skyscrapers were used to distil their rhythm and relationship to the buildings' boundaries. A transformation from vertical to horizontal allowed the repetitive elements to hold in place a linear infrastructure which was derived from a study of the elevator's role in Century City's skyscrapers, depicted within the shadow studies of the site. As a graft the form, not the programme, was used of the Los Angeles freeways and train tracks to find dynamic horizontal layers which can be translated into bicycle paths, running tracks, magnetic railways and crosscalators. The working drawings which consisted of layers of copies from found spatial information, were used to develop working models for the study areas of skin and infrastructure.

In the next stage, the collapse of both working models into yet another structure allowed the first studies of incongruities between skin and structure, establishing an array of spaces in-between. These incongruities were used to insert a critical re-reading of the obtained space. The new model inserts itself into Century City's structure as an architectural parasite in the form of an earth-scratcher that connects two different green spaces through an array of surfaces, anti-programmes and artificial landscapes. Numerous skins cover, connect and shade human activities. This model stands as yet another text available for the reader to interpret. It can be seen as a text about further spatial development for Century City.

MIXED USE DEVELOPMENT

ABOVE LEFT: Skins and boundaries; BELOW LEFT: Structures and infrastructures

DAGMAR RICHTER
WEST COAST GATEWAY
Downtown

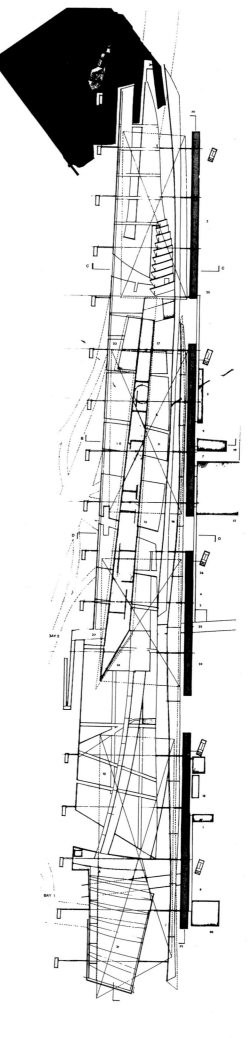

The West Coast Gateway Competition brief requested proposals for reclaiming public space above an eight-lane freeway which, according to conventional log, cut a deep scar into the urban structure of Downtown, Los Angeles. This programme was used to develop a means of spatial representation based on an archaeological investigation of the site and the Downtown area. The process of sedimentation suggested various layers, each linked to different historical moments in the formation of site conditions. Maps of paths, irrigation channels, field boundaries and building volumes were produced and integrated into a cartographic representation in which all spatial layers could be read simultaneously. This, in turn, engendered an array of interpretations from which a new map representing crevices, volumes and fields was created. The different layers of these abstracted landscapes were positioned above the existing freeway on a repetitive scaffolding, at once structure and infrastructure. The uppermost layer, which represents the city's hard asphalt surfaces penetrated by building volumes, was hinged like a drawbridge, introducing the problems and possibilities inherent to a recurrent transformation from a horizontal to vertical structure. The repeated movement of the hinged layer also gave scope to experiment with various wall systems for protecting sensitive areas from the hazards of the freeway.

The architects arrived at what may be described as a veneer or skin architecture. Veneer has played a role in architectural production since Roman antiquity but has recently come into a particular independent existence in the hands of Post-Modern architects who have used it to paste the pseudo-cultural imagery of the Reagan era onto structures derived from functional and economic determinants. Notwithstanding the insubstantiality of the imagery itself, the concept of veneer, indicating an utter independence of skin and structure, suggests a new era of architectural production. Consciously employing a veneer architecture, the design 'covered' the scar of the freeway with distinct layered platforms; in these spaces human activity reclaims as public domain a terrain formerly surrendered to the automobile. For the over one million drivers on the freeway each day, the underside of this Potemkin city reveals a depth of abstract landscapes caught in a play of light.

Selected as finalists in the first phase of the competition, the architects were able to extend their investigation in response to technological as well as financial constraints. In the second phase, the emphasis of the investigation shifted towards the constructive possibilities in the definition of relationships between the different layers. Articulating structure, surface and volume, each was later assigned a specific constructive role, giving it a distinct position within the section.

OPPOSITE ABOVE: Site plan;
RIGHT: Phase I, plan

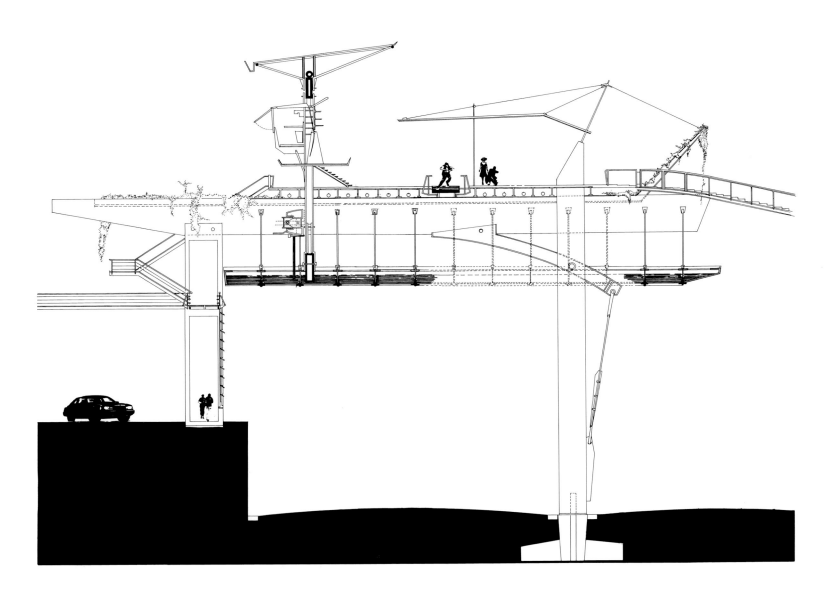
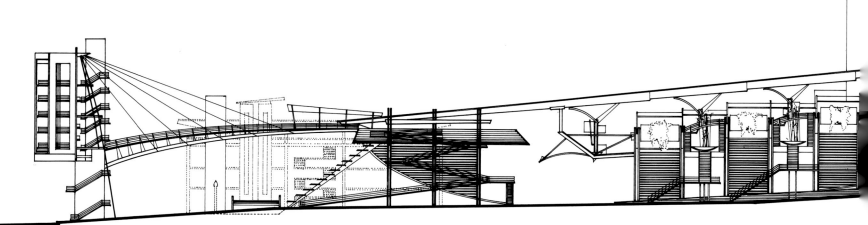

ABOVE: Phase II, detail of section; BELOW L TO R: North elevation

MIXED USE DEVELOPMENT

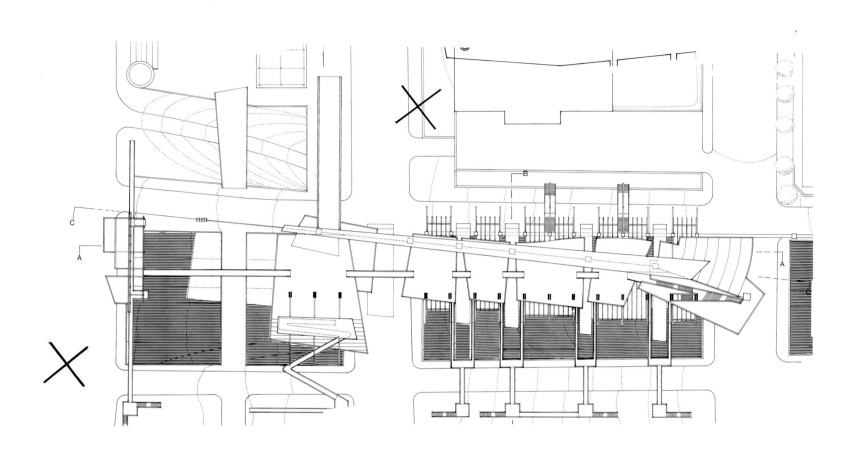

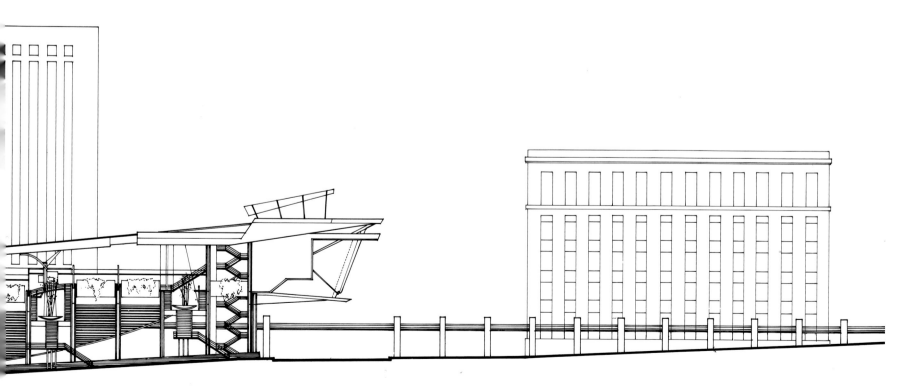

ABOVE: Plan

ERIC OWEN MOSS
HAYDEN TRACT
Culver City

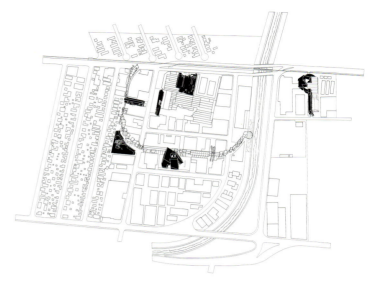

The ownership of this portion of Culver City is shared by private developers and public agencies. The general strategy is to identify it as an 'Architectural-free zone'. The projects included in Hayden Tract comprise 3535 Hayden Avenue, Warner Avenue, Hayden Tower and Hercules.

3535 Hayden Avenue consists of a group of attached warehouse buildings that were to be renovated into a building that would establish a recognisable identity for the record company clients.

Warner Avenue is a colossal relative to its neighbours. Its essential role was planned as both public and civic. The building was to be made from the intersection of three ten-storey 'hammers' connected over a two-storey parking deck. The interior space created was to serve as an enormous court of the performing arts. Surrounding the court were planned civic facilities, offices and a restaurant. The project adjoins the S.P.A.R.C I T Y right of way.

The planning and design effort was to have entirely re-defined and re-constituted a dying industrial area. The architect, developer and the city administration are collaborating to invent new urban criteria, free of the conventional antiquated constraints.

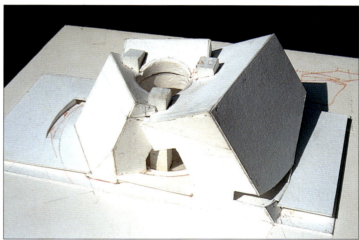

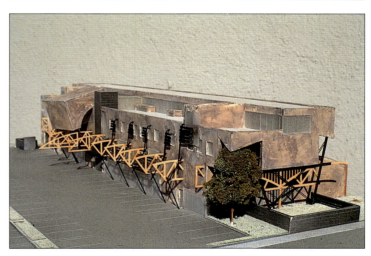

OPPOSITE: 3535 Hayden Avenue; FROM ABOVE: Site plan; Warner Avenue; 3535 Hayden Avenue

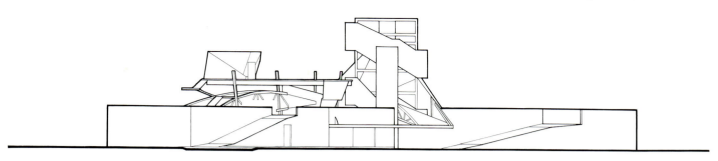

ERIC OWEN MOSS
HAYDEN TOWER
Culver City

The project represents an important planning step in the re-invention of a decaying heavy-industrial area of Culver City. Industrial tenants who occupied the buildings on this and adjacent sites for the last thirty years have gone out of business or are now at work in Laredo, Taipei or Manila. The project is not only an effort to give impetus to a re-definition of a section of West Los Angeles, but by implication is representative of the need to revise economic and land use patterns in many deteriorating industrial portions of American cities.

On the site, a 65-foot steel frame tower once housed an enormous industrial press. Adjoining the tower are two truss-supported sheds originally used for warehousing and manufacturing. The tower skin is to be removed leaving only the frame, the sheds will be demolished. Trusses are saved and stockpiled and a new single-storey concrete-block shed, principally for warehousing, fills the site.

The old wood trusses supported on steel columns are assembled around a steel circulation cylinder, sliced through the deck, that moves pedestrians from parking to the main level warehouse space or to adjoining offices and restaurant. The trusses, radiating from the cylinder, support a new pedestrian walkway on which occupants stroll to office and restaurant areas inside the tower. A freestanding conference building at this level provides private space.

The design strategy investigates use, re-use and abuse of antecedents on the site which is a little like drawing on a sheet on which other drawings exist. One can erase and amend, but not entirely eradicate the previous presence.

ABOVE: East elevation; BELOW: Site plan; OVERLEAF, BELOW L TO R: Ground floor plan; second floor plan; third floor plan; roof plan

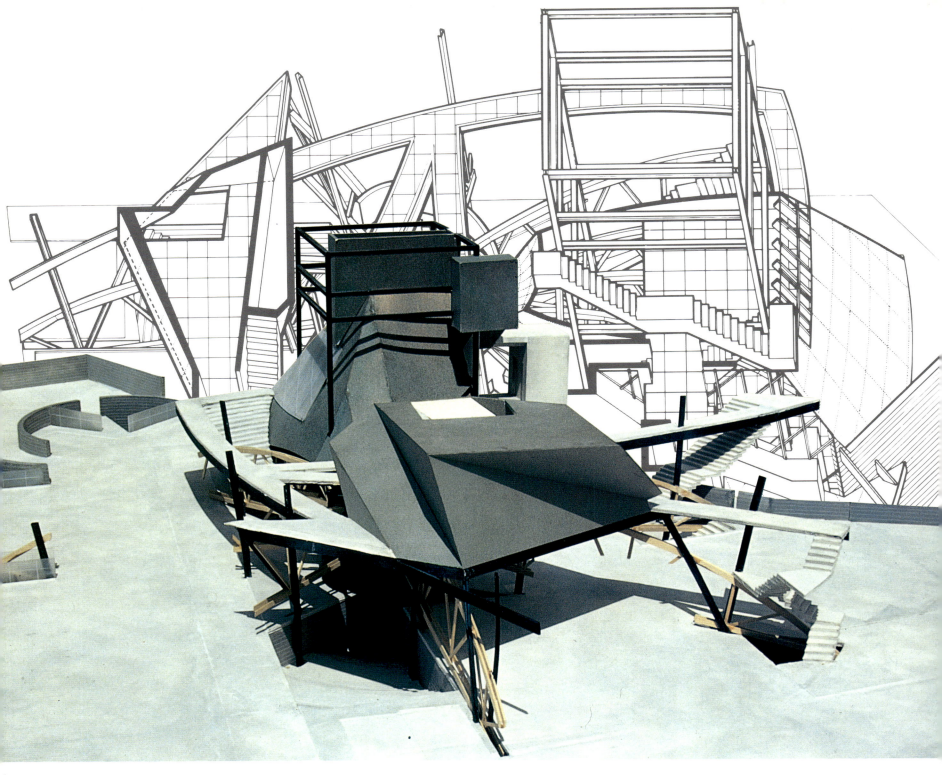
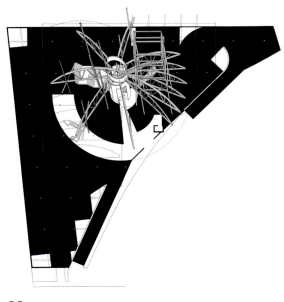
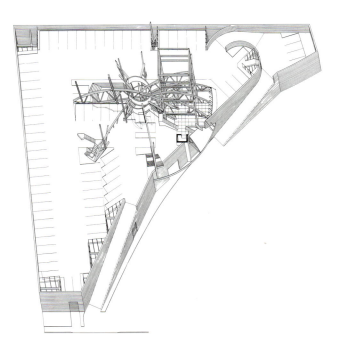

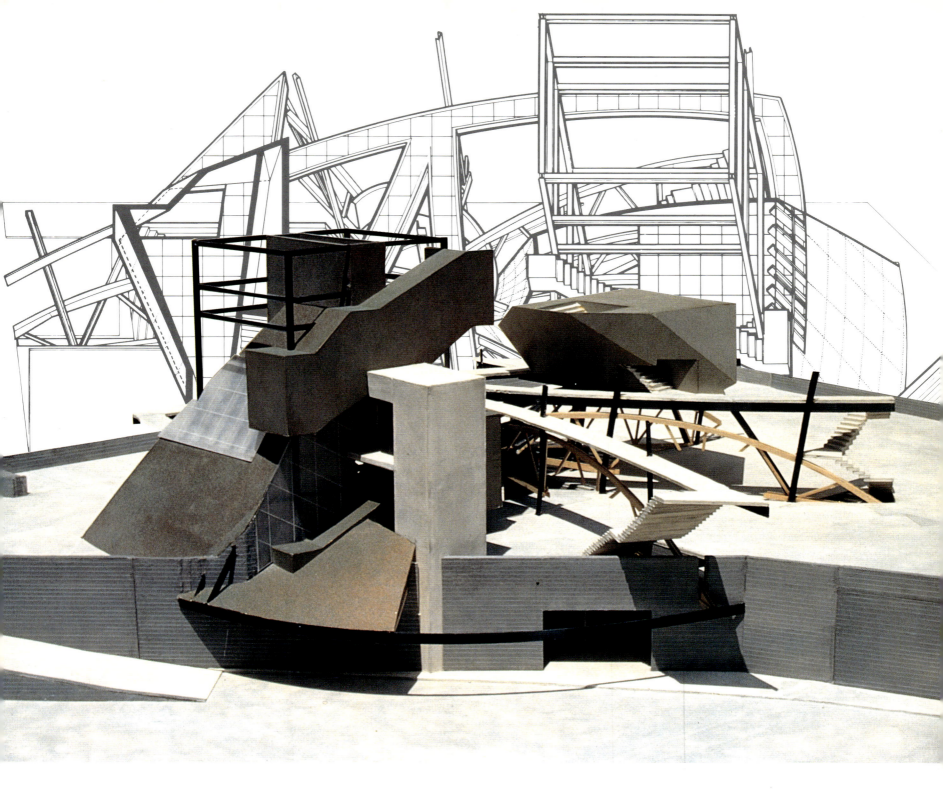
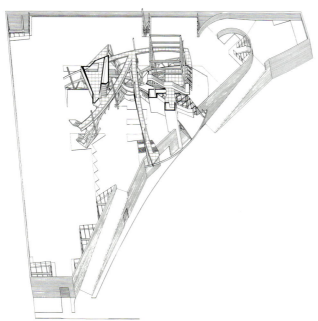
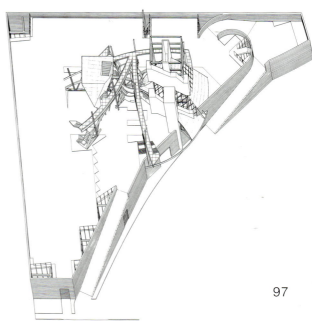

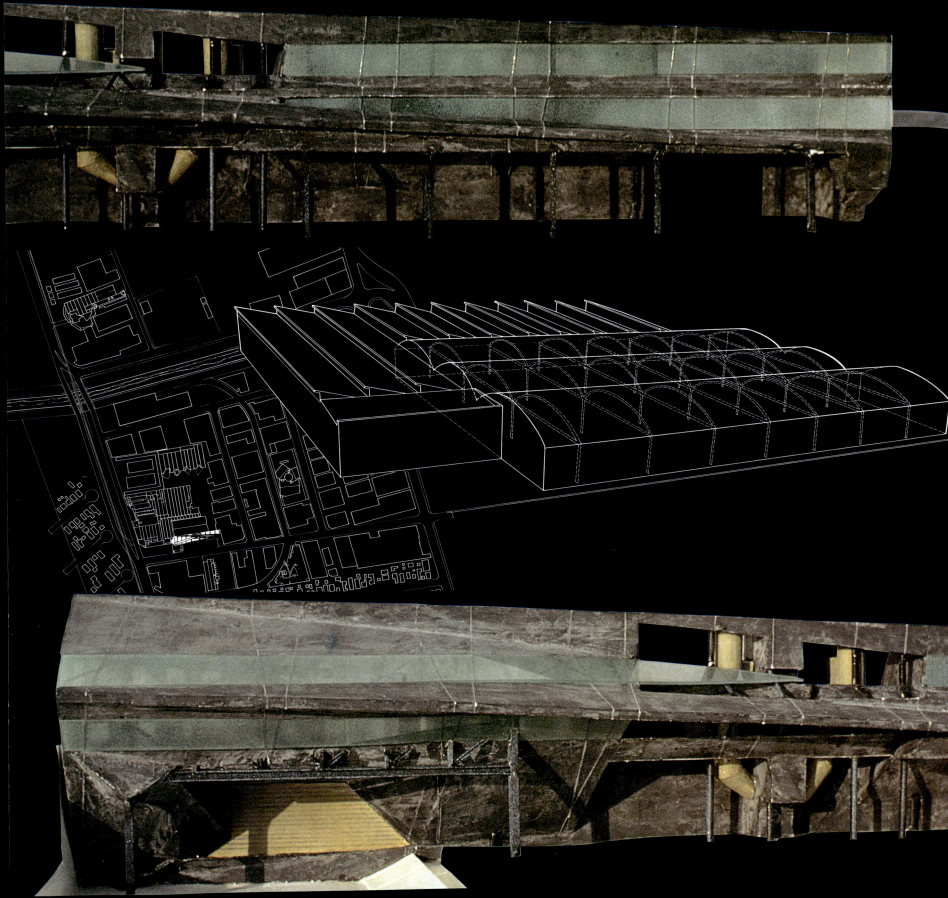

MIXED USE DEVELOPMENT

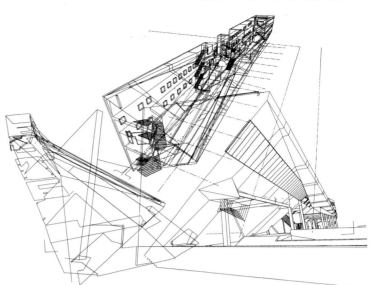

ERIC OWEN MOSS
HERCULES THEATER AND OFFICES
Culver City

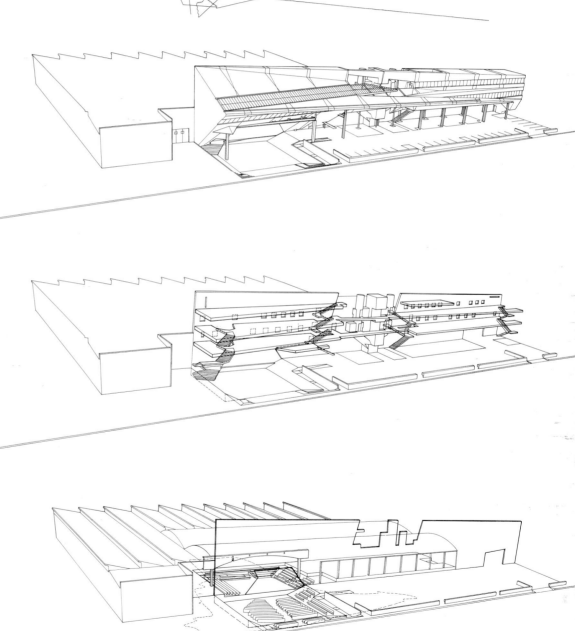

A driving force behind the opportunity to build this project came out of the need to remove toxic waste from the site. An existing light industrial building, with three bays of bowstring trusses, is situated on the site; each bay is about 15,000 square feet.

To facilitate the removal of the waste, one bay (on the west side adjacent to the street) has been removed. Two bays remain. The design of the project seals the open bay with a black masonry wall. Production and office space is hung from the wall as a way to re-coop the lost square-footage for the owner.

The conceptual strategy/aspiration for the project is a kinetic building. The structure moves from the north, triangulated elevation – one leg is the vertical line of the masonry wall – to the south end which is orthogonal. Between the two, the building moves without warping any lines or planes. By adding planes in order to go from three to four, a constantly altering section is achieved.

There are two floors and a feature at the middle which functions as the core. The windows are of the ribbon type, always at the same horizontal zone. Where the building bends, the horizontal follows.

A garden has been formed at the north end of the building site where a deeper hole had to be dug to remove the toxic waste. The site of this deeper excavation becomes the garden. One possibility that was explored for the garden was an open-air theatre, sheltered by the overhanging triangle above. By altering the height of the floor plane of the adjacent building, (for example, dropping the floor) it would have become possible to make a theatre with viewing places for an audience on two sides.

OPPOSITE: Site plan and perspective view; FROM ABOVE: Composite drawing showing sectional perspective and main entrance; main facade overall perspective; main circulation routes perspective; theatre cutaway perspective

ERIC OWEN MOSS
S.P.A.R.C I T Y
Culver City

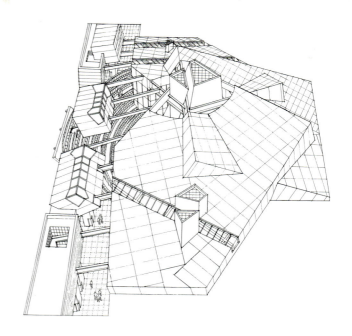

An abandoned Southern Pacific railroad right-of-way, about 50 feet in width, stretches approximately half a mile from the Los Angeles river to National Boulevard. The old tracks run through an area which for the past 50 years has been home to light industry/manufacturing. In the last ten years the industrial users have begun to relocate to areas where rent and labour costs are substantially less, namely Japan, Korea and Mexico.

This area is perhaps a prototype for a number of dated industrial complexes that must re-define or re-invent their urban purpose. The route of S.P.A.R. C I T Y (Southern Pacific Air Rights) moves north-west through a district of warehouses, past an unbuilt site used as a city car park and through an area of UCLA leased artist studios. North, it adjoins a residential area of modest residences, ending at National Boulevard, a major vehicular thoroughfare.

S.P.A.R.C I T Y's strategy is to re-define the area, to reinforce and invigorate, where plausible, existing uses and activities. The project seeks both to begin again and to revive the existing context. These dual objectives are not understood as a conflict of intentions, but as mutually reinforcing goals.

The design approach applied two metaphors; firstly, the Chameleon and secondly, the cars of the freight train that once rolled through the area. The form of the project varies over its length as it extends, amends and reconfirms uses that adjoin the right-of-way: a major commercial gate at National Boulevard, multi-unit housing in the existing residential areas, shops and a theatre adjoining an existing restaurant, street-bridge/office-building (which metamorphoses as artists' lofts and galleries), a hotel and parking, offices and warehouses. These diverse services demonstrate S.P.A.R.C I T Y's proposed development into an office/commercial/restaurant complex at the river.

The ground-level right-of-way itself will become a park and promenade accessing the adjacent buildings along the right-of-way and the vertical circulation to air-rights buildings/bridges above.

Two characterisations exist for the buildings that adjoin the right-of-way: *friendly* and *unfriendly*. If a building is friendly and its owner/tenant selects to join the train, it opens to the right-of-way and the air-rights construction can abut, lean on or extend over the existing building. This suggests a series of new/rehabilitated, restored/reconstituted industrial structures along the line. If the adjacency is unfriendly, S.P.A.R.C I T Y structures and the new park, simply pass by. The original buildings continue to operate, as before, accessed from adjacent streets. If adjacent properties are vacant, the linear structure can extend perpendicular to itself, expropriating and exploring new territory.

This plan is egalitarian and totalitarian. It adds to existing uses, it subtracts, it entices, it compels but does not demand that its neighbours join. It proposes to transform a debilitated area into a major civic component of the West Los Angeles area. S.P.A.R.C I T Y is a conceptual and formal hypothesis. In the end it may appear in pieces, all together or in an altered form. Enthusiastically received by the local City Council, it is an opportunity to reconstitute this portion of a dying, industrially-based city.

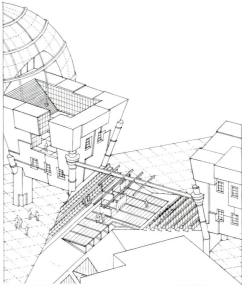

OPPOSITE: Site plan and model; ABOVE: View of amphitheatre; BELOW: View of theatre; OVERLEAF, BELOW RIGHT: View of street-bridge

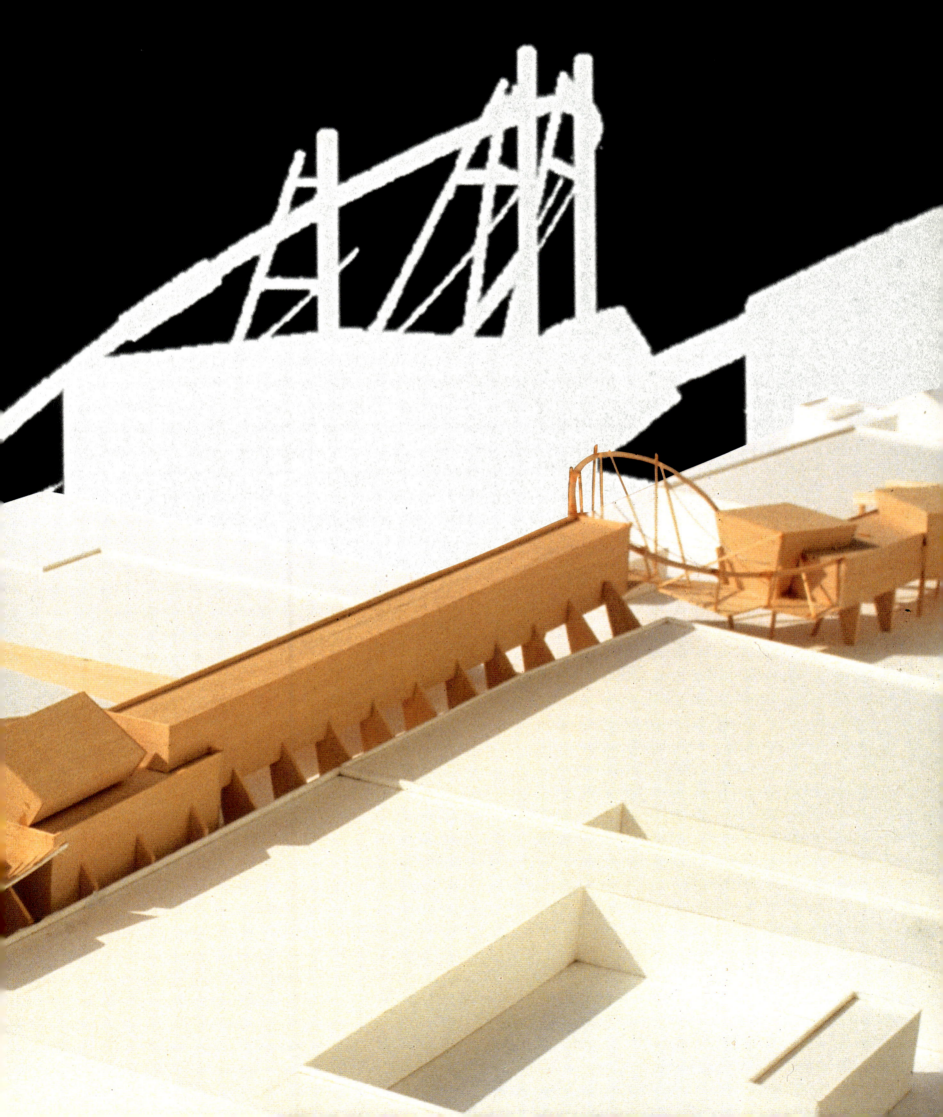

MIXED USE DEVELOPMENT

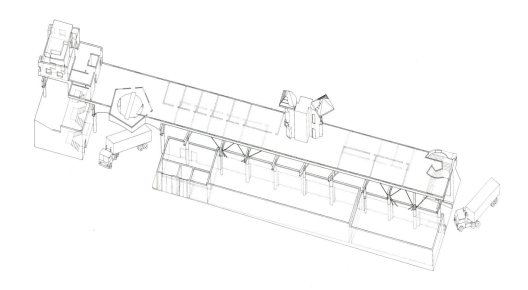

ERIC OWEN MOSS
SAMITAUR I & II
South Central Los Angeles

Samitaur, parts I & II is an office building built over a road in the south-western section of Los Angeles. The area is a mixture of one and two-storey industrial and manufacturing buildings constructed in the 1950s and 60s, interconnected by a network of public and private roads.

The project site is a privately owned road terminated by a complex of one-storey, saw-tooth roofed buildings that house offices, food preparation and storage facilities. Existing single-storey buildings on either side of the road contain light manufacturing. The new office block is lifted on circular steel columns, allowing trucks and cars continued access to the facilities on the same level. The new building will provide expanded office space and will be linked by lift and stairs to production facilities in the old shed at grade level.

Columns supporting the office block are positioned to avoid the loading doors adjacent to the access road. Diagonal bracing at street level and five rigid frames address lateral problems. Tapered steel beams span between the columns. The new first floor is lifted above existing one-storey roofs allowing natural light into the covered street from east and west. It is anticipated that the industrial tenants will be replaced by commercial tenants and the road will become a commercial walking street.

A height limit of 48 feet confines the office to two floors over required truck clearances. Fire regulations limit the building to the width of the private road. The roof access is for service only, although it is likely to become the locale for informal office gatherings offering unrestricted views in all directions.

Three circumstantial conditions require exceptional treatment to the essential office block. First, positioned to address approaching traffic at the street entry, a modified conical section is carved from the orthogonal block, providing exterior deck space and an open stair to the street. Second, on the west face of the office block is a five-sided, two-storey courtyard, planted with grass, irrigated from the beam network above. The modified pentagon is located above a secondary vehicle access point. Third, at the north end of the building adjoining the elevator-stair core, the building block slides over the saw-tooth shed below, supported again on steel columns which penetrate the existing building. Fire codes require a raised first floor height to clear the roof below. The resulting one-and-a-half storey space is the corporate board room.

Truck clearance below and zoned height and width limits above define the essential building block. Column locations are determined by the position of loading dock doors along the road. Beams follow the columns. Truss joisted floors follow the beams. Two office floors are stacked. An elevator connects old to new. At two essential access points the block organisation is countered, and at a third location, no longer over the road, a modified floor height generates the board room.

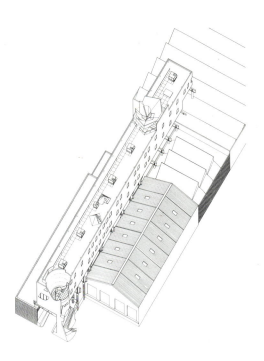

ABOVE AND BELOW: Axonometrics; OVERLEAF L TO R: Sectional axonometrics and plans

LOS ANGELES AS IT MIGHT HAVE BEEN

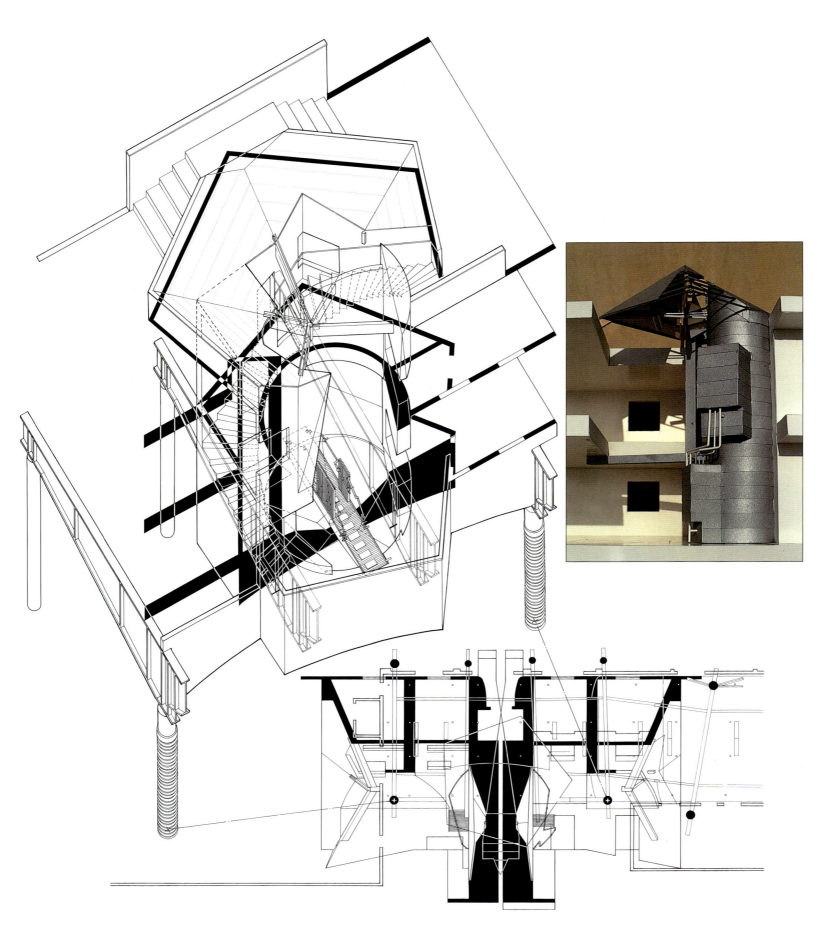

MIXED USE DEVELOPMENT

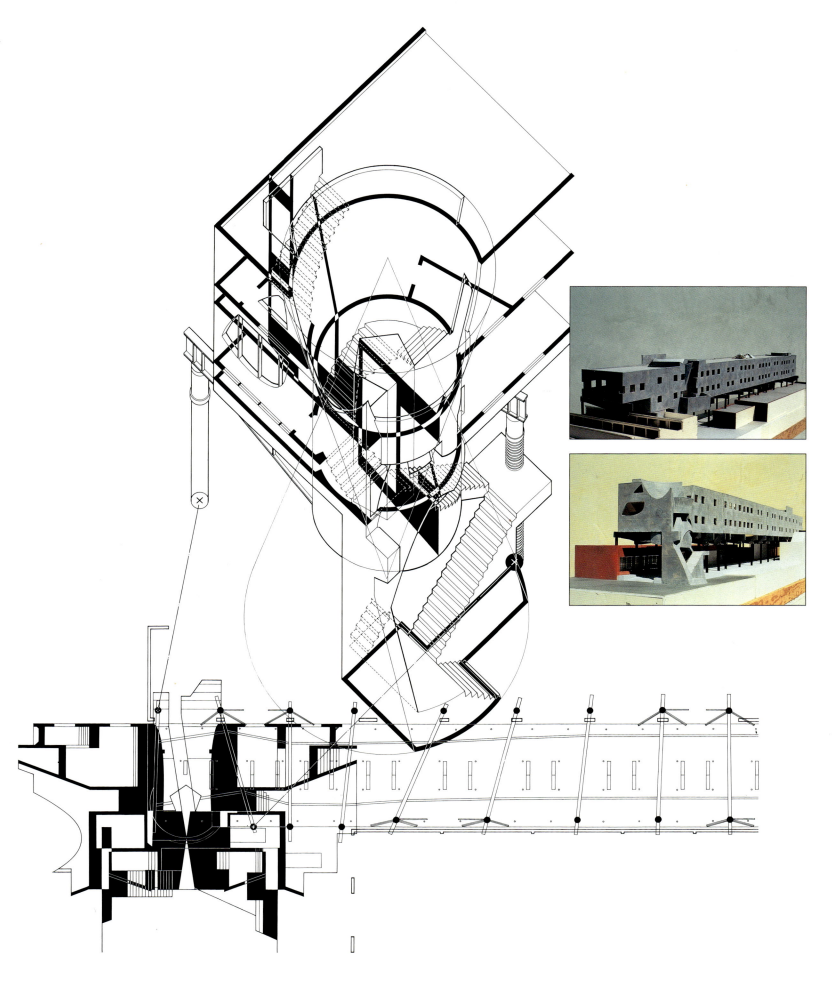

107

MIXED USE DEVELOPMENT

THE JERDE PARTNERSHIP
HOLLYWOOD PROMENADE
Hollywood

Hollywood Boulevard was once Main Street to the world; film premieres staged there in the 1920s and 30s were the epitome of glamour. In steady decline since World War II, the boulevard is currently rebounding with a major redevelopment project by the city, that was timed to celebrate Hollywood's centennial. Hollywood Center is a major catalyst in this rebirth. It includes a hotel, office areas, retail and entertainment space and a Golden Age museum wrapped around famous Mann's Chinese Theatre. Respecting the existing scale and grain of the street, the design breaks down its frontage into a series of pavilions. These pavilions are arranged as events along a winding internal *paseo* with inviting courtyards. Taller structures are at the rear and edges of the site so as not to overwhelm the theatre and street.

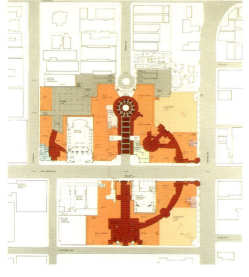

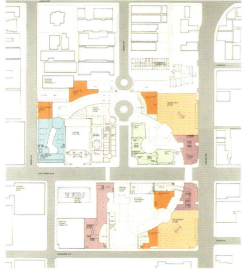

OPPOSITE: Aerial view; FROM ABOVE LEFT: The back lot; the crescent walk; other worlds; FROM ABOVE: Level one; level two; level four; OVERLEAF: North-south section

PRIVATE RESIDENCES

DAGMAR RICHTER
DEVINE RESIDENCE
Hollywood Hills

The project is a substantial addition onto a private residence originally designed by Richard Neutra in 1933 for an art collector named Galke Scheie, in a remote area of the Hollywood Hills overlooking Los Angeles. In 1936 Gregory Ain planned and supervised a small extension on top of the eastern part of the building for the painter Paul Klee, who was expected from Nazi Germany, but never arrived.

The existing building today consists of a living room, a fire-resistant vault which is used as an office, a master bedroom and bathroom, a dining corner and a further three, very small rooms: a child's room with a half bath, a maid's room and a kitchen which was partly designed by Schindler. The client, married and expecting a third child, hired the office to plan a major addition for the young family, which would include bedrooms for all the children, a new master bedroom, a guest unit, a second office, a larger kitchen and more bathrooms. The addition was to be higher than the Neutra building to allow a view to the west and the Pacific.

Originally, the owner wanted to add a new building on top of the Neutra house. However, it was decided that the addition would wrap itself around the Neutra house on the north side, where one of the neighbours had already erected a rather neutral two-storey cubic building. The new structure would be carefully positioned so as not to obstruct this neighbour's view. The design consisted of two main parts: a tower unit that rose two storeys above the Neutra building, giving the planned office a view of the ocean; and a unit, containing the bedrooms, connected at the east side via a staircase to the original house. The plans show the addition dynamically jutting out from the steep incline towards an undeveloped Los Angeles, allowing unobstructed views from each room.

The construction elements and skin were carefully layered to achieve a completely translucent building. A basic steel construction on retaining walls formed a shelf system on which transparent boxes constructed of wood and glass were located like drawers, with a translucent skin applied where necessary, for insulation or privacy.

OPPOSITE ABOVE: Top floor plan; OPPOSITE BELOW: Perspective view from below; ABOVE: Longitudinal section; BELOW: Site plan

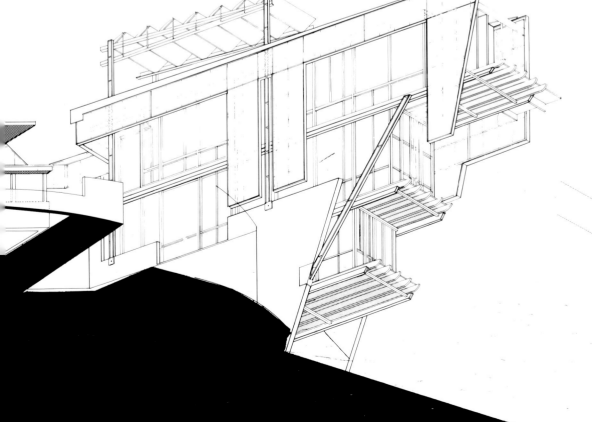

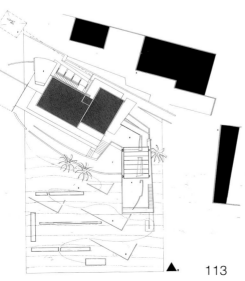

113

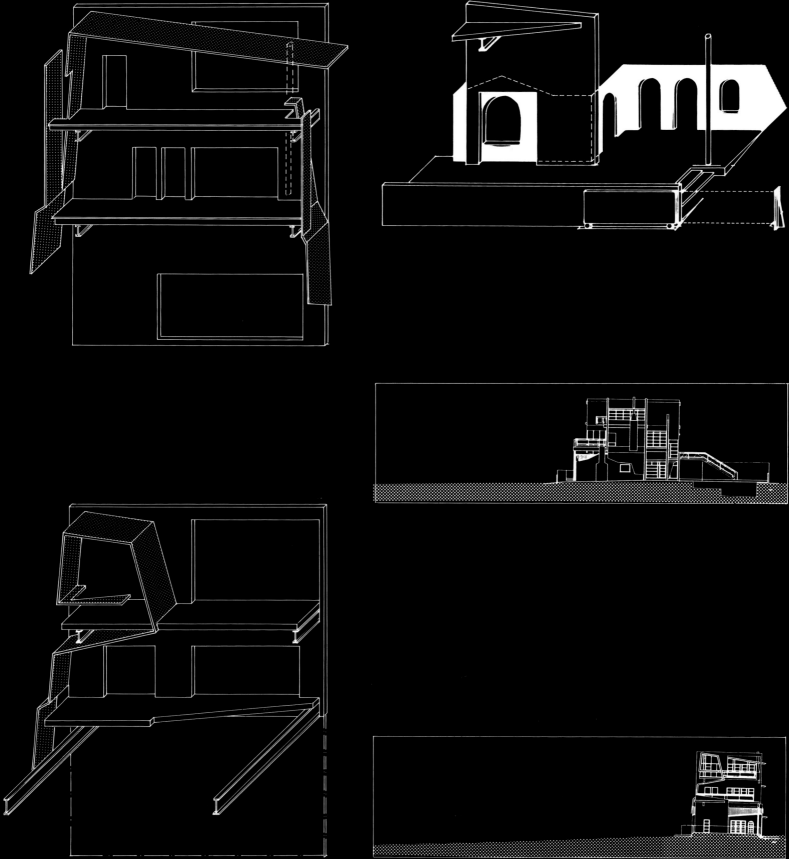

PRIVATE RESIDENCES

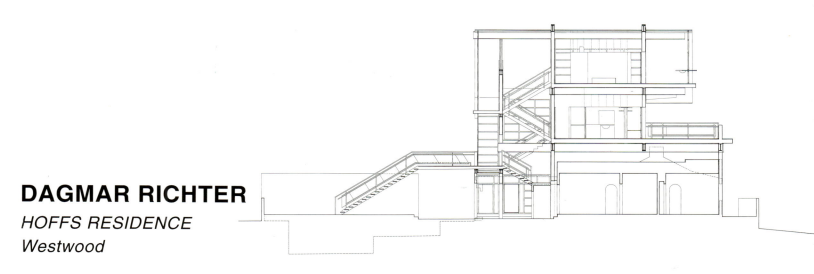

DAGMAR RICHTER
HOFFS RESIDENCE
Westwood

The existing building is a small single-family residence on a standard 50 x 125 square-foot lot in West Los Angeles. It carries a straightforward expression of middle-class domestic life, grounded in an original 1920s neighbourhood. The rustic Spanish style has been applied as a thin veneer easily visible from the street. On the adjacent back lot, Marilyn Monroe is buried in a small cemetery surrounded by high-rise buildings along Wilshire Boulevard.

The neighbourhood is in rapid transition. All traces of former life are being erased completely by developers who erect structures for the sole gain of the 'maximum square-footage allowed'. The existing building, in a subtle way, reflects Los Angeles' ubiquitous film reality. Filmic drama is realised through the application of ornament in the interior as well as the exterior's Spanish style. For his own delight, Joseph Norin, one of the art directors of *Ben Hur*, applied allegorical patterns of the film world throughout the house. This ornamentation truly emphasises the drama of domestic life.

The current owners wanted to add another 1,500 square feet to the existing 1,200 square-foot house. They wanted the filmic allegories of the interior to remain intact, whilst feeling neutral about the exterior. The additional programme consisted of a large studio, a master bedroom and two bathrooms.

Instead of erasing the current sub-structures, a strategy of layering was suggested. The existing building, a cultural subtext of significance, was to be left largely untouched, with an additional layer being added. This gave the opportunity to investigate alternative symbiotic relationships.

Two different landscapes were created: a film set and a simulated 'natural' landscape viewed from above.

The film set consisted of parallel planes erected horizontally and vertically. Some sat on the ground; others floated on a steel shelf. These planes created the background for domestic drama. A few objects were distributed onto tile planes such as fireplaces, a bath/electronic entertainment cabinet-unit and a small stair/guest/toilet unit. In addition, short steel stairs were to span the walls and act as bridges. These objects became the dynamic film furniture, which, for flexibility, contained several rotating and sliding units.

After the planes supplied the background and the objects the foreground, the created space was to be enclosed by a translucent curtain, which would have twisted, folded and wrapped itself tightly in the space between the planes. A new simulated urban landscape of a surreal character would have been created. It was anticipated that this landscape would be specifically viewed from above, as several high-rise buildings are positioned in close vicinity. The house would have changed dramatically between translucency and opacity depending on the light conditions.

The new structure created a relationship with the existing subtext which was symbiotic in nature. The openings of the existing building were framed but not copied by the new wall elements positioned in front of it, creating a row of double images filled with tensions. The translucent curtain, in contrast, slid over the existing building, barely touching it.

OPPOSITE LEFT: Cutaway perspective revealing structural elements; OPPOSITE RIGHT: Cutaway of ground floor and elevations; ABOVE AND BELOW: Section; elevation

115

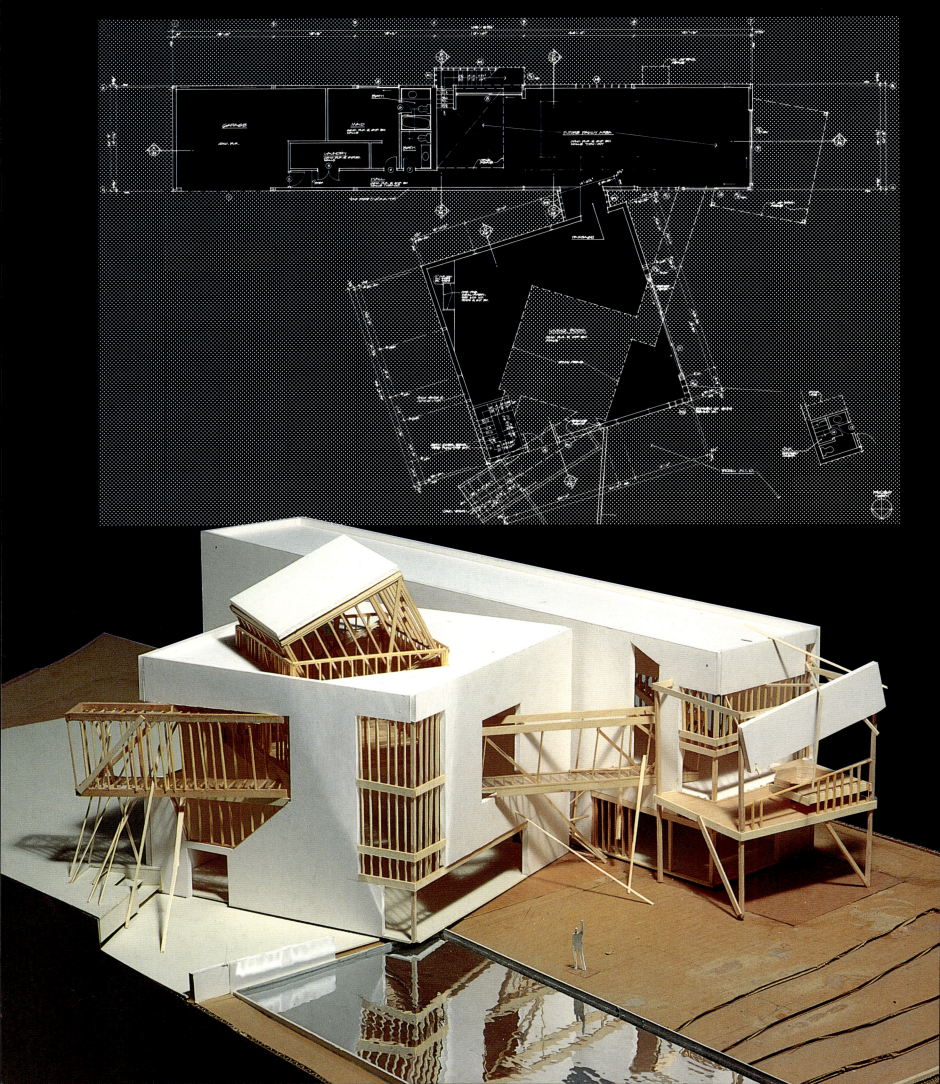

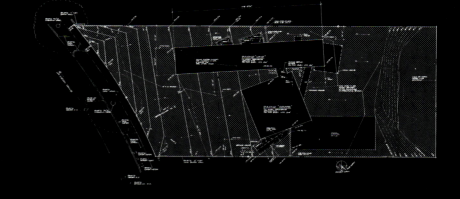

FRANK GEHRY
FAMILIAN RESIDENCE
Santa Monica Mountains

The site is in a residential neighbourhood on a narrow lot that drops off sharply in the rear, opening up to unobstructed views of the Santa Monica Mountains. Responding to the complex programmatic requirements of a family whose lifestyle is both highly public and intensely private, the resultant architectural composition questions the distinction between the complete and the unfinished, the stationary and the static, and the idea of house as both refuge and confrontation. The project also represents an exploration into the use of rough wood tract-house technology (normally covered up) as a tool for sketching with wood.

The house is composed essentially of two separate pieces, a bar oriented to the street at the front of the house, and a cube set at an angle to the bar. The two buildings almost touch, creating a 'crevice space' between them. A series of wood stud bridges, pavilions and lattices ties the structures to each other and to the landscape, which also incorporates a tennis court, swimming pool, staff quarters and on-site parking for thirty vehicles.

Public and private functions are divided between the two main buildings. The cube is basically a single volume reserved for public gatherings, although it does contain some living spaces. A skylight monitor tilts backwards as it perforates the roof of the cube, flooding the area below with natural light. The end wall of the adjacent building is pushed out to form a balcony but the internal volume of the bar remains undisturbed. The relatively narrow width of this building transfers the load entirely onto the exterior walls, allowing all interior surfaces to be placed according to functional and aesthetic considerations. A flexible interior system and a high degree of exclusion from the public spaces were required for this second structure, which houses the private quarters.

Both main buildings are primarily stucco sheathed. Window openings are placed independently of the structure, enabling the wood framing to continue unobstructed and uninterrupted behind the glazing. Elsewhere, exposed structural wood serves to heighten the sense of the sketch.

OPPOSITE ABOVE: Ground floor plans; ABOVE: Site plan

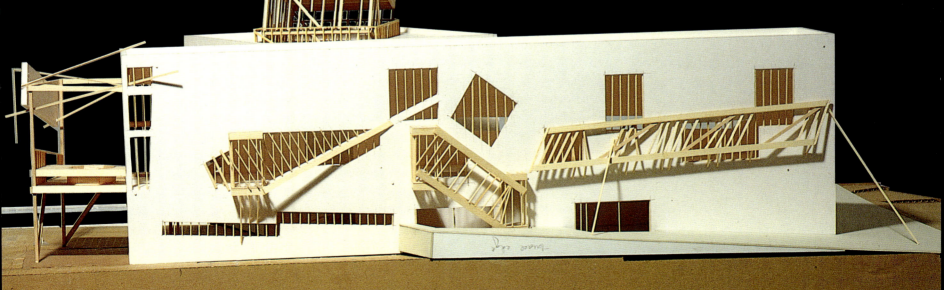

LOS ANGELES AS IT MIGHT HAVE BEEN

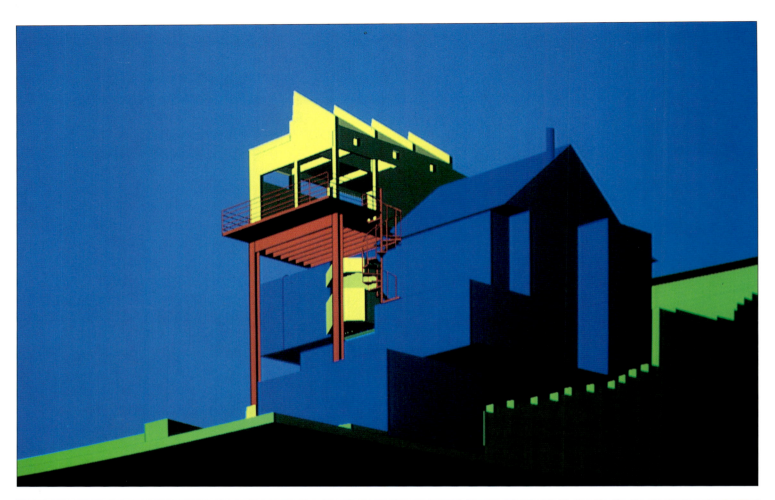

PRIVATE RESIDENCES

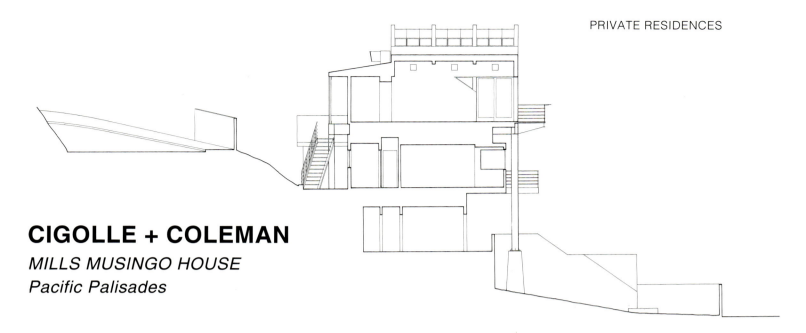

CIGOLLE + COLEMAN
MILLS MUSINGO HOUSE
Pacific Palisades

The existing two-storey house was to have been situated on a small hillside site two blocks from the ocean overlooking the Malibu coastline and Santa Monica Canyon in Los Angeles. The upper floor of the existing house located one level below the street elevation is occupied by the main living elements of the house; the bedroom floor is below. The client, a painter who also works as a film editor, and her husband, a musician and composer, proposed to add a painting studio to the house without changing the interior of the existing house. The addition was conceptually and structurally a separate building, but because of a shortage of space on the lot, and the breathtaking views to the south-west and west, the studio was placed on a steel table which sits over the house. The footings of the existing house were undisturbed by the addition, which meets the ground on four steel columns.

The entry stairway to the studio slides along the property line under a high porch. One enters through a compressed zone which contains painting storage and a lavatory/work room. As a work space for a painter who spends many hours in closed, dark editing rooms, the studio has openings on all four sides, taking advantage of the sea breezes to ventilate the room, and clerestory windows to provide north light. The north wall of the studio is a storage wall for books, materials and props. Three large pairs of doors open to the south and west. The doors may be curtained from the light on sunny afternoons, but provide expansive views of the canyon and ocean in the mornings and evenings and on hazy days, of which there are many. A cantilevered deck extends the studio floor outwards, and a spiral stair connects the studio deck with the living room deck below. An extension of the dining room penetrates the existing wall with a curved volume providing a window to the west outside the wall.

The addition, an object on legs, was established as a counterpoint to the existing house, which grows up the hill as a result of previous additions, and expresses the polarity between light and dark, attic and basement, artist and film editor. The anthropomorphic aspects of the studio derived in part from the client's collection of real, abstracted and imaginary animals; the studio was seen as a suitable addition to the collection. The roof was inspired by Le Corbusier's Ozenfant Studio and House, where the form of the building was expressed by the studio's saw-tooth skylights.

The design concept for the project was explored with computer-generated solid models which enabled extensive visualisations of the project and at the same time, supported the definition and further development of the elements of the design.

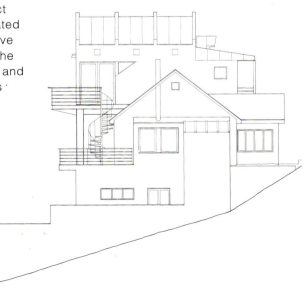

ABOVE AND BELOW: Elevations

119

LOS ANGELES AS IT MIGHT HAVE BEEN

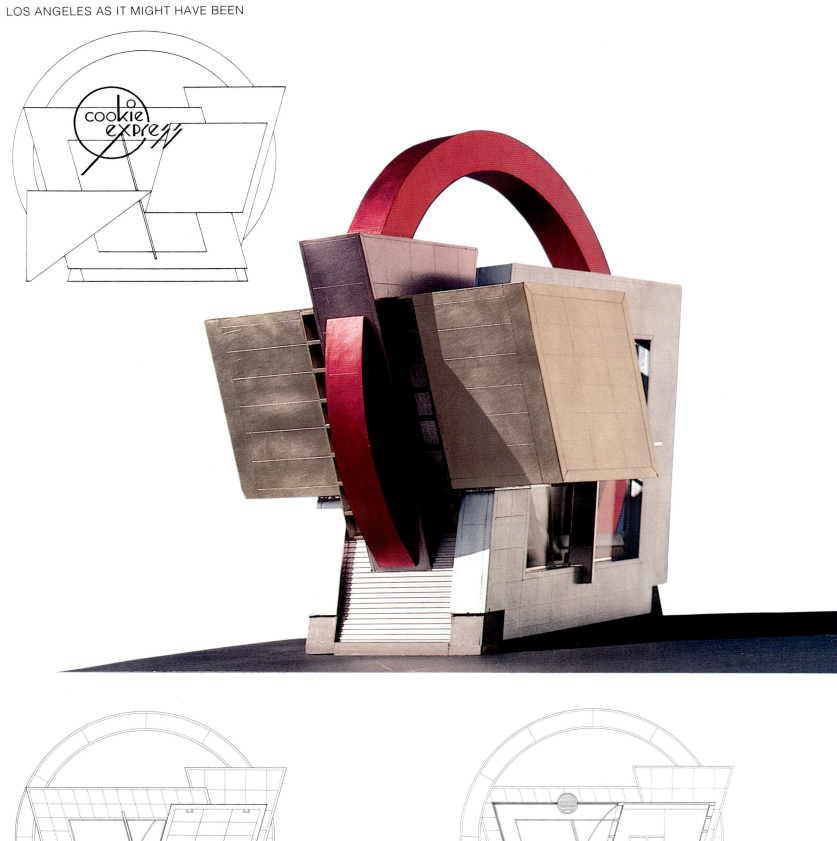

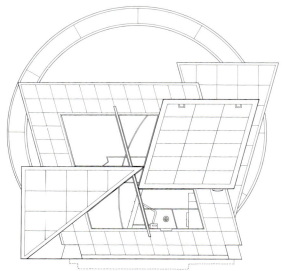
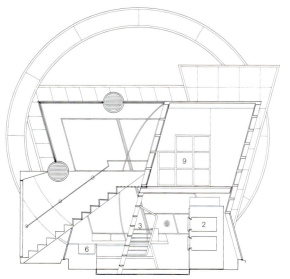

RESTAURANTS, BARS AND SHOPS

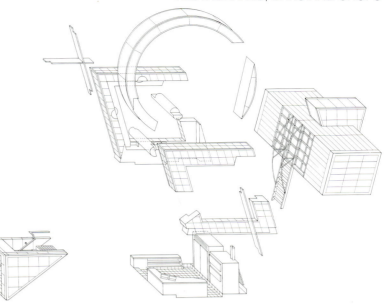

HODGETTS + FUNG
COOKIE EXPRESS

The idea behind this tiny building – the length and breadth of an automobile parking space – was to offer patrons on the move the opportunity to pick up cookies and coffee, whilst in transit from one place to the next. This prototype was to be replicated throughout shopping centre car parks in the South-west.

The unusual configuration was the product of the owner's desire for visibility in the chaotic environment of the strip, to counteract the project's compact and diminutive size and to comply with various local ordinances which mandated a full complement of 'restaurant' facilities.

Hence, the accommodation includes a second-level lavatory and storage area, a legal commercial exit staircase, ovens, refrigerators, sinks and the memory of Melnikov, within the building total of 350 square feet.

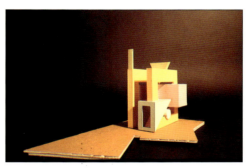

OPPOSITE, ABOVE AND BELOW LEFT: Elevations; OPPOSITE, BELOW RIGHT: Section; ABOVE: Exploded isometric; BELOW L TO R: Roof plan; floor plan

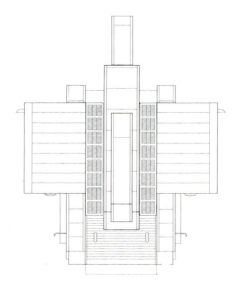
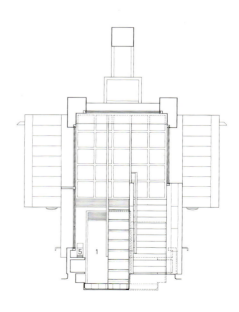

LOS ANGELES AS IT IS

INVENTION AND REINVENTION IN LA
Maggie Toy 124

CULTURAL CENTRES
Frank Gehry
California Aerospace Museum and Theatre 132
Arata Isozaki
The Museum of Contemporary Art 136
Hodgetts + Fung
Towell Library 142
Moore Ruble Yudell
First Church of Christ, Scientist 144
Bart Prince
Pavilion for Japanese Art 148
Fields & Devereaux
The El Capitan Theater 154
Barton Phelps
Corinne A Seeds University Elementary School 156
WED Enterprises
Disneyland 158

MIXED USE DEVELOPMENT
Skidmore Owings & Merrill
The Gas Company Tower 162
Wells Fargo Center 166
Pei Cobb Freed
First Interstate Bank World Center 168
LA Convention Center 172
Frank Gehry
Edgemar Development 176
Moore Ruble Yudell
Plaza Las Fuentes 180
Hodgetts + Fung
UCLA Gateway 186
The Jerde Partnership
Universal Citywalk 188

OFFICES
Frank Gehry
Chiat/Day Temporary Offices 192
Eric Owen Moss
Ince Complex 198
Gary Group 200
Paramount Laundry Building 204
Lindblade Tower 208
8522 National Boulevard Office Building 212
Morphosis
Salick Healthcare Office Building 216
Cesar Pelli
Pacific Design Center and Expansion 220
Hodgetts + Fung
Click Model Management 224
Gwathmey Siegel
The Capital Group 226
Steven Ehrlich
Sony Music Entertainment 228
Kohn Pedersen Fox
550 South Hope Street 232

PRIVATE RESIDENCES
Frank Gehry
Schnabel Residence 234
Gehry Residence 238
Norton House 242
Morphosis
Blades Residence 244
Eric Owen Moss
Lawson/Westen House 248
Frank Israel
Goldberg-Bean House 254
Woo Pavilion 258
Sigrid Miller Pollin
Mount Vernon Avenue Residences 260
Legorreta Arquitectos
Greenberg House 264
McCoy and Simon
Webb Residence 270
Cigolle + Coleman
Canyon House 272
Moore Ruble Yudell

Rodes House	274
Villa Superba	278
Buzz Yudell	
Yudell/Beebe House	280
Hodgetts + Fung	
Viso House	284
Schweitzer Bim	
The Monument	286
Barton Phelps	
Epstein House	290
O'Herlihy & Warner	
Miller Residence	294
Freund-Koopman Residence	298
Central Office of Architecture	
Laguna Beach Residence Addition	302

HEALTH AND LEISURE CENTRES

Morphosis	
Cedars-Sinai Comprehensive Cancer Center	304
Michele Saee	
Dental Centre	308
Steven Ehrlich	
Shatto Recreation Center	310

RESTAURANTS, BARS AND SHOPS

Morphosis	
Kate Mantilini	312
Rotondi	
Nicola Restaurant	316
Nikken America / Charles Cordero AIA / Francesca Garcia-Marques	
Zenzero Restaurant	318
Michele Saee	
Angeli Mare Restaurant	322
Ecru Marina	326
Design Express	330
Ted Tokio Tanaka	
California Beach Rock 'n Sushi	332
Central Office of Architecture	
Brix Restaurant	336

INVENTION AND REINVENTION IN LA
MAGGIE TOY

Los Angeles occupies a curious position within the social and cultural table of America to the extent that it is even ironically claimed that Los Angeles is west of America. Is this because it is everything America dreamed of and more? The city has, for over a century, upheld a free and open policy allowing a mixed bag of ethnic groups to settle there. Whilst this is a very honourable objective, it unfortunately does have large planning implications, as each group stakes out its own territory and protects it. The ideal of a thoroughly integrated community might work in the drawings of the idealist but not in practice, and certainly not across the landscape of Los Angeles. Whilst superficially it might be read that Los Angeles is architecturally confident with its many aggressive schools, it is perhaps insecurity that persuades architects to design constructions which struggle to exert their own personality. The influence of Hollywood – or Hollyweird, as Richard Rayner enjoys describing it – on the town is immense and perhaps stretches further than the obvious comparison of the characters who try to be noticed and those who merely sit back and are noticed. The celluloid city represents the American dream of being able to make it overnight, to pursue a wish – of becoming rich and famous – and make it into reality.

The pressure passes onto the architecture and the architects to create environments that represent this feeling. Frank Gehry explains that he has seen changes over the last three decades as the city has become more sophisticated, but during that transformation it has also become more threatening and more desperate. He also argues that when he first started working in Los Angeles, there was a reluctance to acknowledge what the city really represented. Gehry maintains that he understood the place and therefore could accept it and design accordingly; however, 'a lack of acceptance of Los Angeles' reality hampered my work twenty years ago; it delayed acceptance of my work, which went along with the grain of the place rather than attempting to ignore it, or pretend it should be like New York'. In the end this strategy did break through and Gehry's continued use of it is one of the explanations for his success in the city.

Although it is not advisable to be 'poor' in any city of the world the situation is exacerbated in Los Angeles. As Richard Rayner explains: 'this is no town to be poor in. Every minute someone goes by in their dream car, with their dream life, rubbing your face in it'. One of the contradictions of this city of Oz is that everyone wants to move there to find success, believing that their lives will miraculously change. Everyone is accepted, because this is the city's policy, but only a handful is successful. This sets up an equation which inevitably leads to social unrest.

Traditionally Los Angeles has been characterised as the Granola capital of the United States: full of fruits, nuts and flakes. The latest joke, however, is that it does, after all, have four seasons: riot, fire, earthquake and flood. The frequency of natural and social disaster has stunned even the most hardened Angelenos. Some saw the 'justice uprising' of April 1992 as an inevitable consequence of the state of the city. Charles Jencks explains: 'akin to the classical revolutions – America 1776, France 1789 – it was not the poor who started things, but the conscientious and ambitious. The latter, suddenly finding they had been let down by an unfair judiciary and state police, immediately concluded that to continue in hard work would be pointless'. He carried on to state that this clearly demonstrated that the opportunity for fulfilment of the American Dream is not felt by everyone. The natural disasters of the recent past include the fires in October 1993 and the 6.6 Richter scale earthquake in January 1994, which precipitated both fires and mudslides, leaving the city in chaos on each occasion. Self-righteous moralising invariably follows each disaster. After a series of fires in 1988 and 1989 – which devastated the Desert Hot Springs Riverside County, Apple Valley, San Benadino County, San Carlos, San Diego and the Granada Hills, the Porter Ranch fires and the Los Angeles, Orange and San Benadino fires of June 1990 – Peter H King made some pointed observations on the commentary that followed, in his 'On California' column in the *LA Times*: 'To pass muster on a true Californian tale, there must be references to sub-tropical sunsets and dreamers of the Golden Dream and the center not holding in the place where we ran out of land . . . this treatment is not applicable to any other state. New York blizzards

OPPOSITE: Frank Gehry, California Aerospace Museum and Theatre; ABOVE: LA skyline from Transamerica building; BELOW: The beach scene, Pacific Rim, the plains and the mountains

LOS ANGELES AS IT IS

are not seen as a punishment for various Manhattan sins. Florida hurricanes are not springboards for polemics about the flawed psyche of snowbirds. I watched closely during the Mississippi floods. Not once did I see a reference to the cultural paradox of Iowa . . . No, only our disasters are cast as cosmic retribution, apparently for the sin of living in California in the first place'. That each disaster has been followed by the spectre in both the local and international press of American Armageddon and the end of a national ideal, must be due to the singular position of Los Angeles and California in the American Psyche, as the city the nation loves to hate.

In spite of its rancho past and its complex pre-war history, Los Angeles did not penetrate American or European consciousness until well after the Armistice. Its chief achievement was then seen to be the decision to rely on the automobile and to build the freeways required to do so. The most recent earthquake has revealed just how dependent Los Angeles is on its freeways. A map of the city following the disaster gives the impression of almost strategic cuts to the infrastructure, resulting in maximum disruption to mobility. The dream of the freeways and their use did not turn out quite as expected, although as everyone outside Los Angeles knows, it lives on its car culture: LA loves all its visitors as long as they're not pedestrians. However, the use of the freeways has outgrown its original social and historical perception of being a support-communication network. Car culture has become omnipotent and criminal incidents on the freeway have increased. A road accident has become an opportunity for thieves and worse, so that the natural instincts of concern for others have been subverted and replaced by self-preservation. Also, the speed at which the roads are used has changed dramatically, therefore minor crashes rarely occur as James Steele explains: 'Cars flipped upside down, catapulted over barriers, totally flattened, or crushed like an accordion are a daily sight'. It is time that Los Angeles reverted to emphasising travel around its city but it will not be easy to persuade the public to make this transition.

A surprising consequence of the disaster has been that the first part of the newly-opened metro system has not come into full use, having been almost ignored by the public in its first week of operation. Car-pooling has become mandatory, rather than a matter of choice, determined by the necessity to comply with the limited capacity of the surface streets.

In the tradition of American entrepreneurialism – of which Los Angeles is itself a symbol – the disaster has been turned into commercial gain overnight; alongside the 'I survived the Quake of 94' T-shirts, are books and pamphlets describing 'LA's Alternative Routes'.

One of the most obvious ironies about the Martin Luther King earthquake of 1994, for architects, is that some of the buildings by Los Angeles' most famous architect, Frank Gehry, seem almost to have been improved by it. Perhaps this is the aesthetic he was trying to achieve? His own residence in Santa Monica and the Familian House, for example, followed an aesthetic which could be said to be reminiscent of post-quake constructions. When Gehry was asked in an interview whether he had intended his structures to look like a post-quake construction, he strongly denied these motives explaining, 'I see what I am doing as the equivalent to climbing into the cab and grabbing the wheel of a lorry running away down the highway out of control'. The lorry in this rather 'Indiana Jones' view of the present state of the building arts, is the chaotic state of American contribution to architecture and his self-image is that of the person designed to set it back on course – rather appropriate as an analogy from the architect who is so closely associated with Hollywood. The course of Gehry's architecture was already in the process of dramatic change in his new Disney Concert Hall, which bears closer affinity to a Californian heatwave than the aftermath of an earthquake. This change was caused by a series of experiments similar to those which precipitated the realisation with the Industrial Revolution that the steam engine could be used not only to pump water, but also to drive an axle for locomotive power.

The discovery came about when the Gehry team was asked to provide a mock-up of a portion of a wall of the concert hall for the Venice Biennale 1992. It had previously relied upon axial projection techniques in which x-y coordinates were located by pieces of string stretched through a plastic box. However, it had to search for a more convenient and accurate method which would allow Gehry's 'stream of consciousness' sketches to be converted more directly into models. With the Biennale deadline imminent, the team went to the Aerospace industry, once the backbone of California's industrial strength. It is perhaps ironic that an industry that Gehry has served in the form of one of his best known commissions (The Aerospace Museum and Exhibition Park, 1982-84) should have provided the technology that proved the basis of a creative breakthrough for the designers. The digital computing technique used by aerospace engineers to calculate complex curves and accurately translate them into metallic panels can also be used to transfer curves in sketch models, to cut patterns in stone and to guide the saws. Once this technique was perfected, the steel bracing necessary to support the sample wall from behind was straightforward, and great

OPPOSITE: Morphosis, 72 Market Street, Venice; ABOVE: The Jerde Partnership, Universal Citywalk, Citywalk

efficiency of materials could be achieved. Consequently, contractors who had doubted whether the wall systems specified could be built, were able to see in the sample wall the materials needed and the methods that could be used which allowed them to decrease their tender. The entire hall has now been documented in this way, with working drawings devised by computer. Gehry has also used this technique on all his new projects and thus the angular profiles of his 'post-earthquake' period, have become a thing of the past.

Frank Gehry's influence on other Los Angeles architects has been a matter of contention. He denies that he has been influential, but on this point there seems to be a consensus: more and more of his peers recognise the possibilities of advanced computer techniques and the differences in the way these principles are employed.

The steps that Gehry and his team are making are certainly instructive. Morphosis, for example, has now embraced advanced computer systems for promotional literature about its project and competition submissions – most recently for the Tours Museum competition; Thom Mayne is interested in achieving the most up-to-date publishing medium allowing images to be scanned-in and manipulated on screen; the architecture produced by the Morphosis team has always drawn on the polemical strength and complexity of its home town; Thom Mayne poignantly stresses the necessity for architects to 'comprehend and utilise the complexity of everyday experience . . . It is necessary for architecture to be based in the present and to aspire to that presence'. He also claims that there is no longer any requirement for a regional architecture, arguing that we are all part of the world and that is our 'region', with the level of communication as it is, the definition of regions is distracting and unnecessary. This does not, however, infer that each design should not be site specific; on the contrary whilst the style is universal, each interpretation is individual and unique. His work is based on an organisational system which can represent complex layouts but stems from a strategy of order and continuity, utilising the theories born from James Gleick's *Chaos: The Making of a New Science*. Architects have traditionally drawn inspiration from scientific sources. The stakes have changed over the years as architecture and science have gone through a similar process of bifurcation, and the source field for both has become correspondingly larger, leading to further diversification for the architect.

Gehry seems to remain the godfather of that particular group of architects still at the cutting edge of microchip technology, despite rumours of an avant-garde new generation destined to supplant him. However, it would be unfair to categorise the younger group as 'architects without architecture' as some have been tempted to do, because they have accomplished many building projects. The phase of what was conceived as paper architecture in Los Angeles seemed to end during the early 1990s. As the decade progresses the tendency to rely on heavy graphics (which are often considered as works of art in themselves) rather than actual buildings, is diminishing. As Michael Sorkin explains, 'Unlike its predecessors, the new wave of Los Angeles architecture was widely interpreted before it was created. Instead of seeing the viewpoint of their work elucidated and described, today's group must struggle to produce work which embodies decriptions already made. This can be tough.' It is a challenge in which the protagonists will be assisted by the advance use of technology.

Interestingly the use of advanced computer techniques has called this entire drawing process into question as the drawings stage can no longer be seen as static representations of the finished work. The reinterpretation of graphic convention has had such impact that new ways have been found to show relationships between elements that were previously represented only in certain predictable and familiar forms: they have been reconfigured in calligraphic relationships which have enormous power to convey aesthetic intention.

Coop Himmelblau, the Viennese-based architectural practice which also has an Los Angeles office, talk about the siesmographic quality of its drawing technique and is proud of the fact that the architects design using sketches made while their 'eyes are closed' to convey subliminal intention. Its work in the city remains largely unbuilt as yet, but examples of the work produced outside the city indicates that Coop Himmelblau has taken the opportunities afforded it in this city. The practice relishes the freedom from history that the city promises, and seeks an architecture that is more than the sum of its historical parts; desiring an architecture 'that bleeds, that exhausts, that whirls and even breaks. Architecture that lights up, that stings, that rips, and under stress, tears. Architecture should be cavernous, fiery, smooth, hard, angular, brutal, round, delicate, colourful, obscene, voluptuous, dreamy, alluring, repelling, wet, dry and throbbing'. Coop Himmelblau's influence on Los Angeles architects has travelled across the Atlantic as well, where its designs will soon be realised. The practice's design and drawing principle goes one step further than Gehry's, whose intuitive first abstract sketches have an uninhibited spontaneity.

Eric Owen Moss, one of the so-called 'Southern California School', is more circumspect,

ABOVE: Morphosis, Salick Healthcare Office Building, Beverly Hills; BELOW: Steven Ehrlich, Sony Music Entertainment, Santa Monica

laboriously constructing layer after layer of sketches which together contribute the complex geometries for which he has become known. It has now become widely acknowledged that Philip Johnson referred to him as the 'master jeweller of junk'. His designs demonstrate an unconventional twist, even in comparison to the other architects within the 'School'. Moss enjoys shocking, as well as testing, the observer's intellectual boundaries, continuously searching for new and obscure inspirations. He also insists that the way he is and the way he designs has nothing to do with the city of Los Angeles. It does not matter where he is based, the influences would be the same in that (by his own volition) they would be always different and always changing. He is perpetually questioning what he is doing, bringing in literary figures and others to explain and justify his design. Moss explains how he compared his progress on the Westen House to that of the story of Penelope and Odysseus: 'Penelope put the quilt together during the day and then took it apart at night, a great metaphor for building . . . You're putting something together and you're procrastinating and you build this conceptual procrastination right into the project'. The representation of his work in drawn form is perhaps an art form in itself. Because of the complexity of the built form they represent, it is vital that the designs are clear and thus are frequently drawn in three dimensions. There is a sense that unlike the written and spoken word emanating from this architect, the drawn form – the reality – is where he is clear and can communicate freely.

Previously with Morphosis, Michael Rotondi now not only runs his own practice but also heads the most influential school of architecture in the region, SciArc. The influence of the architecture programme there is being felt internationally. At a time when architects are searching for a direction, schools of architecture are also reassessing their approach. The greatest advantage of this is that it is time for such reappraisal and after a thorough study of the system and its origins, motivation and direction are likely to create a positive result. Rotondi has firmly taken a grip of architectural education at SciArc. The students progress through a 'process' taking on board a series of 'experiments'. Most architects of note working in Los Angeles, as well as the long list of international invitees, can be persuaded to give some of their time to the education of the next generation.

SciArc is not the only educational institution available and a healthy rivalry is maintained with the school at UCLA where Franklin D Israel teaches. Israel has developed a style of design which is very similar to the Eric Owen Moss aesthetic but slightly more controlled. The juxtaposition of elements and colours is more refined, perhaps more self-conscious, motivated by a different agenda.

Following this 'group', a multitude of talent is emerging from the wings. Dagmar Richter teaches at SciArc and demonstrates a cool, demanding architecture which questions a way of authorising a project as each member of team participates systematically in the progress of a design. Koning Eizenberg has developed a reputation for designing clearly in tune with its clients and is one of the few Los Angeles firms who have attempted to address a social agenda with its low-income houses in Santa Monica. the practice has also attempted to create a village-type atmosphere for the Ken Edwards Center for senior citizens in order to avoid the institutional type environment. Michael Saee develops the structural forms of his buildings to be the prominent aesthetic of his design. In his Angeli Mare restaurant, the waved roof form rests upon a strong undulating rib cage of steel supports, the principal visual centre of the scheme. His use of materials combines practical concrete forms with the beauty of wood, the transparent attraction of glass and the cold appeal of metal, with the colours used attaining an overall rustic approach.

The paradox which has arisen within the work of many architects is the age-old dichtomy of intuition and machine technology, a problem with which the most celebrated architects of Los Angeles are grappling, resulting in varying degrees of success. Gehry seems to manage to retain his artistic vision in spite of (in fact, perhaps, assisted by the freedom of) his new found reliance on highly sophisticated techniques. It is difficult to imagine him abandoning his method of using preliminary sketches as the first manifestation of an idea. The desire to combine art and architecture has led Gehry into various collaborations: the scheme for Chiat/Day/Mojo, designed by the Gehry team in association with Claes Oldenburg and Coosje van Brugen, includes overt metaphors. Oldenburg and Van Brugen, who had previously worked on the Spoon and Cherry Bridge, had indicated to Gehry that the partnership of ideas would be exceedingly 'fruitful' and indeed it aided the installation of one of the most iconographic buildings in Venice, exceedingly appropriate for an advertising agency.

The interaction between art and architecture is an important feature of many architects' work and should continue to be encouraged. Gehry is expanding his role still further as a furniture designer and manufacturer. He can be seen posing, dressed as a Canadian Ice Hockey player, advertising his beautiful folded wooden chairs. He frequently leads the way, blazing a trail for architects to learn how to maximise their

ABOVE: Eric Owen Moss, Lawson-Westen House, Brentwood; BELOW: Hodgetts + Fung, Towell Library, Westwood

potential in the present economical climate. Although it was difficult for him in the beginning, he 'recommends young designers whenever [he] can,' in the same manner in which Philip Johnson did for him. 'And there's certainly a wider acceptance of avant-garde architecture in LA. Given this I keep urging the kids not to become disillusioned or cynical about the scene.'

Other architects, those outside the groups being discussed, have been slower in coming to grips with the full implications of computer techniques. To put this in perspective, many of the new buildings in the city have been 'designed' by householders, and the role of the architect has been relegated to an advisor who provides the necessary stamp of official sanction. After the 1994 earthquake, private initiative has inevitably prevailed and it is the people themselves who are rebuilding the city. In the past, re-invention was in the hands of an elite group that wanted to direct the city to its position as one of the most important cities in the US. To do this it depended upon media hype and rewrote Los Angeles' history, turning some of the more unpalatable truths of the past, such as the exploitation of the indigenous population and slave labour, into a vision of bougainvillaea-covered haciendas and farmworkers toiling happily on their vast ranchos in a paradise of natural abundance. In the current re-invention of the city, the irony is that it is the polyglot society that makes up the city who will transform the city as it pursues its aspirations.

Los Angeles is a very fragile city and the consequence of these actions for the city are immense. The accusation that there is no 'there' in Los Angeles – that there is no sense of place – is a reality that needs to be faced and dealt with. Public space is difficult to achieve. The planning of Los Angeles demands that you decide where you want to go and *drive* there accordingly; once you have finished your business there you drive away again. Thus the sense of casually strolling and 'happening' upon a piece of urban space – in true European fashion – is almost unheard of. Although it is what Arata Isozaki attempted to achieve with the Museum of Contemporary Art, the nearest thing to a public space are areas which the public can access for a fee: for example, Disneyland and Citywalk.

The Jerde Partnership has designed Citywalk as a series of potential true-to-life streetlife experiences. Perhaps, as Deyan Sudjic writes – 'for LA's affluent whites . . . waiting in line for a valet-parked car to come back outside a Rodeo Drive boutique is the nearest they come to experiencing street life' – this will be their only opportunity to become streetwise.

In his rather grim and uncompromising assessment of his home town, Mike Davis, in *City of Quartz: Excavating the Future of Los Angeles*, explains how the notion of public space has been destroyed as each 'segment of the community prospects their own, and segregates themselves, against all unknown dangers that might be lurking outside their territory. It is the fear of the event which creates this need for protection. Where there is an actual rising arc of street violence, as in South-central or Downtown Washington DC, most of the carnage is self-contained within ethnic or class boundaries. Yet white middle class imagination, absent from any first-hand knowledge of inner city conditions, magnifies the perceived threat through a demonological lens'. Fear and suspicion are not limited to one class or another, and the problem of how to reunite a deeply segregated metropolis remains the foremost environmental problem the city has to acknowledge and attempt to rectify.

The urban and architectural question now is not so much whether Gehry and his contemporaries can board and take the wheel of the runaway lorry as it speeds down the highway, but whether they can get onto the lorry at all.

Bibliography

Aaron Betsky, *Violated Perfection*, Rizzoli, New York, 1990.
Mike Davis, *City of Quartz: Excavating the Future in Los Angeles*, Vintage, London, 1992.
Frank Gehry, *Buildings and Projects*, Rizzoli, New York, 1985.
Experimental Architecture in Los Angeles, Introduction by Frank Gehry, essays by Aaron Betsky, John Chase and Leon Whiteson, Rizzoli, New York, 1991.
Charles Jencks, *Heteropolis: Los Angeles • The Riots and the Strange Beauty of Hetero-architecture*, Academy Editions, London, 1993.
Wolf Prix and Helmut Swiczinsky, *Coop Himmelblau: The Power of the City*, translated by Robert Halm, Roswitha Prix, Jo Steinbauer and Edda Zimmerman,

Verlagdir George Buchner Buch handlung, Darmstadt, 1988, p95.
Richard Rayner, *Los Angeles Without a Map*, Flamingo, London, 1992.
Michael Sorkin, *Exquisite Corpse*, Verso, London, 1990.
James Steele, *Los Angeles Architecture: The Contemporary Condition*, Phaidon, London, 1993.
Deyan Sudjic, *The 100 Mile City*, Andre Deutsch, London, 1992.
Richard Saul Wurman, *LA Access*, Harper Collins, Dunmore, 1993.
Eric Owen Moss, Academy Editions, London, 1993.
Frank Israel, Academy Editions, London, 1994.
Morphosis: Connected Isolation, Academy Editions, London, 1993.

OPPOSITE: Frank Israel, Bright and Associates, Venice; ABOVE: Burning mini malls; BELOW: South Central LA, the second day of the riots

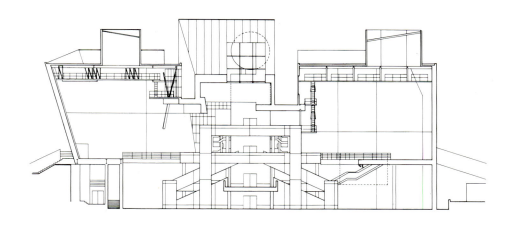

FRANK GEHRY
CALIFORNIA AEROSPACE MUSEUM AND THEATRE
Downtown

The California Aerospace Museum and Theatre is located in Exposition Park, adjacent to the Coliseum and near Downtown Los Angeles. The museum is a major expansion to the Museum of Science and Industry complex. Frank O Gehry and Associates was asked to participate in the master planning of five new museum projects, all to be built in Exposition Park in time for the 1984 Summer Olympics. The Aerospace Museum and Theatre, bid underbudget, was the only one of the originally-planned projects to be completed before the Olympics.

At the time the project was begun, the Aerospace Museum was housed in the 1915 Armory Building. There were few exhibits and little money. The building was to be a spectacular exhibit in itself, in order to give the museum a strong public identity. Since the cost of renovating the existing building was too high, it was decided to place a new exhibit building in front of the older one. A 436-seat Imax Theatre was added, becoming the focus of a new Missile Garden.

The museum building is composed of two 90-foot-tall spaces, each given a different architectural expression, with a gantry-like viewing tower between them and a symbolic sphere rising above the elevator tower. A circular entrance ramp was introduced as a major feature to make both old and new buildings easily accessible. An F104 with US markings was hung onto the facade as an integral part of the design.

The structure is a steel-based frame, with the exterior clad in stucco and painted sheetmetal panels over drywall.

ABOVE: Section; BELOW: Site plan

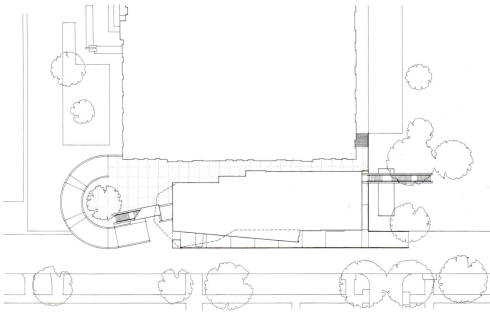

133

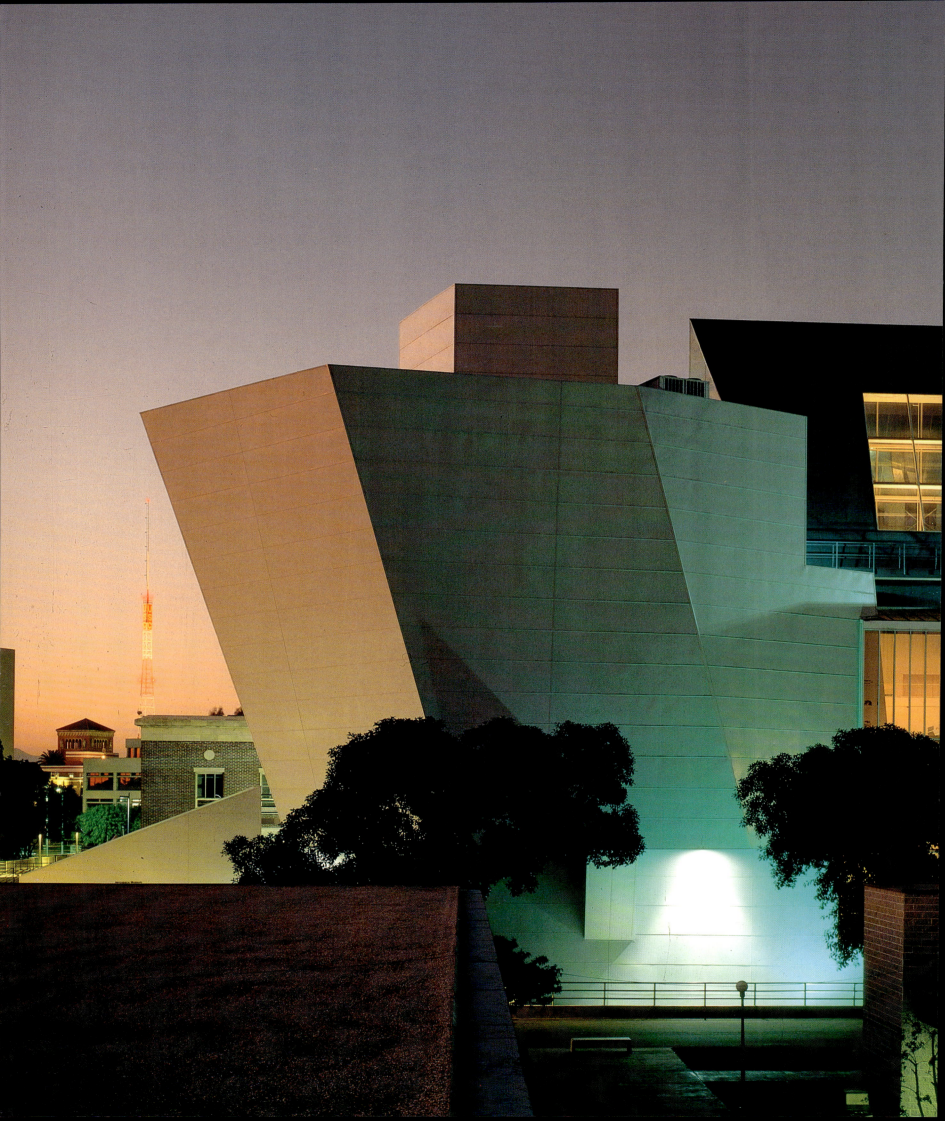

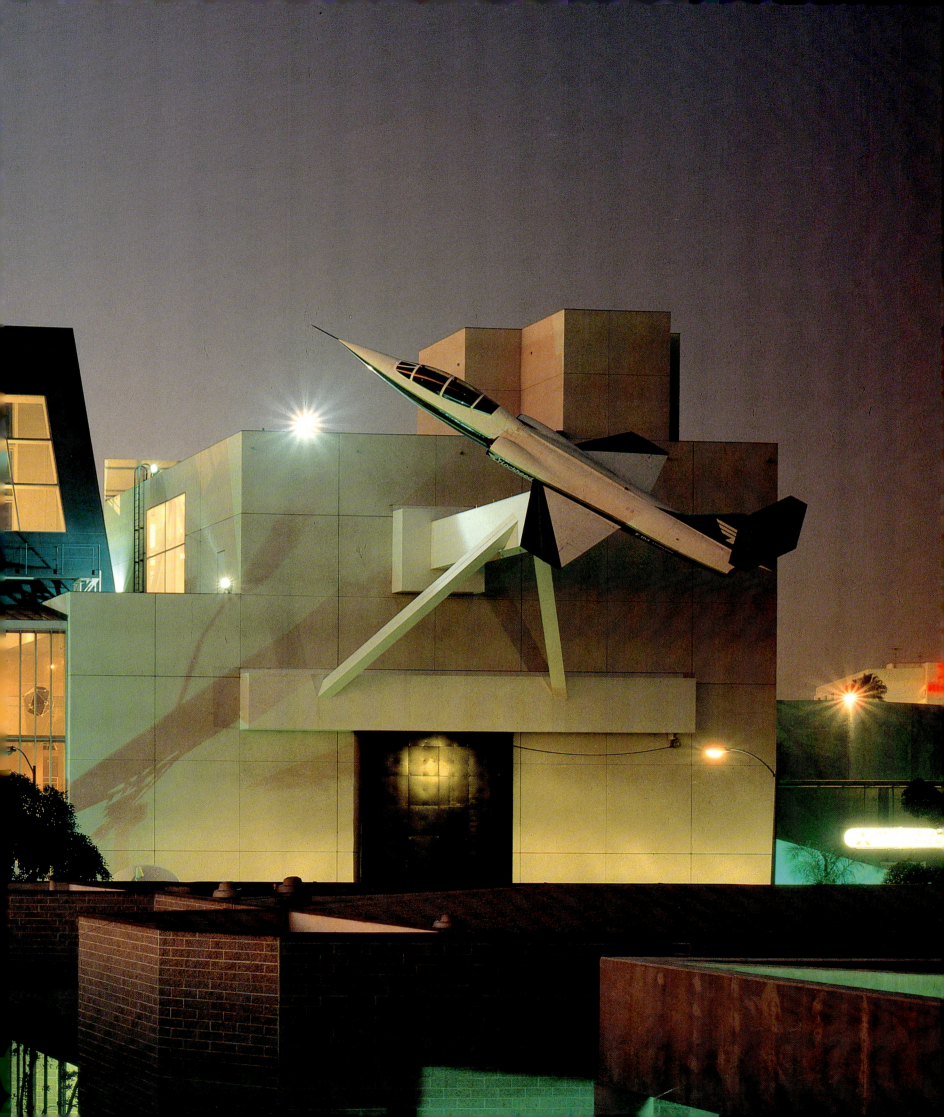

ARATA ISOZAKI
THE MUSEUM OF CONTEMPORARY ART
Downtown

The Museum of Contemporary Art is the first phase of the Bunker Hill redevelopment in Downtown Los Angeles. The main gallery is half-a-level below street level with the entrance court in the centre. The basic design of this gallery consists of two 'Golden Rectangles' which are of Greek origin. Both of these spaces can be subdivided to form smaller galleries spiralling into the Yin-Yang symbol of harmony.

One of the characteristics of this museum is its use of various skylights. The use of both naturally lit and artificially lit galleries enables a variety of objects to be exhibited, according to the different needs of the artists. The floor below the main gallery houses an auditorium with a seating capacity of 250. This can be used for musical or dance performances, video screening or lectures. The lowest floor is a multi-function service area which includes a photographic studio, art storage, workshops and a full-trailer capacity loading dock. The floor above the gallery contains a cafeteria which faces the central court and a museum store which looks onto the sculpture garden. The second floor holds the administrative offices and the third floor holds the curatorial offices and a library.

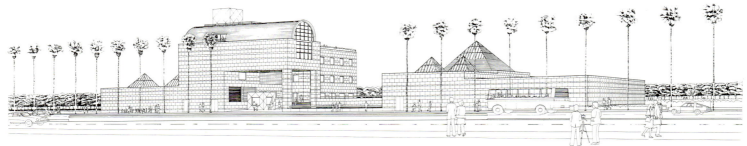

ABOVE: East elevation; BELOW: Perspective view

CULTURAL CENTRES

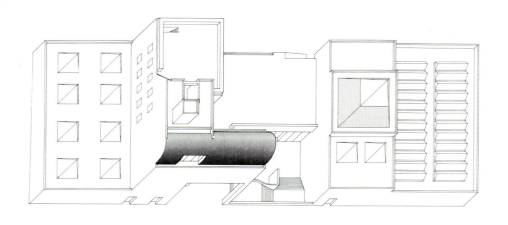

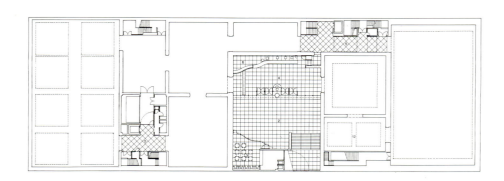
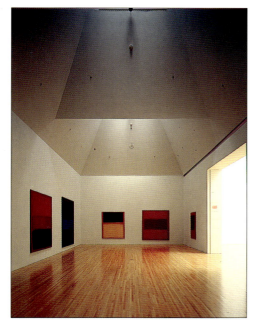

*FROM ABOVE:
Axonometric; gallery
level plan; perspective
of museum court*

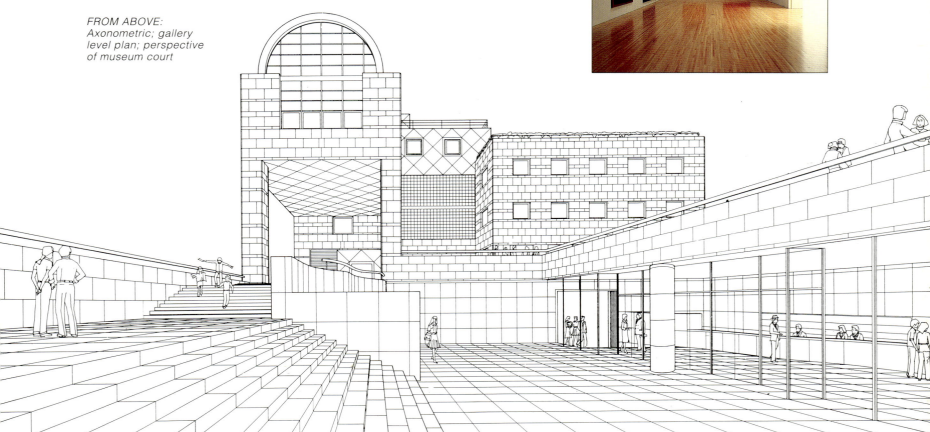

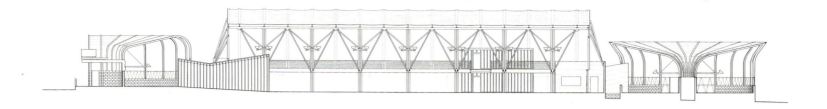

HODGETTS + FUNG
TOWELL LIBRARY
Westwood

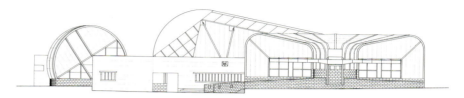

Hodgetts + Fung was asked to devise a temporary structure for UCLA's main undergraduate library during its closure for seismic renovation. The building programme integrated several significant factors, including a rigorous deadline, a demandingly low budget and a difficult site. A critical hub of campus activity, this was to be a new facility on an already crowded campus. The design needed to read as unquestionably temporary while maintaining the identity of a functioning library. With that in mind, the programme evolved into a cluster of smaller structures which complemented the scale of the existing buildings while providing an opportunity for a range of future uses.

The tented landforms that comprise the complex are a series of linked structures which functions as an assembly of individual components conceived to look different and unpredictable from all directions. The main tensile structure is in the shape of a sloping shed and is home to the library stacks and other student services.

Towell Library is 'rough tech', as materials and details of assembly were utilised for decorative emphasis. A braced steel substructure not only supports the main structure and stabilises the roof ribs at mid-span, but also undulates during an earthquake. The fabric covering, a brightly-coloured yellow and white industrial standard polyester substrate, features a separate layer inside to enhance insulation.

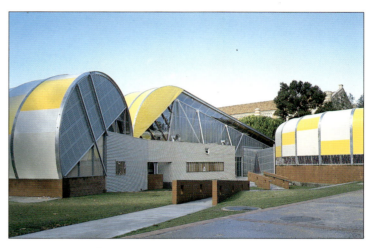

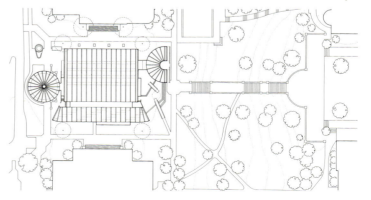

ABOVE: Longitudinal section; east elevation; BELOW: Site plan

MOORE RUBLE YUDELL
FIRST CHURCH OF CHRIST, SCIENTIST
Glendale

Two Christian Science congregations in a small, prosperous Southern California town united to build a new church. A small site made accommodation of programme and parking requirements a challenge.

The architects' approach was to group the various uses around a courtyard, through which the main auditorium, Sunday School building, offices and meeting rooms are all entered. Arrival from the parking areas on two levels is at one corner, marked by a tower that brings light down a stairwell to the lower level. The entrance to the foyer of the auditorium is at the courtyard's opposite corner, extending the sequence of movement. The foyer itself is a glassy bay that embraces the courtyard and in the evening creates a glowing pavilion of light along the street.

The auditorium, which seats 250, is filled with filtered clerestory light by large openings which recall the Arts and Crafts tradition of the region's architectural heritage. The central aisle of the auditorium runs on the diagonal, increasing the sense of spaciousness. The Sunday School building, across the courtyard from the auditorium, has a nursery and a flexible area that can be used for large gatherings, whilst at the same time offering privacy to smaller groups. Ancillary meeting rooms and offices complete the enclosure of the courtyard on three sides while, on the fourth, broad steps and a ramp open out to the street.

A small site and limited budget have not hindered the creation of a tranquil, memorable church that is responsive to its place, its tradition, and its congregation.

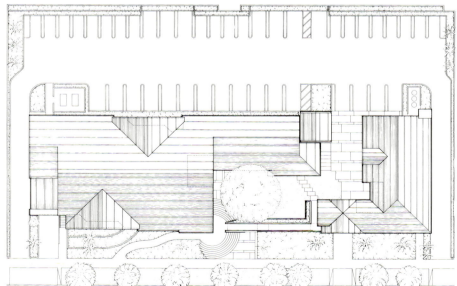

ABOVE: West elevation; BELOW: Roof plan

BART PRINCE

PAVILION FOR JAPANESE ART
Beverly Hills

The Pavilion for Japanese Art at the Los Angeles County Museum of Art opened to the public in September 1988. It was known during construction as the Shin'en'Kan Collection Gallery, or the Shin'en'Kan Pavilion. The schematic design that this building was based on was worked out by Bruce Goff for Joe Price for a site in Oklahoma, although it was always considered a possibility that the building might be built elsewhere. Prince and Goff had planned to associate as architects to carry out the project and worked together on it in the months prior to the death of Bruce Goff in 1982.

The completed building is a separate structure or pavilion connected by raised walkways to the existing museum buildings. It rests on a poured-concrete mat foundation which sits above the water table of the adjacent tar pit, distributing the loads in an earthquake. It was necessary to have an elaborate methane gas venting and detection system beneath this mat to eliminate the build-up of gasses which seep up from the tar deposits below. The mat supports the perimeter masonry and poured-concrete walls as well as the six large column masts which reach up through the roof to carry the curved steel box beams from which the roofs are suspended by cables.

Suspended roofs eliminate the need for perimeter structural supports around the gallery spaces. The walls are hence able to become non-load-bearing translucent panels which allow the light to filter into the building in much the same way as it does through a *shoji* screen wall in Japan. The main east gallery is one large space with ramps leading from one level viewing area to another. On each of these levels are two large *tokonomas* where the artworks are displayed. The viewing areas are separated from the *tokonomas* by an open space with a pool beneath. This keeps the viewer a safe distance away from the art, thus eliminating the need for the usual glass protection which creates reflection. The large west gallery has similar translucent walls but is a single level space, allowing for changing exhibits and large sculptures. Below this space is another smaller gallery and the entrance lobby and bookshop. It was necessary to add an entire floor below the main entry level to house the large mechanical rooms and restrooms. It is on this level that the non-public storage vault, scholars' study room and library are located with light entering around the perimeter from above, through the same translucent panels as those used throughout the building. In the original design when the building was smaller and more like a private museum, these spaces were located where the large west gallery is now. Built as part of an existing museum complex it was desirable to have additional public exhibition space and necessary to have elaborate mechanical, electrical, security and back-up systems which required a large amount of space. Hence, the need for this ground level floor.

At the time of Goff's death the scheme was defined at small scale on three sheets of drawings. These consisted of two floor plans and one elevation drawing. The completed building has integrated the spatial and architectural idea of those original drawings in harmony with the requirements of the building codes, mechanical, electrical and security systems without compromise and can be recognised as such. The *art* was the client and every important decision was based on what would be best for it. By the same token, the building is not complete without the art which becomes an integral part of the whole design.

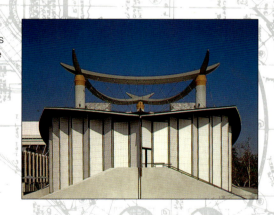

BACKGROUND: *Third level floor plan*

LOS ANGELES AS IT IS

BELOW: Longitudinal section

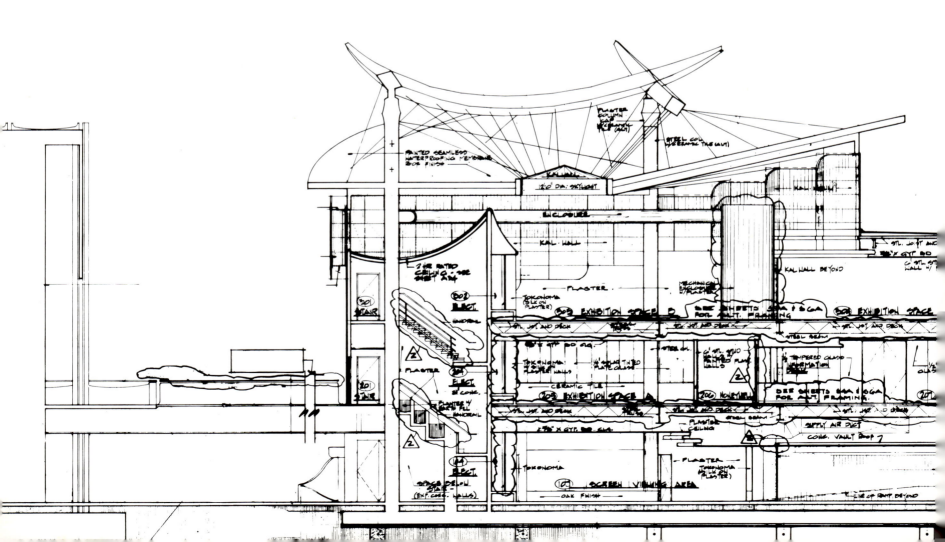

CULTURAL CENTRES

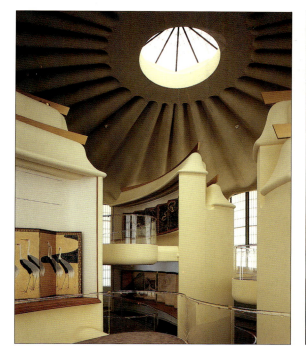

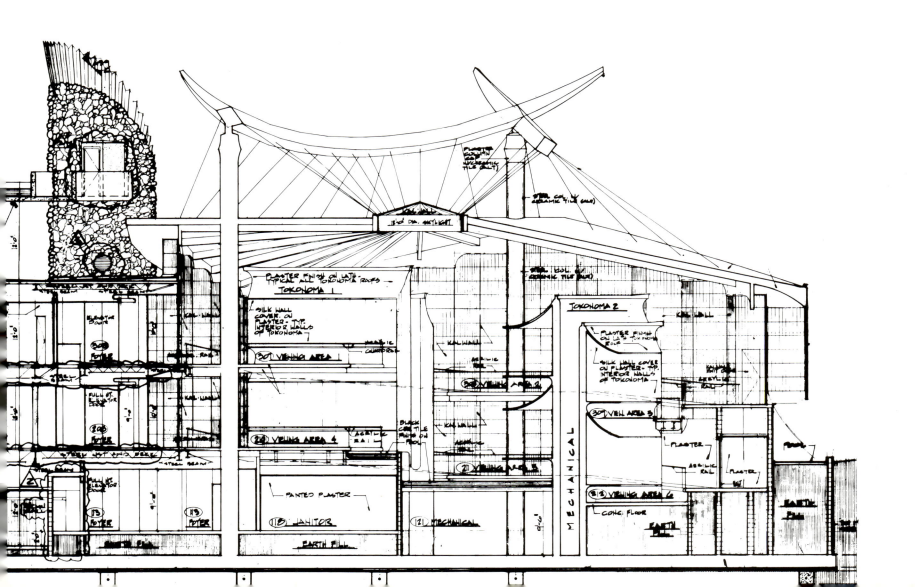

FIELDS & DEVEREAUX
THE EL CAPITAN THEATER
Hollywood

This project represents the restoration and transformation of 'a past its prime' historic stagehouse into a financially viable and visually energetic motion picture showcase. The collaboration of Pacific Theaters Corporation with Fields & Devereaux as the architects and the design talents of Buena Vista Productions, a division of Walt Disney Studios, resulted in a multi-award-winning project. The auditorium and lobby, which over the years have received many partial remodellings, were transformed to their original 1926 glory.

After removing layers of ageing false walls, the gilded decorative tracery of the original proscenium fan arch was fully restored and lighted dramatically. The main floor of the auditorium seats 650 people and the balcony seats 440. The opera boxes, long ago destroyed, have been rebuilt. The main lobby features newly restored finishes and a renovated snack bar, with the redressed promenade for the balcony functions as a second lobby. The wood-panelled tudor lounge was restored and is now used for special première gatherings.

The building's historic entry was also restored to its original Chiagueresque ornate-style and a new box office was built in the manner of the ornate decoration. Replacing the 1960s metal front, a new marquee canopy in the style of the 1926 original heralds the cinema's original name, 'The El Capitan Theater' with the show titles. In addition, the heating and air conditioning systems were brought up to date, along with the electrical, lighting and fire sprinkler systems. The project was completed in June 1991.

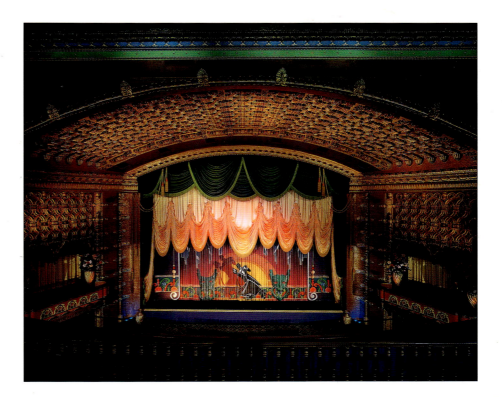

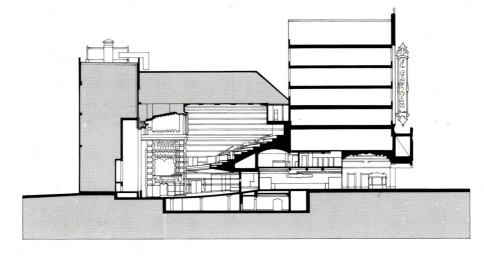

Section

CULTURAL CENTRES

BARTON PHELPS
CORINNE A SEEDS UNIVERSITY ELEMENTARY SCHOOL
Westwood

The Elementary School of Education at UCLA was founded over a hundred years ago and is best known for its early adoption of the social studies-based instruction methods promoted by John Dewey.

The programme for new facilities was developed as part of the dramatic reconfiguration of the North Eastern UCLA campus. The UES Relocation replaces classrooms, research areas and playgrounds (by Neutra and Alexander, 1958) lost to a new graduate school. A two-storey, curving composition which follows the contours of the bank in which it is set, derives its form from a three-part classroom module articulated by natural light at joints between the three volumes.

Using the same floor area as the building it replaced, the concrete-block classroom module provides new options for spatial variety and flexible use. The 'small room' at the centre of each module differs from adjacent rooms in volume, daylighting and finishes, providing an intimate area for music, reading, or computer use by small groups. Circumstantial elements at the lower level – patios, canopies, stairs and ramps – soften the formal geometry.

Sunlight was carefully accommodated as the *spirit* of the building, differentiating the upper and lower rooms through the course of a day or season, animating the structural frame and materials, and loosening the overall form of the building to allow the square rooms to 'move' around the curving bank of their prehistoric riverbed site.

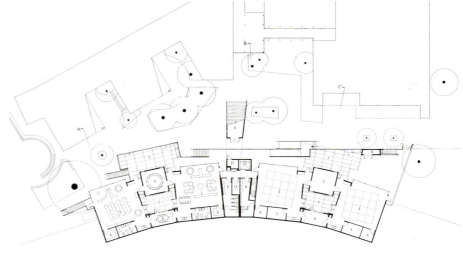

ABOVE: West elevation; BELOW: Lower level plan

157

LOS ANGELES AS IT IS

WED ENTERPRISES
DISNEYLAND
Anaheim

Disneyland is located approximately twenty-seven miles south-east of the Los Angeles Civic Centre. The magic lands and public areas occupy eighty-five acres of land, with guest parking for 15,167 vehicles on another one hundred acres.

The magic of Disneyland comes to life in eight 'themed' lands: Adventureland, with its exotic regions of Asia, Africa and the South Pacific; Critter Country, a down-home, backwoods setting for 'Splash Mountain'; Fantasyland, a happy kingdom of storybook enchantment where one enters through the Sleeping Beauty Castle and confronts the infamous characters from Cinderella and Pinocchio to Alice in Wonderland; Frontierland, which is entered through the swinging doors of a Western saloon, where an exciting realm of pioneers transport us back to the heritage of the Old West; Main Street USA, a composite of small-town America, *c*1900, with shops with wooden floors and glass display cases at precisely the right height for children's noses; New Orleans Square, home to ghosts, pirates and quaint shops where Dixieland music is played daily; Tomorrowland, a fantasy world of the future with trips to Mars and a $20 million high-speed journey to the stars with a NASA simulated entrance – a veritable panorama on the move.

Finally there is Mickey's Toontown, a three-dimensional cartoon world, 'hometown' to Mickey Mouse and the rest of the cartoon characters. Everything is exaggerated in the Toontown – as in all of Disneyland – to convey the cartoonish elements. Straight lines or conventional architecture cannot be found here.

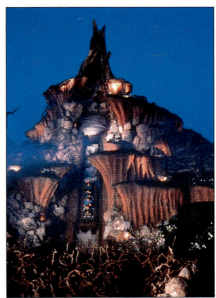

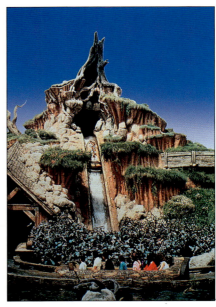

CULTURAL CENTRES

161

SKIDMORE OWINGS & MERRILL
THE GAS COMPANY TOWER
Downtown

The sleek Gas Company Tower pierces the Downtown Los Angeles skyline. Sheathed in blue/grey granite, the 52-storey tower is the second office building in the Maguire Thomas Partners' library redevelopment plan. The building is topped with an elliptical grey/blue dome identifying the joint venture partner and primary tenant, The Gas Company.

Tenants and visitors are welcomed into one of the most impressive lobbies in the city, lined with restaurants and shops. The concourse level features polished grey granite juxtaposed with aluminium panels and stainless steel pillars, evoking an elegant and contemporary ambience. A blue flame chandelier, The Gas Company logo, is the focal point for the Grand Avenue rotunda.

A spectacular 100-foot abstract mural by the artist Frank Stella, commissioned by Maguire Thomas Partners and painted on a co-operative neighbouring building, is an innovative addition to Downtown Los Angeles' public art. It also has the added advantage of creating outstanding 'views' for the first ten floors of tower.

With the library redevelopment plan, Maguire Thomas Partners launched a Traffic Management Programme that is now the standard for the city. The firm built a large, secure parking structure outside the central core, adjacent to freeways that bisect Downtown. Commuters simply board one of Maguire Thomas Partners' comfortable shuttles for a quick ride to Downtown. In the afternoon, a sophisticated traffic control information system in the garage lobby alerts commuters to traffic delays and pinpoints the quickest routes home.

ABOVE: Axonometric of lobby; BELOW: Planometric

MIXED USE DEVELOPMENT

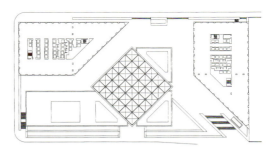

SKIDMORE OWINGS & MERRILL
WELLS FARGO CENTER
Downtown

A striking profile atop Los Angeles' Bunker Hill, Wells Fargo Center is one of the most successful business complexes in the city. The 54- and 45-storey trapezoid towers, clad in polished Finnish granite, serve as the Southern California headquarters for the Wells Fargo Bank and IBM, both partners in the development headed by Maguire Thomas Partners.

The towers are joined at ground level by The Court at Wells Fargo Center, a three-storey atrium housing a stunning sculpture collection by contemporary masters in an elegant garden setting. The shops and restaurants at The Court were carefully selected to meet the business and personal needs of the tenants and their employees. From early morning until after hours, the court is alive with Downtown socialising, dining and shopping.

From valet parking by uniformed attendants to around-the-clock polishing of brass appointments, every detail at Wells Fargo Center is carefully attended to. Tenant service is a top priority with requests monitored by computer and handled by well-trained staff.

Wells Fargo Center is a testament to Maguire Thomas Partners' method of conducting business. The initial investment in planning and design, materials, public spaces and state-of-the-art systems has been rewarded. The project was fully leased when completed in 1985, attracting leading international and national firms. Today, it continues to be one of the city's pre-eminent business locations.

ABOVE: *Plan at gallery roof level; Ground floor plan*

167

MIXED USE DEVELOPMENT

PEI COBB FREED
FIRST INTERSTATE BANK WORLD CENTER
Downtown

The most challenging project undertaken by the developers, Maguire Thomas Partners, is the Los Angeles Central Library redevelopment plan, which requires fifteen years for completion.

Downtown's architectural icon and the cornerstone of the central business district, the historical Central Library was outdated, overcrowded and had fallen into serious disrepair. City leaders considered demolishing it and replacing it with two office towers. Maguire Thomas Partners, determined to save this landmark Bertram Goodhue building, joined ARCO to commission an extensive study by national experts of how to preserve the library.

The former continued to spearhead the project by developing two office towers which are providing $125 million, the bulk of the financing required for the library's restoration and expansion. The first of these two buildings, the 73-storey First Interstate Bank World Center, is the tallest building in the west. The distinctive crown-shaped tower is the national headquarters of Pacific Enterprises Inc, the developer's joint venture partner.

The Bunker Hill Steps, the city's most exciting public space, descends four storeys along the base of the tower. Reminiscent of the Spanish Steps in Rome, the majestic staircase provides a vitally needed urban planning link in Downtown, joining the Bunker Hill financial district to the traditional central business district below.

Another important public space included in the plan is the restoration for the Library West lawn to its original gardens, as designed by Goodhue.

ABOVE: Downtown redevelopment masterplan

169

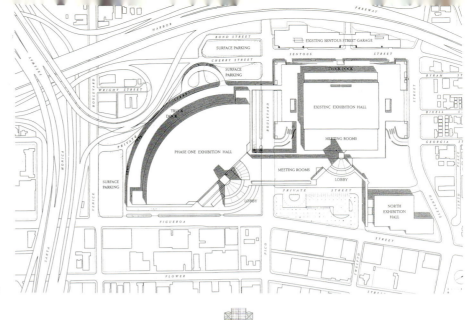

PEI COBB FREED
LA CONVENTION CENTER
Downtown

Located at one of the busiest freeway intersections in Los Angeles, this 2.5-million-square-foot expansion is ranked among the top ten convention centres in the United States. It provides a 350,000 square-foot space for reception and registration facilities, an exhibition hall, a ballroom, administration offices and an executive conference room. The expansion also provides extensive new parking spaces and loading docks, a private road system for shuttle buses and taxis, food courts and numerous other amenities.

The major challenge confronted in this project was the positioning of the new exhibition hall on the same level, but across the street from, the existing facility. The new hall was designed with a curved outer wall which responds to high-speed freeway traffic, and glazed public spaces on the opposite side which weave an essential relationship between the building and the surrounding community. Two glazed entry pavilions, one inserted in front of the original structure, serve as gateways to both LACC and Downtown. Physical connection between the old and new exhibition halls is achieved by a meeting room bridge over Pico Boulevard, a major organising element that facilitates the movement of people, equipment and vehicles through the entire complex.

The expansion has enriched LACC with a major public plaza and a unique image responsive to the climate, the liveliness, the automobiles and freeways – to those things that are uniquely Los Angeles – so that the convention centre evolves directly out of the city and helps to define it in the public realm.

ABOVE: Site plan; BELOW: Section

FRANK GEHRY
EDGEMAR DEVELOPMENT
Santa Monica

The project, an art museum and commercial development on two levels, with both on-grade and subterranean parking, occupies the site of a former dairy. It consists of several structures, each with a distinct architectural character. Some of the structures face Main Street and others face an internal courtyard.

A major design issue was to maintain the small-scale character of the existing surroundings, a commercial zone of primarily small shops and restaurants. The street and adjoining sidewalks are heavily travelled by day and night. For this reason, parking is screened and the existing scale is maintained by lining the 250-foot-wide street frontage with five small, visually separate structures relating to the scale of the existing shops. The three-tower elements are positioned to enhance views and draw potential customers into the centre courtyard. The slender proportion and open character of these higher elements interject minimally into views of the ocean from the hillside residences behind the project.

Along Main Street, the central element of the complex is a wall fragment of the former dairy, now a shop. Previously the facade was plaster but the original fragment collapsed during construction so it was rebuilt sheathed in copper and green glazed tile. Also new is an openwork tower above. Next to the tower, clad in galvanised metal, is a curved shape containing shops and a terrace above for the second level office block, surfaced in natural grey stucco. Two other towers, a greenhouse structure, and the elevator lead the eye back into the court.

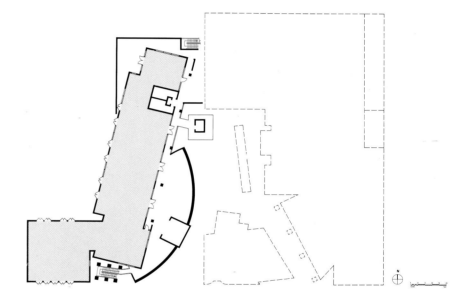

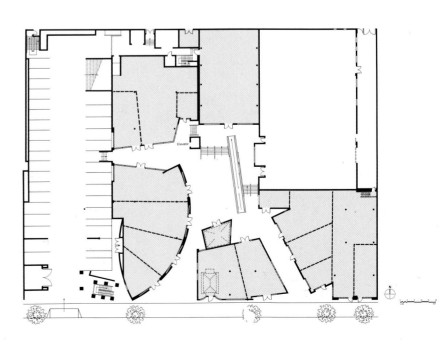

ABOVE: Office level; BELOW: Main Street retail level

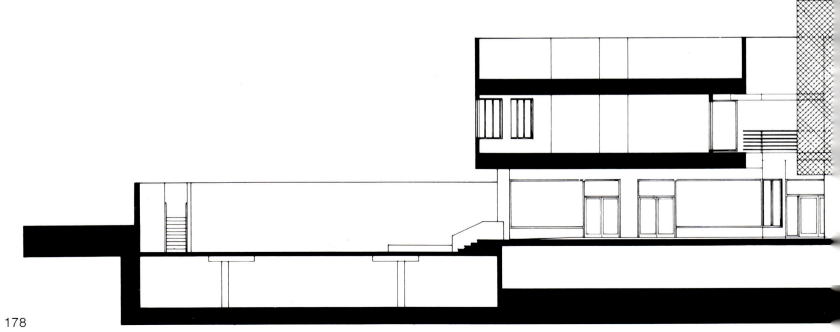

MIXED USE DEVELOPMENT

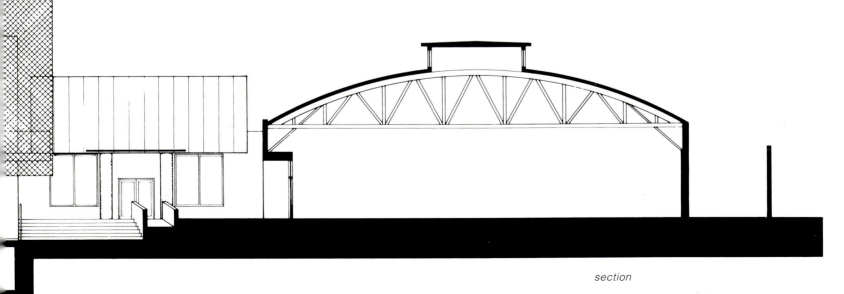

section

MOORE RUBLE YUDELL
PLAZA LAS FUENTES
Pasadena

Plaza Las Fuentes, in the heart of Pasadena's historic district includes new office space, retail space, hotel and conference facilities, and public gardens, designed and scaled carefully to reinforce the adjacent City Hall as a civic landmark and a focus of urban activity.

The configuration of the project seeks to fulfil the original city master plan, which set the City Hall as a civic jewel in the centre of a grand public garden. View corridors are carefully maintained, linking parts of the projects, especially its public gardens, to the City Hall. Major uses address the City Hall and its civic neighbours, and buildings respect the existing street grid. A series of courts ties the life of this street pattern to the attractions of a new retail promenade and related gardens.

This promenade, a pedestrian street, stretches through the project, linking a series of courts. The heart of this sequence is a generous civic court located on axis with City Hall. It is a central stage for the life of the project and a major public gathering place for Pasadena, suitable for outdoor performance. At the north end of the *paseo* is a court giving access to a 360-room hotel and conference centre. The south end is anchored by office and restaurant uses.

The city required a connection to its tradition of Mediterranean architecture. The scale and design of the project take their cue from the adjacent City Hall. Arched arcades, deeply inset openings, stucco walls and tile roofs evoke the spirit of the region's architectural heritage in a refreshing manner, responding specifically to this particular site, context and time.

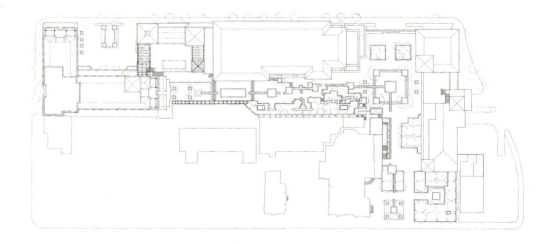

ABOVE: Los Robles Avenue elevation; BELOW: Roof plan

MIXED USE DEVELOPMENT

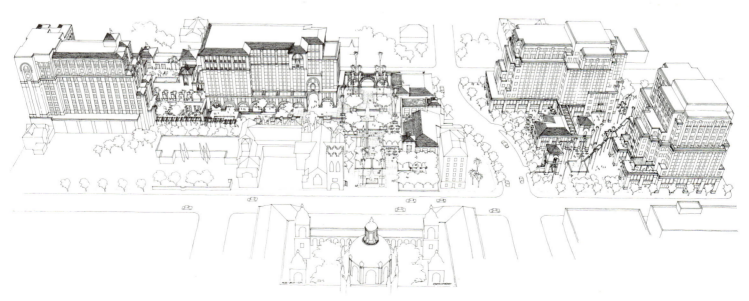

Aerial view

MIXED USE DEVELOPMENT

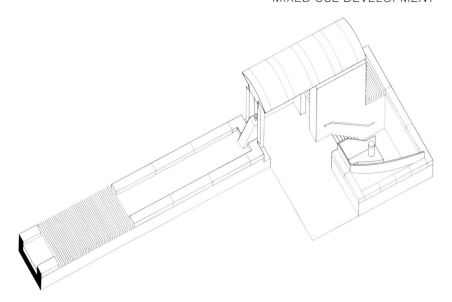

HODGETTS + FUNG
UCLA GATEWAY
Westwood

The recently completed UCLA Gateway masterplan in Westwood integrates the complex issues of identity, management, function and aesthetic, creating cohesion for a heavily-trafficked public space in the context of existing and new site relationships and user issues. The UCLA Gateway incorporates a waterscape environmental installation, which serves as both a metaphor for the complex and a critical connection between the myriad physical features of the campus.

The first completed phase of the Gateway masterplan coordinated the siting of four medical facilities. A broad lawn and a screen of trees emphasised the southern entrance by providing definition to the campus from Westwood Village. Behind the signature wall, a quiet courtyard framed with water leads to a line of lanterns symbolising the university motto, 'Let there be Light'. A contemporary palette of brick, precast concrete and sandblasted stainless steel suggests continuity with the original campus buildings.

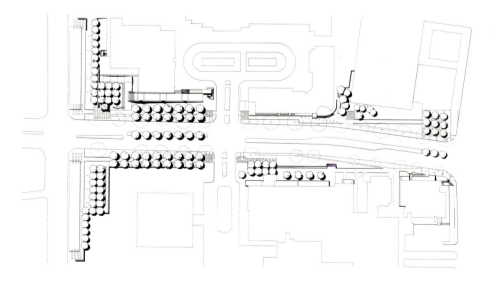

ABOVE: Axonometric of the water installation; BELOW: Site plan

THE JERDE PARTNERSHIP
UNIVERSAL CITYWALK
Citywalk

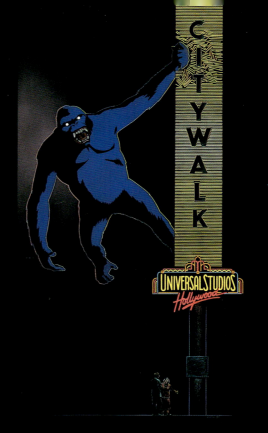

As phase one of the larger MCA/Universal City project, Citywalk, is a 1,500-foot-long strip covering a three-block area bordered by two freeways, located at the critical hinge of the basin and the valley. It is a central link to the scattered parts of the cast movie studio complex. It is designed to distil the ephemeral quality of Los Angeles street life as it allows ongoing elaboration and change. Citywalk is built up of layers of signs, art and diverse visual information. Its tight pedestrian scale and open ambience encourage movement through shops and venues, both day and night.

Contained within the site is a massive studio complex for making films and music, all the headquarter buildings for the administration and executive branch of the entertainment business. There is also the Universal Tour, giving an inside view of film making and the theme park with the largest theatre complex (a 2,500 seat public amphitheatre) in North America.

The MCA project appeals to a collection of special interest groups: the family, the tourist, the non-specific citizen. In the search for defining the nature of Los Angeles it has become clear that the metropolis is so vast that its edges are imperceptible. If one cannot perceive edges, one cannot connote place; without place there is no object of focus. Los Angeles, in fact, is revealed as a set of nested places, small centres drawing their energy and theme from the psyche of the citizens and the geography and topography of the place. Universal City is a micropolis, nested within the many micropoli of the City of Los Angeles.

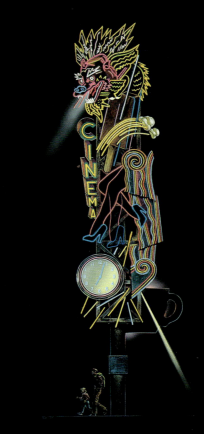

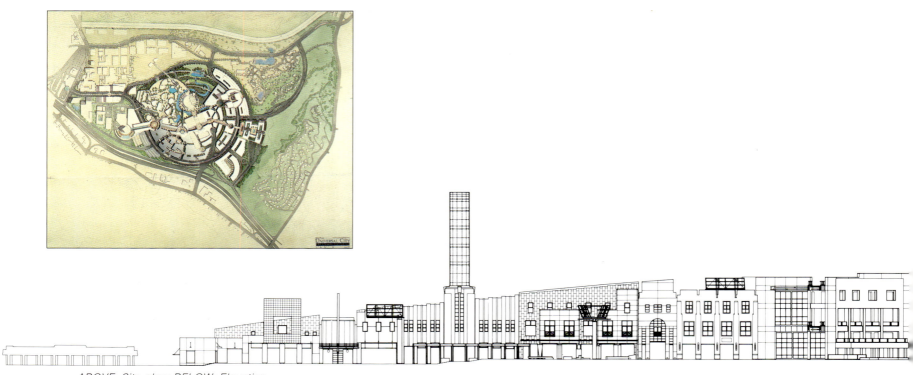

ABOVE: Site plan; BELOW: Elevation

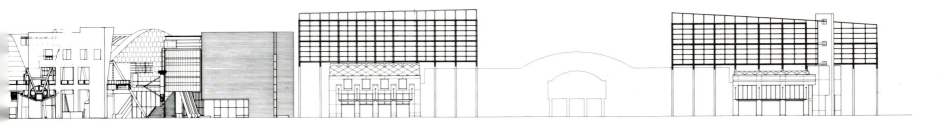

FRANK GEHRY
CHIAT/DAY TEMPORARY OFFICES
Venice

The Chiat/Day temporary offices are located in a complex of renovated tilt-up concrete warehouse buildings in Venice. The 42,000-square-foot main warehouse has 24-foot-high ceilings and is designed to accommodate the majority of the staff and their activities. Building 'A', 3,800 square feet, contains shipping and receiving and storage areas, while Building 'B' houses client reception and client conference rooms complete with audio/visual and kitchen facilities.

The scope of work was primarily interior. However, new skylights and storefront glazing at 'loading dock' doors introduce natural light into the windowless warehouse and the entire exterior has been repainted to distinguish it from its neighbours. The electrical power, data and communication cables are managed by a raised cable-tray supported by steel columns. The wood stud construction is sheathed with a variety of finish materials such as sheet metal, brilliantly painted drywall, MDO plywood, and 'finn-ply' plywood.

The main warehouse interior space is organised by a 'main street' axis running north/south, flanked by open-plan workstations and enclosed spaces. An enormous 54-foot-long 'fish' form is constructed with wooden ribs sheathed in galvanised sheet metal skin. It is the principal in-house conference room. A plywood 'battleship' with uplit canopies dominates and anchors the centre of the warehouse. The contrast in scale of these objects, coupled with the circulation arteries, suggests the experience of a village landscape built within the volume of the warehouse. The circulation become the objects which separate the office areas.

The main client conference room, a series of three interconnected building/objects contained within the existing concrete shed, is in Building 'B', which flanks the entry pavilion. The entry is sheathed in galvanised scales, the end pavilion is covered in dark reddish finn-ply, and the middle pavilion is sheathed in sheared cardboard blocks. This cardboard covers the entire interior giving it a very sculptural, quiet, warm ambience. A 'canoe' light fixture hangs over the green granite conference table which was designed for this space and shaped to reflect the boat floating above. A 'log' light floats alongside and illuminates the display walls. Built-in cardboard furniture forms an informal seating area behind the conference table and a glass fish lamp glows in the corner. On the opposite end wall, television screens and state-of-the-art audio/visual equipment is flush-mounted into the cardboard walls. Remotely operated skylights allow for control of natural light. At night especially, the building objects are read as a still-life composition from outside.

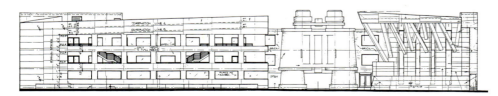

ABOVE: Preliminary sketch; BELOW: West elevation; OVERLEAF OPPOSITE: Upper roof plan

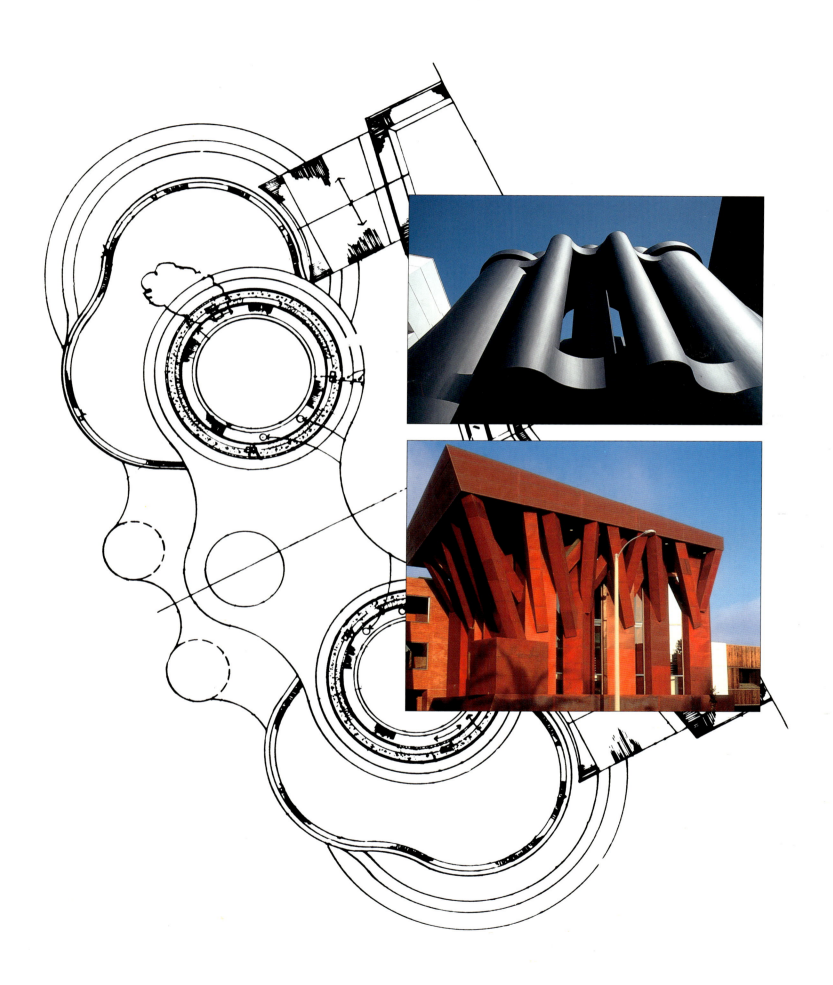

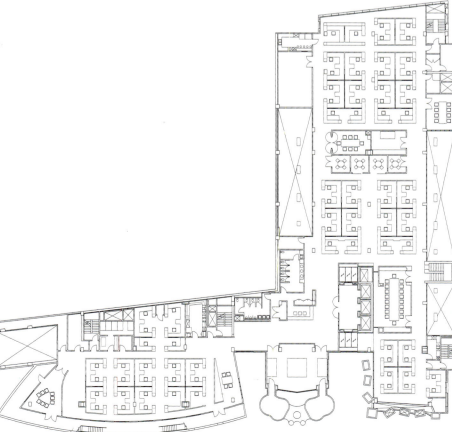

Ground floor plan

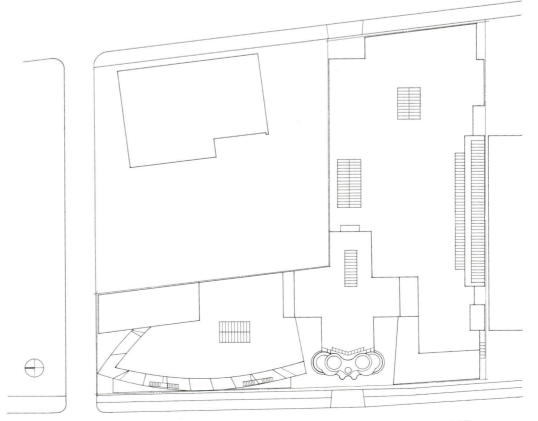

Roof plan

ERIC OWEN MOSS
INCE COMPLEX
Culver City

The Ince Complex is a group of four existing buildings: Paramount Laundry office building, Lindblade Tower, Gary Group office building and GEM, the largest being the Paramount Laundry office building, and consisting of approximately 60,000 square feet.

Individually, these four buildings represent renewal, remodelling, restoration, demolition and reconstitution. Together, they create a space, a Los Angeles quadrangle. Into this space fits a fifth building, the Ince Theatre for the performing arts and cinema.

The Ince Theatre is made up of three spheres. The theatre itself is in the south part of the building, the seating in the north. A public entry stair leads underneath the seating area and then up into it. It can be accessed both from the north directly from the car park, or from the south by way of a ramp. The possibility for a restaurant exists for the upper deck. There is also a possible link via bridge to an office building to the north.

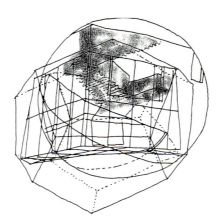

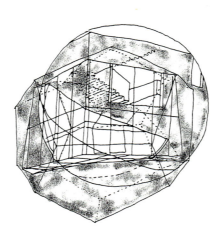
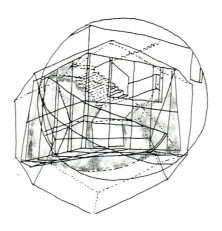

OPPOSITE: Gary Group office building; FROM ABOVE: Site plan; models of GEM; conceptual sketches

OFFICES

ERIC OWEN MOSS
GARY GROUP OFFICE BUILDING, INCE COMPLEX
Culver City

The Gary Group office building is the third piece of a four-building office complex involving both new construction and remodelling. The first two buildings, Paramount Laundry and Lindblade Tower are completed and occupied. The result has been a significant revitalisation of a deteriorating area in Culver City. The Gary Group is an advertising and promotion agency.

The building is conceived as a picturesque novel with a series of discontinuous adventures involving the same participants. The novel can be opened at any point and read either forwards or backwards.

The building has two entrances. The first is cut from an almost freestanding concrete block wall inclined to the leeward, resting on C-shaped steel ribs implanted in an adjoining wall. A clock is attached to the west end of the inclined wall, facing the car park. The second entrance, cut in a wall embellished with chains, wires, pipes, re-bar, block planters and flowers, confronts the car park. Inside, immediately south of the inclined wall, is a group of work stations arranged within a cruciform plan/gable section. At the centre of the cruci-gable is a pool, open to the sky, watered from above by steel shower-heads which drop the water through a marble chute into the pool.

Adjoining the cruci-gable area is a hall terminated by a private meditation room. South of the hall is a two-storey area that includes both private offices and open counters for graphic artists. The vaulted roof, supported by two bowstring trusses, is carefully interrupted by two enormous aluminium, glass and sheet-metal funnels that deposit natural light inside.

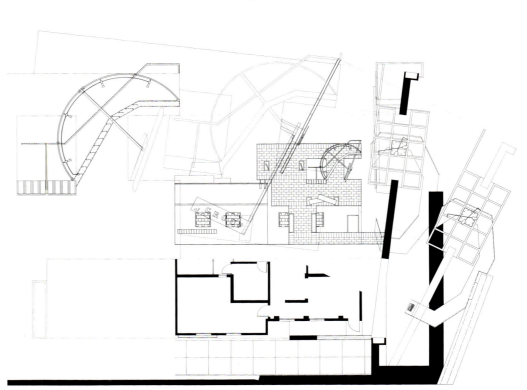

Composite scheme drawings

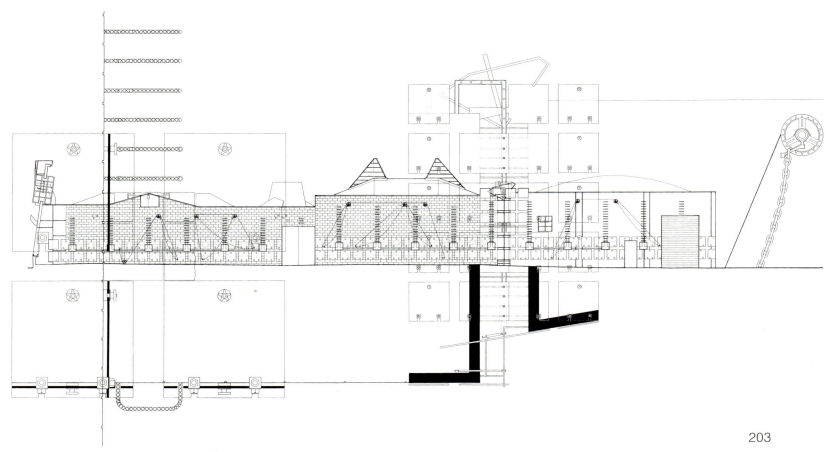

203

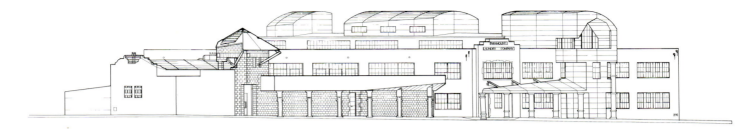

ERIC OWEN MOSS
PARAMOUNT LAUNDRY BUILDING, INCE COMPLEX
Culver City

An existing warehouse, built in 1940, with poured concrete walls and a wood truss supported roof is located in this Culver City neighbourhood of studio production facilities. Part of the Ince complex, the building is approached from the north, via the Santa Monica Freeway from which it can be clearly seen.

The lobby is capped with a simple vault, adjusted in plan towards the direction of freeway view and traffic flow. This plan adjustment generates a modified vault in section which is extended above the old roof, identifying the new components of the building below. This modified roof vault is positioned over the entrance lobby above a bridge and over a new rear exit stair. Where the vault is inserted, the existing roof sheathing is removed and the vault and supporting walls extend vertically above the original roof, visible from the floors below.

The new second floor projects into the central space and is supported by columns which also support the bridge. The new third floor consists of separate areas placed at opposite ends of the central volume which occurs just below the bottom chord of the existing wood trusses. The two third floors are then linked by a bridge, at the centre of which are two benches. The bridge is aligned with the new vaulted roof which brings natural light through new clerestory windows to the bridge from the north.

The building is a combination of wood, steel and reinforced concrete construction. The vault is covered with galvanised sheets of steel. The new columns supporting the entry canopy and the bridge are vitrified clay pipes filled with reinforced concrete.

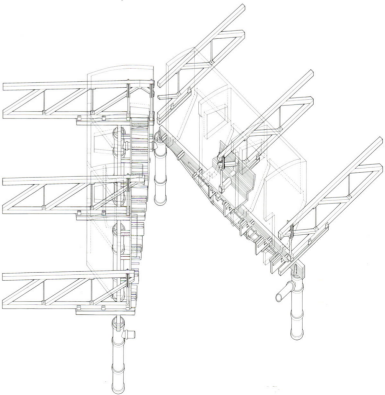

ABOVE: Elevation of Paramount Laundry and Lindblade Tower; BELOW: Part axonometric showing structure

ERIC OWEN MOSS
LINDBLADE TOWER, INCE COMPLEX
Culver City

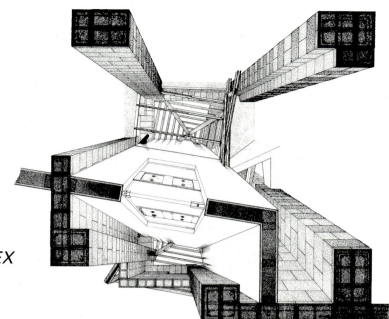

A dilapidated warehouse, originally built in the early 1940s in Culver City, has been remodelled. The new facility provides a flexible work-space for a local graphics company. The exterior wall of an adjoining office was also remodelled.

Windows are minimised. Two skylights and a courtyard with roll-up glass door provide natural light and air.

The company intends to continuously modify the use of the interior as required by new projects. The high, truss-supported roof at the north end contains movable tables for layouts. Conference tables can also be arranged for open meetings and reviews of work in progress. The remainder of the space utilises desks, tables, benches, shelves – movable work stations of various kinds. Power, telephone and computer terminals are located at close intervals in walls and floors. Office furnishings can be removed and tables arranged for catered meals. De-mountable partitions could be installed if needed. Two bathrooms are provided. At the south end is a large roll-up door enclosing a storage area the width of the space.

The tower provides a formal entry. A secondary service entrance is provided in the west wall behind the clay column colonnade. The tower also signals the building's presence to a primary commercial street and to Santa Monica freeway to the north. A portion of the tower roof is covered; a portion of the roof is open to a skylight below, positioned over the entry door.

A split one-face red concrete block was used to construct the tower and a portion of the street wall. The remaining walls are wood studs covered with a steel trowelled cement plaster finish both inside and outside. Original wood trusses supporting the north end roof were repaired and re-used. The roof of this area is a modified standing seam, galvanised steel sheet. A portion of the tower roof is open to a glass skylight occurring inside the tower at the section line of the steel panelled roof. Where the tower roof opens to the skylight below, wood roof beams are covered with galvanised steel. Where the tower roof is closed, the roof is a factory-painted white steel. A line of vitrified clay covered reinforced concrete columns fronts the main street.

The exterior wall of the adjacent office space is of 24 x 4-foot sheets of a bonded epoxy and wood particles (strand board), covered with a clear grey sealer. The two spaces share a common interior wall, also in strand board. The new bathroom space with HVAC units above is galvanised steel sheets over wood studs.

The HVAC system is composed of two gas-fired high efficiency furnaces, two high efficiency condensers and two electronically programmable thermostats with remote sensors for energy conservation.

This building provides conservation of existing building scale and type, modified for both a new external identity and a flexible, diverse interior for a new user.

ABOVE: Worm's-eye view of tower

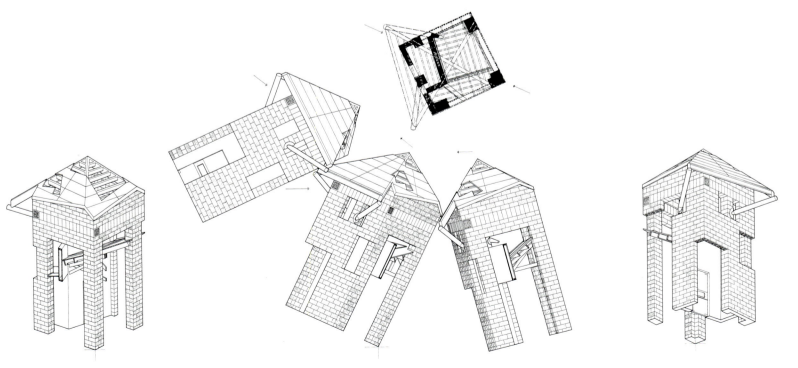

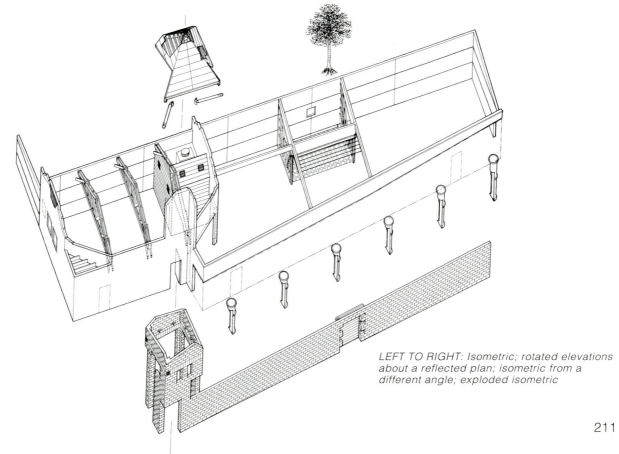

LEFT TO RIGHT: Isometric; rotated elevations about a reflected plan; isometric from a different angle; exploded isometric

ERIC OWEN MOSS
8522 NATIONAL BOULEVARD OFFICE BUILDING
Culver City

On National Boulevard, a main thoroughfare in Culver City, five warehouses adjoin one another to form a single building. The first building was constructed in the 1920s and the others followed during the 1930s and 40s. All were long span spaces with clerestory windows facing either east or north.

There was never any design attempt to co-ordinate an earlier building with a later one. Buildings were simply added as additional square footage was required. By 1986, the building – used as a plastics factory – was filled with partitions, hung ceilings, ducts, sprinkler lines and rooms of every size. The exterior was dilapidated.

The owner decided to have the building re-constituted for commercial use. A steel canopy was stretched across the street elevation, propped on struts extended from the existing wall. An elliptical entry court was cut into the original building, exposing a piece of truss structure to the street. A pedestrian entry ramp from the street leads into the court, then through the entry door to a causeway organised around an existing column system. The causeway leads to a middle lobby, newly skylit, with a perimeter wall of block and plaster, related in plan form to the entry ellipse. Turning south, there is a second causeway which leads to a large meeting room. A third ellipse has been built into an existing room with walls of concrete block. The original block is sometimes painted, sometimes sandblasted.

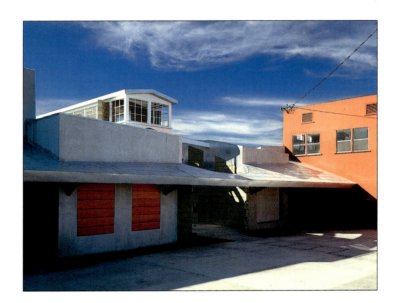

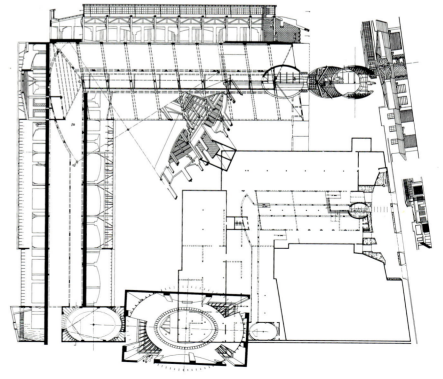

Composite scheme drawing

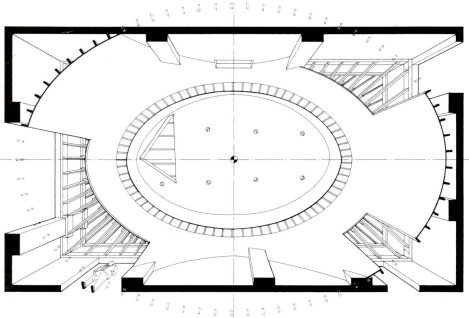

Worm's-eye view of meeting hall

214

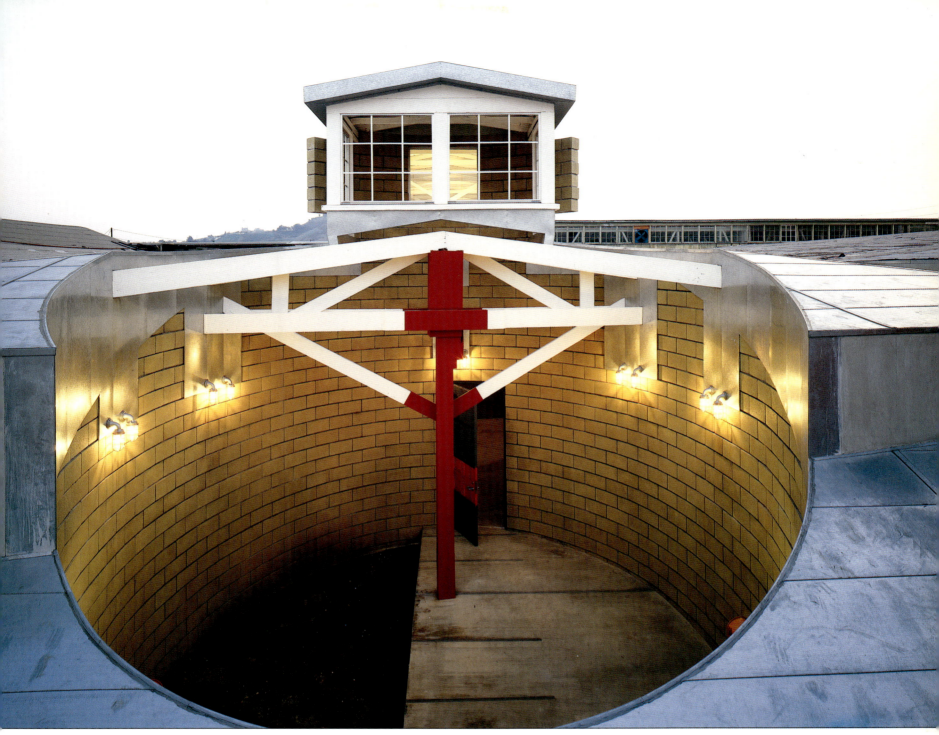
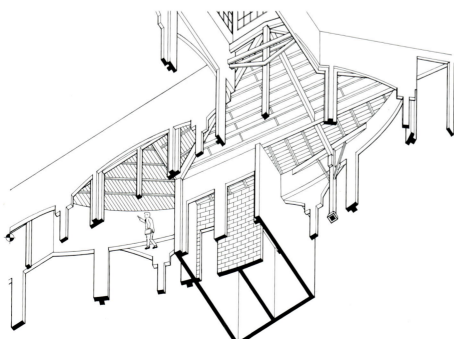

Axonometric of circulation space and lift lobby

MORPHOSIS
SALICK HEALTHCARE OFFICE BUILDING
Beverly Hills

The challenge of creating a public presence through the formal and pragmatic transfiguration of an existing building became the departure point for the design. Onto a generic, prototypically Los Angeles urban site came the commission to develop a possibly even more prosaic structure. The initial instinct was to challenge the generic by creating a more differentiated entity to replace it.

The strategy concentrated on identifying and resolving a series of existing formal conditions, including an emphasis on the expression of the corner site, an engagement of the awkwardly-placed mechanical penthouse volume and a discrimination of the facades. In place of the undifferentiated box of horizontal slabs which existed prior to intervention, a series of opaque and transparent vertically-oriented components was positioned, essentially functioning to divide the formerly monolithic structure into two separate buildings. Each facade was addressed to minimise or maximise solar heat gain, producing extremes of opacity on the south and west, in contrast to the transparency of the east and north. The east facade reveals the irregular nature of the existing steel frame which is used as a datum for the new envelope. Previously undifferentiated aspects, including the segments of entry, the corner condition, the roof boundary and day/night lighting conditions were seen as opportunities to express the integration of discrete parts and as analogous to, and mimetic of, patterns of accretional urban growth.

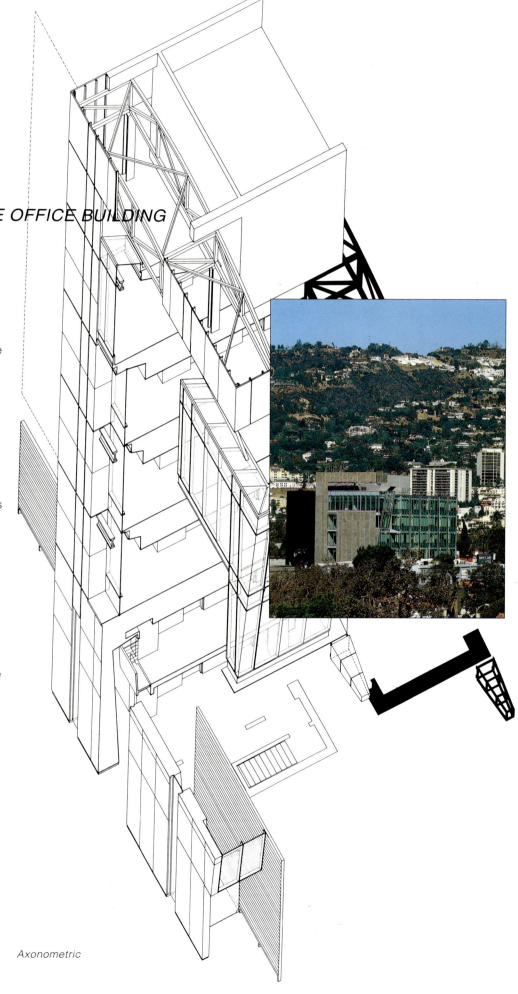

Axonometric

LOS ANGELES AS IT IS

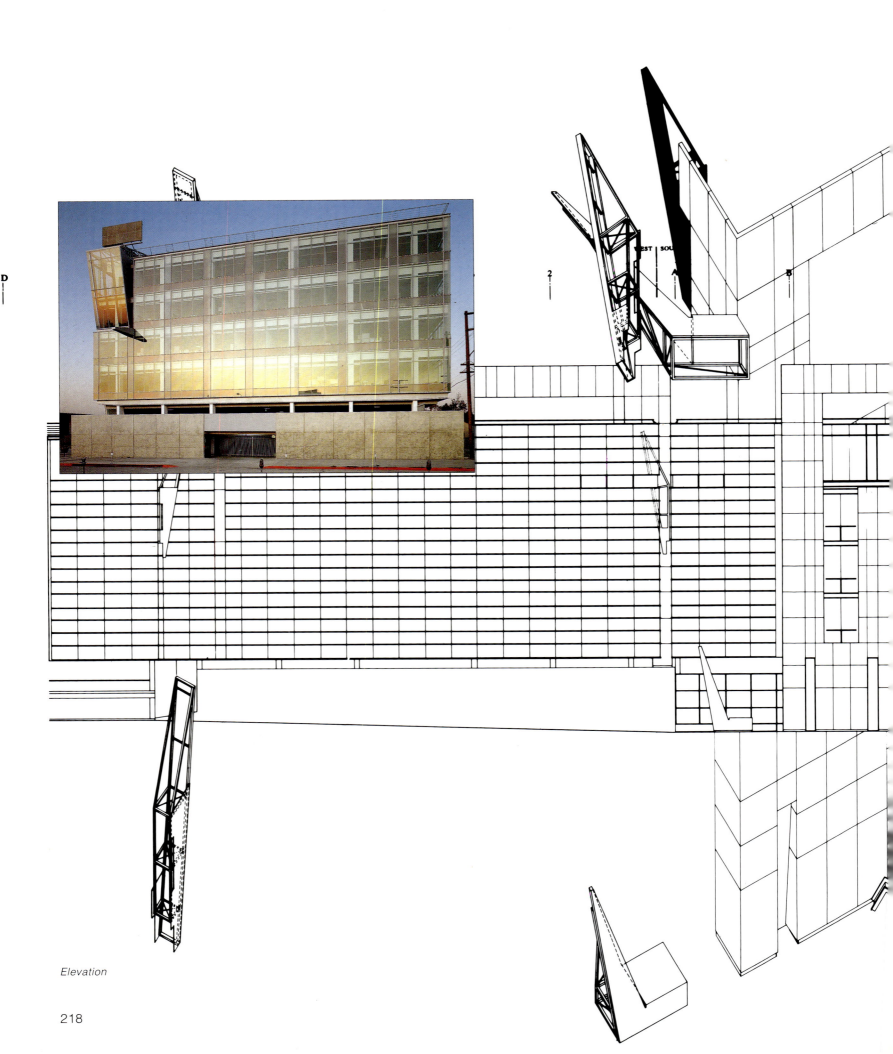

Elevation

218

OFFICES

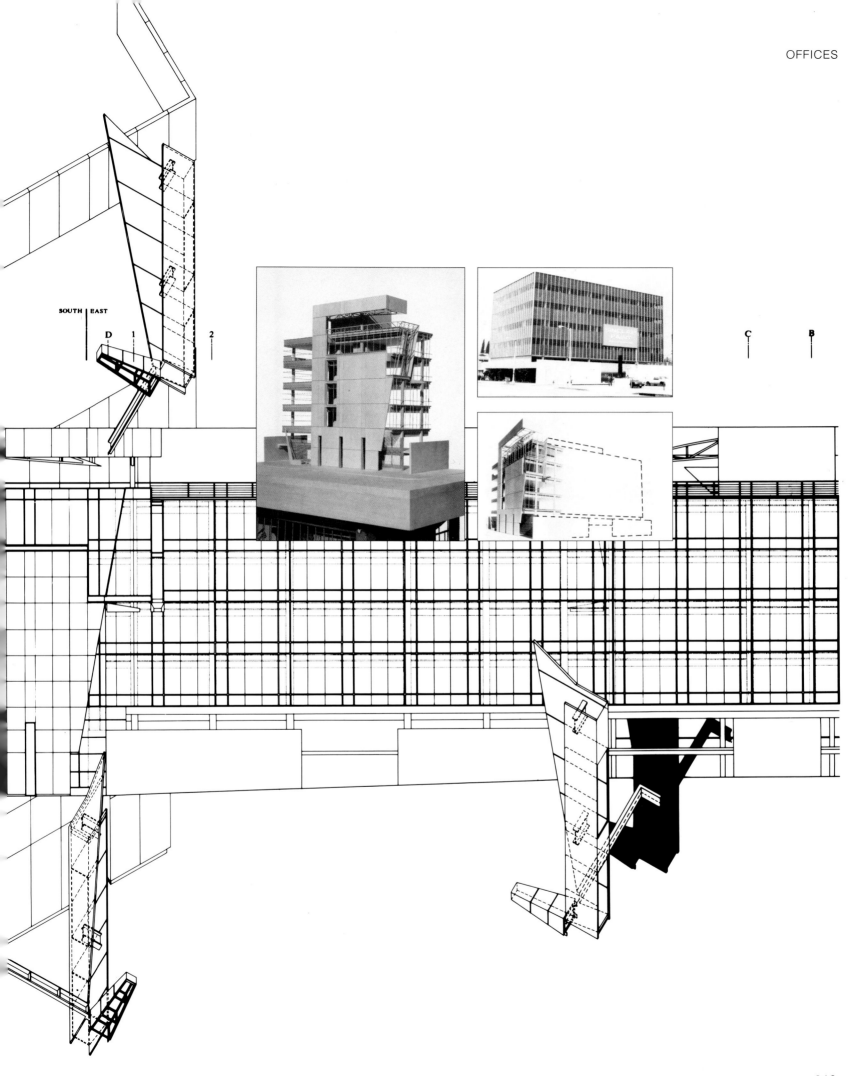

LOS ANGELES AS IT IS

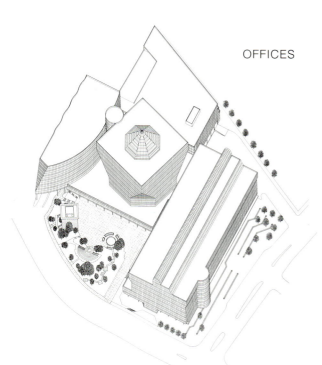

CESAR PELLI
PACIFIC DESIGN CENTER AND EXPANSION
West Hollywood

Affectionately referred to as the Blue Whale, Phase I of the Pacific Design Center is located in the heart of the City's well-established trade centre, providing showroom space to serve the needs of professional interior designers, specifiers, decorators, architects and dealers involved in contract and residential design.

From the second to sixth levels, a permanent array of showrooms display furniture, decorator items, gifts and accessories. The corridors on each floor contain glass-walled kiosks for additional show space. The Galleria mall areas on the fifth and sixth floors are covered by a skylit barrel vault which extends the full length of the building.

The Center was conceived as a single, free-standing structure. The decision to expand it raised the complex issue of how to add to a distinctive landmark. Due to the isolated form of the original building, both Phase II and III additions were designed as a series of oversized fragments to form a collection of pieces.

Each addition has a unique shape and colour, although materials, scale and detailing correspond to the original blue structure. Phase II, the Green Building expansion, is clad in green spandrel glass and includes a showroom area, car park, conference centre, public plaza and an outdoor amphitheatre. It is connected to the original building at the terrace and first floor levels. Phase III is clad in red and includes additional showroom space and a car park. Each phase is organised as a series of stacked two-level atria.

ABOVE: Axonometric; BELOW: Section (Phases I, II and III)

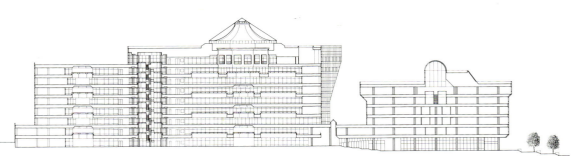

LOS ANGELES AS IT IS

OFFICES

223

HODGETTS + FUNG
CLICK MODEL MANAGEMENT
West Hollywood

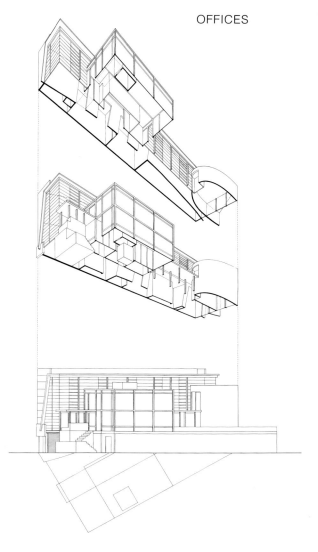

Hodgetts + Fung was chosen to design the Los Angeles offices for Click Model Management, a New York-based talent agency whose client roster features artists who are either in the film or modelling industry. Posing an intricate programme in a frenetic setting, the building was to be constructed on a very tight site within a compact block, crammed with buildings which varied in scale, use and appearance. In order to complement the eclectic, densely populated neighbourhood, the solution utilised a variety of exterior building materials including stucco, steel, concrete block, glass and wood. To address the split usage of the facility itself, a scheme was created that featured buildings within a building.

The grouping itself rests on a plinth which functions as a garage. Three volumes with contrasting shapes which rest on top of the ground floor parking form the *piano nobile*. These volumes are collectively enclosed by a simple rectangle composed of a glass curtain wall, and are connected to each other by a bridge-like structure. The first volume is a cube which contains the lobby, offices and an indoor/outdoor courtyard. The second is a parabolic conference space. A hull-like shape forms the solid service wall which contains the building's mechanical features as well as a kitchen, restrooms and other non-public spaces.

The bridge functions as a connection between the conference area and offices. It is an integrating element of the structure, piercing the interior spaces of these two volumes – creating the mezzanine in the conference parabola and the office floor in the cube. The bridge doubles as an outdoor terrace, maximising the use of adjacent outdoor 'rooms', ultimately increasing the functional area of the overall building significantly.

Finally, the glass rectangle which covers the individual volumes provides a practical and aesthetic connection between the distinct architectural elements.

FROM ABOVE RIGHT: Perspective diagram; section; street elevation; BELOW: Second floor plan

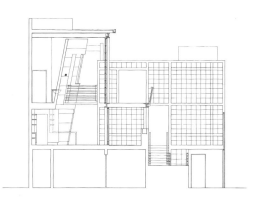

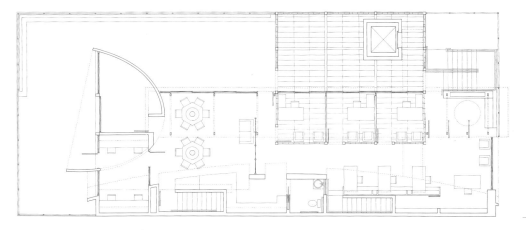

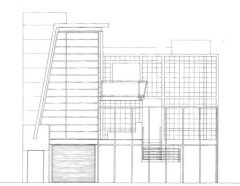

GWATHMEY SIEGEL
THE CAPITAL GROUP
West Los Angeles

This two-floor, 45,000 square-foot office for a pension management and investment firm responds to the client's egalitarian vision. The four corners of each floor are designated common spaces – conference rooms, cafeteria, library and board-meeting room – leaving four perimeter zones on each floor to be divided into equal-sized offices.

A two-storey entry and reception space is articulated by an open stairway to a glass-block bridge which is connected to circulation galleries filled with contemporary art. Natural light penetrates the galleries from interior clerestory windows in the office walls. Adjacent to the galleries are open workstations and another layer of file and support space.

The perimeter offices were designed for maximum efficiency and flexibility. An integrated cabinet and millwork system of wood panelling and translucent and transparent glass establishes the aesthetic of the entire space.

STEVEN EHRLICH
SONY MUSIC ENTERTAINMENT
Santa Monica

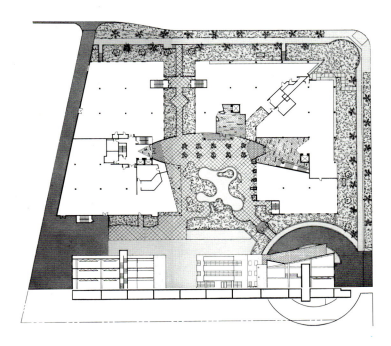

This 100,000-square-foot complex houses 200 employees of Sony Music's new West Coast headquarters in Santa Monica. The programme includes executive offices, a recording studio, performance space and indoor/outdoor dining areas. The structure is an orchestration of three buildings forming an interior court – a verdant waterscaped arboretum.

The public facade presents three distinctly shaped buildings, each housing the Epic, Columbia and Sony Music labels, unified by a consistent architectural language of sandstone cladding, horizontal fenestration, piloti, large panels of translucent green glass and horizontal metal awnings. The project is influenced by streamlined Modern architecture which flourished in Santa Monica in the 1930s.

The visual focus of the project is the 20th Street and Colorado Avenue corner, where a soaring triangular wedge counterpoints a carved stone curve. The contrast of opposite forms symbolises the meeting of East and West. The juxtaposition of the two-storey curved and three-storey acute-angled buildings resolves the street corner. The mass (at the street facade) of the Columbia and Epic buildings is fragmented into smaller elements by the shaping of the taut spandrel glass into the cleft stone.

Employees enter all three buildings by subterranean parking. Each building has its own elevator. Guests enter through the corporate elevator lobby. On special occasions guests and celebrities enter at the rotary drop-off through a sculptured gate which leads into the courtyard. Each lobby has its own unique coloured selections of stone flooring, wood panelling and burnished plaster.

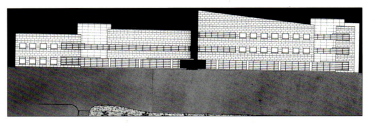

ABOVE: Site plan

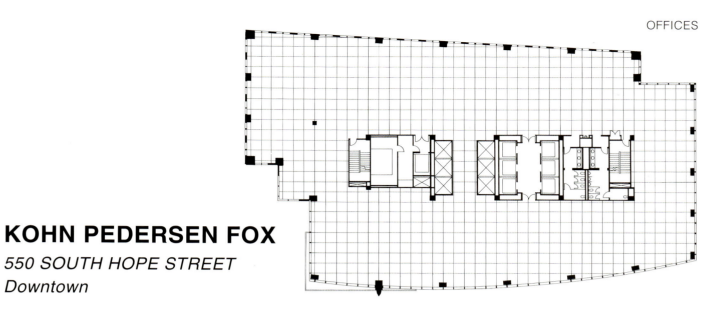

KOHN PEDERSEN FOX
550 SOUTH HOPE STREET
Downtown

This 27-storey office building is adjacent to the Los Angeles Public Library of 1926 and opposite the California Club of 1929. The building was designed to relate to this historical context through gestures of scale and the use of beige and red-orange granites. 550 South Hope is organised around a central slab of the same width as the California Club which allows the two buildings to be read as a pair that frames the tower of the library as the terminus of Hope Street. This reading is reinforced by a base element which defines the street wall and produces a relationship to the adjacent, smaller building. Retail shops and a two-storey lobby are located at ground level while a court garden located at the mezzanine level provides a pleasant dining atmosphere.

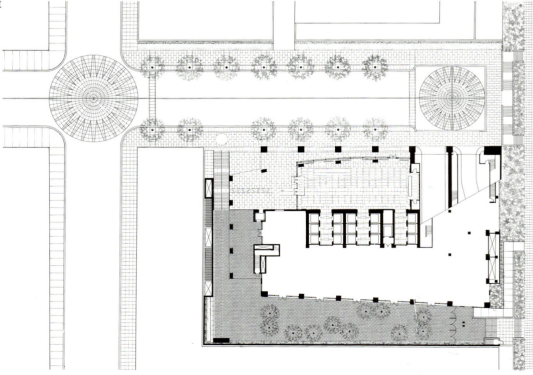

ABOVE: *Typical plan*; BELOW: *Site plan*

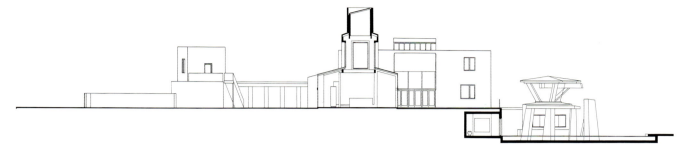

FRANK GEHRY
SCHNABEL RESIDENCE
Brentwood

Located on a quiet street in the Brentwood Hills, this village-like arrangement of forms is a direct response to the elaborate building programme and the desire to create a variety of outdoor spaces to extend the perception of the size of the lot. This strategy suggests that different programme elements can be represented as distinct objects. By varying both shape and surface, these objects have each been given a specific architectural character and are played against one another both spatially and sculpturally.

The focal point within the walled, two-level garden is a cruciform structure sheathed in lead-coated copper panels which houses the entry, living and dining rooms and a library. A central three-storey sky-lit space accentuates the openness of the structure, while the north arm of the crucifix is connected to a simple two-storey stucco volume which contains the kitchen, a two-storey family room and two bedrooms. The building is connected, by a copper-clad colonnade, to the garage at the front of the site and, via a partially underground stairway, to the master bedroom on the water below.

Three freestanding elements are placed in the upper garden: a sky-lit guest apartment crowned with a copper dome and flanked at the entrance by copper columns; a long blue-tiled lap pool raised partially above ground and a studio/bedroom with a sawtoothed roof.

Appearing to float in the shallow lake carved into the hillside one level below the rest of the site is the secluded master bedroom pavilion with its sculptural skylight and shade-giving copper-clad columns, creating a serene, light-filled retreat.

ABOVE: Elevation

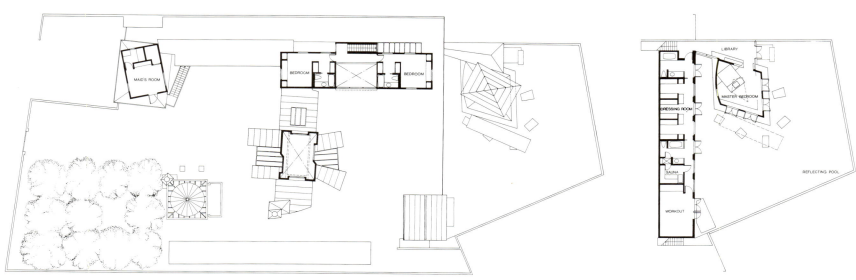

LEFT TO RIGHT: First floor plan; lower-ground floor plan; ground floor plan

FRANK GEHRY
GEHRY RESIDENCE
Santa Monica

The site is in a residential neighbourhood on a narrow lot that drops off sharply in the rear, allowing unobstructed views of the Santa Monica Mountains. Responding to the complex requirements of a family whose lifestyle is divided between the highly public and intensely private, the resultant architectural composition questions the distinction between the complete and the unfinished, the stationary and the static, and the idea of house as both refuge and confrontation.

The house is composed essentially of two separate parts, a 20 foot x 110 foot bar oriented to the street at the front of the house, and a 40-foot-square cube set at an angle to the bar. The cube is basically a single volume reserved for public gatherings. A skylight monitor tilts backwards as it perforates the roof of the cube, flooding the area below with natural light. The end wall of the adjacent building is pushed out to form a balcony but the internal volume of the bar remains undisturbed. The relatively narrow width of this building transfers the load entirely onto the exterior walls, allowing all interior surfaces to be placed according to functional and aesthetic considerations. A flexible interior system and a high degree of exclusion from the public spaces were required for this second structure, which houses the family's bedrooms and private quarters.

The house is primarily stucco sheathed. Window openings are placed independently of the structure, enabling the wood framing to continue unobstructed and uninterrupted behind the glazing.

ABOVE: Isometric; BELOW: Preliminary concept sketch

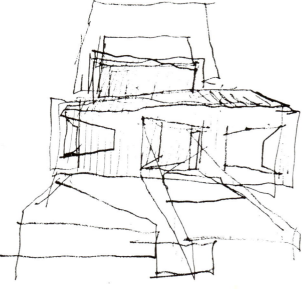

LOS ANGELES AS IT IS

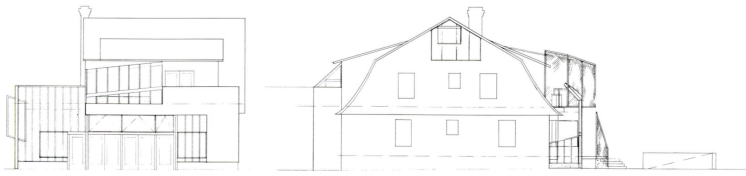

West and south elevations

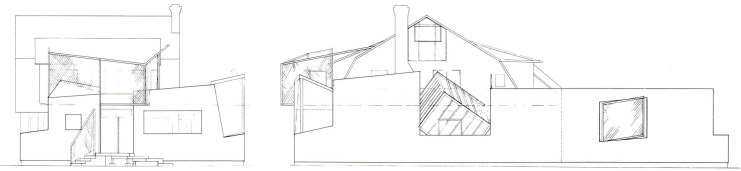

East and north elevations

LOS ANGELES AS IT IS

PRIVATE RESIDENCES

FRANK GEHRY
NORTON HOUSE
Venice

This three-storey house is built on a typically narrow beachfront lot, bounded by a heavily-trafficked boardwalk to the west and an alley at the back. The owners requested access to the ocean views without sacrificing privacy from passers-by and neighbours to the north and south.

A blue-tiled box structure forms the ground-floor base to the simple stacking of programmatic elements. The house contains a studio in the front, with two bedrooms and a double-car garage at the back. Living and additional bedroom areas on the second and third levels are raised from the street and are set back from the beachfront walk to increase privacy and allow for terraces which provide views of the ocean.

The wide second level deck also acts as a visual buffer between the boardwalk and the living-kitchen-dining areas, and is continuous with these areas when the glass doors are open. The kitchen's deep skylight offers visual access to the third floor bedrooms and opens up the long narrow living area. A flight of stairs ascends from the western edge of the main deck to a freestanding study whose form echoes those of nearby lifeguard stations and is a powerful compositional element, especially when viewed from the terrace of the third-floor master bedroom. Two terraces at the back of the house and easy access to the roof provide further privacy with panoramic views of the eclectic neighbourhood.

Diverse exterior materials include concrete block, glazed tile, stucco and wood logs. These varied textures and colours reflect the visual chaos of the building's complex urban context.

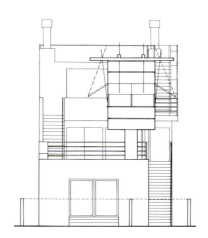

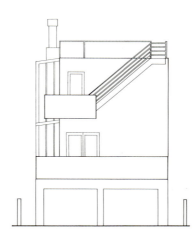

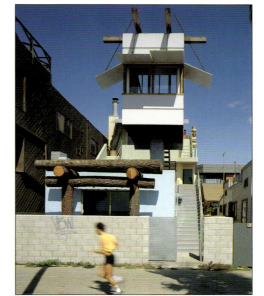

FROM ABOVE: Third floor plan; west elevation; east elevation

PRIVATE RESIDENCES

MORPHOSIS
BLADES RESIDENCE
Santa Barbara

A large exterior room has been created which embraces an augmented natural landscape, conveying a sense of sanctuary. Experientially, this strategy provides an opportunity for the occupant to witness the enigmatic interactions of nature; one is made aware of the value of diversity and difference. This perception of integration allows one to cope with the haphazardness of complex life. Through the fusion of the exterior and interior worlds, the individual gradually becomes oriented and learns to maintain balance. This interaction aspires to bridge the gap between the subjective experience of one's inner world and the objective experience of one's outer world.

The building arrangement, while alluding to the specific characteristics of this site, ultimately demonstrates its tentativeness to fixity by making overt reference to our temporary status as occupants. The work is a manifestation of an organisational strategy capable of representing a high degree of differentiation within a framework of order and continuity. The complex of pieces expresses states of both harmony and tension in the sense that this co-existence of difference (between the wilful architectural elements and the augmented landscape) is inherently in conflict. These architectural landscape elements confront, but are simultaneously at home with, the untouched grounds. The fractured characteristic of the solution provides a perpetual open-endedness and unfinished quality to the project. It is part of an accretive process that anticipates the next intervention.

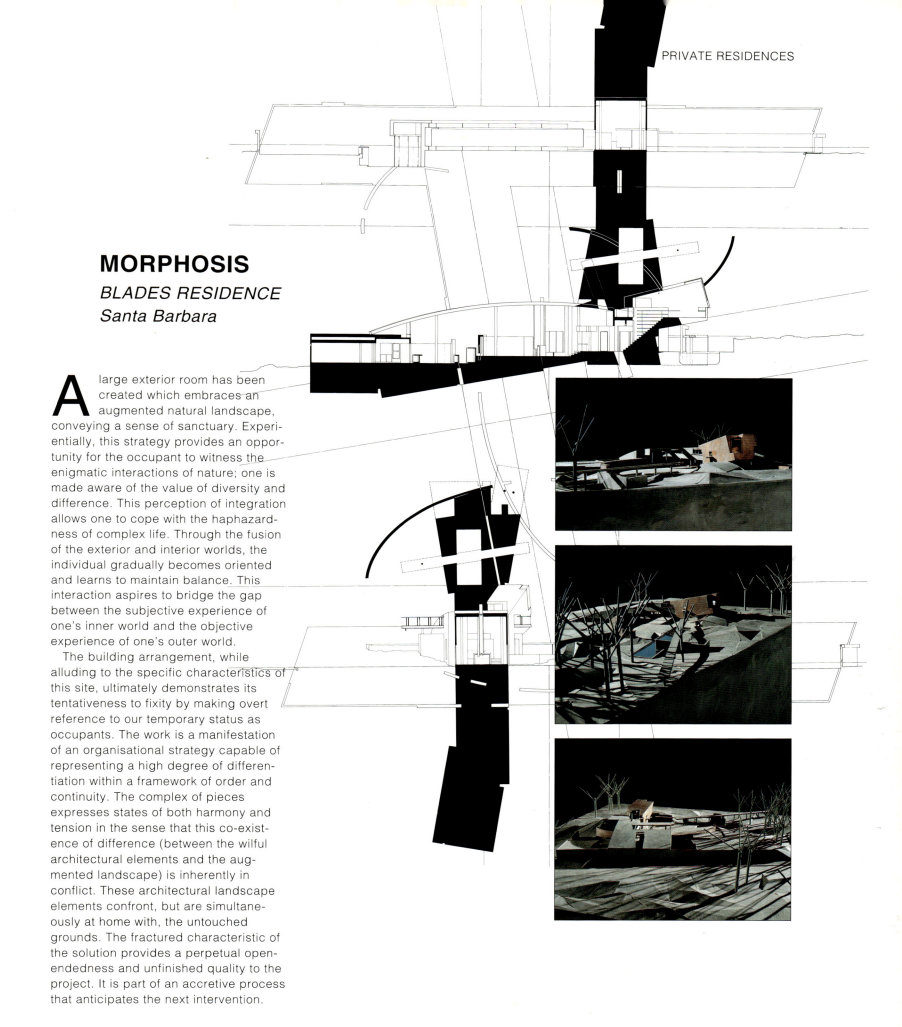

ABOVE: Sections; OVERLEAF: Plan

PRIVATE RESIDENCES

ERIC OWEN MOSS
LAWSON/WESTEN HOUSE
Brentwood

The clients were closely involved with the design of this house. The kitchen is the space in which they tend to entertain the most, so it was important to make it the focal element of the building. The room is cylindrical in shape with a conical roof, but the centre of the cone is not the centre of the cylinder. The top of the cone is cut away vertically, creating space for a deck with an ocean view. The cut presents a curved parabolic element which would create a vaulted roof if pulled out towards the street. The only literal instance of this occurrence taking place is one fully extended rib at the entrance.

A mapping of the kitchen in the plan sets a series of points, suggesting plan options, or rules. However, as the rules are interpreted in the section, the connection between the hypothetical logic of the plan and the reality of the section seems to diminish. Hence, the sectional consequences do not reflect the plan. The geometric order of the cone/cylinder kitchen depends first on the centre of a square, which is the geographic centre of the site. The centre of the square is also the centre of the cone. The apex of the vaulted roof is drawn through that centre point. A ring beam concentric to this centre supports the conical roof. The kitchen cylinder is adjusted to the south, tangent to one edge of the square. Cone and cylinder amend one another, creating a volume which is both.

The original scheme for the building had three rectangular elements, the residue of which appears sporadically in the final kitchen section.

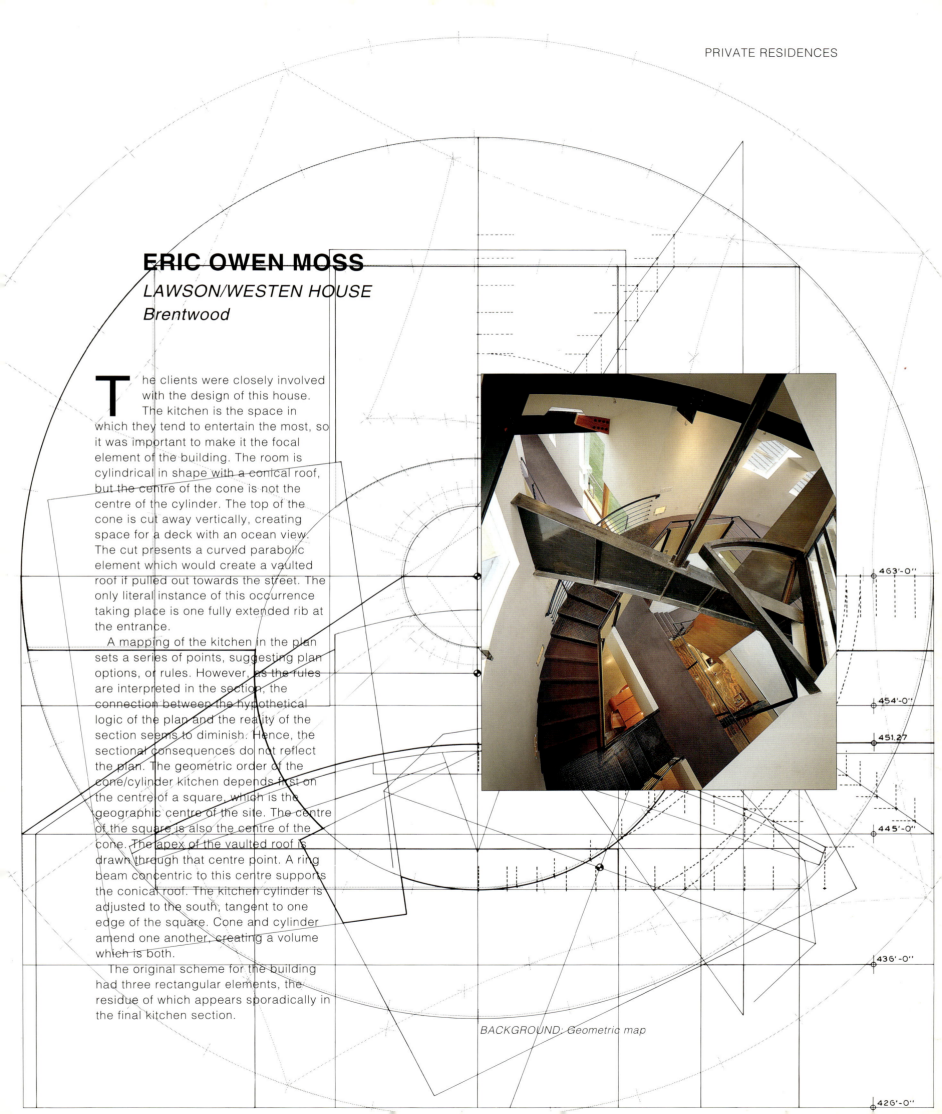

BACKGROUND: *Geometric map*

FRANK ISRAEL
GOLDBERG-BEAN HOUSE
Hollywood

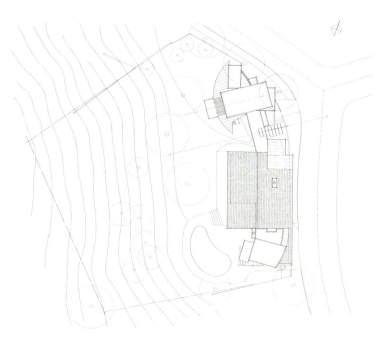

This project consists of an addition to a single-family residence in the Hollywood Hills. The existing house sits on a curved, gently sloping site. The clients asked the architect to remodel the existing house, while adding a private realm that completely transforms the site, projecting a series of dramatically articulated, three-dimensional volumes beyond the original house and into the garden. Another small bedroom is planned for the opposite end of the existing house as a small roof pavilion.

Linking the new with the old, an undulating plaster wall both invites and denies communication between the public and private spaces. Set around the curve of the wall and the site, the original and new wings focus on the distant views. Spaces within the home are delineated through structural and sculptural elements – a studio is elevated on four posts which form the canopy chamber for a bed below, and a telescopic cone of bonded steel forms a fireplace which functions as an eddy within the spatial flow.

The materials reinforce the variety of forms. A gridded rectilinear studio perched on the highest point of the site is covered in cedar plywood with redwood battens. The master bedroom has curved walls and a skewed, vaulted roof, all clad with bonded sheetmetal panels.

Entry to the house is signified by a small pool-shaped garden. A tilting steel and glass canopy shades the street terrace and the visitor. The entrance also serves as the centre of movement throughout, a place from which one can proceed to the garden or the house, to a public or private domain.

ABOVE: Site plan; OVERLEAF, BELOW LEFT: East elevation; OVERLEAF, BELOW RIGHT: West elevation

LOS ANGELES AS IT IS

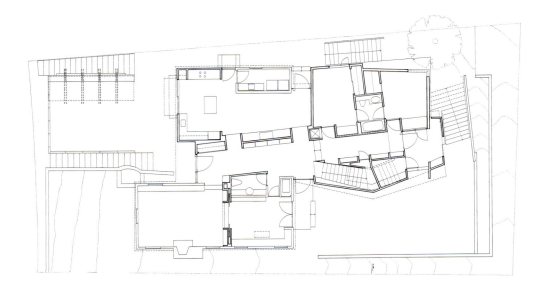

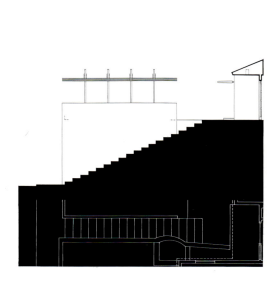
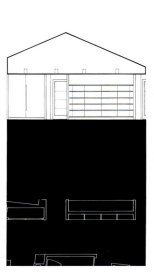
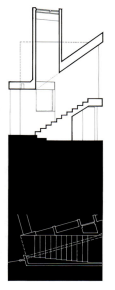
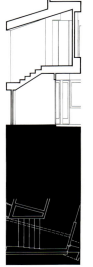
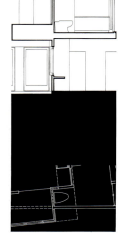

FRANK ISRAEL
WOO PAVILION
Silverlake

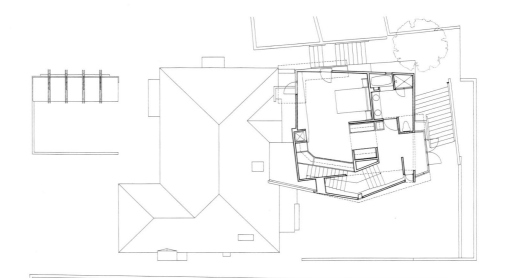

A 1,400-foot addition to a bungalow on the north side of Silver Lake, the Woo Pavilion adds a few new dimensions to the notion of a 'pavilion in a garden'. The addition is shielded from the street and placed at a dramatic conceptual distance from the original home.

The clients needed to expand the original residence in a number of ways, principally to contain their ever-expanding collection of books and also to provide an 'original' environment for their children. This intriguing combination of concerns gave rise to the architect's scheme, in which hundreds of feet of bookshelves are integrated into a dramatic passageway, creating a new generative space for the Woo family. This 'literary' passageway offers them ready access to experience of the past and present as they confront and create the future lives of their children.

One reaches the addition through a new axis, cut through the original house. The axis runs at a slightly oblique angle from the front door to the new structure at the back. The addition creates three new bedrooms: two on the first floor and a new master bedroom on the second. Bath and storage spaces were added on both levels as well.

The library-hallway runs along one edge of the two lower rooms and then up a curving stairway – modelled after a nautilus shell – to the master suite. A glowing lightwell over the staircase draws one up to the second-floor spaces and sheds light on the stairway and bookshelves (without damaging the volumes).

The upper level of the addition was conceived as a total retreat for the Woos, with a beautiful view of Silver Lake and an abundance of natural light. The major space, the largest in the house, is the master bedroom and studio with a large corner window. In addition to a private balcony, a small 'child's space' was introduced to enable the children to make a gradual progression from crib to bedroom, whilst remaining close to their parents.

The architects tried to reflect the gentle and enlightened philosophy of the clients in the exterior disposition of the pavilion and in its placement on the site. The pavilion was pulled to one side of the property, improving its view of Silver Lake and allowing an open, outdoor 'room' on the other side. Clad in stone-dashed stucco, the walls of the addition appear to buckle and pull away in places, revealing – and illuminating – an interior world.

OPPOSITE ABOVE: Floor plan; ABOVE: Floor plan of pavilion; BELOW: Longitudinal section

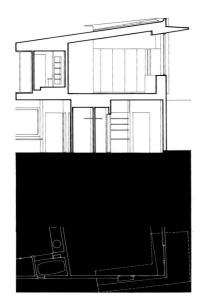 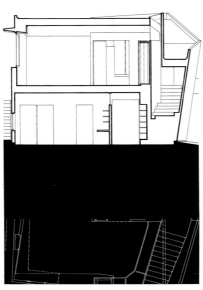 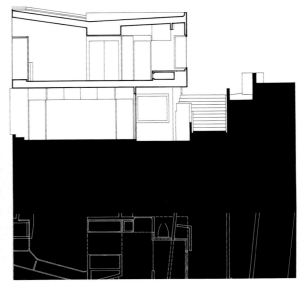

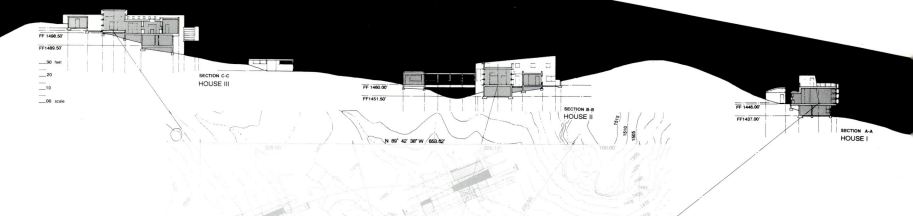

SIGRID MILLER POLLIN
MOUNT VERNON AVENUE RESIDENCES
Riverside

The intent of this small residential subdivision was to realise an alternative method for hillside development in Southern California by forming a coherent architecture which interprets the specifics of the site and region whilst also minimising grading of natural contours.

Each house is approximately 3,000 square-feet. The Tower House (House I) and the Boat House (House III) are designed for a family of four, whilst the Bridge House (House II) is designed for a family of seven. The three houses form an implied arc at the north side of the site which encircles a large open space. Each structure has a distinctly different relationship to the sloping terrain. House I is situated parallel to its slope and retains against it, House II spans a small ravine and House III is launched perpendicular to its hill. The siting and programme for each house allows for individuality and variation. The nine-and-a-half acre site is full of natural variety, including a gentle knoll, a grassy valley, a rocky ravine and a county parkland bordering the site.

Each house has a high volume living space with high ceilings and windows revealing dramatic views to the valley below. Common materials are used for each house with red stucco walls coding the spine; concrete block, redwood and light stucco defining the other smaller spaces; and one unprogrammed, whimsical space has been included to be used over time as the residents see fit. The forms of the houses become an interpretation of the surrounding powerful rock formations, an experiment in the simple but strong relationships between topography and building.

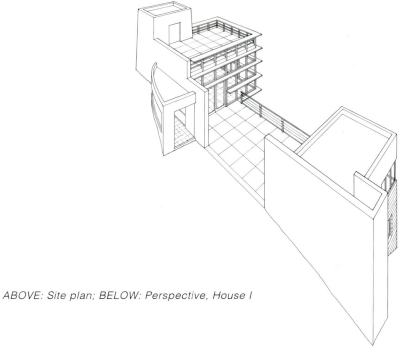

ABOVE: Site plan; BELOW: Perspective, House I

Perspective, House II

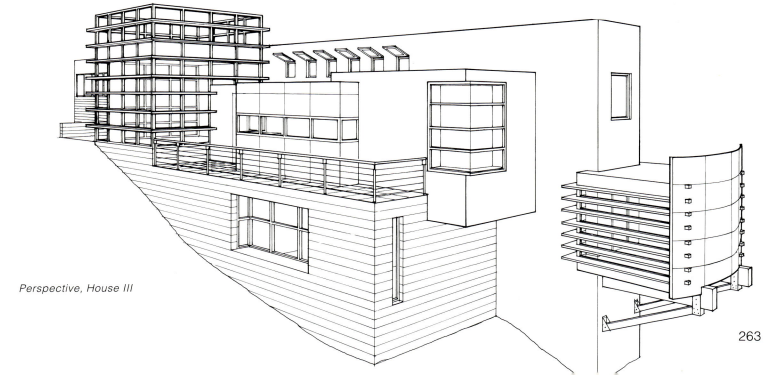

Perspective, House III

PRIVATE RESIDENCES

LEGORRETA ARQUITECTOS
GREENBERG HOUSE
Brentwood

Located in a residential area of Los Angeles, this house was designed to create its own environment. The entrance is through a courtyard enclosed by walls of different angles and heights. The asymmetry is emphasised by the location of a group of palm trees. The importance of the garage door is recognised with a bright yellow wall.

The back of the house is the result of the free location of the two towers, the library and the studio, all of which enhance an open terrace. Below, the pool and the jacuzzi tower complete the interplay of volumes and colours.

Intimacy and human scale in design were carefully considered throughout the house. This constant theme is balanced by the use of very different types of windows, patios and colours, giving each room its own atmosphere and personality. Hence, everyday life offers several different environments throughout the day.

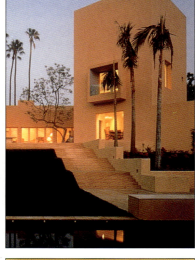

ABOVE: Site plan

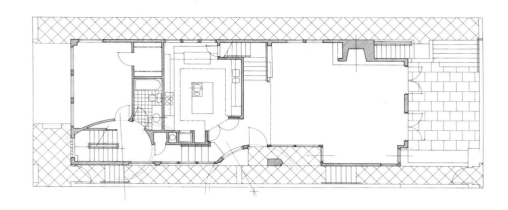

McCOY AND SIMON

WEBB RESIDENCE
Marina del Rey

The residence includes approximately 6,800 square feet on three levels and a semi-subterranean parking garage. The site is 35 x 90 feet, located in Marina del Rey, half a block from the beach, with an allowable footprint for the building of 67 x 26 feet. The site fronts a pedestrian street to the south with a service alley to the north.

The Webb residence explores ideas of space, volume, and surface, as well as the response to the opportunities and challenges of the context.

The house is located in an eclectic neighbourhood of small beach cottages, large condominiums, and ostentatious private homes. The design was driven primarily by an effort to address the beauty beyond the built context, in the quality of the light and the horizon of the ocean. The building is organised around a promenade from the entry walk to the outdoor room of the roof terrace, providing a view of the horizon. The primary path of this promenade is the long stairway on the east side of the house.

The simple mass of the building is a counterpoint to the subtleties of the interior volumes, which incorporate changes in section to maximise the height of the primary rooms and to compress the secondary rooms within the height limit regulations. The surface of the house is designed to emphasise the surface of the walls, not only to capture the light and shadows, but also to maximise the scale of the primary windows. The proportion and scale of the exterior walls is complex in order to reveal the subtle contrasts between the interior and exterior, and to explore the effects of surface and transparency.

ABOVE: Ground floor plan

CIGOLLE + COLEMAN

CANYON HOUSE
Pacific Palisades

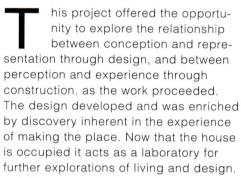

This project offered the opportunity to explore the relationship between conception and representation through design, and between perception and experience through construction, as the work proceeded. The design developed and was enriched by discovery inherent in the experience of making the place. Now that the house is occupied it acts as a laboratory for further explorations of living and design.

A house and studio designed by two architects for themselves attempts a reconciliation of oppositions within a framework of a critical transformation of programme, site and architectural syntax in which the programme, site and formal syntax for the house evolves through a process of metamorphosis which embodies the notion of being inbetween, of looking back to the origin of the idea or form while projecting a potential set of new alternative variations.

The house is set on a steeply sloped site. A tower and a block are placed on a hill, the tower at the bottom, rotated to face the ocean, and the block near the top, parallel to the street and facing the canyon. The tower, standing free of the hill, is the house of the individual, a house of origin and of destination. The block is a loft container, made up of platforms built out of the hillside and embedded in it, containing spaces for other activities and attachments which one develops over time. In addition to the tower and the block, two pairs of walls complete the definition of spaces.

The first floor, which is at the top, at the level of the road, contains two automobiles on one side and several tables on the other side. A stair hall is incised into the block. The stairs descend through a volume defined at the ceiling by wooden baffles which filter sky, clouds and light through glass panels into the stair volume and to the levels below. The stairway is an open steel structure with limestone-filled treads.

At the second floor the stairs open into a space with one long solid wall and one short opaque glass wall with a fireplace embedded in it. The other long side of the rectangular room is formed by a row of columns and a series of glass panels, which slide back completely to open the room onto an outdoor platform. The frame and the transparent glass both delineate and make ambiguous the line between inside and outside.

The third floor, the lowest level, consists of a room containing hanging clothes and a dressing table, a stage and an end to the stairs. The bottom run of the stairs follows the slope of the hill; the vertical volume of the stairs connects the sky and the earth, and grounds the building to the land.

The sectional organisation of the programme for the house into working, living and sleeping levels is overlaid with a sequence of spaces defined by walls and volumes. Two types of spaces are developed: spaces within the walls of preconceived volumes, and spaces between walls, those which are resultant both in intention and conception. In this way, there is an attempt to create both the predictable and the inbetween places where the unexpected, the unprogrammed is encouraged to occur. The design provides the range of places which a self-sufficient environment like a live-work house must include: places of security and places to be at risk, places of contemplation and of interaction.

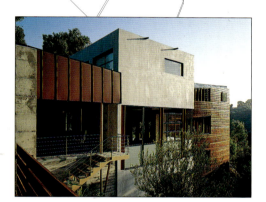

ABOVE: Isometric

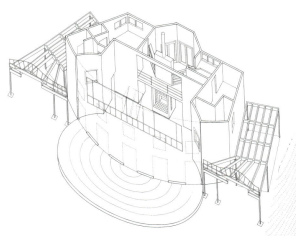

MOORE RUBLE YUDELL
RODES HOUSE
Brentwood

This house was designed for a bachelor English professor who wanted a serene and formal home on a modest budget. The house evolved from the limitations of its site – a flat, trapezoid-shaped orchard with hills rising steeply on two sides. The orchard is loose-fill and impossible to build upon; hence, the only way the house could meet its low budget was to span the hill.

This span was first designed with trusses within the exterior walls. It then evolved into a series of three trussed bridges which pierced the long symmetrical curve of the facade, the inner wall of the living room, and the rear of the dining room conservatory. In the final scheme, the truss construction was not affordable and the span was achieved with a buried bridge of caissons and grade beams. However, the owner and the architects had taken such pleasure in the play of the straight trusses and the curved facade that it is recollected with a plane of lightweight lattice which invites vegetation and serves as an armature for lighting.

In a very small house the gourmet owner wanted generous provisions for cooking and dining, and a grand living-room. To save space he was happy to settle for an alcove bed in the pattern of Thomas Jefferson's. Upstairs a guest room and bathroom are across the bridge from a small study.

In front of the house an oval patio serves as stage for performers visiting the client's university, while guests sit in an orange grove laced with fragments of a terraced amphitheatre. Modest materials – stucco exteriors and plaster interiors – are animated by pastel walls and vegetation.

ABOVE L TO R: Axonometric; site plan

PRIVATE RESIDENCES

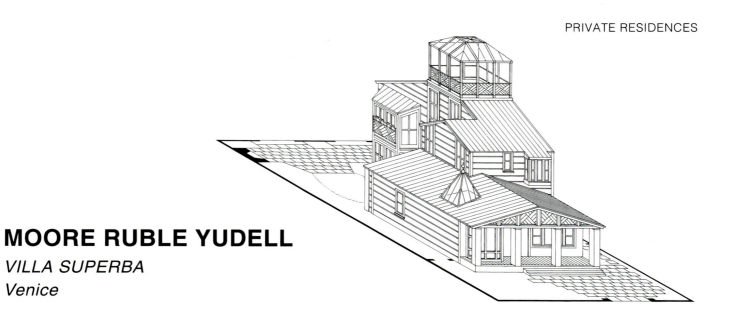

MOORE RUBLE YUDELL
VILLA SUPERBA
Venice

With this expanded Venice bungalow the architects hoped to set a good example for a neighbourhood in which charming smaller houses are often sacrificed for oversized stucco boxes. In concept, the original house is joined by a second, taller one crowned by a rooftop sleeping porch. The original bungalow was rebuilt with the same lapped siding, while its wall-house companion was scaled up with painted plywood and horizontal battens. In the front, a remodelled grander porch and glass pyramid on the roof face the street behind a shallow garden of palms and jacarandas. At the back, a walled courtyard entered through glass bays has banana trees, an outdoor fireplace and a small fountain. The superimposition of the two 'houses' and the interlocking of gardens, porches and window-bays generate inside-outside ambiguities that are continued throughout. A hallway becomes a porch for the kitchen and stairway, the upstairs bedroom has its own house-like identity, and the rooftop pavilion, a tent-like *dach-salletl*, changes with the seasons.

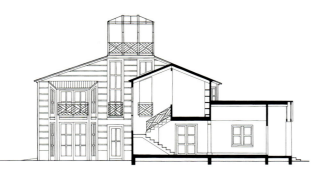

ABOVE: Isometric; LEFT: North elevation/section

PRIVATE RESIDENCES

BUZZ YUDELL
YUDELL/BEEBE HOUSE
Malibu

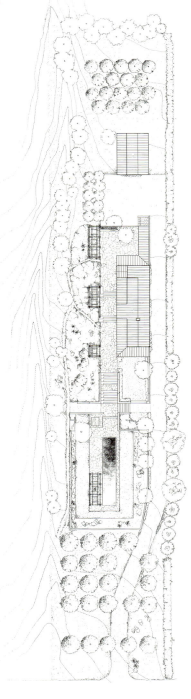

This house was designed by and for an architect and his wife, a graphic designer and avid gardener. Set in a hillside lot bordered to the west by a dry creek, the house evolved from the constraints and pleasures of the site. From east to west it unfolds as layers of habitation: from carefully proportioned rooms, to a sunny gallery broad enough for seating and dining, to a stepping street, on to a set of pergolas that functions as garden rooms of varying character, then to cultivated gardens and finally to the stream-bed and uncultivated chaparral.

The north-south transformations are equally important. The lot is graced due north with a serene mountain view and a complementary view south to the ocean. Movement along this axis connects a series of outside courtyards. One drives towards the mountain, along the eastern wall of the house, to the parking court, and then through a sequence of courts heading back towards the ocean view. Inside, the gallery and library emphasise the mountain-to-ocean axis. Outside, the terraced street links a series of courts.

The house itself is developed in close response to concerns of proportion and light. Its extruded shape was both economical and reminiscent of farmhouses in California and other warm coastal climates. Its tower and library reach for the ocean and mountain views.

The richness of experience derives from the overlay of the east-west transformation (formal rooms to native landscape) with the north-south, mountain-to-sea movement. The interplay of geometry and landscape creates a place that is at once serene and full of unfolding experiences.

ABOVE: Aerial perspective and cutaway view;
BELOW: Roof plan

HODGETTS + FUNG
VISO RESIDENCE
Hollywood Hills

One cannot build in the Hollywood Hills without respect for those who have built there before. In this home there are echoes of Rudolph Schindler, Cameron Menzies and Richard Neutra, who helped to establish a vocabulary and style suitable to the unique social and topographic environment found in the hills and canyons of Los Angeles. For this project a typical builder's vernacular was sought in the search for an inexpensive but elegant design for a hillside dwelling.

Painted stucco, aluminium sash and standard details are used throughout. Openings are of a modest dimension, in keeping with the builder's tradition, but configured in a manner to suggest unique volumes. A carefully described geometry articulates a series of overlapping living spaces and intersections and articulation of materials also respects common practice. A precipitous site and crowded adjacent properties were definitive conditions in the physical lay-out of the house. By the orientation of living volumes towards selected views, a configuration was defined which eliminated undesirable context while underscoring the client's enthusiasm for the Griffith Observatory and the Hollywood sign.

Internally, a cylindrical volume ratchets to become a foyer on the first level, a bridge-like transition on the main level, and a study on the upper level, while proving a strong visual axis of resolution for the splayed geometries of the primary accommodation. A dense, yet continuously evolving staircase keyed to the cylinder offers access to a complementary sequence of landings, overlooks and necessities including a subterranean washstand.

ABOVE: Section; BELOW: Ground floor framing plan

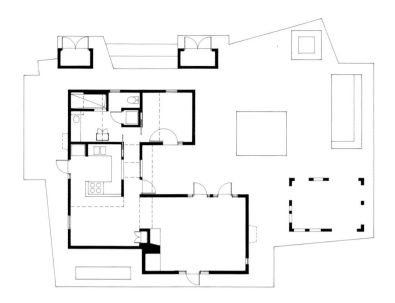

SCHWEITZER BIM
THE MONUMENT
Joshua Tree

The Joshua Tree National Monument is a park unlike other national parks. Devoid of leafy trees, green grass and large expanses of water it stretches out instead across the high desert as an expanse of sand carpeted with giant boulders whose interstices are filled with cactus, thorny brush, yucca plants and Joshua trees.

Composed of simple geometric forms, this 950 square-foot house on a ten-acre site is not intended to function so much as a container for living, but as a series of rooms to supplement the main space, the landscape.

An outside porch-like structure, painted a rich burnt orange, provides shade during the day and a vantage point for beautiful sunsets over a distant ridge. The living room is enclosed by 24-foot-high olive-green walls punctured by irregular openings which provide fractured views of the rocks and sky. An L-shaped volume, painted purple-blue, contains in one leg a small dining area and a kitchen with sleeping lofts overhead, and in the other, the bathroom and a single bedroom. The house is constructed of simple materials, painted stucco walls, exposed aggregate concrete floors and the colours are the colours of the desert: orange, blue and olive-green. The interior colours are subtle variations on the exterior theme which enhance the monastic solemnity that imbues the space.

Simplicity of form and the creation of a symbiotic relationship with the desert is the goal of this architecture. The building and the land are intended to be read as one living space. RM Schindler's ideal of the house as a permanent camp is very much alive at the Monument.

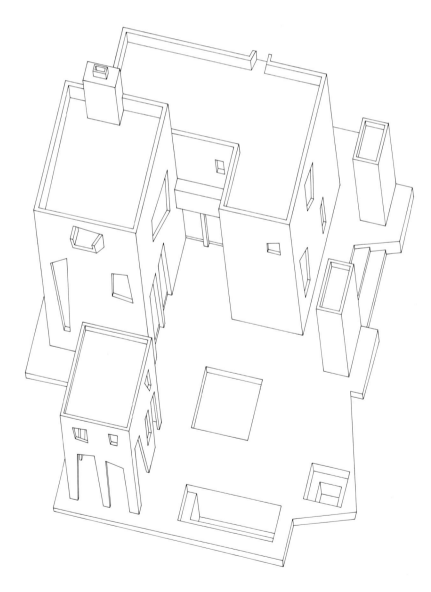

ABOVE: Ground floor plan; BELOW: Axonometric

BARTON PHELPS
EPSTEIN HOUSE
Beverly Hills

The site is a high canyon overlooking the city to the south. Deep deposits of alluvial fill, along with building department requirements for a walled debris basin, combined to shape the narrow three-storey block, pushed into the rock of the steep hillside it parallels. A blind elevation results from the retaining wall that runs the length of the first two floors and is countered by the open floor plan, extensive fenestration, and cantilever projections on the other sides.

The configuration imposed by geology and topography resulted in a variety of siting conditions that suggested different images. The two-storey garage/studio wing extends the facade as a tall, protective wall which postpones a full view of the site until one passes through a portal at the base of the rocky slope. Inside, a raised terrace loosely contained by an assemblage of detached volumes, claims the centre of the canyon. Seen from the garden in the ravine above, the uphill 'office building' dominates and connects the house to the distant high-rise landscape of Wilshire Boulevard. The single-storey bedroom floor opens under broad eaves onto a lawn that allows it to look and work like a ranch house somewhere in the flats.

The use of materials expresses the stratified organisation of the house as well as the vertical connections between layers. To emphasise the natural complexity of the materials, walls, floors and ceilings are treated as separate planes.

Freed from the constraints of consistency, each house-part is tailored to its part of the site; reinforcing distinctive aspects in order to enhance the sense of its natural beauty.

ABOVE: Floor plan; OVERLEAF L TO R: Elevation and section

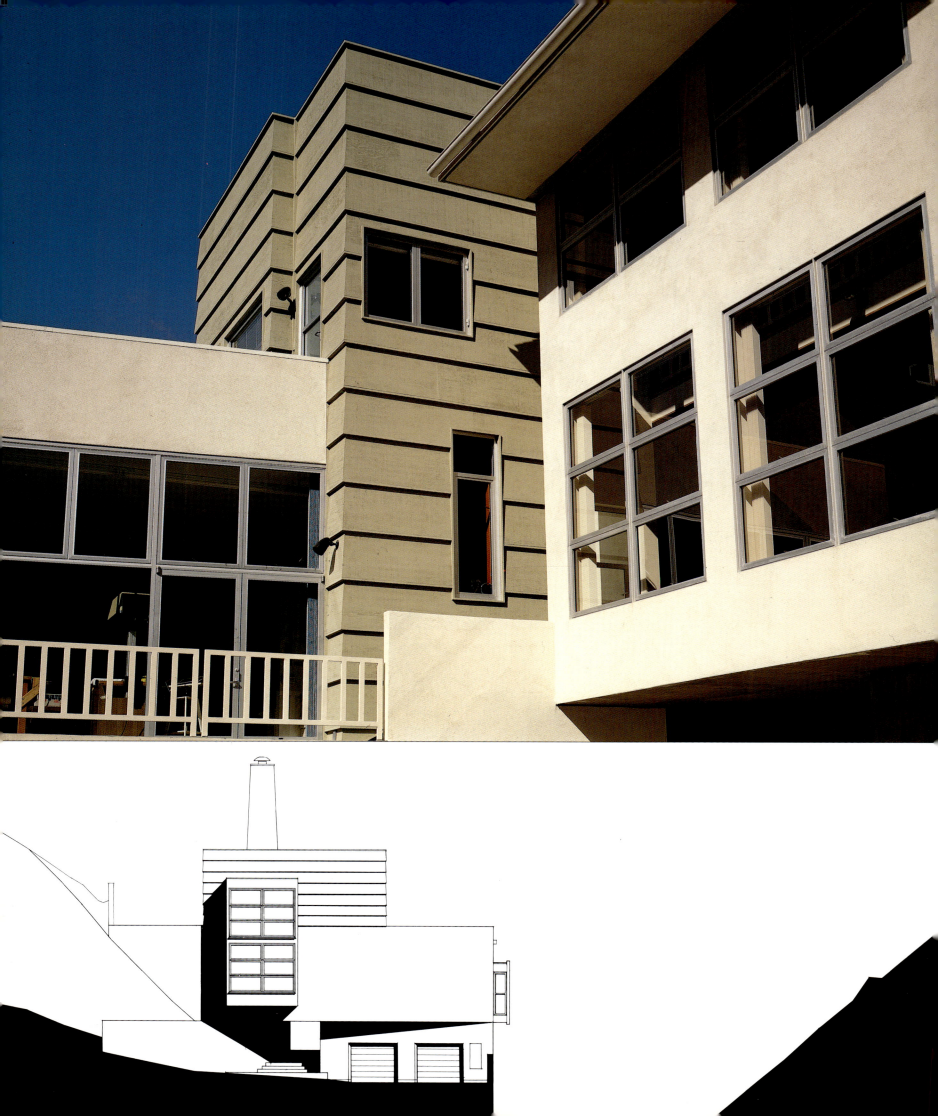

PRIVATE RESIDENCES

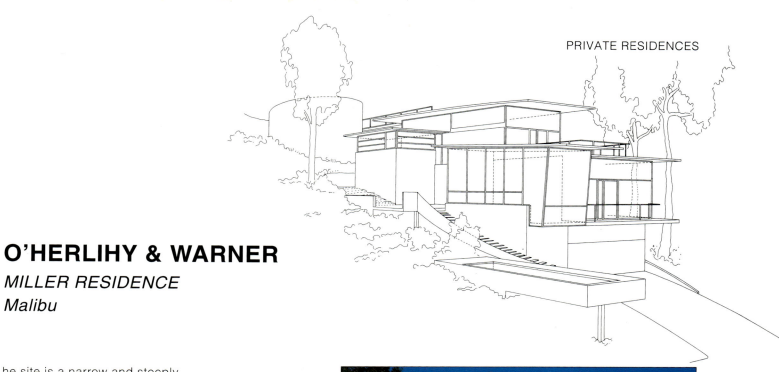

O'HERLIHY & WARNER
MILLER RESIDENCE
Malibu

The site is a narrow and steeply sloping lot approximately 50 feet by 160 feet next to the Pacific Ocean. The clients, a married couple with two children, required a 5,000 square-foot residence and guest house to be built on the site, with specific requests for roof terraces and maximised views of the ocean.

Given the steep slope of the site and its relation to views, structure, volume and light were taken as the root of the architectural solution. The house continues the slope in stereometric terms. Working with proportion and light, the living spaces are broken up into a series of volumes delineated by different materials. In order to emphasise the translucency of the house and provide visual privacy while permitting light, the various glass planes are glazed in different types of glass. The east and west elevations are of translucent U- and sandblasted glass, while the north and south elevations are of green and clear glass to maximise the views. The interior life of the house is activated by extending itself to the exterior via these visual but materialised walls.

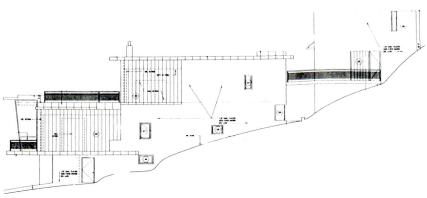

ABOVE: Perspective view; BELOW: Elevation

O'HERLIHY & WARNER
FREUND-KOOPMAN RESIDENCE
Pacific Palisades

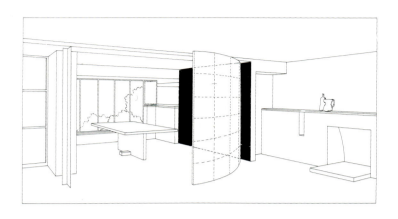

This addition and renovation of a Pacific Palisades residence attempts to create an ensemble of living volumes which engage the natural virtues of the site. The existing, inward-looking house is oblivious to its beautiful wooded site on an ancient alluvial bluff in the Santa Monica Mountains. The new bedroom/library addition reaches out over the descending hillside, with the prismatic library volume on top completely enveloped beneath the broad canopy of existing pines. The new swimming pool and low garden walls also serve to extend the house into the landscape.

ABOVE: Dining room perspective; LEFT: Ground floor plan

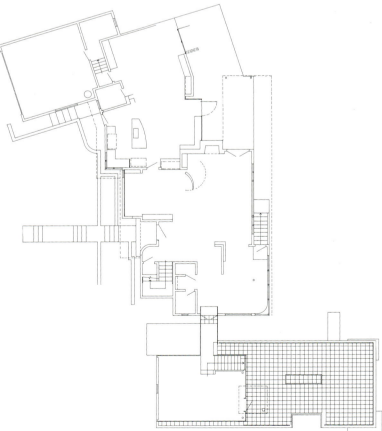

PRIVATE RESIDENCES

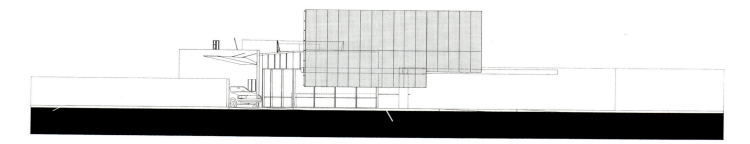

CENTRAL OFFICE OF ARCHITECTURE
LAGUNA BEACH RESIDENCE ADDITION
Laguna Beach

Four contiguous lots reside on a bluff overlooking the Pacific Ocean. A neighbouring house exists on a rise directly above the site in question, while the existing house opens out onto the pool deck and the ocean views beyond.

A new master bedroom and bathroom with increased privacy, a study and a pool house containing a guest bathroom were requested by the client, as well as the use of minimal maintenance materials in the project.

The architects found it necessary to section the site into two distinct portions: on one side of the division was the neighbouring house and the driveway used to approach the site; on the other, the existing house and the pool area which has the potential to become an outdoor living space in the Southern California tradition. The addition was designed to screen the living space from the driveway and the neighbours, while reinforcing the outdoor room. High fibre cement panel walls mark the dividing line of the site. The more enclosed rooms are outside these walls while inside the walls is the master bedroom which completely opens to the outdoor room via a set of full-height pivoting glazed doors. The connection between the existing house and the addition is a short hallway which follows the dividing wall. The materials used were wood-framing, stucco, terrazzo, ceramic tile and stainless steel sheet. The interior cabinets and general woodwork are of white oak with black granite surfaces.

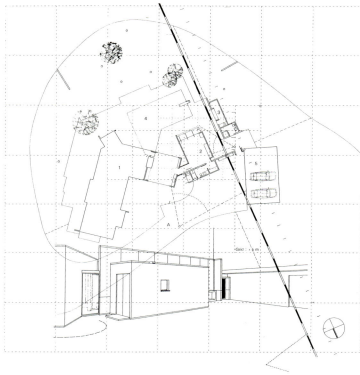

ABOVE: South-west elevation; site plan and perspective from pool; BELOW: Site plan and perspective of entry sequence

HEALTH AND LEISURE CENTRES

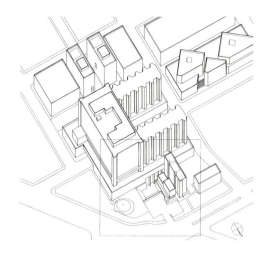

MORPHOSIS
CEDARS-SINAI COMPREHENSIVE CANCER CENTER
Beverly Hills

The site for the new building is located on the north-east corner of the Cedars-Sinai Medical Center. Bounded by an existing car park, heli-pad and three medical centre buildings the facility also utilises subterranean level space within the existing medical tower. The Center is an outpatient facility combining diagnosis, treatment and counselling within one setting. In order to maximise efficiency and eliminate duplication of services, direct connection to the Medical Center is imperative as it is used by cancer patients who are maintaining relatively normal lifestyles during treatment.

Two basic design objectives summarise the approach to the project: first, a design strategy which can clarify and organise a difficult site impacted between three existing buildings while requiring continuity between the new building and the existing subterranean space. Second, an architecture which enhances one's comprehension of location and choice of movement within a complex multi-departmental facility which is part of a much larger medical centre. The architectural language emphasises the Z axis and the sectional quality of the building, natural and artificial light and an overt reference to construction.

The two major spaces of the building (lobby and chemotherapy atrium) were conceived as quasi-exterior places and form the datum for the total scheme and the complex's relationship to the sky and ground. The hope is for an architecture that can occupy the mind, affect the spirit and act as a foil to the patient's current circumstance by removing him or her from self-occupation.

ABOVE: Axonometric; BELOW: Composite drawing showing axonometric of details; OVERLEAF, BELOW L TO R: Composite drawings showing sectional axonometric and axonometric of details

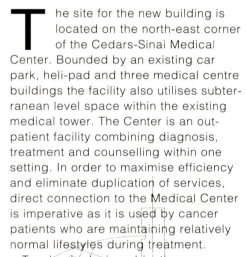

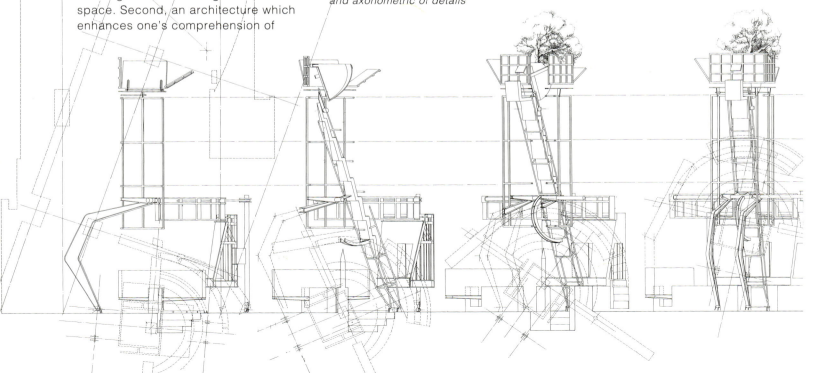

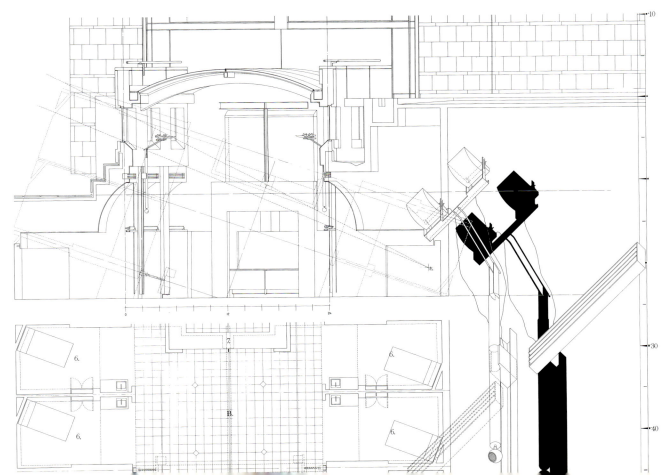

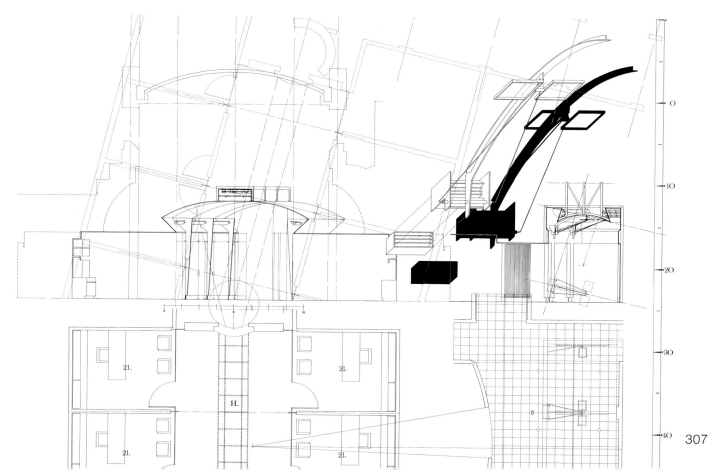

MICHELE SAEE
DENTAL CENTRE
Beverly Hills

The interior design for this dental centre destroys the traditional concept of dentists' offices. The clinic occupies 4,000 square-feet in a converted apartment building overlooking a small mews. Its function demanded specialised equipment and mechanical services at each dental station; in addition, reception and waiting areas, patient files, an x-ray room and a photo laboratory had to be located within a few feet of the treatment areas.

Saee's solution was an abstracted 'free plan', in which sculptural objects define space and circulation. As most of the patients lie on their backs, much ingenuity is devoted to the ceiling, with floating forms, recessed planes, acute reveals and unexpected fissures, lit by unseen windows.

Saee has made full use of the bright Southern California sunshine by exploiting luminosity and shadow. The roof is pierced to install multiple skylights and the walls have been thickened to create recesses for existing windows. In some areas, walls shield the windows from view, reflecting light onto other surfaces.

Visitors enter the clinic up a single flight of wooden stairs stained a translucent green, a colour that is continued through the lobby and into the inner hallway. Saee has rejected rectilinear spaces and the openness of the plan incorporates five dental stations in the same room, separated from one another by tall partitions. Within each cubicle, recumbent patients enjoy a vista across the mews, the wall of which has been generously glazed. The tile roofs and gardens of the surrounding neighbourhood also gives a feeling of space uncommon in so many dental surgeries.

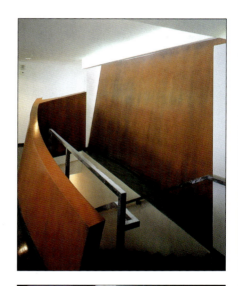

STEVEN EHRLICH
SHATTO RECREATION CENTER
Downtown

This community and recreation centre is set in an open park, in an ethnically mixed, tough, inner-city neighbourhood. The City of Los Angeles has been very concerned about the graffiti and vandalism problems, hence the challenge was to be defensive but not offensive in the design and construction of the building. The centre is located in an area where neighbouring buildings were destroyed in the LA riots, but this project has not been harmed, even from graffiti – a tribute to the community having a vested interest in their recreation centre.

The plan is a simple rectangle, with the cross-section bringing a softness to an otherwise hard urban environment. Anthropomorphic allusions to a whale and serpentine mechanical ducts inside the 'belly' are a play on the fact that it is a recreation centre.

In order to deal with the complex issues of defence and identity, concrete block was chosen as a durable, economical and structural exterior and interior wall surface. This material has been structurally woven into an abstract expression, with three different blocks making up the palette. A sand-coloured fluted block forms a 'watermark' as well as energy fissures that spread upwards through the structural clay-brick block. The 'pattern' of the structurally-woven masonry material was born out of the collaboration of the architect and artist. It conveys this building's identity within a community where graffiti is a part of its ancient roots in the form of calligraphy and its Aztec culture.

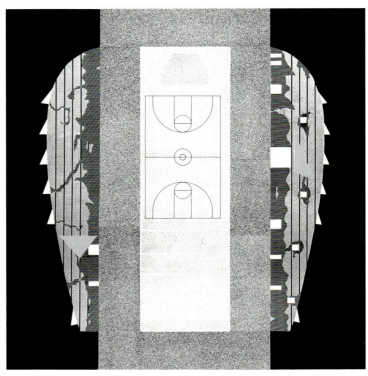

ABOVE: Site plan; BELOW: Composite drawing of floor plan and elevations

RESTAURANTS, BARS AND SHOPS

MORPHOSIS
KATE MANTILINI
Beverly Hills

The client requested 'a roadside steakhouse for the future, with a clock', a hybrid cafe/restaurant/diner to be placed in a 1950's bank building on Wilshire Boulevard in Beverly Hills. Rather than merely renovating the interior, the architects created an active *poche* wall which engulfed the old frame and was designed on a four-person booth increment. An oculus was cut into the ceiling and into that oculus a notionally kinetic orrery was placed. This metal construction describes the plan of the building on the floor. A curving wall over the long bar and kitchen area depicts – at the request of the client – the pre-War fight promoter for whom the restaurant was named.

The space in which this takes place is aggressive, obsessive and active, though it is tempered by a certain coolness and a business-like politeness. It is a simple open hall, vaguely exterior in character, reflecting its public intention. The massiveness of the booth-wall gives the whole structure a permanence, while the grid of the interior is carried to the outside, so that the skin has a cactus-like appearance, vacillating between surface and volume. This project requires a 'reading' in terms other than those of sight alone.

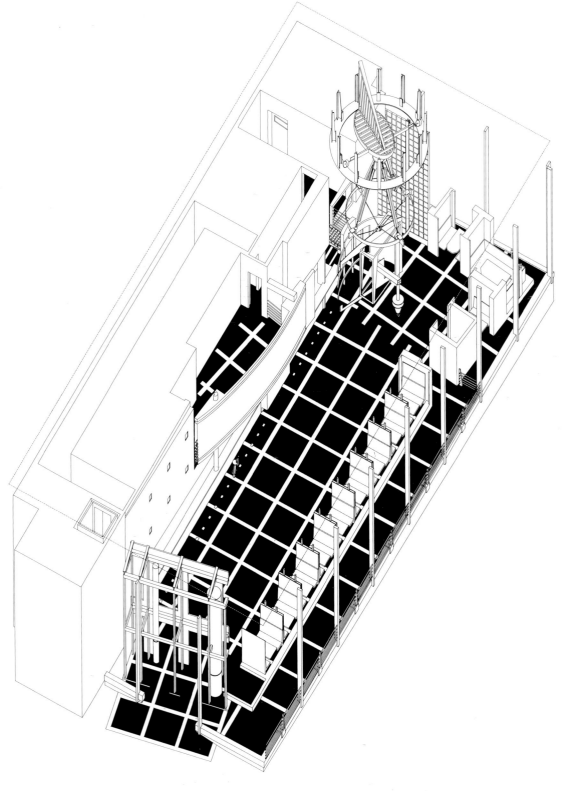

RIGHT: Axonometric; OVERLEAF: Composite drawing of section, plan and exploded axonometric of detail

313

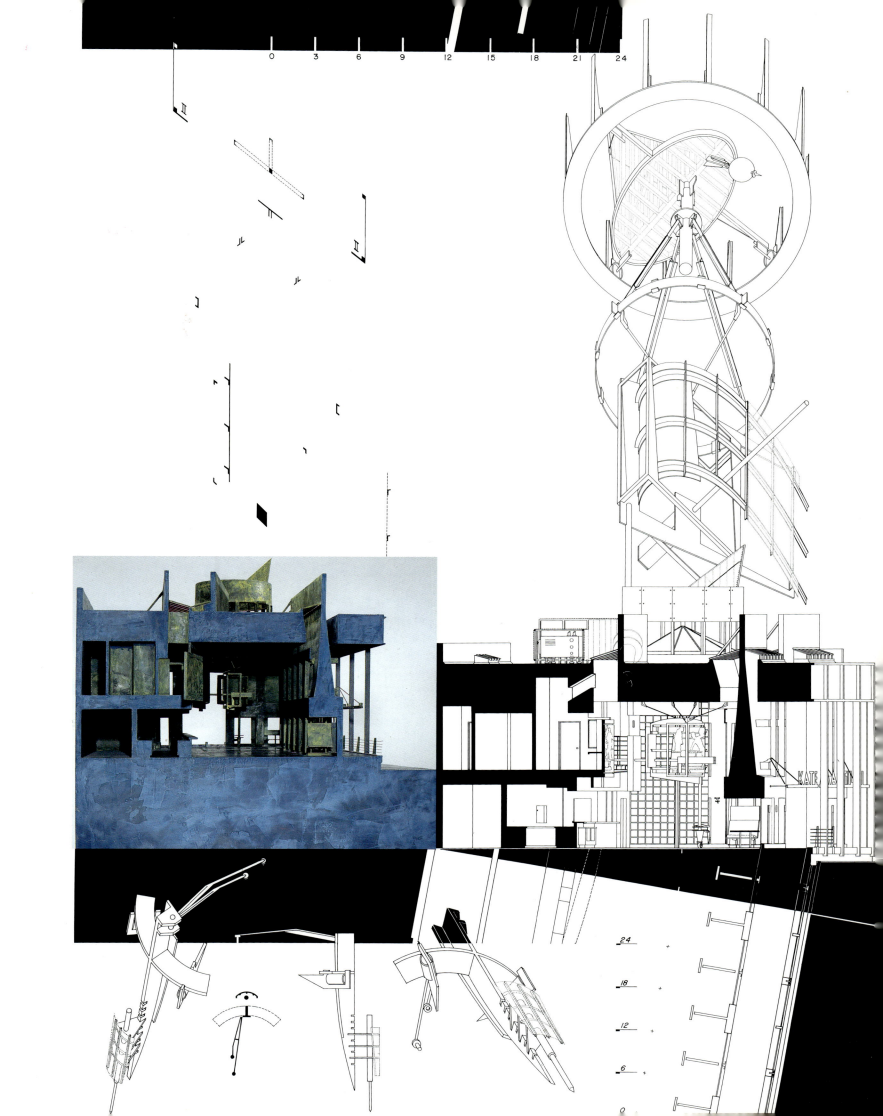

ROTONDI
NICOLA RESTAURANT
Downtown

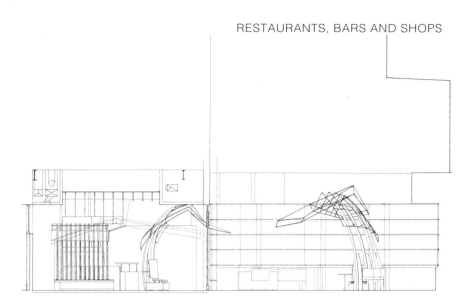

Nicola is a 100-seat restaurant and food service operation in a 52-storey high-rise building in downtown Los Angeles. The featured cuisine can be described as 'contemporary food with ethnic influences'. The public dining area, located on the ground floor, is divided between a rather confined interior space and a six-storey high glass enclosed atrium space.

The design, by Michael Rotondi with Brian Reiff, is the result of discovering and constructing ordering systems that are both latent and imposed to the existing conditions and programmatic requirements. The restaurant, being divided into areas such as kitchen, service, bar, waiting area/entrance, restrooms and both interior and exterior dining areas, is unified through the geometry of organisation and constructed systems. Initially, a map was derived that laid out the principal ordering systems that would describe the characteristics of the place (functional and spatial). Then, through the experimental use of woodwork, metal, stone and drywall, the space was given form based on the geometry of the ordering map and by imagining the movement of the body through space. The objective is to create conceptual and perceptual coherence.

In nature, complex systems are layered interdependently to compose essential beauty. We believe that discovering this principle which exists in architecture, will be the fundamental experience at Nicola.

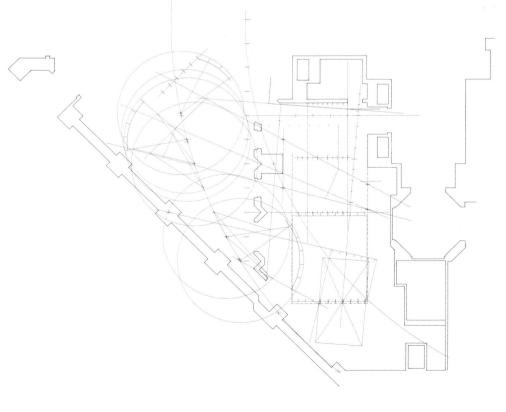

ABOVE: Section; BELOW: Ordering systems

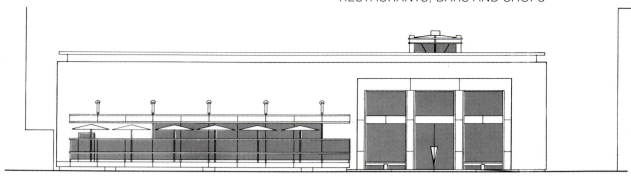

NIKKEN AMERICA / CHARLES S CORDERO AIA / FRANCESCA GARCIA-MARQUES
ZENZERO RESTAURANT
Santa Monica

The basic design was to remodel and upgrade the existing restaurant. The formal edifice fronts Ocean Avenue, Palisades Park and the Pacific Ocean beyond. It consists of a primary rectangular mass which contains two axially aligned volumes paralleling ocean views, a main dining room and reception/bar area. This primary axis is terminated by an exhibition kitchen at one end and a bar at the other. Both are detailed with burled wood, custom-made glass and polished granite counters. The transparency of the 'crackle' glass wall separating the dining and bar areas contributes to the notion of 'interlocking volumes' where a curved wood ceiling above the bar and a plaster ceiling above the dining room overlap and blur the clear distinction of either volume, creating a fluid spatial sequence. Both volumes relate directly to external spaces.

The dining room opens completely onto the patio/dining terrace and the reception/bar area is axially aligned perpendicular to the primary axis, terminating at one end with a courtyard and at the other with entry doors framing views of the Pacific beyond. This creates a biaxial layout, the focus of which is a conical light monitor. The interrelation of exterior and interior spaces is 'thematic'. A flamed granite and limestone paving module with alternating metal accent strips organises the plan layout, extending from interior to exterior.

Strategically placed art objects, sun control and theatrical night lighting create an inherent outward disposition taking advantage of the Southern California climate, contributing to an 'urban theatre' along Ocean Avenue.

ABOVE: Front elevation

RESTAURANTS, BARS AND SHOPS

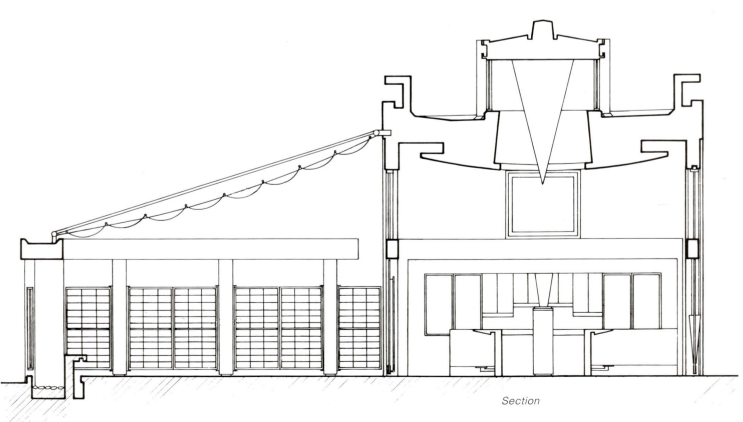

Section

321

MICHELE SAEE
ANGELI MARE RESTAURANT
Marina del Rey

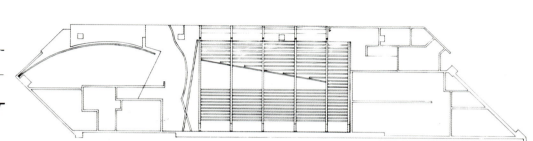

Angeli Mare is situated in the Marina Marketplace shopping mall, seating 90 people in the dining room and 30 in the bar. Creating Angeli Mare took Saee through the process of making an identity for a restaurant with its own specific message. The kitchen and the bar embrace the dining room which is in the middle of the space. The function of each part is very specific and the interaction of the parts is very important for the function of the restaurant.

The exterior image is simple and clear with each part having a separate identity. The contextual aspect of the restaurant does not rely on its surroundings but rather on a concept which grew out of its geographic location (near the ocean) among other ideas. The dining room was designed to express a certain feeling of being underwater. The wave-like ceiling in the dining room covers exhaust shafts, HUAC ducts, sprinklers, speakers, plumbing pipes and other elements. The steel columns and beams add another layer to the ceiling, giving an outdoor feeling to the dining room by the creation of a trellis effect. The long narrow beams are also a source of direct and indirect lighting in the space. The wine rack separates the dining room from the bar, accenting the outdoor idea by creating a sculpture garden effect.

The combination of a city which lacks hierarchy and creates an arena for experimentation, and the intensity which involves others to craft Saee's projects, generates the most energy in the architect's work.

ABOVE: Section and ceiling plan; BELOW: Beam detail

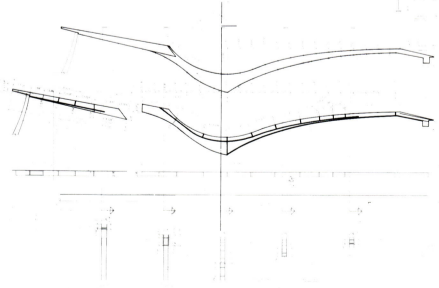

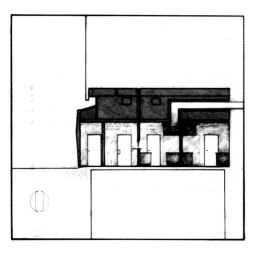 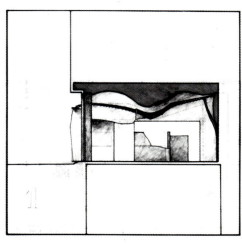 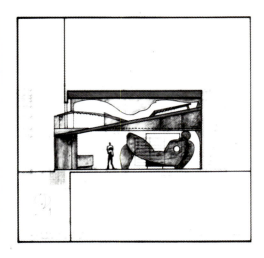

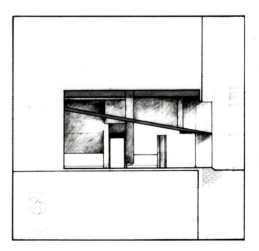
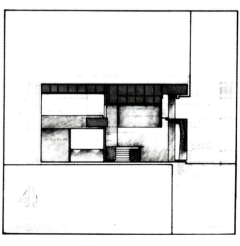

Sections

325

RESTAURANTS, BARS AND SHOPS

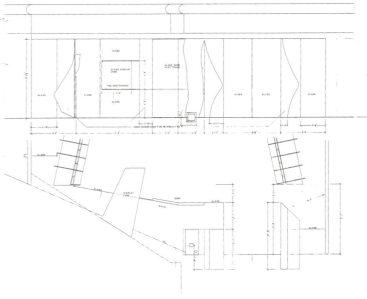

MICHELE SAEE
ECRU MARINA
Marina del Rey

Located in the Marina Marketplace shopping mall a few doors along from the Angeli Mare Restaurant, Ecru punctures the otherwise uneventful two-storey open shopping mall with its sculptural forms that invade the pavement: a glass vitrine protrudes out of the store, supported on a fin of structural glass that pierces the glazed shop front. Plywood sculptures, inspired by an Indian figurine, stand at an angle to the convex glass door.

The store is divided into three strips: the nave is bracketed by undulating, plywood-panelled walls mounted on wooden ribs and the elongated spaces on either side of the store are reached via slots in the ribbed walls and serve as changing rooms with fabric partitions.

Near the entrance of the shop is a contoured column from which a massive glass and wood display case is cantilevered, and at the other end, a stand of pivoting mirrors. Angled display credenzas of wood incorporate faceted benches. Part of the floor in the main space was covered with wood to level a two-inch difference in grade. The remainder of the floor is stained and sealed concrete. The ceiling is made of warped gypboard, evocatively shaped like the bottom of a boat. Saee's graceful custom boom lighting throws the sculpted ceiling into relief; the recessed lights in the exterior canopy are set into eye-shaped cavities in keeping with the anthropomorphic motifs elsewhere.

ABOVE: Partial plan and elevation

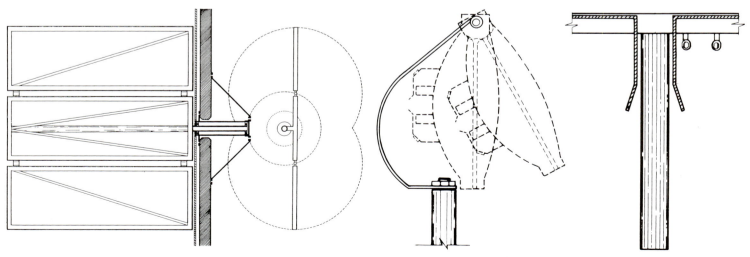

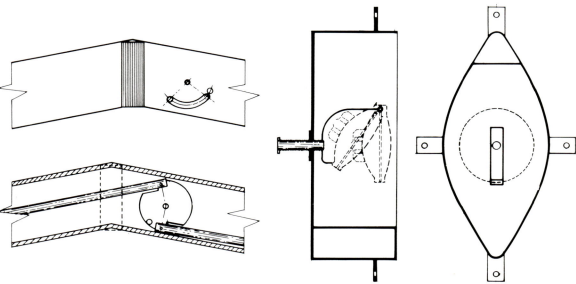

Details

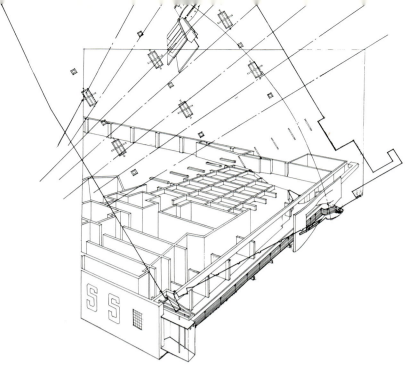

MICHELE SAEE
DESIGN EXPRESS
Downtown

A 40,000 square-foot industrial building alongside a set of train tracks was converted into a showroom for high fashion furniture. The front of the building was designed as a facade facing a major boulevard. The only modulation of the cavernous space is created by a series of glass and steel vitrines. Welding and grinding marks and graffiti found on site were left intact. Together with the wood ceiling and concrete forms, these raw forms and the steel interventions contrast with the highly refined furniture on display.

As Design Express reveals, as much here as in his other projects, the overall design process for Michele Saee is the product of a thought, an intention, a desire to explore; but the process of making and seeing those thoughts in practice leads one to understand the reality of life and ourselves. We need to learn to see things inside out and outside in.

ABOVE: Cutaway

TED TOKIO TANAKA

CALIFORNIA BEACH ROCK 'N SUSHI
Hollywood

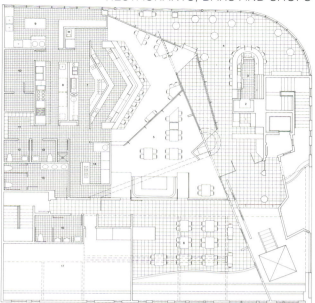

This rock'n roll sushi restaurant is located in the heart of Melrose Avenue, taking its place in the milieu of hip boutiques, galleries and restaurants.

Kazu, the owner, wanted to bring the California beach scene to this trendy shopping street. The beach spirit is captured in its free-flowing plan, and its multi-layered forms and bright colours hit the senses like a succession of waves. Props and metaphors abound. Enter by the lifeguard station and meet the surf and sand, complete with sharks, surfboards and outdoor sunshine.

Movement as a theme is interpreted by the sensuous plan and forms. *Kumo* (Japanese for clouds) hang overhead; waves and mountains are created with reflective glass, glossy plastic laminates and metal railing. Even the triangle and diamond-shaped tables look like the shimmering reflections of the sea.

The art work provides bright beach colours and a childlike impression of the pop characters found at the beach scene. If all this is not enough to alter the mood, the loud MTV music and multi-screen videos certainly give a definite rhythm to it.

The making of sushi is a performing art, and the sushi counter becomes a stage with an array of bubbling water tubes acting as a backdrop. Within this beach theatre, the punk-haired sushi chefs dazzle and entertain while artistically presenting the riches of the sea. California Beach presents Eastern food on Western shores in an atmosphere of fun and amusement.

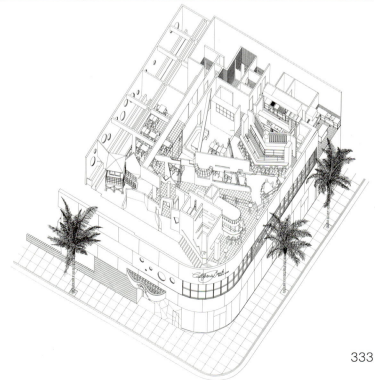

ABOVE: Floor plan; BELOW: Axonometric

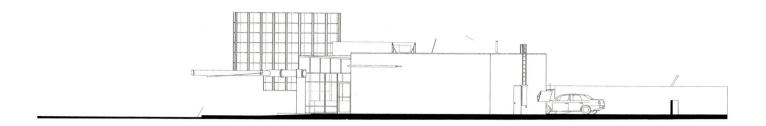

CENTRAL OFFICE OF ARCHITECTURE
BRIX RESTAURANT
Marina del Rey

Brix is a 1,300 square-foot drive-through health food restaurant in a typical commercial lot located in a mixed one- and two-storey commercial zone near a major intersection. The restaurant consists of large kitchen, a small serving and dining area, an office and a drive-up window.

This area of the city is unstructured and lacks any desirable architectural/urban principles worth reinforcing. To counter this chaotic structure it was necessary to present a unified and recognisable street elevation to potential customers as they drove by at relatively high speeds. This was accomplished by the intervention of a long floating wall/screen placed between the street edge and the face of the building. The semi-transparent mask constructed of perforated metal and various steel sections, operates simultaneously at two levels: it acts as a filter dampening the visual and audio noise generated in the street, and as a found urban object pulled from its normative functional context, it is an empty sign allowing for the layering and collapse of the three dimensional building behind it. During the day one can track the movement of the shadow of the silhouetted object while at night the glass dining room becomes a light box projecting artificial light through the screen. Given that the programmatic area for the restaurant is quite small, the design strategy amplifies the presence of the building on the site, successfully defining the street edge.

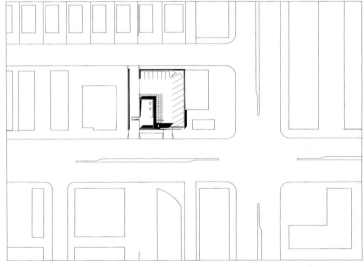

ABOVE: North-west elevation; BELOW: Site plan

LOS ANGELES AS IT WILL BE

LIFE IN A SOCIAL EXPERIMENT
Maggie Toy — 340

CULTURAL CENTRES
Richard Meier
The Getty Center — 348
Morphosis
Science Museum School — 352
Frank Gehry
Walt Disney Concert Hall — 354
Eric Owen Moss
SMSC — 356
Moore Ruble Yudell
Hollywood Entertainment Museum — 358

TRANSPORT
Ellerbe Becket
Metro Red Line — 360

MIXED USE DEVELOPMENT
Moore Ruble Yudell
Playa Vista Masterplan — 364
Moule & Polyzoides
Playa Vista — 368
Hodgetts + Fung
Hudson-Wilcox — 372

PRIVATE RESIDENCES
Rotondi
CDLT 1, 2 Cedar Lodge Terrace — 374
Carlson/Reges Residence and Gallery — 376
Eric Owen Moss
Aronoff House — 378
Coop Himmelblau
Rehak House — 382
Melrose I — 384
Moule & Polyzoides
Arnaz Condominiums — 386
Frank Israel
Drager House — 388
Baldwin House — 390

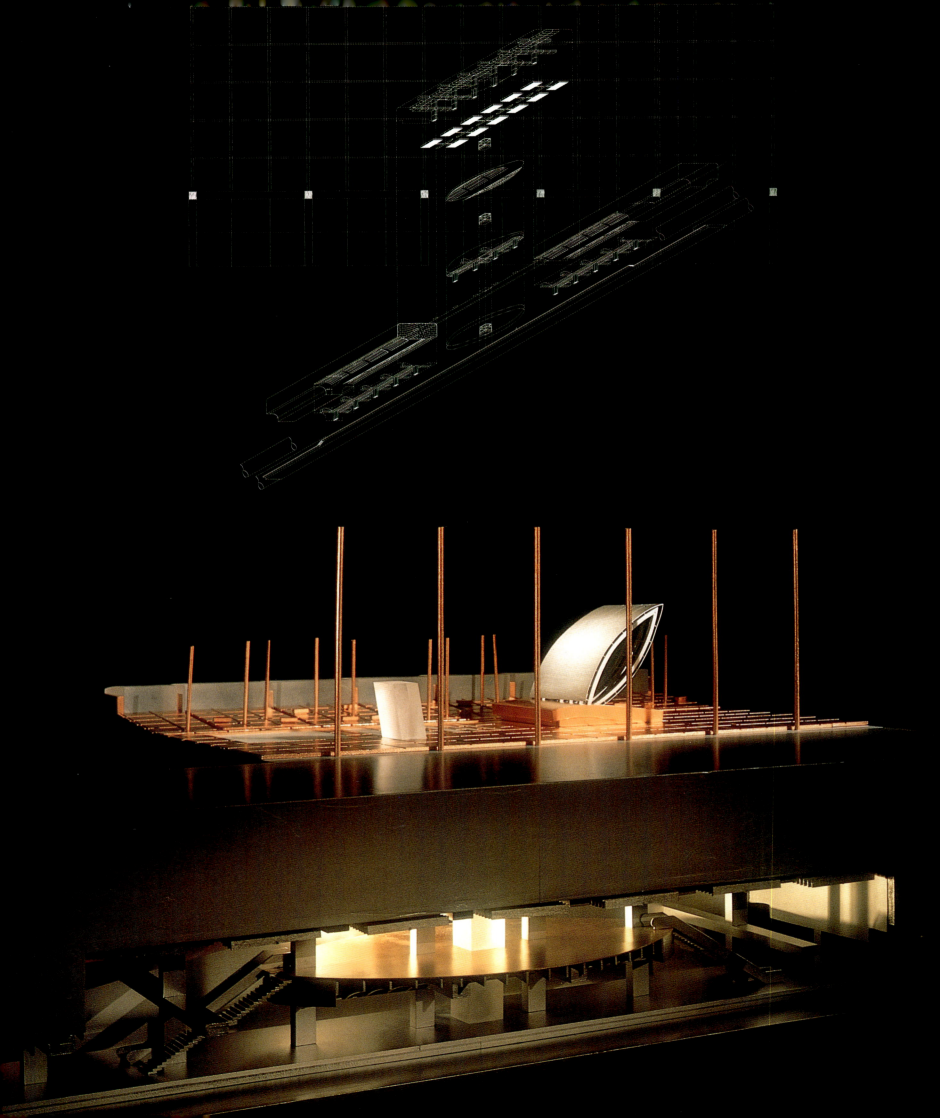

LIFE IN A SOCIAL EXPERIMENT
MAGGIE TOY

Mythology is a triumph of belief over reality, depending for its survival not on evidence but on constant reiteration . . . they endure because they serve social needs.   Helena Kennedy

Los Angeles is the most polyglot city in the world today, with the local Chamber of Commerce statistics confirming that there are more Thais living there than in Bangkok, more Koreans than in Seoul and more Mexicans than in Mexico City. This unprecedented cultural mix has obviously had considerable effect on the evolving architecture, whether it responds to this mixture or deliberately ignores it. Each distinct ethnic group chooses to perpetuate the social patterns and traditions carried within it from a previous context. In spite of planning initiatives which have attempted to centralise the city's infrastructure – such as the metro link – Los Angeles remains a series of disconnected suburbs, with each of these fragmented still further into more specific ethnic enclaves. The most recent statistics suggest that the Asian community is the most volatile group within those cities within the city. Chinese, Koreans, Japanese and Thais, who represent over ten per cent of the total population of Los Angeles, have increased by 110 per cent over the last ten years. This group is followed, over the same time frame, by Hispanics at 37.8 per cent of the population, a 62.2 per cent increase, and Blacks representing 11.2 per cent of the total, which amounts to a 5.2 per cent increase. The group which has decreased in its representation in Los Angeles over this ten-year period consists of non-Hispanic Whites and native American Indians, and Eskimos and Aluets; totalling 41.3 per cent of the population – a decrease in numbers by 13.9 per cent.

A map of Los Angeles County – such as those featured in Charles Jencks' *Heteropolis* – outlining the geographical concentration of the groups, reads like a diagram of the influence of numerous Shoguns in feudal Edo. The lines of demarcation are quite definite with position, in connection to physical and natural amenities clearly determined by economic factors. The white population, for instance, is predominantly located near the Pacific, stretching from the Palisades in the north through to Santa Monica in the centre and the beach communities strung out along the south-west, all the way to the Orange County border. In dramatic contrast, the black population is concentrated in the south-central part of the city. Its boundaries have been 'red-lined' by financial institutions which refuse to grant mandatory loans inside these economically-established areas.

The Hispanic population is predicted to double, exceeding 80 per cent of the total population by the turn of the century. Its own confident prediction is that Los Angeles, which began as a Hispanic-Mexican City, will come full circle and end up as one. This group is mainly restricted to the interior, but has more apparent mobility for reasons that are still unclear.

The fastest growing of all groups is the Asian community, which has staked out areas such as 'Koreatown' occupied by 'Americans' between Westen, Vermont and Wilshire. Coincidentally, this was one of the major flash points of the riots of April 1992, indicative of the fact that the real issue behind the violence was not so much prejudice as economics. Anger resulting from friction between the African-Americans and Koreans was brought on by commercial competition for rapidly-shrinking markets due to the change in racial mix of the city. Neither the riots nor the desperately underfunded *Rebuild LA* programme – led by the 1985 Olympic organiser Peter Ueberroth – has served to dissipate the tension. It is almost inevitable that there will be further incidents, since the ingredients have not changed. The palpable tension that fills the air, as the Asian community continues to grow and prosper, is perceptibly increasing.

Although the traditional ethnic powerbase is actually decreasing in size, it has been reinforced by recent mayoral elections, and therefore continues to act as before. In recent attempts to renew enthusiasm for a master strategy to the plan of the Downtown area, this group has ignored the reality of Downtown now bracketed by the Barrio on the eastern edge and 'Little Guatemala' on the north-west. This has resulted in phenomena such as large commercial zones in the central business district which have been given to a single segment of the population and attempts, by the rapidly crumbling power base, to change this equation into one that would be more acceptable to them. Attempts to find a happy medium have so far

OPPOSITE: Ellerbe Becket, Metro Red Line, Vermont/Santa Monica Station

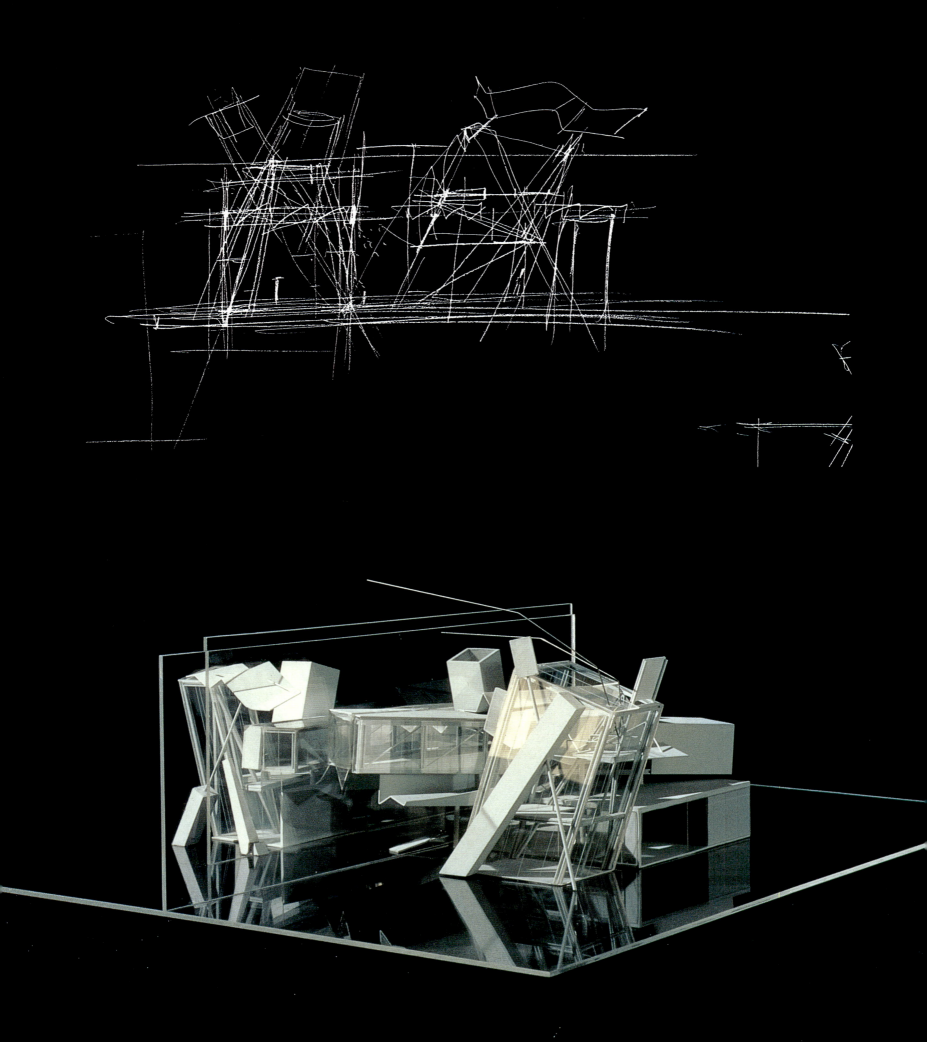

been of the half-hearted, sanitised kind working towards a cultural approach that borders on tokenism.

The future of any city is difficult to predict; but it is especially difficult with Los Angeles. One is certain that the ethnic mix of the city will intensify and continue to influence changes in politics and the world view. When economic conditions are good, the tendency is to credit such diversity. Financial prosperity in the past has been partly attributed to the fact that Los Angeles is a 'melting pot' – or to use the popular metaphor – 'tossed salad', of separate but nevertheless related ingredients.

In times of economic hardship, however, the search for scapegoats rises and illegal immigrants are the first target. As Kevin Starr explains, this attitude prevailed in the 1930s towards 'Dustbowl immigrants', and culminated in the dispatch of 126 police officers to seal-off California's land borders. Any American who could not prove his or her net worth was prevented from entering the state. Like the Chinese, the Japanese and the Dustbowlers before them, illegal Mexican immigrants are perceived not only as a threat to the economy, but also as a threat to a certain, established way of life. This perceived threat has deep psychological roots. As Starr points out: 'what previous generations struggled for across a lifetime – the chance to live and work in America – is stolen by means of false papers'. One only has to visit the American border between San Diego and Tijuana to witness the nightly exodus of young men moving northwards, defying the ingenious but inadequate border patrols. The traffic of people across the Bury freeway dividing the two countries, has itself been cause for concern to the US police force who has had to deal with a horrifying level of accidents. Signs were erected for motorists depicting a man, a woman and a child 'fleeing', as a warning to slow down. Ironically and often tragically, Mexicans interpreted the signs as places to cross and this particular piece of roadside iconography proved literally fatal. The broader picture, of which the illegal Mexican immigration issue is a part, is the underground economy, and black market papers and permissions. One argument is that Mexicans are doing the jobs that Americans do not want to do. Another opinion is that jobs created by the Mexican immigrants far outweigh the jobs taken by them. The picture today is complex. Mexican immigrants are stratified into a tier system: those who have established themselves into a city (usually after great hardship); the new arrivals; and those who remain in a marginal situation, resented by their compatriots.

Other ethnic groups must go through a vetting procedure of airport immigration. Rather than the traditional East Coast gateway, the West Coast is now the popular point of entry for prospective immigrants into the country. The deeper reasons serve as a barometer for the shift in geographical power since the disruptions caused by industrialisation in the 19th century and the rural-urban migration that ensued, caused great poverty and an exodus to the promise of a better life. Today, people coming from the Pacific Basin leave areas perceived globally as 'Rapidly Industrialising Countries' (RICs). The geographer Thomas Jablously has said: 'The influx of immigrants to Los Angeles creates challenges for the city similar to those faced by New York, Boston and Chicago when they absorbed newcomers from Southern and Eastern Europe at the end of the 19th and beginning of the 20th century'. The challenges today are to create a sense of community in an environment that fosters a proliferation of ghettos. In Los Angeles, perhaps more than any other city, large distances between ethnically-defined areas are covered only by freeways and broad surface streets which the poor new arrival has little chance of penetrating.

In such physical surroundings it is easy to see how the lack of interaction afforded by such physical surroundings works against the ideal of a single community. By way of contrast, their proximity to one another and the necessity of public transport and centralised services, meant that the immigrants were forced to 'integrate' to some extent. In this extreme case of decentralised, multi-faceted and diversified culture, it is understandable that any new arrival may not immediately be imbued with a coherent sense of American identity. Today that identification must come, not from the immediate surroundings, or from daily interaction with 'American citizens' but from a more phenomenal source – TV and films. Ironically the latter is the major industry that the city is busily engaged in creating.

Films have been making predictions on the position of Los Angeles in the future. Ridley Scott's *Blade Runner* showed Harrison Ford dodging the effective 'thought police' system and falling in love with a robot. Frightened robots were exterminated because of the perpetual fear that the humans would be taken over by them. All this took place against a backdrop of towering constructions which still failed to penetrate the smog, and a haunting voice tempting the inhabitants away with promise of a new life on another satellite. Mike Davis argues that this genre of film, full of predictions, indicates that inevitable 'images of carceral inner cities (*Running Man*), high-tech police death squads (*Blade Runner*), sentient buildings (*Die Hard*), urban bantustans (*They Live*), Vietnam-like street wars (*Colors*), and so on, only extrapolate from actually existing trends'.

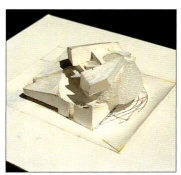

OPPOSITE: Coop Himmelblau, Melrose I, West Hollywood; ABOVE: Frank Gehry, Disney Concert Hall, Downtown; BELOW: Eric Owen Moss, SMSC, Santa Monica

LOS ANGELES AS IT WILL BE

Such visions are born of what we see around us. The assumption that this is the direction in which Los Angeles is heading is hardly a positive comment on the 'city of the future'. Nonetheless they are frighteningly apposite. The repetitive scenario – dark smog-filled days; tall dominating, oppressive buildings; no public space; no means for social intercourse; an acceptance of ethnic warfare and everyday violence – describes an anarchic future for the city. All the factual information available confirms this scenario. Crime rates, for instance, continue to increase as Charles Jencks outlines: 'Even in 1992, in spite of the gangland truce and expressions of goodwill following the riots, homicide and crime rates continue to soar yearly'. However accurate it may be, the representation of Los Angeles life by both the movies and the intellectual assessments of scholars such as Mike Davis and Peter Plagens, does not emotionally assist in its rebuilding. This task, however, must be faced if any new direction away from hell is to be found.

The governing of Los Angeles echoes the disparate city itself. Professor Jane Pisano has observed: 'We have created powerful single-focus regional institutions to solve single problems. . . [The authority of cities] is being replaced by a very fragmented system of governance which is neither effective nor accountable to people'. It is worth noting that many of the immigrants bring the experience of ineffective government with them and are hence more accustomed to self-determination than to any reliance on any rational administrative system.

The architects who work in Los Angeles have a clear and potentially influential role to play in meeting the challenge of easing relations between the disparate groups that occupy the city. Schemes that bring communities together outside the established enclaves are more in the spirit of the future, as they can take a major lead in the process of initiating a sense of cross-cultural integration. Another Hollywood epic springs to mind when the responsibility of the architect is called upon to drastically change and shape the city. In Ayn Rand's *The Fountainhead*, Howard Roark plays the dreadfully chauvinistic character who pursues his beliefs for the future of the environment at all odds, until at the happy ending he is able to create his style of architecture without even the restriction of a budget. Architectural power is only as effective as the financial backing power behind it but there are possibilities of an architectural contribution to improve the city. The Howard Roark saga chronicles a time in architecture when there was a move to replace all that was bad in building with one omnipotent, international style of architecture and planning. Now that the errors of that movement have been learnt, the emphasis in Los Angeles needs to be on the maintenance of the representation of the pluralistic society contained therein. The architects carving the future city can be seen to be achieving this pluralistic aim. If this pattern could be extended to all sectors of the community, the process of degeneration could be slowed down.

The Green Party of Los Angeles has put together a proposal for the reconstruction and rebuilding of Los Angeles called *Cooperate LA*. The manifesto, written by Dennis Bottum, Mike Feinstein and Watt Sheasby, outlines the extreme tensions in Los Angeles and presents possible alternatives to the present annihilistic direction. This scheme confirms its belief that the Ueberroth scheme will not work and details the methods which it believes will succeed: 'Only policies that promote community self-determination and self-reliance can lead us to a just and sustainable society'.

Its proposal outlines that all reconstruction and redevelopment should incorporate three key principles. Firstly, on the issue of self-determination, economic and political decisions should be made by the communities which they affect. Secondly, there needs to be a concerted effort to conserve the natural wealth of animal and land resources and to effect improvements for the environment for future generations. Finally, economic structures should be established which support local ownership and control, assist in the self-reliance of the community and plough back profits into the community.

The Green Party outlines ten methods by which these principles should be realised, one of which includes affordable housing. This suggests that the present plan by the Department of Housing and Urban Development to privatise public housing demonstrates an abandonment of responsibility. At the moment property taxes are levied on sites which consequently remain undeveloped. Buildings are allowed to decay and lie idle to avoid being taxed for improvements. If taxes were transferred from property to land, the land prices would decrease, taking the speculative advantage out of holding the land. Coupled with the lower building tax, this would mean lower housing costs which would ultimately enable more housing units and would also rejuvenate and promote efficient land use in urban areas. This solution corresponds to the Green Party's determination to improve the use of land in general and to design on a human scale. To create an improved sense of place in Los Angeles, the Green Party insists on the promotion of increase in open space, pedestrian oriented design, cycle usage, mixed use planning to decrease commuting, energy-efficient building and transport routes: all aspects that can be taken on by the architect and planner.

OPPOSITE ABOVE: Coop Himmelblau, Open House, Malibu; OPPOSITE BELOW: Moore Ruble Yudell, Playa Vista Masterplan, Marina del Rey (Developers: Maguire Thomas Partners); ABOVE: Hodgetts + Fung, Thames House, Hollywood

LOS ANGELES AS IT WILL BE

Other instruments for improvement include better community-police relations, political reform, education versus incarceration and community development co-operation. Its report is an accurate but encouraging assessment of Los Angeles as it is now and how it could be in the future. It is easier to be negative about the existing situation in Los Angeles and the Green Party has placed itself in a position which invites criticism from the 'dark scenario writers'. If these measures were heeded, the end product might be the survival and blossoming of a city that has at least superficially personified the American Dream.

Predictions for the future of Los Angeles are as extreme as its own characterisation. A recent article in *Time* magazine described the city as a place 'where suburbs merge together in a giant urban sprawl, commuters are gridlocked in freeways, pollution is rife and massive influxes of immigrants burden the schools; where disparity between rich and poor is intense and the only affordable homes for miles around are miles from people's jobs'. Pushed to its furthest extreme, a scenario of unbridled violence and chaos has been developed by futurists as their prediction of the ultimate destiny of Los Angeles.

The recent discovery of thousands of homeless living under a freeway that had been enclosed by side walls brought one aspect of this nightmarish vision into uncomfortably sharp focus. Similar stories of legions of displaced people living in the underworld of New York's heating and ventilation shafts, basements and abandoned subway channels, while equally tragic, could not convey the shocking disjunction of stultifying destitution beneath a symbol of progress, freedom and literally, mobility. When the socialists interviewed the people under the freeways who had organised themselves into small communities based on their joint survival strategy, they reiterated the callousness of the society that they felt peripheral to, that it was 'too hard out there'.

The litany of perplexing problems in the 'paradise' continues: Los Angeles has, according to Professor Pisano, 'by far the worst air quality of the nation' and problems of waste disposal and water quality are magnified by rapid population growth. The county region that constitutes Los Angeles is growing twice as fast as the rest of the country, with over 13.4 million inhabitants. According to the *LA 2000* report (written in 1988), these figures are projected to reach 18.1 million by the year 2010.

Architectural styles of the past have, to a certain extent, been directed by fashion. The existing pluralistic condition has precipitated a state of searching for a direction. Whilst I am fairly sure that many of the architects concerned would not admit to this, or indeed, would not be aware of it, a certain direction is being gleaned from the increasing interest in what drives the universe and how it is organised. The recent investigation of the Chaos Theory for example, explores an awareness that perhaps it is not driven through patterns and organised systems but has a spiritual root. Although this is an architectural idea, it is also followed through into behaviour patterns. Churches become fuller during periods of lean times for example; the search for a greater force than we understand to plead to and to delegate responsibility to is certainly a prevalent need in times of hardship. Could architecture search for direction within this multiplicitous context, which parallels the search for an unknown all powerful force and lead us to salvation?

Despite, and perhaps even because of, the problems faced by Los Angeles, many see the city as an important model of the city of the future. Significantly this optimism is epitomised by Angelenos themselves, who take little notice of the pessimists and are in a continual process of self-improvement. Although Los Angeles is the only city in America to deliberately obliterate its river (this too in the name of progress – the army corps and engineers decided that it should run in an orderly and controllable concrete channel) the 'friends of the LA River' have taken on the Herculean task of restoring it; a project rivalled only in scope by John Nash's serpentine connection between Buckingham Palace and Regent's Park in London.

The building schemes we can expect to see in the immediate future include a selection of projects which engender a sense of community spirit. Much talk is made of the Disney Center by Frank Gehry, as it addresses the whole issue of public space and community spirit. It is an important building in the city and its interaction with the space around it suggests an attempt to encourage a sense of place and perhaps of pride in the city. It is a positive piece which, it is hoped, will encourage the sense of community outlined by the Green Party, amongst others.

The Metro project by Ellerbe Becket also attempts to revive this spirit in the public transport system in Los Angeles, encouraging the use of a shared resource to invoke a sense of pleasure in travel and to provide a more ecologically sound alternative to the system currently in use. We also expect to see the completion of Richard Meier's Getty Center, placed majestically amongst parks and open space. It is similar to the Ellerbe Becket scheme in that it creates a sense of community, although one wonders how limited the community it serves will be.

Of course there is no certainty that all these schemes will be completed – there are few certainties in the future: that is what makes it so

Moule & Polyzoides, Downtown Strategic Plan

compelling – but this selection goes some way in presenting what will probably happen in the architectural environment of future Los Angeles.

Following the January 1994 earthquake, seismologists tend to agree that there is a 50 per cent chance of another one in the next twenty years, scoring eight or even more on the Richter Scale. Furthermore, there is as great a chance of a seven-point rupture occurring in the manner of the 1933 Long Beach quake that killed up to 23,000 people. Natural and unnatural calamities not only reflect the unprecedented co-operative spirit in Angelenos, but as the 1994 earthquake has shown, promise a spirit of survival and bravado in the face of adversity. Los Angeles is defying both geographical obstacles and the disillusionment that could ultimately force its inhabitants to seek a more secure future elsewhere. This defiance might be the most salient motif of both the city and its people.

Bibliography
Ayn Rand, *The Fountainhead*, Granada, St Alban's, Herts, first published 1947
Charles Jencks, *Heteropolis*, Academy Editions, 1993
Franklin D Israel, Academy Editions, 1994
Moore Ruble Yudell, Academy Editions, 1993
Mike Davis, *City of Quartz: Excavating the Future in Los Angeles*, Vintage, London, 1992
LA 2000: A City for the Future, Los Angeles 2000 Committee, 1988
Joel Garreau, *Edge City: Life on the New Frontier*, Doubleday, New York, 1991
'The Periphery', *Architectural Design*, March/April, 1994
Kevin Starr, *Blueprints for Modern Living: History and Legacy of the Case Study Houses*, MIT Press in conjunction with the Museum of Contemporary Art, LA, Cambridge, Mass, 1989
Peter Plagen, 'The Ecology of Evil', *Art Forum*, December 1972
Helena Kennedy, *Eve was Framed: Women and British Justice*, Vintage, London, 1992
Los Angeles Architecture: The Contemporary Condition, James Steele, Phaidon Press, London, 1993

Still from Blade Runner

CULTURAL CENTRES

RICHARD MEIER
THE GETTY CENTER
Santa Monica

When the personal estate of John Paul Getty passed into trust in 1982, it was decided to expand its mandate beyond the confines of a single museum in order to more accurately reflect his wish that it should assist in 'the diffusion of artistic and general knowledge'. From its inception, the museum has concentrated on holdings in a limited number of areas, preferring to strengthen specific interests rather than seek general coverage.

The trustees purchased 110 acres in the foothills of the Santa Monica Mountains. Meier's schematic design consisted of six separate buildings connected by tram to a parking structure for public use at the base of the mountain, organised around terraced gardens landscaped with indigenous plants on the lower elevations of the site. The final design was presented in 1991.

Each of the six buildings is clustered along two ridges, with the museum located at the point where they intersect. The museum will dominate the eastern elevation and is organised around a tall, circular lobby, located in such a way as to provide visual orientation of the five, two-storey high galleries located around a garden court. In four of these five 'pavilions' the galleries are organised around atriums which are either open to the sky or covered by glass. Enclosed and covered walkways will link the lobby, the pavilions and the courtyard, allowing for a variety of paths through the museum.

Richard Meier's personal vision of the project is that it is 'essentially classical'. With its regular rhythms and axial organisation, the Getty Center will embody that realm of the rational and the human.

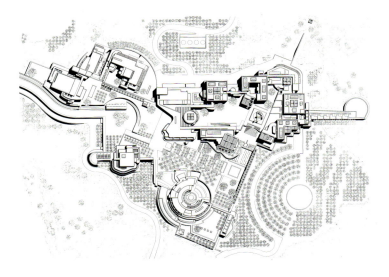

ABOVE: Axonometric; BELOW: Site plan

349

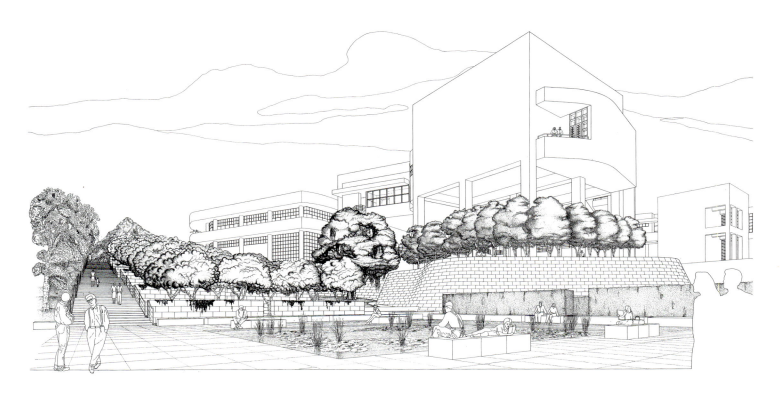

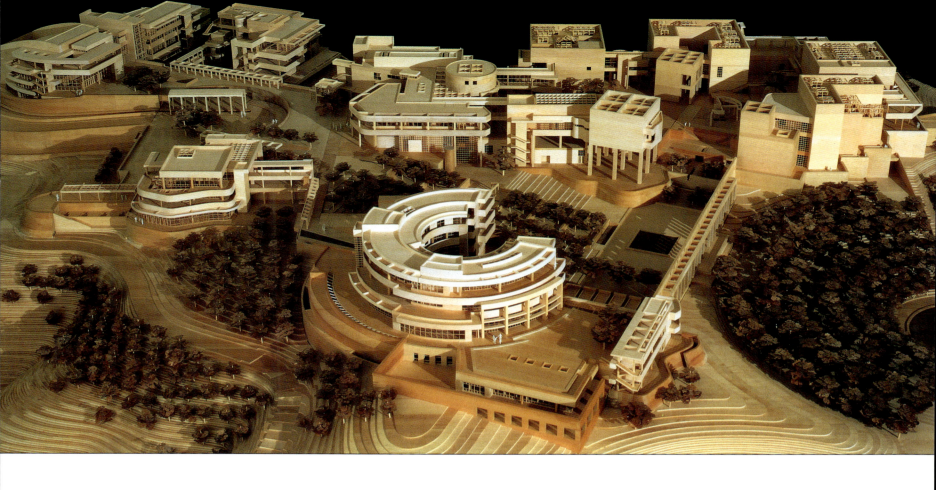

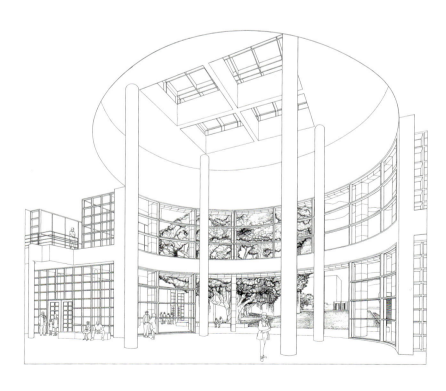

OPPOSITE: Perspective view of the central gardens, looking north; LEFT: Perspective view of the central lobby

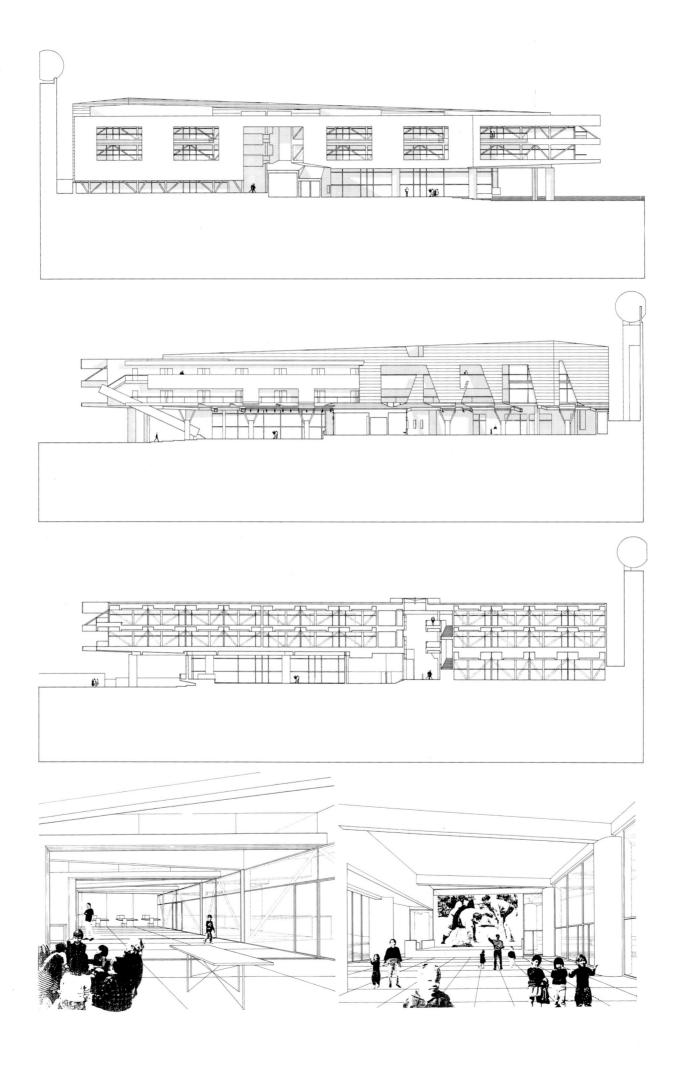

MORPHOSIS
SCIENCE MUSEUM SCHOOL
Downtown

The design for the Science Museum School provides the opportunity to make a connection between the project as an educational institution and an architecture which can communicate specific ideas that become interactive with the process of education. The architects were interested in integrating ideas of technology as they relate to building and nature into one cohesive environment. The existing landscape of Exposition Park (the Rose Garden) provided an opportunity to integrate the landscape into the basic organisational idea of the building. Given the tough environment of the Downtown area, the building was deliberately organised so that the school feels like an extension of the Rose Garden. Visually and mentally, this aspires to create a contemplative atmosphere for the school population.

The main building is situated in a linear manner creating two different facades to the east and west while a conceptual extension of the Rose Garden extends through the site creating a more informal 'green' area between the campus and the school.

All public areas and the kindergarten are on the first floor connected to a central lobby; classrooms are located on the second and third floors. The administration is placed centrally in the main building allowing maximum control, while the media centre, seen as the 'electronic brain' of the school, links with the administration and occupies the area directly behind the armoury portico. The portico of the armoury building was incorporated into the new building to reinforce the notion that the architects build best when it is on a foundation of the past.

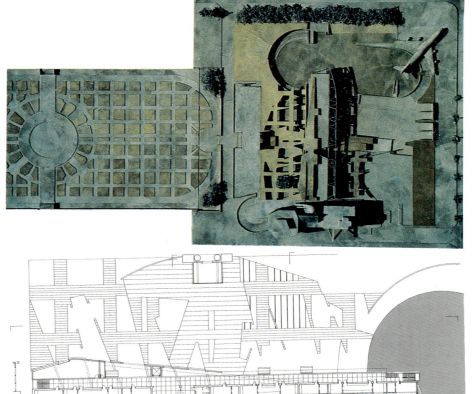

OPPOSITE FROM ABOVE: East elevation; west elevation; section; classroom module perspective; multipurpose room perspective; BELOW: Second floor plan

LOS ANGELES AS IT WILL BE

FRANK GEHRY
WALT DISNEY CONCERT HALL
Downtown

Located on a historically and culturally prominent downtown site, the Walt Disney Concert Hall is to become the Los Angeles Philharmonic's permanent home. The Concert Hall will be situated on historic Bunker Hill at the intersection of First Street and Grand Avenue, adjacent to the existing Music Center of Los Angeles. The 200,000 square-foot project began as an invitational design competition during which many of the fundamental design tenets were established, including an open and accessible 'front door', a sympathetic and inclusive attitude in the building's relationship to the Music Center's existing Chandler Pavilion, a pedestrian scale frontage along Grand Avenue, a generous and open backstage/musician area and a large garden in which the Hall rests.

The Concert Hall will not be located in the centre of the site, which consists of one city block. The majority of the site will be devoted to gardens, accessible not only from the Hall but from the adjacent streets, providing an oasis within the surrounding urban environment. An entry plaza will be located at the corner of First and Grand to relate the facility to the existing Music Center and a secondary entry plaza will be located at the corner of Second and Grand to provide primary access to the gardens. Unlike most concert halls, the building lobby will be dispersed along the street and will remain open during the day; large operable glass panels will provide maximum accessibility to various amenities including a pre-concert performance space. This area will be used for performance-related lectures, educational programmes and other scheduled and impromptu performances throughout the day.

The focus of the current design is the 2,400-seat Concert Hall, whose interior and form are a direct expression of acoustical parameters, resulting in both visual and acoustic intimacy. Wood seating blocks surround the orchestra platform and, together with the sail-like wooden ceiling forms, give one the impression of a great ship. A pipe organ will occupy a central position between seating blocks at stage rear. Skylights and a large window in the rear of the Hall allow natural light to enhance daytime concerts.

The exterior of the Concert Hall will be clad in a flower-like wrapper of French limestone and stainless steel. The building's orientation, combined with the curving and folding exterior stone, will present highly sculptural compositions as viewers move along Grand Avenue and through the surrounding gardens and plazas. An extensive backstage technical area surrounds the Hall and opens onto a private musicians' garden. The backstage door will open onto a semi-public garden and the largest rehearsal room will be placed near this entry to be used for small scale public performances. This openness of the backstage will encourage interaction between artists and the public. A 2,500-car garage on six levels will be constructed below the Hall with access from three surrounding streets. Concert-goers will arrive in the foyer from the garage by way of an escalator cascade which provides unique opportunities for art installations and brings daylight into the underground garage. Completion is scheduled for 1996.

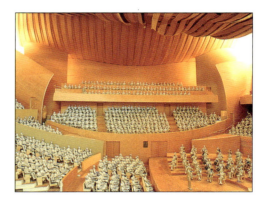

LOS ANGELES AS IT WILL BE

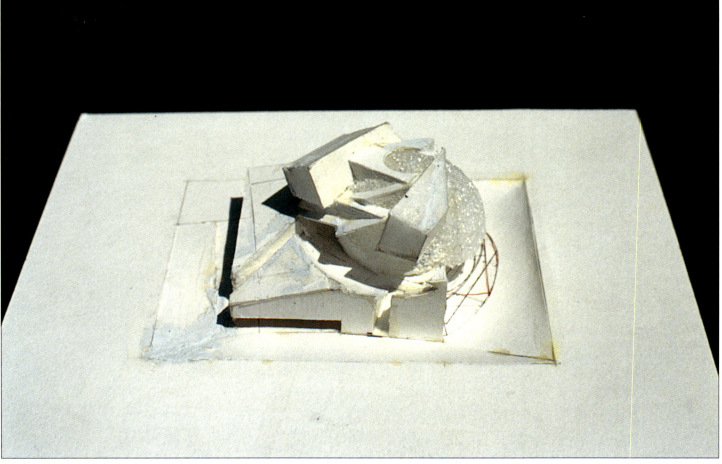

ERIC OWEN MOSS
SMSC
Santa Monica

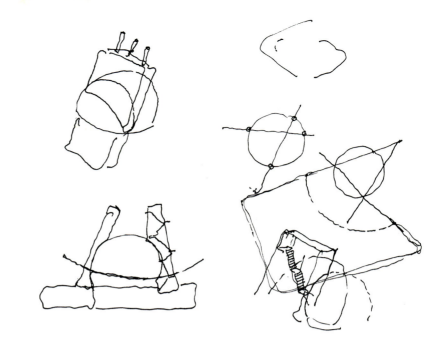

Both the project programme and the site organisation are in the preliminary planning stages for the SMSC (Santa Monica Science Center). The project's sketches and models are both literal and suggestive.

The focus of the project will be a 250-seat planetarium theatre using a Digistar projector and software. Additional telescopes likely to be included are a coelostat solar telescope, a one-metre reflecting telescope and possibly a small radio telescope.

Space will be provided for both conferences and exhibits and there will also be a retail area, classrooms, laboratories and production space. The Center will be used by local corporations, students, scientists and the general public.

ABOVE: Conceptual sketches; BELOW: Autocad 12 conceptual diagram evolved from sketches

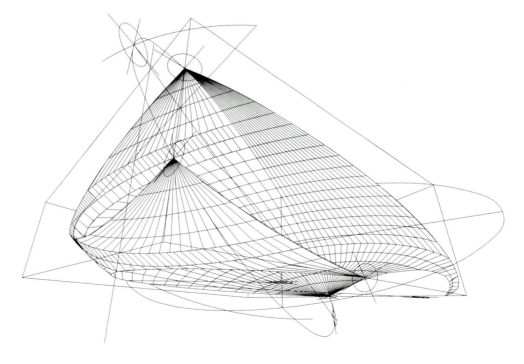

LOS ANGELES AS IT WILL BE

CULTURAL CENTRES

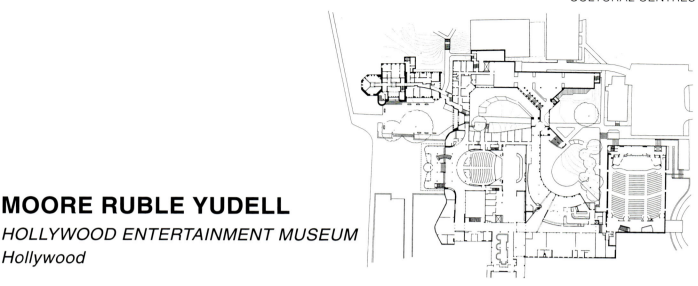

MOORE RUBLE YUDELL
HOLLYWOOD ENTERTAINMENT MUSEUM
Hollywood

Hollywood Entertainment Museum, scheduled for opening in autumn 1995, chronicles the historic and future eras of the broadcast media in Hollywood. The project involves the preservation and reuse of the original 2,700-seat Warner Theater by architect G Albert Landsburgh which, at the time of its opening in 1927, was the largest live stage and movie palace space in the city. It later housed the first radio station in the area. Located in the heart of Hollywood, the theatre itself will serve as the entry and focal point for the museum tour. The project contains a 'backlot' experience on the site to recreate the activity of a film set as well as to provide a place for special gatherings, openings and other events.

The basic philosophy of the Hollywood Entertainment Museum is to preserve and celebrate the closely intertwined histories of Hollywood as a place and as the central focus in the development of the entertainment industry. Renovating the great theatres and re-establishing its place along one of the most famous boulevards in American history are crucial. The underlying goals of the design are to use this theatre as a living cultural institution and to contribute to the revitalisation of Hollywood Boulevard and the surrounding neighbourhood.

The theatre space will be cleared of the subdivision walls and floors built in the 1970s to reveal the original volume and decorative treatments. Circulation will pass through the historic building with glimpses for the visitor into some of the important spaces as an introduction to the main exhibits that will be housed in the new three-storey structure built along the north side of the theatre.

The new museum building, containing the chronological story of the entertainment industry in Hollywood, will evoke the spirit of the original sound stages – large industrial-like spaces that provide the backdrop and support for the various sets and exhibits. The building is intended to complement the existing theatre without mimicking the historic style. It is placed against the taller, blank northern wall of the theatre building and has two tower elements that both recall the radio towers on the existing building and can serve as light beacons for the museum. The structural planning module will be expressed on the exterior as a series of truss-like columns with a carefully detailed infill panel system.

Visitors dropped off by bus or parked on the lot may gather in the 'backlot' plaza area and then walk through the covered passage to the Hollywood Boulevard entrance. Museum-related shops and restaurant facilities will be located in the storefront spaces along Hollywood Boulevard and Wilcox Avenue. The administrative offices will be placed on the upper floors of the original office block facing Hollywood Boulevard. The theatre basement will contain some mechanical and electrical rooms as well as back-of-house functions such as exhibit preparation areas.

With the Pacific Warner Theater returned to its original grandeur and retained as a functioning jewel and keystone of the project, and with the construction of a new adjacent building housing the specific exhibits, Hollywood will gain a new destination and an anchor for visitors to this important part of our civic heritage.

OPPOSITE LEFT, FROM ABOVE: Plaza area; view from Hollywood Boulevard; entrance; tower viewing platform; OPPOSITE RIGHT, FROM ABOVE: Cahuenga Boulevard elevation; north elevation; Wilcox Avenue elevation; Section through museum and existing theatre ABOVE: Site plan

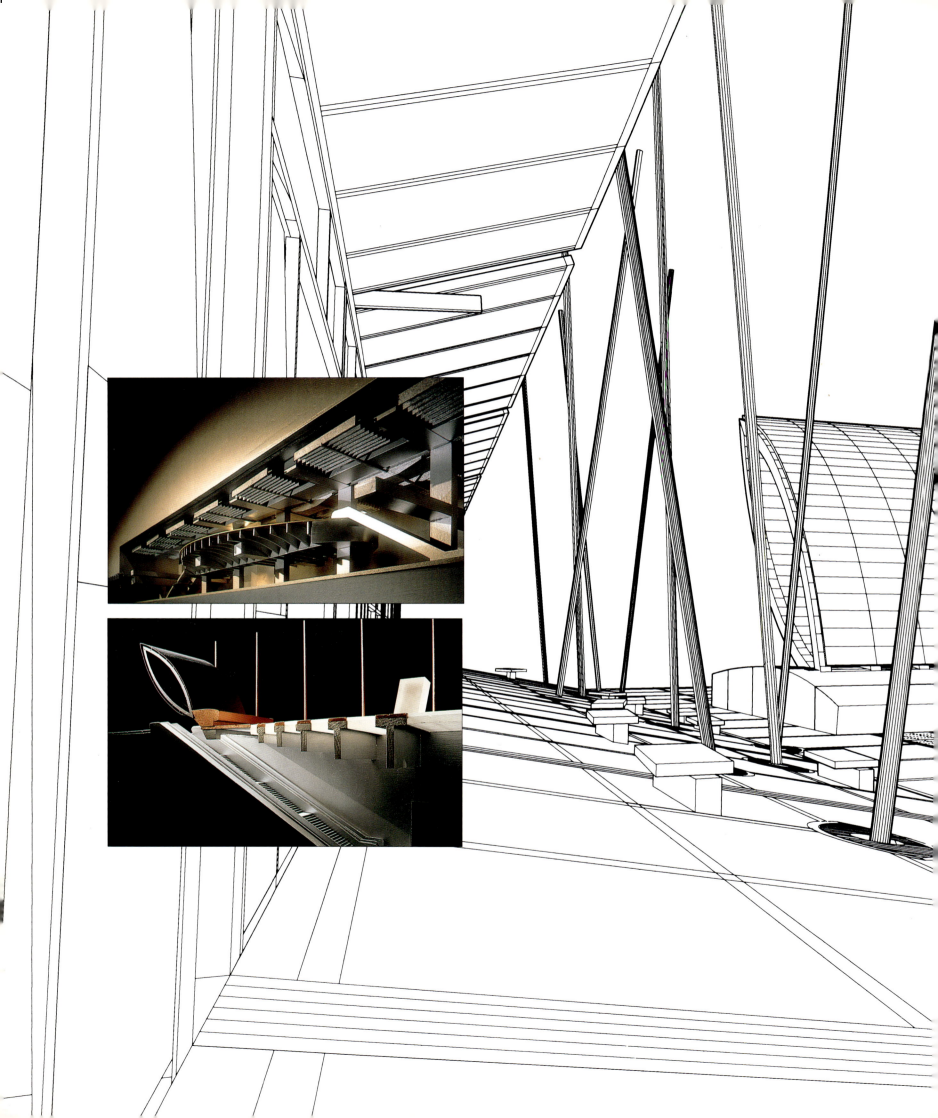

TRANSPORT

ELLERBE BECKET
METRO RED LINE
Vermont/Santa Monica Station

The Vermont/Santa Monica Station in Hollywood is part of a plan to improve connections in Los Angeles via rapid transit trains.

Ellerbe Becket is providing architectural design services for this project which comprises a public plaza on Vermont Avenue, a forty-foot long underground station and a circulation space which connects the two spaces. A stainless steel canopy, cantilevered thirty feet above the plaza, signals the entrance to the station.

For Los Angeles, the construction of the Metro Rail constitutes a new typology for the metropolitan area. This urban intervention affords an opportunity to address different urban forms and spatial experiences which have not existed before. This project attempts to understand and define some of these issues and to approach a solution of subtle complexity.

One of the largest stations on the Red Line, running from Downtown Los Angeles to North Hollywood, Vermont/Santa Monica is located one block from the Braille Institute and is adjacent to the Los Angeles City College. Due to its proximity to these institutions, the project incorporates art programmes of the college and utilises architectural elements of light, sound and materials to aid visually-impaired users.

BACKGROUND AND OVERLEAF: *Computer generated perspective views*

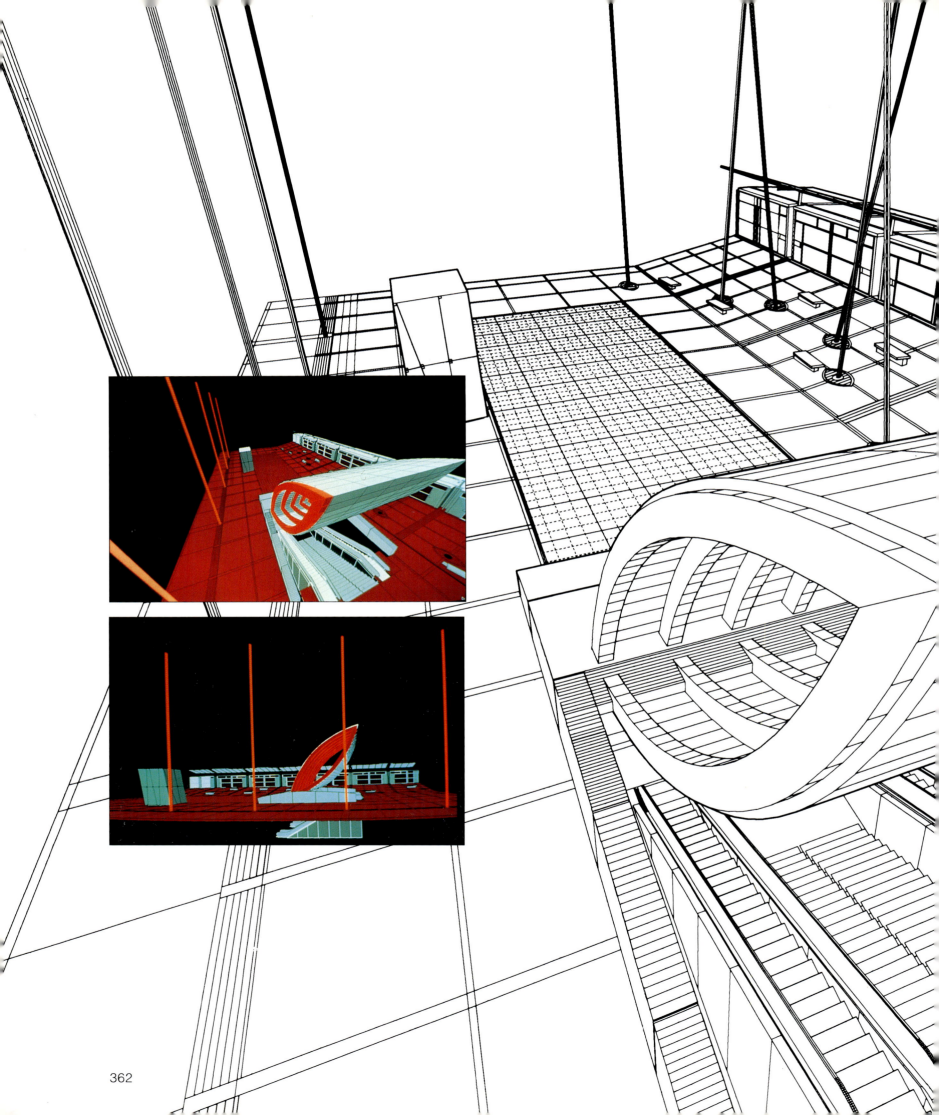

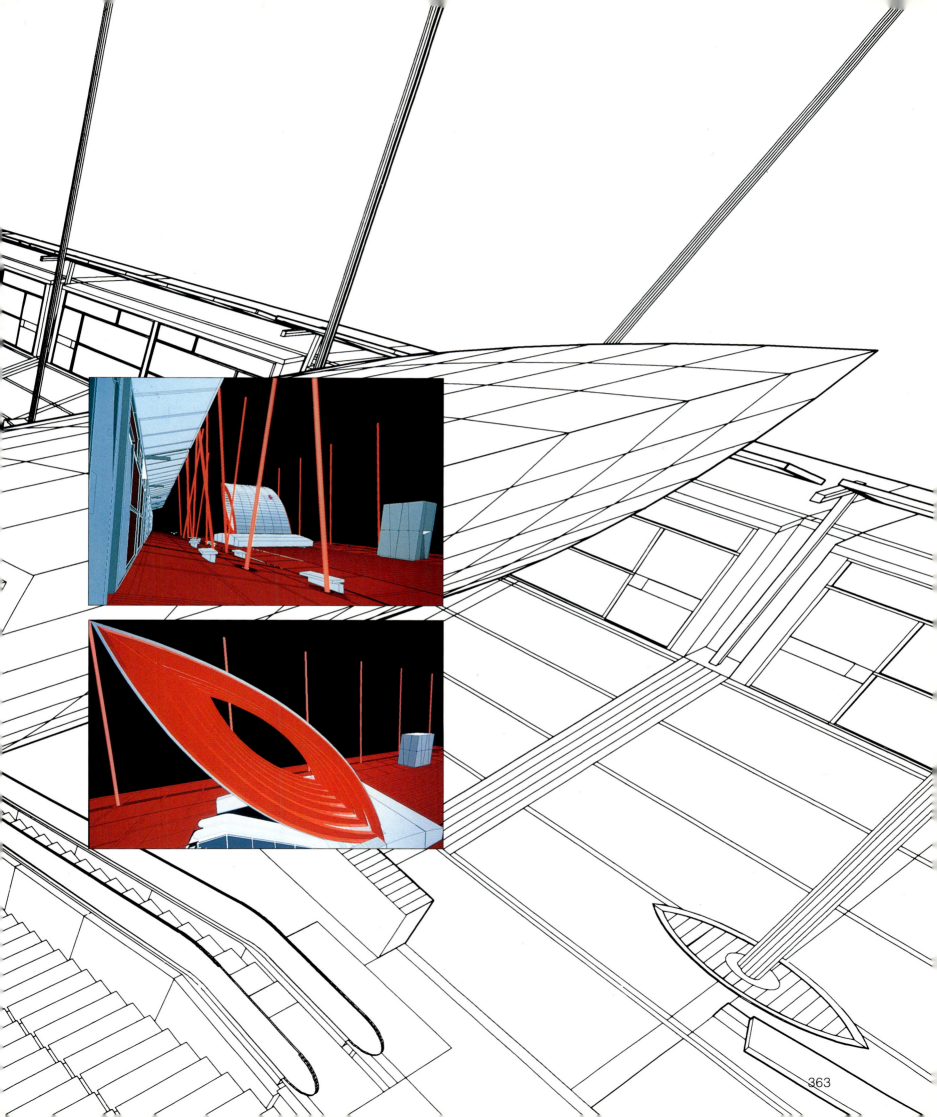

MOORE RUBLE YUDELL
PLAYA VISTA MASTERPLAN
Marina del Rey

Playa Vista is a major new urban development encompassing nearly 1,000 acres of largely undeveloped land at the heart of Los Angeles' Westside. In 1989 the architects were asked to participate in the creation of a masterplan that would include 11,750 units of housing, five million square feet of office space, 720,000 square feet of retail space, 2,400 hotel rooms and a forty-acre marina. Their challenge was to address social and environmental concerns within the economic constraints of the clients, in order to create an appropriate urban model for new development.

The first challenge was understanding what contributes to the sense of community in a place and how traditional patterns of development might inform approaches to such contemporary issues – from public transportation to waste treatment and recycling. Their strategy came to include a combination of traditional techniques including mixed-use, mid-density, mid-rise planning and the re-establishment of the importance of civic and cultural amenities as essential elements of the community.

Over 270 acres of existing wetlands on the site are to be preserved. On the remaining land an ordered system of blocks and streets weaves the new community into the fabric of the surrounding city. Retail civic and office uses are distributed among residential areas so that each unit of housing is within walking distance of transit, stores, schools, open space or places to work. A diversity of housing drawn from successful southern Californian precedents offers choices for housing and includes approximately twenty-five per cent affordable units.

OPPOSITE: Site masterplan

LOS ANGELES AS IT WILL BE

MIXED USE DEVELOPMENT

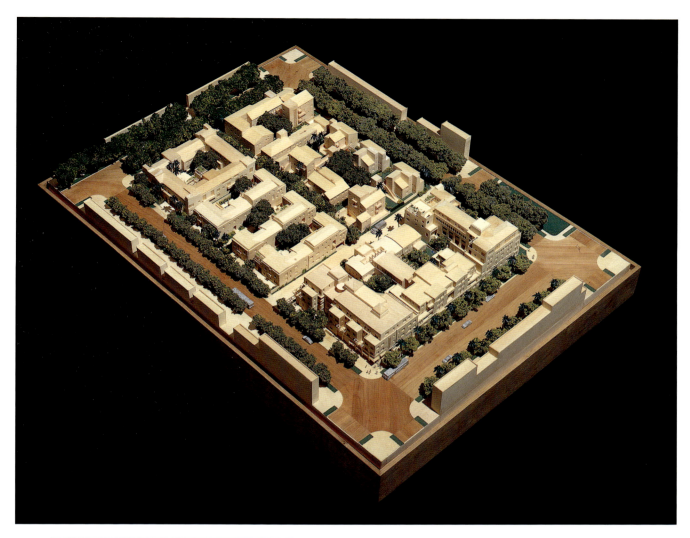

367

LOS ANGELES AS IT WILL BE

MIXED USE DEVELOPMENT

MOULE & POLYZOIDES
PLAYA VISTA
Marina del Rey

Playa Vista represents one of the most ambitious efforts to date towards reversing today's prevalent and destructive pattern of auto-oriented sprawl. Located on the former site of Howard Hughes' airport and factory between Venice, Marina del Rey, Playa del Rey and Culver City, the proposed community incorporates a broad range of planning and environmental initiatives.

As part of an assembled team – including Andres Duany and Elizabeth Plater-Zyberk, Legorreta Arquitectos and landscape architects Hanna/Olin – which is willing to work with the citizens to achieve innovative results, the Playa Vista masterplan defines a balanced community of low- to mid-rise buildings with a strong emphasis on the provision of a generous public realm. Playa Vista uses a defined hierarchy of street and open-space types to shape its neighbourhoods. Though predominantly residential in character, they also include office, retail, recreational, cultural and civic uses. An office campus, village centre and marina will also be included.

Over half of Playa Vista's site has been set aside for various forms of open space. These include major parks and playing fields, smaller neighbourhood parks and squares, cycling and jogging trails and pedestrian promenades. A restored bluff, wetland preserve and riparian corridor serve as greenbelts for the community. The plan also includes a low-emission internal shuttle service that will be linked to regional transportation systems. In addition, car pooling, ride sharing and public transit incentives are to be actively promoted.

ABOVE: Playa Vista masterplan

LOS ANGELES AS IT WILL BE

East elevation; courtyard section

MIXED USE DEVELOPMENT

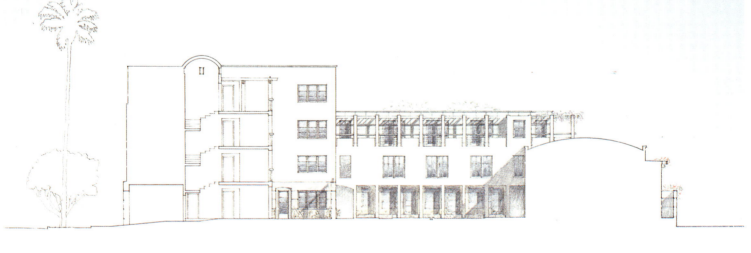

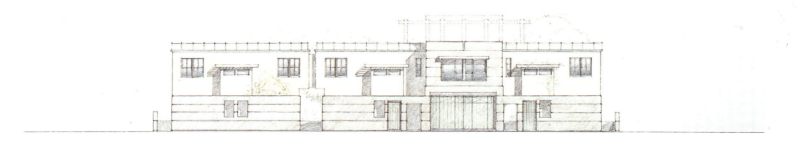

Courtyard section; alley elevation

HODGETTS + FUNG
HUDSON-WILCOX
Hollywood

The intention is to create a community hub by linking together the Department of Transportation commuter parking facilities, an open-air market place, prestigious office space and affordable housing. The synergy of the project is designed to reinforce existing community patterns – thus avoiding the typical development strategies. By respecting the boulevard's variegated street facades and strengthening pedestrian usage, the project generates a prototype for future development on adjacent blocks in Los Angeles.

*ABOVE: East-west section;
BELOW: Perspective view*

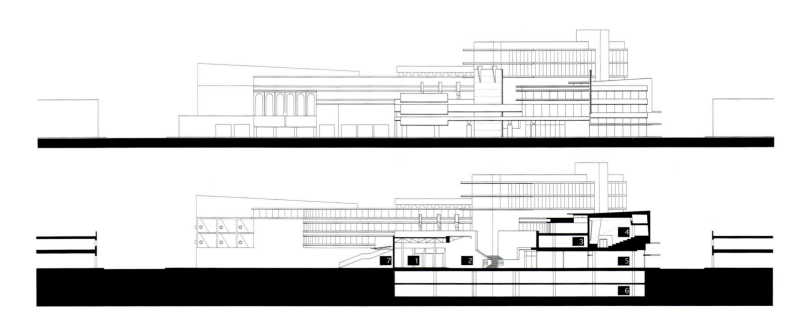

PRIVATE RESIDENCES

ROTONDI

CDLT 1, 2 CEDAR LODGE TERRACE
Silverlake

This house addition is not complete, perhaps it never will be. The motivation to begin was a combination of circumstance and desire. The house needed to be enlarged, but first Rotondi was compelled to investigate a set of ideas which had been accumulating, believing that these would serve that purpose.

This project would be constructed with minimal drawings – mostly diagrammatic, establishing basic spatial order and elemental relationships in plan and section. This project would be worked on, conceived and built full scale, in real time, simultaneously, providing the opportunity to work *improvisationally*.

The work would proceed, in principle, on the basis that each idea is in fact the impetus for the next; that ideas are a vehicle for form-making, that the ultimate test of any idea is to build it. Considering this, it seemed essential to try and close distance in time between the moment of conception and the act of its inception, with the act of looking at it. They all become in this special case contemporary. This simultaneous condition might permeate the actual material – concrete, wood, steel and plaster – so any observer could follow the traces of the architect's immediate gestures.

The structures Rotondi creates are hybrid in nature and form, constructed of many similar and disparate elements which converge to make an artefact that is inextricably complex.

The building is made in a manner that when you come upon it, you see what it is, and how it is made. It has position – it organises the space around it and that which it appropriates.

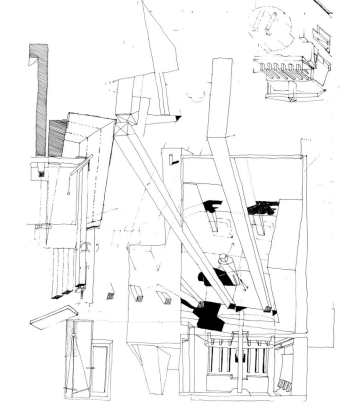

Sketch

375

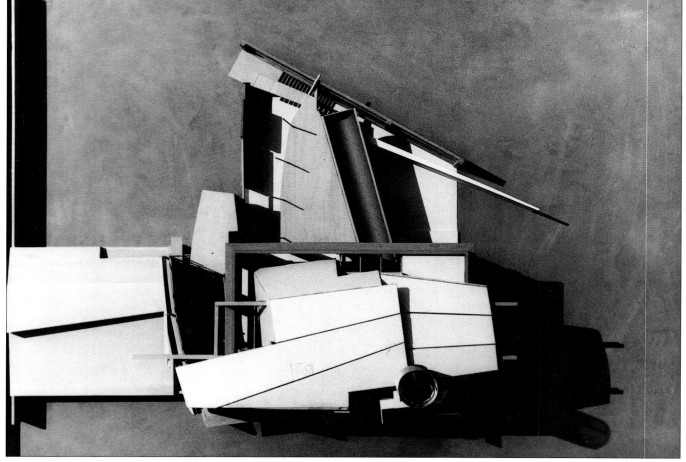

PRIVATE RESIDENCES

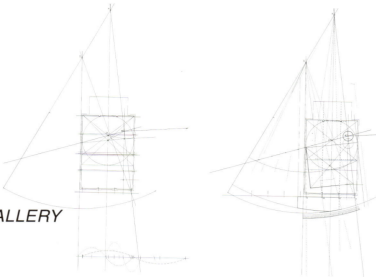

ROTONDI
CARLSON/REGES RESIDENCE AND GALLERY
Downtown

The Carlson/Reges project is the result of a unique client/builder and architect collaboration. The clients have lived for some time in what was once an electric company cabling structure north of Downtown Los Angeles. The clients requested that their expanding collection of paintings and sculpture was accommodated in a manner which would allow public showings without compromising their privacy, and would take advantage of the materials they had stockpiled nearby.

Given these criteria, the project pursued the possibilities of volume and scale rather than the complexity of minute details. The acoustic and environmental problems associated with living in a large open space in the midst of an urban/industrial landscape also had to be tackled.

The process began with a modelling and drawing analysis that addressed two separate but simultaneous areas of concern. The first modelling depicted bodily and emotional responses to the possibilities of the site and existing structure. The result of this exploration was a series of volumetric elements: the shield protects the translucent kitchen and the interior from the strongest southern sun, blocks the noise and dirt of the adjacent train switching yard, and forms a protected vertical garden.

A three-dimensional geometric analysis was undertaken concurrent with the 'experiential' modelling. Information generated from this analysis of existing conditions was layered with the body input with the intention of creating a complex but singular volume to unify the separate elements that were being generated from the study models.

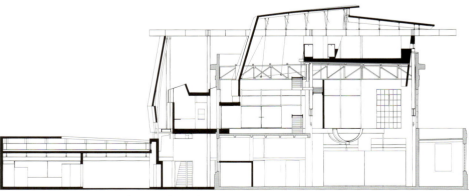

ABOVE L TO R: Existing order and relationships; new order and relationships; BELOW: Section

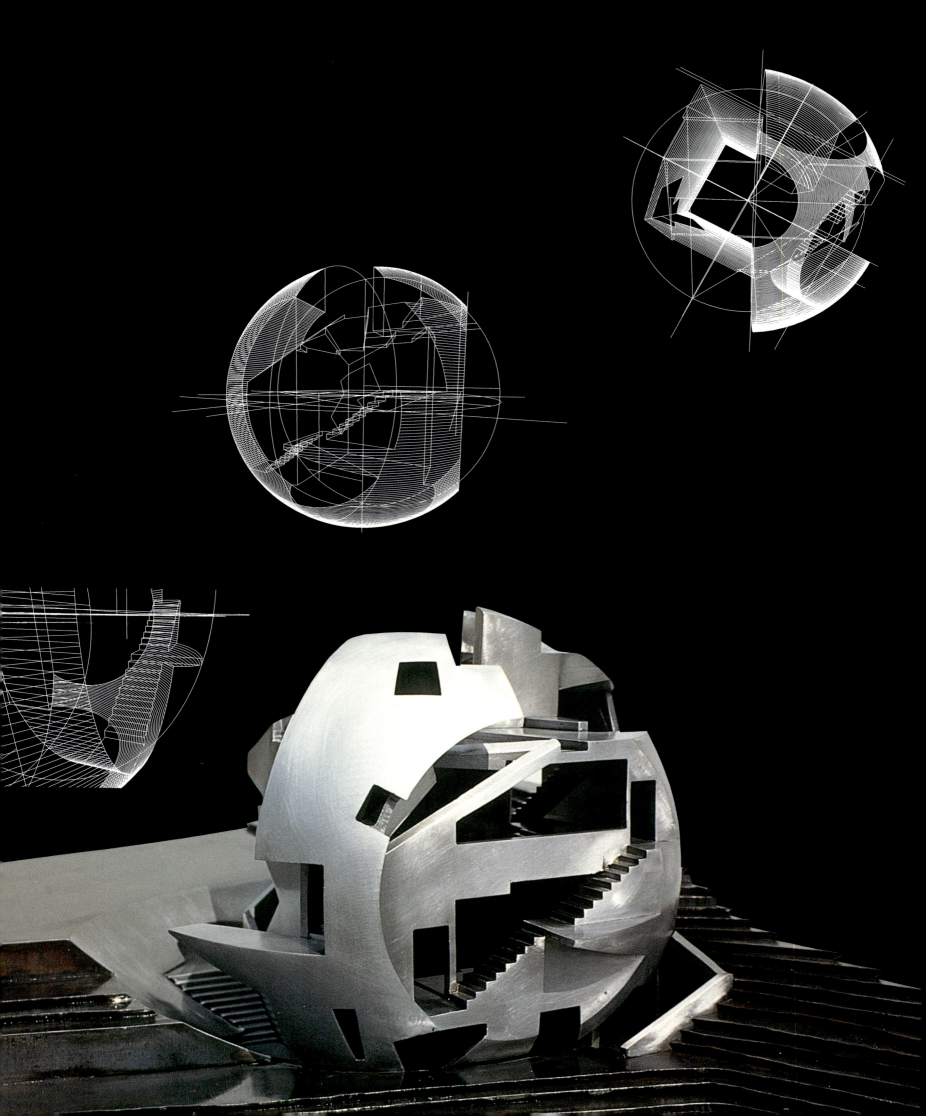

ERIC OWEN MOSS
ARONOFF HOUSE
Santa Monica

This nondescript tract house on the northern side of the Santa Monica Mountains is part of a property that stretches northwest of the existing slope to the Santa Monica Conservancy, a beautiful wooded area extending for several miles, protected in perpetuity from development.

The new guest house is a pleasurable toy for its owners, their employees, guests and children. The building can be climbed on, examined and used as a viewing platform. Its location and the configuration of floors and windows take full advantage of the spectacular views of the forest. It is positioned at the transition from the flat to the sloping portion of the site, and is also adjacent to the south-west property line, thereby exploiting the vista without interrupting the existing house's view.

The project contains three floors: the top level studio/executive offices for the owners; an office floor at grade for a business with three employees and a separate apartment below. The roof is oriented towards the Conservancy area and the San Fernando Valley, and is accessible from all levels via a stairway which runs along the perimeter of the house. The middle level is the office floor, used during the work day in conjunction with the owners' offices on the top floor. The apartment at the lowest level has lift access, a covered deck area and an open patio. All levels may be accessed from the middle level lobby or from the exterior.

Placed precariously at the top of a slope; stabilised by the conical cut; a threat to roll as a sphere; re-anchored by the cube, the guest house is a stable instability.

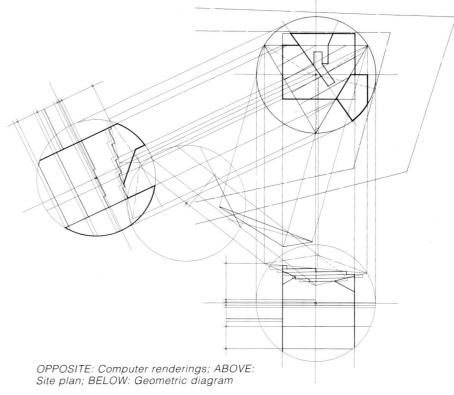

OPPOSITE: Computer renderings; ABOVE: Site plan; BELOW: Geometric diagram

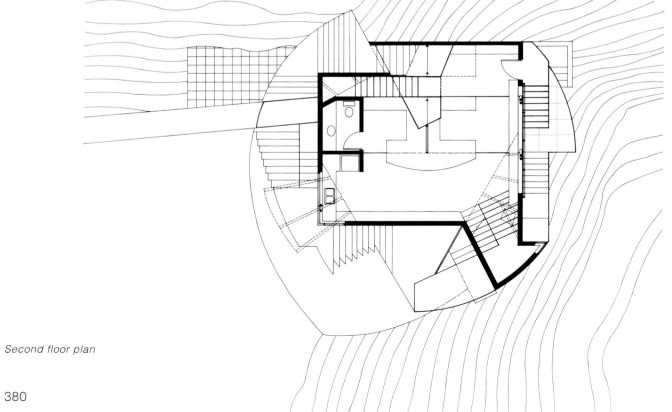

Second floor plan

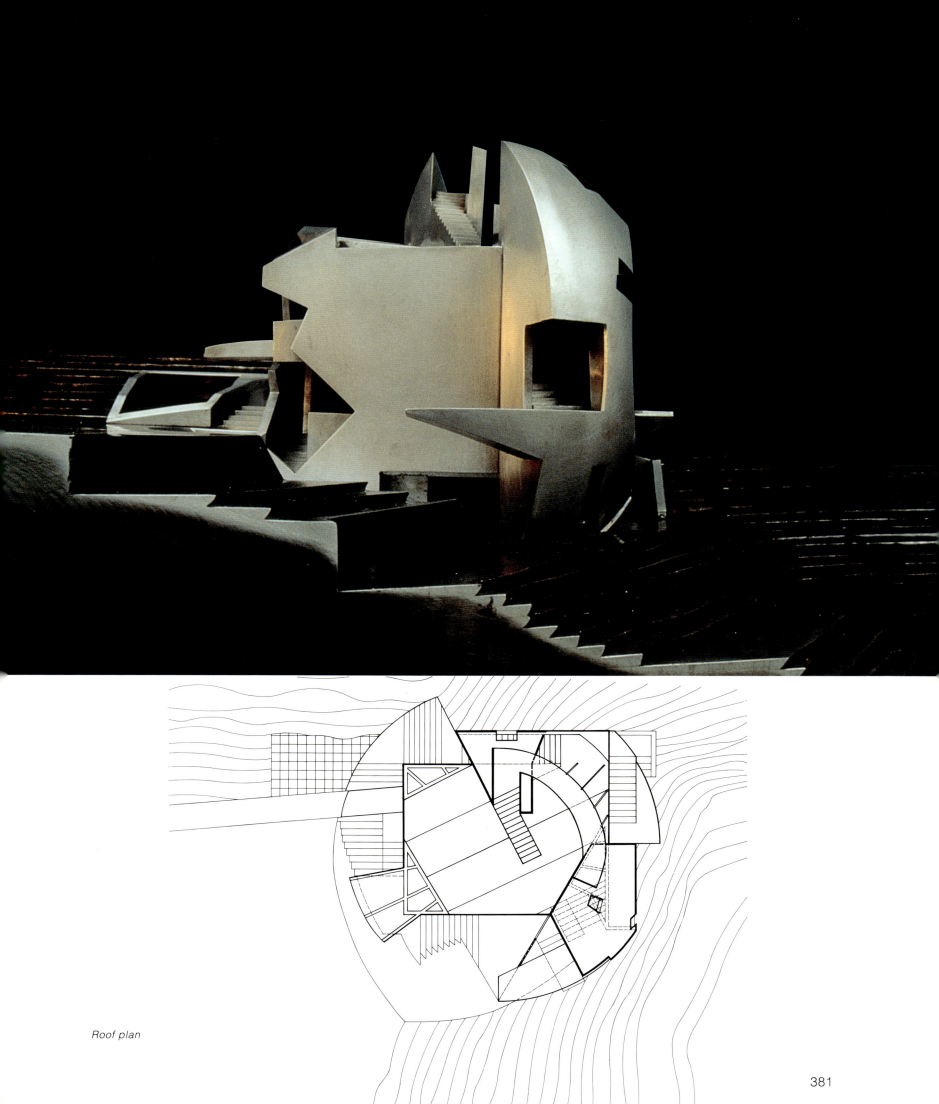

Roof plan

LOS ANGELES AS IT WILL BE

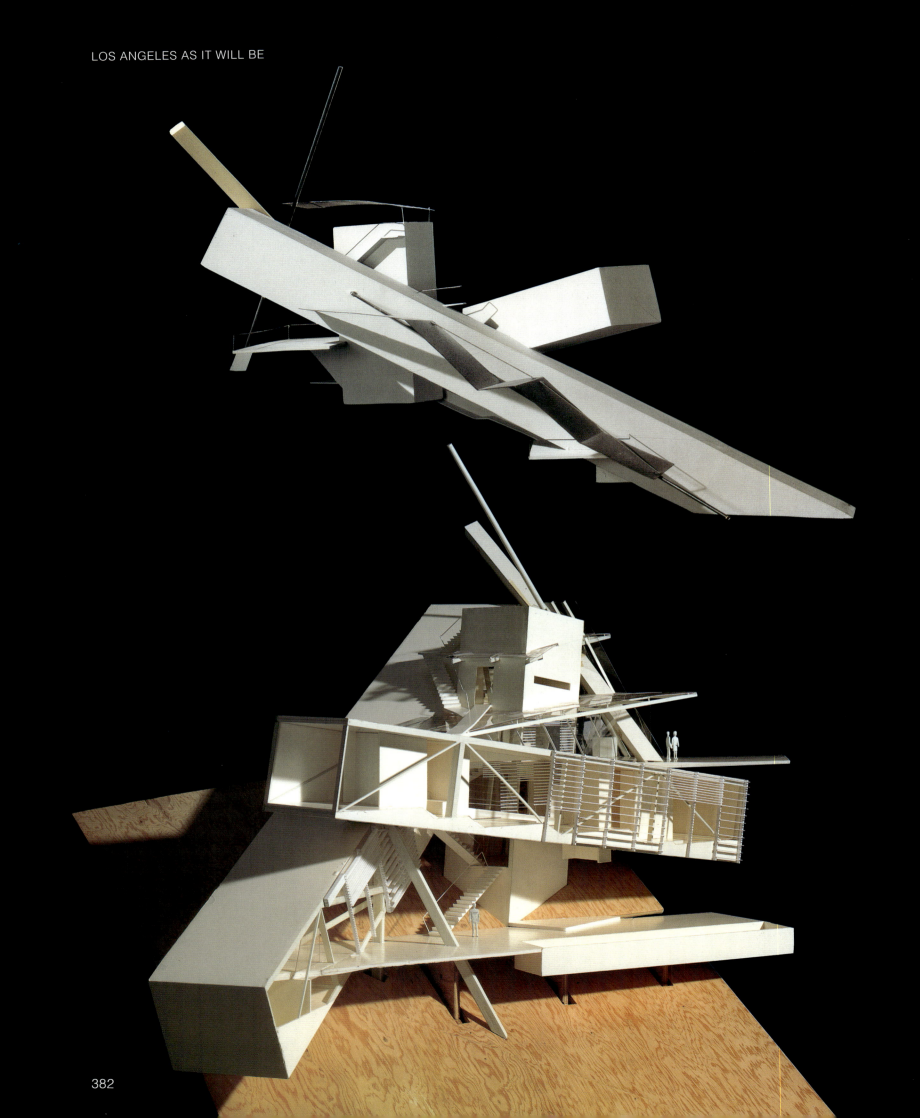

382

PRIVATE RESIDENCES

COOP HIMMELBLAU
REHAK HOUSE
Malibu

The building site, begun in 1990 and still in progress, is very inconveniently divided. An ... juts through it, creating a ... plateau and a southern slope. ... hitects decided to design the ... in accordance with the precipi- ... uthern slope. The first sketch and ... del depict the concept. Two arms – the city-view arm and the ... arm – are affixed to the slope in ... pe of an 'x'. Flying platforms, ... ble roof tops and a tower all tie ... me together.

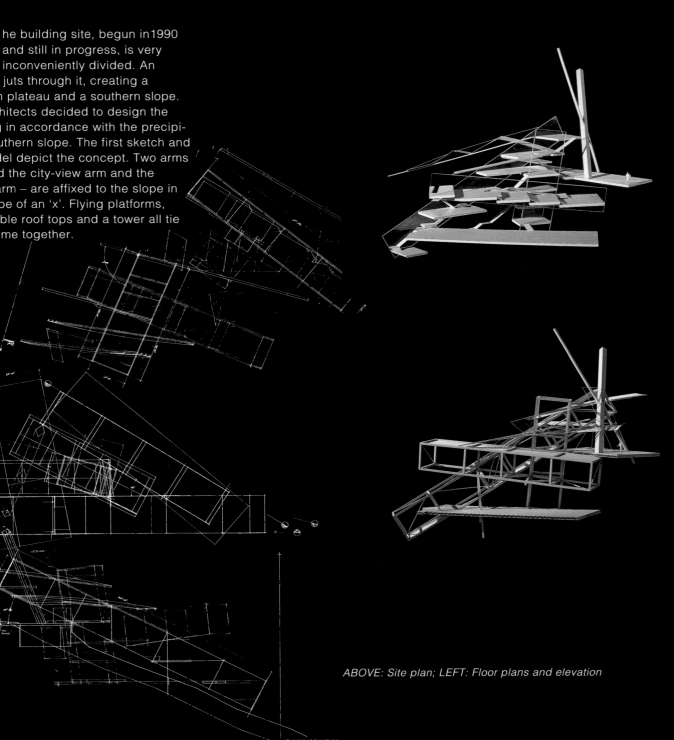

ABOVE: Site plan; LEFT: Floor plans and elevation

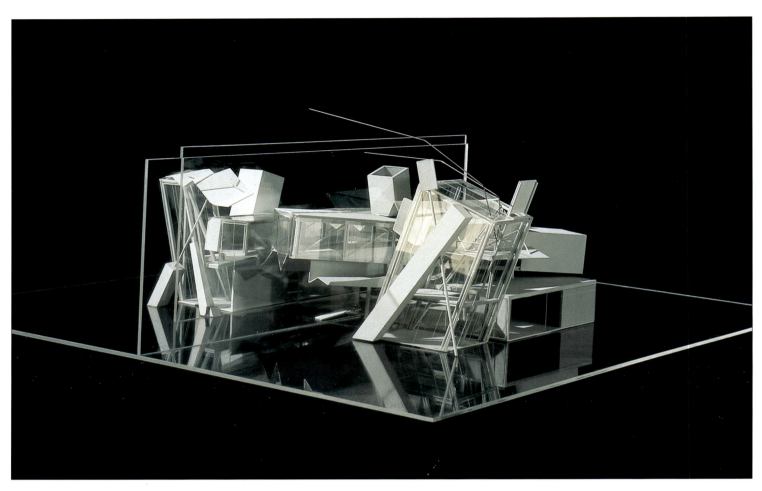
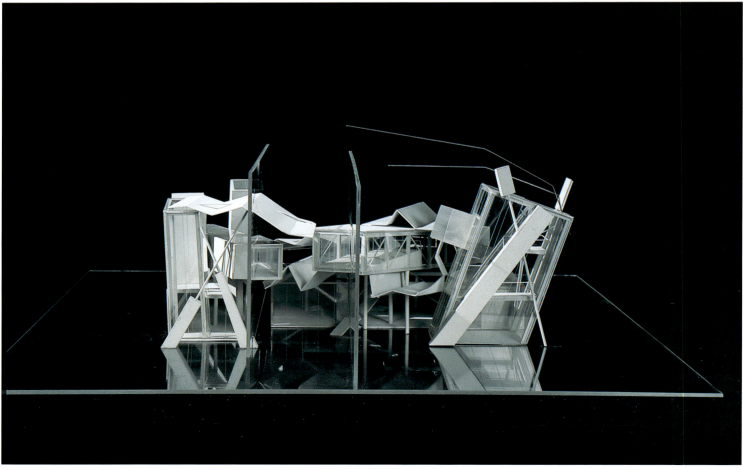

COOP HIMMELBLAU

MELROSE I
West Hollywood

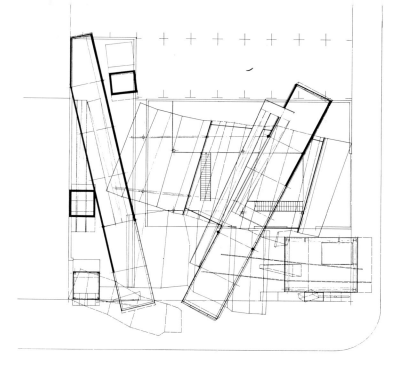

This multi-purpose commercial building, which was begun in 1990, contains a bar, restaurant, boutiques and bookshop and is situated on Melrose Avenue. The design concept of the project avoids the simple cramming-together of several boxes. Rather, it conceives of a complex unit of volume contained in a two-storey building. At a later stage, the room-dividing is to be carved out of the total space, more or less arbitrarily, depending on the purposes then designated. The steeply inclining glazed tower has moveable platforms suitable for ever possible alteration of the spatial situation.

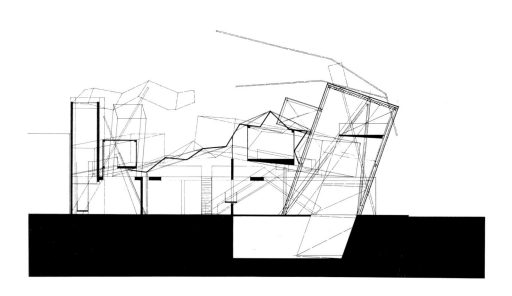

ABOVE: Plan; BELOW: Section

PRIVATE RESIDENCES

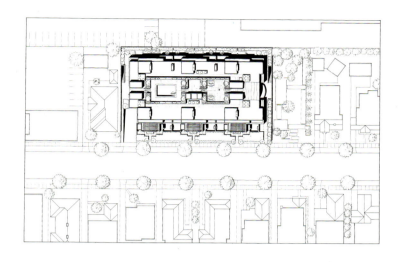

MOULE & POLYZOIDES
ARNAZ DRIVE CONDOMINIUMS
Beverly Hills

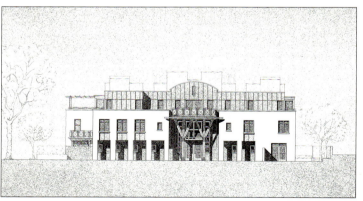

This project wrestled with the impending densification of several multi-family neighbourhoods throughout Los Angeles. Situated on a street of duplexes, quadplexes and some single-family houses, this project, composed of several aggregated lots, heralds a new era of increased building lot coverage and volume. Creating better and more liveable multi-family housing stock citywide was explored and the architects attacked the problem from the point of view of manipulating the building masses on the street and park sides as well as carving out usable open spaces for the individual units, the entire building and the community.

As a way of countering the typical 'six pack' solution of destroying the ground plane with driveways and parked cars, this building places the parking below grade and splits the driveways on either side of the building to minimise curb cuts at the pavement. The building then defines a deliberate streetwall made up of individual unit entrances, patios and living room windows. The entrance faces the adjacent neighbourhood park as a way of activating it.

The individual units are organised as double-loaded townhouses taking up the first and second floors. Two-storey living rooms are articulated as individual small buildings which maintain the massing of the duplexes down the street. They also let natural light deep into the interior of the units. The third floor is made up of flats with exterior terraces while the roof has a pool, jacuzzi and gardens.

The building's forms, materials and attitude of garden spaces continue the legacy of the work of Irving Gill, Charles and Henry Greene and RM Schindler.

FROM ABOVE: Site plan; facade detail; north elevation

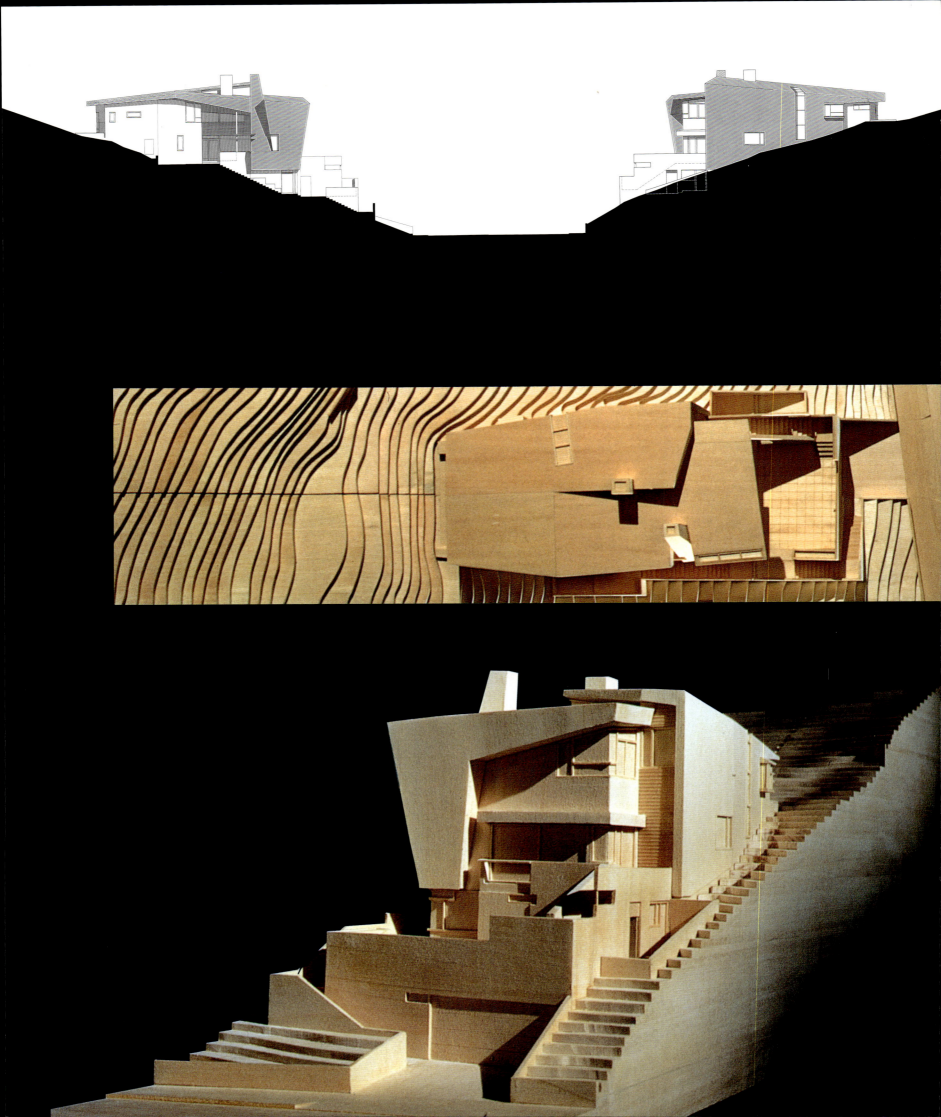

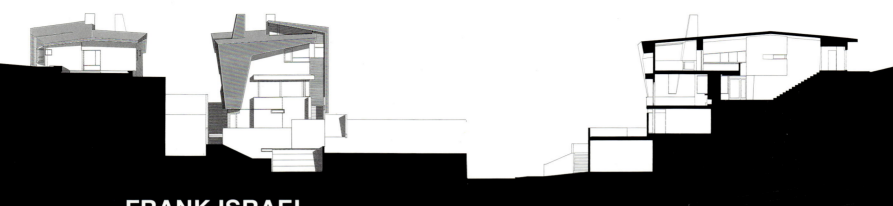

FRANK ISRAEL
DRAGER HOUSE
Berkeley

Stepping up the Berkeley hills with views of the San Francisco Bay, the Drager House is a new house on an old site which is haunted by the tragedy of the Berkeley fire of 1991. This house is an entirely new gesture, not an homage to the original colonial tower building. It is terraced up the hill to take full advantage of the site. Built of stucco and copper shingles, it blends into its setting by camouflaging itself into the eucalyptus and pine groves.

Inside, a large monumental staircase begins in the family room and ascends to the living room level, opening up to a large hallway from which one climbs to the bedrooms above. This staircase also leads to an outdoor terrace from which one can proceed to the upper play area and garden. The house which is nearly 5,000 square feet is sculpted into its setting. The roof appears to slip away creating a series of skylights and clerestories. Clad in copper, this sloped surface bends into the facade of the building, creating an ambiguity between what is volume and what is surface.

ABOVE L TO R: Elevations, section; RIGHT: Roof plan

PRIVATE RESIDENCES

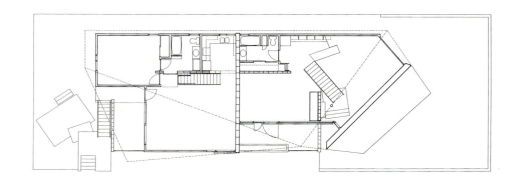

FRANK ISRAEL
BALDWIN HOUSE
Venice

This beach house in Venice actually consists of two houses that abut a small street and an alleyway a few blocks from the ocean. Designed for a photographer and his family, the Baldwin House (1991) also includes a two-bedroom rental unit.

The two-storey studio space sits across the street from Bright and Associates, paying homage to that project by using many of the same materials. The rental unit is accessed from a private garden at the back of the site, and the entire complex will be unified by a large, sweeping sheet-metal roof, made of anodised titanium to achieve an iridescence akin to the skin of a reptile or fish. This gesture acknowledges the proximity to the sea, imbuing the house with an appropriate sense of grandeur.

To support the vast roof, two major masonry walls cut through the plan, dividing the interior into two units, and into service and served spaces within each. The down-turning sweep of the roof shelters the largest of the interior spaces from the south light to provide a studio for the photographer.

The cruciform structure of the two primary walls is sculpted away in places to modulate movement and light, and the ground slab is gently terraced up from the entrance void.

A darkroom, bathrooms and storage spaces are stacked along the north side on three levels, enclosed by a light skin of wood and metal panelling. Windows close the reveals between the roofing and panelling systems, ensuring that each one is read independently.

ABOVE: Plan of level two; BELOW: Elevation

LOS ANGELES AS IT MIGHT HAVE BEEN

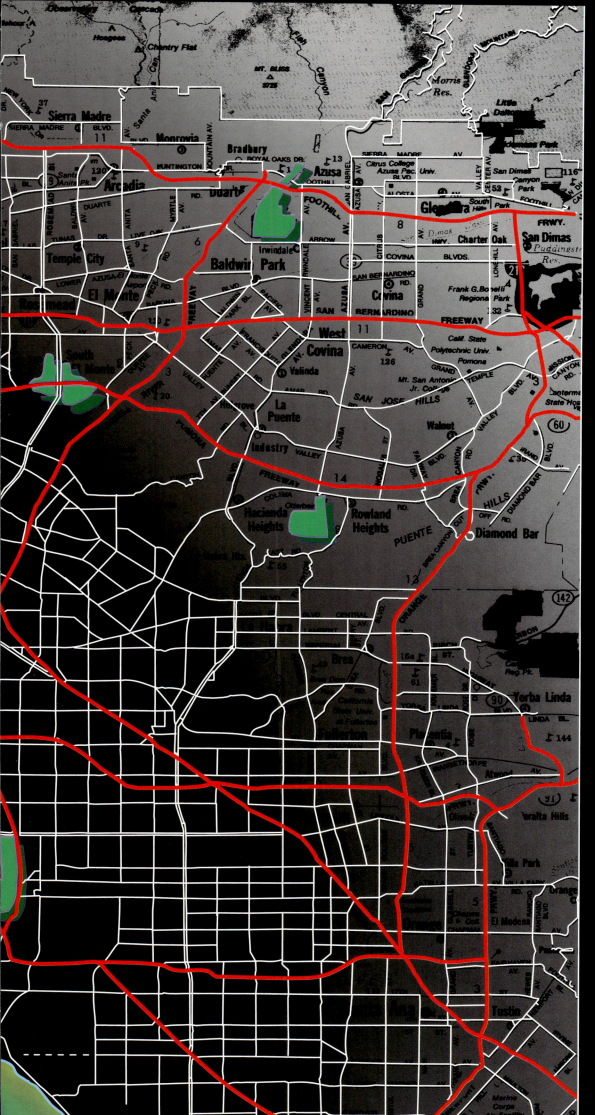

LOS ANGELES AS IT MIGHT HAVE BEEN

Yuzen Vintage Car Museum 76
Arts Park LA 80
Steel Cloud 82
Century City 84
West Coast Gateway 88
Hayden Tower 94
Hercules Theater and Offices 98
S.P.A.R.C.I T Y 100
Samitaur I & II 104
Hollywood Promenade 108
Devine Residence 112
Hoffs Residence 114
Familian Residence 116
Mills Musingo House 118

LOS ANGELES AS IT IS

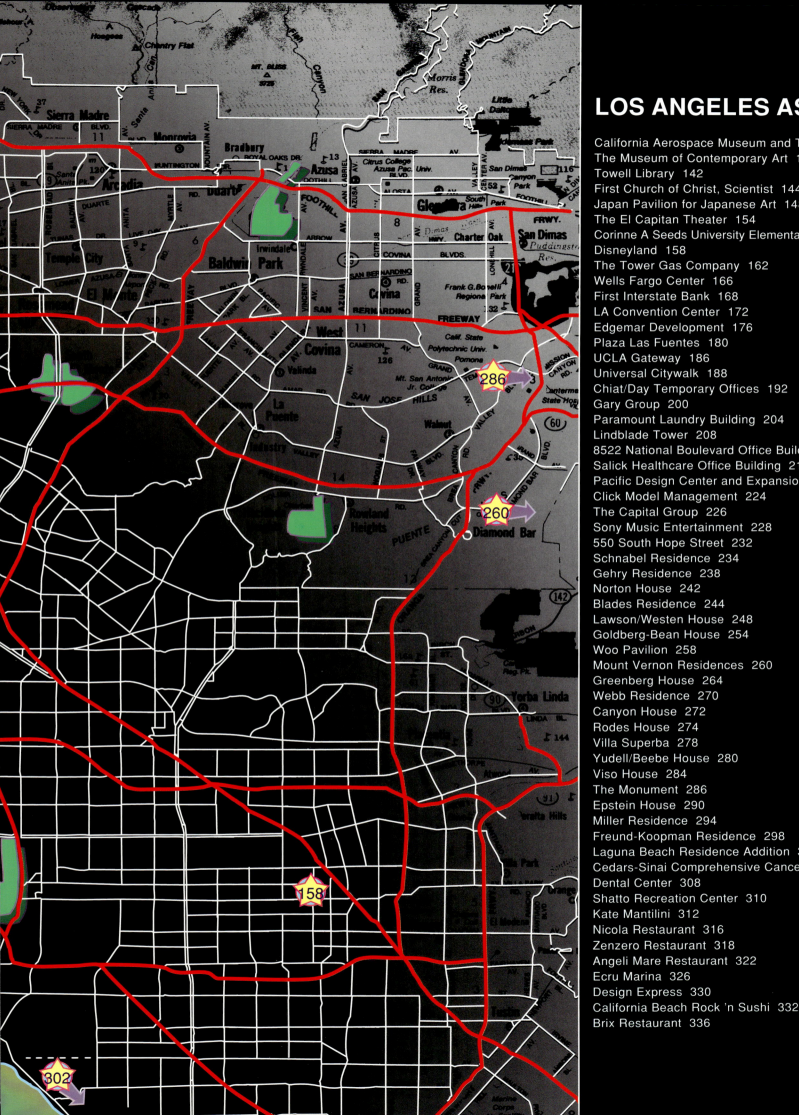

LOS ANGELES AS IT IS

California Aerospace Museum and Theatre 132
The Museum of Contemporary Art 136
Towell Library 142
First Church of Christ, Scientist 144
Japan Pavilion for Japanese Art 148
The El Capitan Theater 154
Corinne A Seeds University Elementary School 156
Disneyland 158
The Tower Gas Company 162
Wells Fargo Center 166
First Interstate Bank 168
LA Convention Center 172
Edgemar Development 176
Plaza Las Fuentes 180
UCLA Gateway 186
Universal Citywalk 188
Chiat/Day Temporary Offices 192
Gary Group 200
Paramount Laundry Building 204
Lindblade Tower 208
8522 National Boulevard Office Building 212
Salick Healthcare Office Building 216
Pacific Design Center and Expansion 220
Click Model Management 224
The Capital Group 226
Sony Music Entertainment 228
550 South Hope Street 232
Schnabel Residence 234
Gehry Residence 238
Norton House 242
Blades Residence 244
Lawson/Westen House 248
Goldberg-Bean House 254
Woo Pavilion 258
Mount Vernon Residences 260
Greenberg House 264
Webb Residence 270
Canyon House 272
Rodes House 274
Villa Superba 278
Yudell/Beebe House 280
Viso House 284
The Monument 286
Epstein House 290
Miller Residence 294
Freund-Koopman Residence 298
Laguna Beach Residence Addition 302
Cedars-Sinai Comprehensive Cancer Center 304
Dental Center 308
Shatto Recreation Center 310
Kate Mantilini 312
Nicola Restaurant 316
Zenzero Restaurant 318
Angeli Mare Restaurant 322
Ecru Marina 326
Design Express 330
California Beach Rock 'n Sushi 332
Brix Restaurant 336

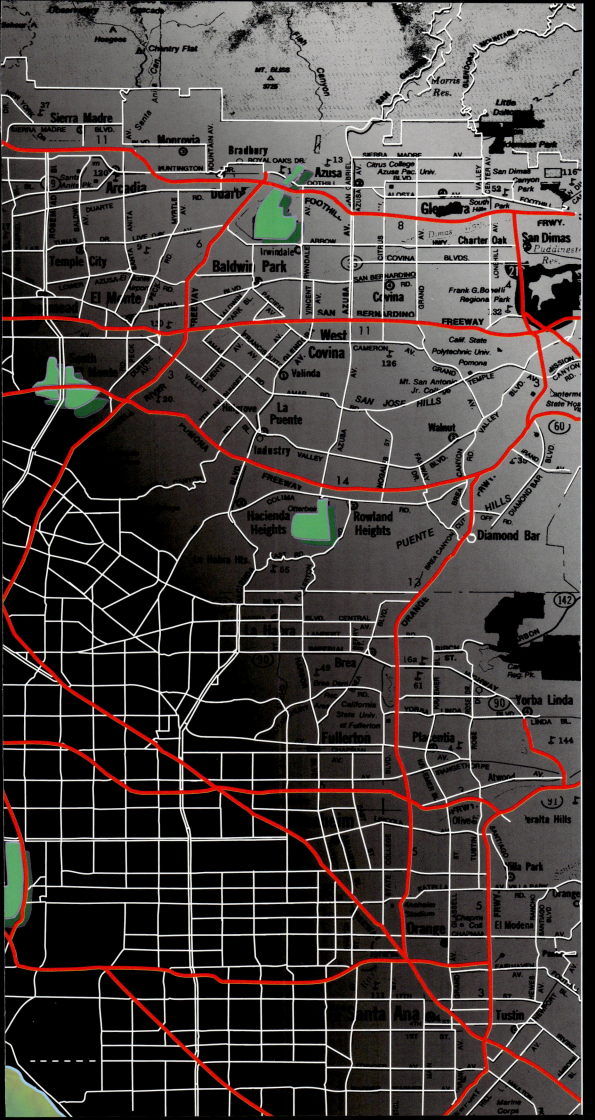

LOS ANGELES AS IT WILL BE

The Getty Center 348
Science Museum School 352
Walt Disney Concert Hall 354
SMSC 356
Hollywood Entertainment Museum 358
Metro Red Line 360
Playa Vista 364
Hudson-Wilcox 372
CDLT 1, 2 Cedar Lodge Terrace 374
Carlson/Reges Residence and Gateway 37
Aronoff House 378
Rehak House 382
Melrose I 384
Arnaz Apartments 386
Drager House 388
Baldwin House 390

ARCHITECTS' INDEX

Nikken America / Charles Cordero AIA / Francesca Garcia-Marques
Zenzero Restaurant   318

Studio Asymptote
Steel Cloud   82

Ellerbe Becket
Metro Red Line   360

Schweitzer Bim
The Monument   286

Central Office of Architecture
Laguna Beach Residence Addition   302
Brix Restaurant   336

Cigolle + Coleman
Mills Musingo House   118
Canyon House   272
Rodes House   274

Fields & Devereaux
The El Capitan Theater   154

Steven Ehrlich
Sony Music Entertainment   228
Shatto Recreation Center   310

Kohn Pedersen Fox
550 South Hope Street   232

Pei Cobb Freed
First Interstate Bank   168
LA Convention Center   172

Hodgetts + Fung
Arts Park LA   80
Cookie Express   120
Towell Library   142
UCLA Gateway   186
Click Model Management   224
Hudson-Wilcox   372

Frank Gehry
Familian Residence   116
California Aerospace Museum and Theatre   132
Edgemar Development   176
Chiat/Day Temporary Offices   192
Schnabel Residence   234
Gehry Residence   238
Norton House   242
Walt Disney Concert Hall   354

Coop Himmelblau
Rehak House   382
Melrose I   384

Arata Isozaki
The Museum of Contemporary Art   136

Frank Israel
Goldberg-Bean House   254
Woo Pavilion   258
Drager House   388
Baldwin House   390

The Jerde Partnership
Hollywood Promenade   108
Universal Citywalk   188

Legorreta Arquitectos
Greenberg House   264

Richard Meier
The Getty Center   348

Skidmore Owings & Merrill
The Tower Gas Company   162
Wells Fargo Center   166

Morphosis
Yuzen Vintage Car Museum   76
Salick Healthcare Office Building   216
Blades Residence   244
Cedars-Sinai Comprehensive Cancer Center   304

Kate Mantilini	312		CDLT 1, 2 Cedar Lodge Terrace	374
Science Museum School	352		Carlson/Reges Residence and Gateway	376

Eric Owen Moss
Hayden Tract	92		**Michele Saee**	
Hayden Tower	94		Dental Center	308
Hercules Theater and Offices	98		Angeli Mare Restaurant	322
S.P.A.R.C I T Y	100		Ecru Marina	326
Samitaur I & II	104		Design Express	330
Ince Complex	198			
Gary Group	200		**Gwathmey Siegel**	
Paramount Laundry Building	204		The Capital Group	226
Lindblade Tower	208			
8522 National Boulevard Office Building	212		**McCoy and Simon**	
Lawson/Westen House	248		Webb Residence	270
SMSC	356			
Aronoff House	378		**Ted Tokio Tanaka**	
			California Beach Rock 'n Sushi	332

Cesar Pelli
Pacific Design Center Expansion — 220

O'Herlihy & Warner
Miller Residence — 294
Freund-Koopman Residence — 298

Barton Phelps
Corinne A Seeds University Elementary School — 156
Epstein House — 290

WED Enterprises
Disneyland — 158

Sigrid Miller Pollin
Mount Vernon Residences — 260

Buzz Yudell
Yudell/Beebe House — 280

Moule & Polyzoides
Playa Vista — 368
Arnaz Apartments — 386

Moore Ruble Yudell
First Church of Christ, Scientist — 144
Plaza Las Fuentes — 180
Villa Superba — 278
Hollywood Entertainment Museum — 358
Playa Vista Masterplan — 364

Bart Prince
Japan Pavilion for Japanese Art — 148

Dagmar Richter
Century City — 84
West Coast Gateway — 88
Devine Residence — 112
Hoffs Residence — 114

Rotondi
Nicola Restaurant — 316